BIPLANES, TRIPLANES & SEAPLANES

THE AVIATION FACTFILE

BIPLANES, TRIPLANES & SEAPLANES

GENERAL EDITOR: JIM WINCHESTER

Grange
BOOKS

First published in 2004 for Grange Books
An imprint of Grange Books plc
The Grange
Kingsnorth Industrial Estate
Hoo, Nr Rochester
Kent ME3 9ND
www.grangebooks.co.uk

A catalogue record for this book is available from the British Library.

ISBN 1-84013-641-3

Produced by
Amber Books Ltd
Bradley's Close
74–77 White Lion Street
London N1 9PF
www.amberbooks.co.uk

Printed in Singapore

Contents

INTRODUCTION

Left: Regarded as one of the most beautiful aircraft ever built, the Beech Staggerwing was first flown in 1932 and remains a classic.

Right: The Fokker Dr.1 Triplane proved a dangerous tool in the hands of German aces on the Western front.

Below: A preserved example of the Curtiss JN-4 'Jenny' – the aircraft that brought aviation to the people and typified the barnstorming era.

Biplanes

The first successful aircraft had two pairs of flying surfaces largely because the box structure of the braced wings overcame the strength limitations of the available lightweight materials, mainly spruce and beechwood. The structure had to be light because early engines produced little power for their weight. For example, the engine on the Wright Flyer was a model of efficiency for its time, but gave only 9 kW (12 hp.) for its 90 kg (200 lb) weight. Biplanes also gave a lot of wing area and thus lift for a given wingspan. They also required a lot of skill and resources to build and had to be carefully rigged in the field in order to fly predictably. Monoplanes were simpler and lighter, but were not trusted by some aviators and military commanders. After several structural failures, the Royal Flying Corps even banned them. The monoplane eventually achieved dominance, but biplane fighter aircraft, including the Gladiator and Polikarpov I-153, continued to be produced and to fight into the early 1940s. One specialized naval aircraft, the Swordfish, remained in production until the end of World War II. Despite their apparently outdated layout, biplanes continue to be produced for specialist uses, offering as they do strength and manoeuvrability, attributes useful in aerobatics as well as agricultural aviation.

Triplanes

Although several pioneers believed that if two sets of wings were good, fifteen must be better, the 'multiplane' failed to get off the ground – in many cases literally. The largest practical number of wings proved to be three, but the triplane was to be little more than a colourful footnote in aviation history. Designed to provide the pilot with a better view while retaining the agility and manoeuvrability of a biplane, the

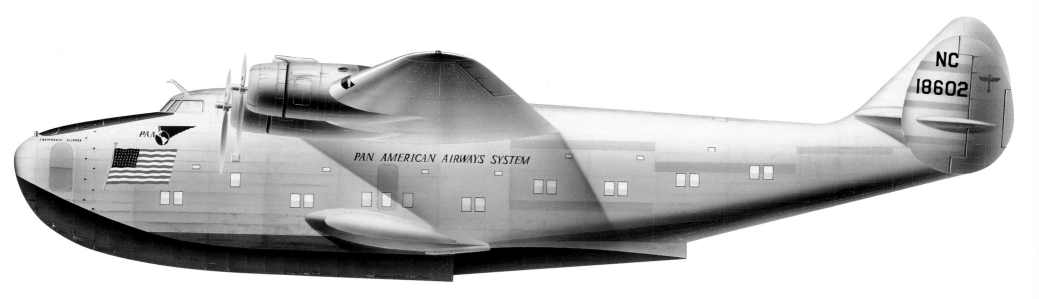

Above: Between 1939 and 1946 Boeing's Model 314 Clippers provided long-distance air travel in luxury for the privileged few.

Far right: The sturdy Martin PBM Mariner saw combat in every theatre of World War II.

Right: The Blohm und Voss BV 138, nicknamed the 'Flying Clog', performed a useful reconnaissance role during World War II.

appearance of the Sopwith Triplane in late 1916 led to a 'triplane frenzy' among manufacturers. At least 15 German and Austro-Hungarian companies built 'Tripes' in response, of which the Fokker Dr.I was the only real success. A small number of pilots, notably Collishaw and von Richthofen, made the triplane famous out of all proportion to the numbers built – fewer than 500 examples of the Sopwith and Fokker combined.

Seaplanes

The aeroplane was invented before the airfield or aerodrome. While some of the first aviators operated from beaches or farm fields, others such as Samuel Langley chose floatplane designs because they figured that water was more forgiving of error.

The fastest aircraft in the world in the 1920s and early '30s were the floatplanes that competed for the famed Schneider Trophy, such as the Curtiss R3C. Operating from water gave almost unlimited space for the long take-off runs these high-performance racers required and obviated the need for long, smooth runways, which simply didn't exist at that time. For the same reason, the first long-range airliners were largely flying boats. Even as commercial and military airports were built in Europe and America, flying boats were vital for supporting colonies and outposts in Africa, the Far East and the Pacific. Although their civil heyday was in the 1930s and military use peaked during World War II, the big flying boats and amphibians had something of a revival in the immediate post-war years. A few large amphibians remain in service in Japan and Russia today, mainly in the maritime patrol role, and thousands of light floatplanes continue to serve tourists, fishermen and remote communities in parts of the USA and Canada.

AIRCO

DH.2

● Single-seater ● Pusher-engined fighter ● Fully aerobatic

▲ Both the two-seat DH.1 and single-seat DH.2 used a pusher propeller layout, which allowed a clear field for forwards fire. By dispensing with the observer, the DH.2 became a fast and agile fighter.

A rotary engine mounted in the pusher position drove the propeller of the DH.2. This was the second pusher fighter designed by Geoffrey de Havilland and built by Airco. The pusher concept has been tried a number of times in aviation history, but has rarely produced a combat aircraft on par with a 'tractor'-engined equivalent. The DH.2 was an interesting design, but it never became one of the great fighters of World War I.

AIRCO DH.2

Exposed engine position ▶
The DH.2's engine and propeller were installed inside the open fuselage structure of the aircraft.

▼ 'Fly-by-wire'
A mass of control wires and rigging cables characterised the DH.2. A number of early aircraft were lost when their rotary engines broke-up in flight and flying fragments damaged the vulnerable wing and fuselage structure.

▲ Royal Flying Corps fighters
No. 24 Squadron took the DH.2 to war in early 1917, but by August 1918 there was none left in service. This collection of replicas includes the contemporary Bristol Scout, Bristol M.1C and SE.5a.

▲ No Lewis gun
A single Lewis machine-gun was normally mounted in the position shown by the white fairing mounted on the cockpit lip.

Fabric covering ▶
Sunlight shining through the fabric covering reveals the wooden structure of the wings.

FACTS AND FIGURES

➤ Geoffrey de Havilland was forced to choose a pusher layout because British interrupter gear was not available.

➤ Many of the DH.2's components were simply scaled down from the DH.1.

➤ No. 29 Squadron lost four out of 16 DH.2s when flying to France in a snowstorm.

➤ Oswald Boelcke was killed in a flying accident when engaging a DH.2.

➤ In the prototype a ballast weight of 13.6 kg (30 lb.) was needed in the nose as the DH.2 was tail heavy without its machine-gun.

➤ In April 1916 the DH.2 was found to be a match for the Fokker monoplanes.

Fighting the Fokkers

A smaller version of Geoffrey de Havilland's earlier DH.1 fighter, the DH.2 retained the pusher configuration of its predecessor to create a clear field of fire for its Lewis gun. In 1915, British aeronautical engineers had not yet designed a practical 'interrupter' to enable a machine-gun to fire through the propeller.

Although the Lewis gun did not endanger the propeller, its initial installation in the DH.2 provided a host of problems for the pilot. A mounting was provided on each side of the cockpit and the pilot was expected to set up the gun on whatever side would give him the best chance of hitting the target. The pilot was challenged to maintain control of the aircraft while struggling to move the gun from side to side.

The DH.2 was never easy to fly or to shoot from, but it gave British pilots a fighter with which to seize the advantage against Germany's Fokker monoplanes. Eventually, the Lewis gun was mounted in the centre in front of the pilot, and the DH.2 held its own in battle until more modern German types appeared.

Below: Pilots were completely exposed to the elements in the DH.2, but the field of view was excellent. Pilots soon began to use the gun as a fixed weapon, moving the whole aircraft to aim it.

Above: With its Lewis gun in place, a DH.2 comes in to land at the end of a patrol.

DH.2

Towards the end of 1915 No. 24 Squadron began receiving its first DH.2s. This aircraft was one of the first batch to join the unit, which pioneered operations with the DH.2.

DH.2

Type: single-seat scout fighter

Powerplant: one 75-kW (100-hp.) Gnome Monosoupape rotary piston engine or one 82-kW (110-hp.) Le Rhône rotary engine (late models)

Maximum speed: (Gnome engine) 150 km/h (93 m.p.h.) at sea level

Cruising speed: 126 km/h (78 m.p.h.)

Endurance: 2 hours 45 min

Service ceiling: 4265 m (14,000 ft.)

Weights: empty 428 kg (942 lb.); maximum take-off 654 kg (1,441 lb.)

Armament: one forward-firing 7.62-mm Lewis machine-gun with canisters holding 47 rounds

Dimensions:
span	8.61 m (28 ft. 3 in.)
length	7.68 m (25 ft. 2 in.)
height	2.91 m (9 ft. 6 in.)
wing area	23.13 m² (249 sq. ft.)

Once pilots had adopted the tactic of aiming the aircraft and not the gun, the gun was fixed in position. Some movement up and down was allowed for minor aiming corrections, however.

Although they looked fragile, the tubular-steel tailbooms were comprehensively rigged, which made them strong yet flexible.

The DH.2 had a single fin and rudder and an unusually large tailplane.

Not only was the pilot expected to juggle his Lewis gun from side to side while maintaining control of the aircraft during combat, but he also had to change the heavy 47-round ammunition drums.

Both the top and bottom wings were fitted with ailerons. Once initial structural problems had been overcome and pilots had mastered its tricky handling, the DH.2 proved to be a manoeuvrable fighter.

Most DH.2s were powered by the Gnome Monosoupape rotary engine, but some of the later aircraft featured the 82-kW (110-hp.) Le Rhône engine.

A steerable tailskid aided ground handling, which was also improved, together with flight performance, by a larger rudder on production machines.

COMBAT DATA

MAXIMUM SPEED

Airco DH.2s were able to prevent air-superiority by the all-conquering Fokker monoplanes by virtue of their forward-firing gun, good manoeuvrability and high speed. Nieuport's Type 11 was faster still, but saw comparatively little service.

DH.2	150 km/h (93 m.p.h.)
E.III	140 km/h (87 m.p.h.)
TYPE 11	155 km/h (96 m.p.h.)

MAXIMUM POWER

Most aero-engines of the period produced a similar power output. More powerful engines were larger and therefore heavier. It was down to the aircraft designer to produce a light, efficient airframe to maximise available power, thereby giving optimum performance.

DH.2	E.III	TYPE 11
75 kW (100 hp.)	75 kW (100 hp.)	60 kW (80 hp.)

ENDURANCE

Escort missions were sometimes flown by fighting scouts such as these, but the majority of air-to-air victories were gained when pilots set out to find and engage enemy fighters. Long endurance gave a pilot more time to find targets and greater combat persistence.

DH.2	E.III	TYPE 11
2 hours 45 min	1 hour 30 min	2 hours 30 min

British pusher-engined fighters

VICKERS F.B.5 GUNBUS: This 1914 design represents the first British aircraft intended from the outset for air-to-air fighting.

GRAHAME-WHITE TYPE 11: The Type 11 was an unsuccessful attempt at producing a fighter in the 1915/16 period.

BLACKBURN TRIPLANE: Designed as a Zeppelin airship killer, the Triplane did not perform well and only one was built.

VICKERS TYPE 161 COW GUN FIGHTER: Built to carry the 37-mm COW gun, this 1931 fighter was the ultimate in pusher designs.

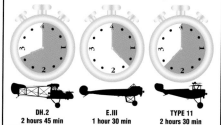

AIRCO

DH.4

● Day bomber ● British and US production ● Powerful engines

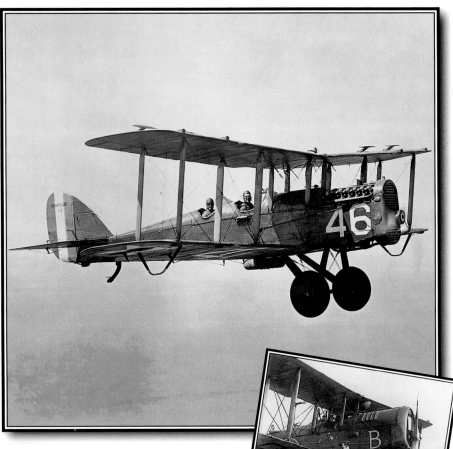

O ne of the most successful aircraft of World War I, the DH.4 was the first British bomber designed for the role. After its first flight in August 1916, the DH.4 was transformed by the Rolls-Royce Eagle engine, which enabled the aircraft's performance to match that of contemporary fighters. Nearly 7,000 were built, more than half of these in the US. Production continued after World War I, when several air forces, together with early airlines, retained the DH.4.

▲ After their success in France during World War I, British-built DH.4s and American-built DH.4s found further service in foreign air forces, including those of Belgium, Greece, Japan and Nicaragua.

PHOTO FILE

AIRCO DH.4

▲ DH-4B air mail pioneer
Surplus DH-4s were converted for the US Postal Department to establish an air mail service; the front cockpit held mail bags. This aircraft has wingtip landing lights.

▲ 'Liberty Plane'
With hundreds of surplus DH-4s available after World War I, many found their way into civil operation. DH-4s were used not only as mail carriers, but also as airliners and crop-dusters.

▲ Steel-framed DH-4M-1
A.S.23007 was one of a number of American-built DH-4s rebuilt by Boeing and Atlantic Aircraft during the 1920s, with steel-tube fuselages. These aircraft were designated DH-4M-1s and -2s, respectively.

▲ Cabin-equipped DH-4A
DH-4As carried a pilot and two passengers. Nine were converted from DH-4s, serving with the RAF and on early routes across the English Channel.

Army air ambulance ▶
Among numerous DH-4 variants to enter US military service were a number of DH-4Amb-2s which were able to carry two stretcher cases.

FACTS AND FIGURES

➤ A total of 30 aircraft were built for the US Postal Department, with increased-span wings and two 149-kW Hall-Scott engines.

➤ DH.4s were fitted with engines ranging in power output from 149 kW to 391 kW.

➤ Total US DH-4 production reached 4,846; 15 were built in Belgium; 1,449 in the UK.

➤ A DH.4 shipped to New Zealand became the first aircraft to fly over that country's highest mountain, 3760-m (12,330-ft.) Mount Cook.

➤ The Airco DH.4 prototype flew in August 1916 from its base at Hendon, London.

➤ For coastal patrol tasks, the RNAS fitted floats to at least one DH.4.

de Havilland's day bombing master

Staggered wings were used on the DH.4 to give the pilot a good view of the ground for bombing. One or two Lewis guns were fitted in the observer's cockpit, and one or two forward-firing Vickers guns were mounted on the fuselage sides. In this form the DH.4 made an immediate impression over the Western Front in 1917.

Nearly 1,500 were built in the UK, and almost 5,000 with 298-kW (400-hp.) Liberty 12 engines, in the United States, where the US Army used DH-4s until 1932. The US Navy and Marine Corps also used the type.

After the war, RAF aircraft were retired, and many were transferred to other countries. More than 1,500 of the American aircraft were modified as DH-4Bs, while Boeing and Fokker Atlantic built 285 modernised DH-4Ms with steel-tube fuselages. There were more than 60 modified versions, including single-seaters, dual-

Above: In 1923, USAAC DH-4s conclusively demonstrated air-to-air refuelling for the first time. The receiver was aloft for over 37 hours.

control trainers and air ambulances. A total of 100 DH-4Bs were also used to establish the US air mail service, the aircraft serving until 1927.

Above: The DH.4 was operational from April 1917. On 6 April, No. 55 Squadron flew from Fienvilliers on a mission to bomb Valenciennes. Its performance matched that of fighters of the time.

DH.4

N5977 was one of a batch of 50 DH.4s built by Westland Aircraft with Rolls-Royce Eagle engines. It carries the markings of No. 2 Squadron, RNAS, immediately prior to its redesignation in 1918 as No. 202 Squadron, RAF.

American interest in the DH.4 was high; almost 5,000 were built with 298-kW (400-hp.) Liberty 12 engines fitted. In all, 1,885 were shipped to France.

The placement of the main fuel tank between the pilot and the gunner proved a disadvantage as it hampered in-flight communication. It was also prone to catching fire if hit by enemy guns, earning the aircraft the nickname 'The Flaming Coffin'.

DH.4s were defensively and offensively well-armed. RNAS aircraft carried two forward-firing 7.7-mm (.303 cal.) Vickers machine-guns above the engine (RFC machines carried only one) and one or two 7.7-mm Lewis machine-guns in the rear cockpit.

The DH.4 was a conventional two-bay biplane with a wood and fabric structure, although its forward fuselage was skinned with plywood for strength. The tailplane was adjustable, allowing the pilot to trim the aircraft in flight.

Originally intended to be powered by an uprated Beardmore engine of 119 kW (160 hp.), the first DH.4 actually flew with a 172-kW (230-hp.) BHP powerplant. However, it was Rolls-Royce's 186-kW (250-hp.) Eagle 12-cylinder engine that took the DH.4 to fame.

Underfuselage/wing bomb racks on the DH.4 had a 209-kg (460-lb.) capacity. As No. 55 Squadron, Royal Flying Corps received its first aircraft, Royal Naval Air Service examples were also being delivered. These aircraft undertook bombing, gun ranging (for ships), reconnaissance and photographic tasks.

DH.4

Type: light day bomber

Powerplant: one 280-kW (375-hp.) Rolls-Royce Eagle VIII water-cooled 12-cylinder engine

Maximum speed: 230 km/h (143 m.p.h.) at sea level

Endurance: 3 hours 45 min

Range: 700 km (435 mi.)

Service ceiling: 6705 m (22,000 ft.)

Weights: empty 1083 kg (2,383 lb.); maximum take-off 1575 kg (3,465 lb.)

Armament: (RNAS aircraft) two forward-firing 7.7-mm (.303 cal.) Vickers machine-guns and one or two 7.7-mm Lewis machine-gun(s) in the rear cockpit, plus up to 209 kg (460 lb.) of bombs

Dimensions:
span	12.92 m	(42 ft. 4 in.)
length	9.35 m	(30 ft. 8 in.)
height	3.05 m	(10 ft.)
wing area	40.32 m²	(434 sq. ft.)

COMBAT DATA

ENDURANCE

The DH.4 had a good range and endurance performance compared to the contemporary Albatros C.V/16. The post-war American-built DH-4M retained this ability.

DH.4	C.V/16	DH-4M
3 hrs 45 mins	3 hrs 15 mins	3 hrs 45 mins

ARMAMENT

While RFC DH.4s were equipped with three machine-guns, RNAS aircraft used four, like the later US-built DH-4M. The Albatros was lightly-armed by comparison, although it could carry a 'light bombload'.

DH.4 3 x 7. 7-mm (.303 cal.) machine-guns
209-kg (460-lb.) bombload

C.V/16 2 x 7.92-mm machine-guns

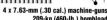

DH-4M 4 x 7.63-mm (.30 cal.) machine-guns
209-kg (460-lb.) bombload

POWER

The chief benefits of the post-war DH-4M were its more powerful engine and more robust steel-tube fuselage structure. With the Liberty 12 installed, it had twice the power of the C.V/16.

DH.4	C.V/16	DH-4M
280 kW (375 hp.)	164 kW (220 hp.)	313 kW (420 hp.)

British land-based bombers of World War I

AVRO 504: In November 1914, four modified RNAS 504 trainers from a base in France made a raid on Zeppelin sheds at Friedrichshafen.

ROYAL AIRCRAFT FACTORY BE.2: This two-seat reconnaissance type was adapted as a bomber, but was vulnerable to enemy fighters.

SHORT BOMBER: A land-based version of the Short 184 floatplane, the Bomber flew missions with the RNAS from late 1916.

SOPWITH 1½ STRUTTER: Armed with a forward-firing gun, this Sopwith design equipped RNAS and RFC units as a bomber and escort.

AIRCO

DH.9 AND DH.9A

● Two-seat bomber ● World War I ● Popular civilian aircraft

An ambitious attempt to improve the DH.4, the Airco DH.9 was a bomber expected to play a major role in the Great War. It had the advantage of using wings, tail and landing gear similar to those of the DH.4, which made it easy to produce, but the type suffered from having inadequate engines and remained inferior to the plane it was meant to replace in the newly-established Royal Air Force. The DH.9A, however, was a much improved model.

▲ Serving briefly in the day-bomber role at the end of World War I, the DH.9A, known as the 'Nine-Ack', stayed in production after 1918 and in the 1920s served as an army co-operation aircraft in Iraq and on the North-West Frontier. UK-based bomber and auxiliary squadrons were also equipped with the DH.9A.

▲ **Post-war versatility**
After World War I, many DH.9s were sold on the civilian market; some were exported, including this floatplane conversion which was sold to the British and Egyptian Tea Co. Ltd.

▲ **Large wing**
The later versions of the DH.9 and DH.9A had a very good service ceiling, made possible by the large wing area.

Civil service ▼
Belgian airline SNETA's DH.9C flew between Croydon and Brussels, with wing-mounted luggage racks and a DH.4 cabin.

Flexible load ▲
During World War I the DH.9 was used to distribute propaganda leaflets behind enemy lines – one of the earliest examples of psychological warfare. DH.9s of No.110 Squadron dropped over 10 tons of bombs on German cities in 1918.

▲ **Close formation**
In 1923 the DH.9A was a state-of-the-art day-bomber; crews from No. 39 Squadron are seen here practising formation flying.

Mock attack ▶
At the Hendon Pageant in 1929 No. 208(AC) Sqn conducted bombing demonstrations with their DH.9As against a mock fort and tanks.

FACTS AND FIGURES

➤ The DH.9 was introduced to combat service in France with British squadrons in April 1918, and the DH.9A in June.

➤ The prototype for this series began flight tests in July 1917.

➤ The total production of the DH.9 exceeded 3,200 aircraft.

➤ War surplus DH.9 and DH.9As served in many countries, including Afghanistan, Canada, Estonia, Greece and Latvia.

➤ Hispano-Suiza manufactured about 500 DH.9s for the Spanish air force.

➤ Ultimately, DH.9s were produced at the rate of one every 40 minutes.

PROFILE

The nine and the 'Nine-Ack'

The DH.9 was produced because of the concern about daylight attacks on London by German bombers. Seeking to improve its own bomber force, the Royal Flying Corps invested heavily in the DH.9, a handsome but under-powered aircraft based on the proven (and famous) DH.4.

Flown with several engine types, the DH.9 was always hamstrung by inadequate power. Intrepid British crews, flying with squadrons in France, achieved some success against

the Kaiser's forces, but suffered heavy losses which were blamed on the flaws of this promising but disappointing biplane.

DH.9s were more effective in Macedonia, Palestine and at home in the United Kingdom, where they flew coastal defence and anti-Zeppelin patrols. The last RAF DH.9s were used as ambulances in Somaliland, but these were withdrawn by July 1919.

The DH.9A, however, was one of the most successful

strategic bombers of the period. Considerably more powerful engine types and a larger wing area ensured much improved performance. Though used only briefly before the Armistice, the DH.9A was standard equipment in the RAF until 1931.

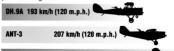

Above: Despite its ungainly appearance the DH.9A gave valuable service in India, the Middle East and North Africa. Reconditioned in 1925, this aircraft enjoyed a very long service life.

Above: After the war some DH.9As were 'tropicalised' for service in Iraq and on the North-West Frontier. This aircraft has an extra radiator under the nose and an overload fuel tank under the starboard upper wing.

DH.9A

Type: two-seat light day-bomber

Powerplant: one 298-kW (400-hp.) Liberty 12 inline piston engine

Maximum speed: 193 km/h (120 m.p.h.) at 3048 m (10,000 ft.)

Endurance: 5 hours 45 min

Range: 1000 km (620 mi.)

Service ceiling: 5105 m (16,750 ft.)

Weights: empty 1012 kg (2,226 lb.); maximum take-off 1508 kg (3,310 lb.)

Armament: one fixed forward-firing 7.7-mm (.303 cal.) Vickers machine-gun and one or two 7.7-mm Lewis guns fitted on a Scarff ring in the aft cockpit, plus up to 299 kg (660 lb.) of bombs

Dimensions: span 14.02 m (46 ft.)
length 9.14 m (30 ft.)
height 3.44 m (11 ft. 3 in.)
wing area 40.32 m² (434 sq. ft.)

Most DH.9s were powered by the Rolls-Royce Eagle or the slightly more powerful Liberty 12 engine built in the United States.

In the DH.9 the pilot no longer sat in the potentially dangerous position between the engine and fuel tank, as in the DH.4. With the cockpit set further back, he could also communicate with the gunner far more easily.

The silver colour scheme carried by this 'Nine-Ack' is typical of RAF army co-operation aircraft in the Middle East during the 1920s.

DH.9A

J7832 was operated by No. 45 Squadron, RAF, based at Helwan, Egypt, in 1928. It was tasked with aerial policing in co-operation with the army.

The 'winged camel' symbol on the nose of this aircraft is that of No. 45 Squadron, RAF. This symbol formed part of their official squadron badge, alluding to colonial policing duties in the Middle East.

Armament consisted of two machine-guns: the pilot's 7.7-mm (.303 cal.) Vickers firing through the propeller and the observer's single or twin 7.7-mm Lewis gun.

Initially fitted with a 171-kW (230-hp.) engine, the DH.9 was unable to climb above 3962 metres (13,000 ft.) with a full military load of fuel, oil, water and armament.

ACTION DATA

MAXIMUM SPEED
The DH.9A was designed to have a superior service ceiling rather than a high top speed. The other two types were fitted with more powerful engines.

DH.9A 193 km/h (120 m.p.h.)
ANT-3 207 km/h (128 m.p.h.)
Bre.19A2 235 km/h (146 m.p.h.)

SERVICE CEILING
In action from bases the DH.9A was able to elude enemy fighters with its altitude capability, which was exceptional for the period.

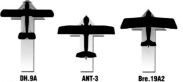

DH.9A 5105 m (16,750 ft.) | ANT-3 4950 m (10,900 ft.) | Bre.19A2 5000 m (16,400 ft.)

ARMAMENT
Compared to other light day-bombers of the era, the DH.9A had a comparable gun armament, but a relatively light bombload. The Breguet 19 had superior defensive armament.

DH.9A 299 kg (660 lb.) bombs and 2 x 7.7-mm (.303 cal.) MGs | ANT-3 500 kg (1,100 lb.) bombs and 2 x 7.62-mm (.30 cal.) MGs | Bre.19A2 400 kg (880 lb.) bombs and 3 x 7.7-mm (.303 cal.) MGs

Early Airco/de Havillands

DH.2: When the first DH.2 flew in 1915 the British had yet to develop interrupter gear to allow a gun to be fired forwards through the propeller arc. The DH.2 was a successful single-seat fighter with a pusher propeller and armed with a Lewis machine-gun.

DH.4: One of the outstanding designs of World War I, the DH.4 had handling and performance that made it almost impossible to intercept when it entered service in France in March 1917. Thousands were built in the United States after the war.

DH.10 AMIENS: A twin-engined bomber based on the smaller DH.3, the Amiens was just too late to see war service. Peacetime duties included an airmail service between England and occupied Germany; others served on the North-West Frontier.

ALBATROS

C.I-C.XII

● Artillery observation ● Bomber ● Long service history

▲ Pilots came to respect the C Series aircraft as they built up a reputation for viceless handling and the ability to bring their crews home despite suffering considerable damage.

To take advantage of the more powerful engines available to the Germans in 1915, Albatros designed a two-seat general-purpose aircraft named the C.I. The design was so good that it spawned a number of successors which served until the conclusion of World War I. With a sturdy wooden fuselage the C Series aircraft could take a considerable amount of punishment. Several of Germany's most famous pilots started their operational careers in the type.

ALBATROS C.I-C.XII

▼ Production milestone
In 1917 Albatros celebrated the construction of their 2,500th aircraft by decorating this C.V. This version was powered by a 164-kW eight-cylinder Mercedes engine.

▲ Modified C.I
This aircraft has a modified fin and rudder with a vertical trailing edge. Unusually, the aircraft is being flown from the rear cockpit.

Restricted view ▶
The large engine, with its vertical exhaust, gave C.III pilots very restricted forward vision.

▲ Heavily braced
The biplane wings were supported by wooden wing struts and a multitude of bracing wires.

Versatile aircraft ▶
The Albatros C.III was the most important general-purpose German aircraft of 1916.

FACTS AND FIGURES

➤ The world's most famous ace, Baron Manfred von Richthofen, flew as an observer in a C.I on the Russian Front.

➤ The C.Ib dual-control trainer version was built mainly by Mercur Flugzeugbau.

➤ The Albatros series was identifiable by the distinctive 'chimney' exhausts.

➤ Although initially regarded as a 'stop-gap' machine, 350 C.VIIs were still serving with front-line units as late as February 1917.

➤ Serving in all battle areas, the C.VII was often used as a light tactical bomber.

➤ The C.X was fitted with oxygen equipment, allowing high-altitude reconnaissance.

Germany's multi-role master

Designed at a time when the full capabilities of the aeroplane were not fully appreciated, the Albatros C.I was an advanced aircraft for its day. Entering service in 1915, the Albatros was used for reconnaissance, bombing, photography, artillery observation and, for a brief period, as an escort.

One reason for the C.I's popularity with crew was its excellent rearward-firing gun on a moveable mounting, which, for the first time, allowed the observer to take defensive action against hostile aircraft.

Among the famous pilots who flew the C.I was Oswald Boelcke, who developed the technique of positioning his aircraft to enable the observer to fire at enemy aircraft.

The C.I was followed in production by the C.III, which became the most prolific of all Albatros two-seaters. Similar in form to the C.I, this aircraft featured a more powerful engine and revised tail surfaces which increased agility.

The less successful C.V and C.VI designs were followed by the C.VII, which again featured a more powerful engine and control improvements. The last two major types, the C.X and C.XII, were highly capable machines but they retained many features from the original C.I.

Left: To help prevent noxious fumes from the engine reaching the cockpit, this C.I featured extended exhausts which released fumes over the wing.

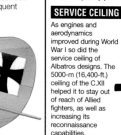

Above: This Swedish version of the Albatros C.I was designated SK 1 and was used as a trainer in the 1920s. It is seen here preserved at the Malmslatt Museum in Sweden.

C.III

Type: two-seat general-purpose biplane

Powerplant: one 111.9-kW (150-hp.) Benz Bz III or one 119.3-kW (160-hp.) Mercedes D III piston engine

Maximum speed: 140 km/h (87 m.p.h.)

Endurance: 4 hr

Initial climb rate: 9 min to 1000 m (3,300 ft.)

Service ceiling: 3353 m (11,000 ft.)

Weights: empty 851 kg (1,872 lb.); loaded 1353 kg (2,977 lb.)

Armament: one 7.92-mm machine-gun on a flexible mount in the rear cockpit and (on later aircraft) one 7.92-mm forward-firing LMG 08/15 machine-gun, plus up to 91 kg (200 lb.) of bombs

Dimensions:
span	11.69 m	(38 ft. 4 in.)
length	8.00 m	(26 ft. 3 in.)
height	3.10 m	(10 ft. 2 in.)
wing area	36.91 m²	(426 sq. ft.)

C.III

Seen in a typical factory-finish colour scheme, this C.III was delivered in early 1917. The type commanded great respect from Allied pilots who found it very difficult to shoot down.

The pilot, seated in the front cockpit, flew the aircraft using wheel and rudder-bar type controls. Instrumentation was comprehensive for the period and included altimeter, fuel gauges, tachometer, clock and compass.

The trainable Parabellum machine-gun of the C.III was a very useful weapon and allowed the observer to fire at attackers approaching from behind.

Although similar to its C.I predecessor, the C.III featured completely revised tail surfaces. The new, more rounded unit was a hallmark of subsequent C Series Albatros aircraft.

The majority of C.IIIs were fitted with a Mercedes D III engine, which was mounted on stout wooden bearers. A short chimney-type manifold exhausted the engine fumes vertically. Later versions were fitted with a fixed forward-facing machine-gun which fired through the propeller arc.

The vee-type main undercarriage was constructed of steel tube. A 'claw'-type brake was fitted in the centre of the axle and was operated by a lever in the cockpit.

The C.III's great strength was due to the construction of the fuselage. This comprised four main fuselage longerons covered with plywood panels which did not need internal bracing.

COMBAT DATA

POWER

Developed before the outbreak of World War I, the B.I was relatively underpowered compared to the later C Series. The ultimate C.XII had excellent performance thanks to its powerful engine.

B.II 74 kW (100 hp.)
C.I 119 kW (160 hp.)
C.XII 194 klW (260 hp.)

SERVICE CEILING

As engines and aerodynamics improved during World War I so did the service ceiling of Albatros designs. The 5000-m (16,400-ft.) ceiling of the C.XII helped it to stay out of reach of Allied fighters, as well as increasing its reconnaissance capabilities.

B.II 3000m (9,840 ft.)
C.I 3353 m (11,000 ft.)
C.XII 5000 m (16,400 ft.)

ENDURANCE

The B.I was one of the best observation aircraft of 1914/15. One of its main assets was its excellent endurance, allowing it to cover a large area during reconnaissance missions. Later C Series aircraft generally had poorer endurance because of their 'thirsty' engines.

B.II 4 hours
C.I 2 hours 30 min
C.XII 2 hours 15 min

Albatros family

D SERIES: The D Series of fighting scouts were highly respected by the Allies and saw action from 1916 until the end of the war.

G SERIES: Albatros produced three bomber designs during World War I. This example, a G.II, was built only in prototype form.

L SERIES: Post-war Albatros aircraft were given L prefixes. This example is a L.72 biplane which transported freight between German cities.

W SERIES: Fitted with twin floats, the W.1 was basically an unarmed reconnaissance seaplane version of the B.II landplane.

ALBATROS

D.VA

● Single-seat biplane fighter ● Wooden fuselage

▲ *Introduced in the mid-summer of 1917, the Albatros D.V was the German air service's answer to the Allies' SE.5a and Spad, both of which had gained the upper hand against the earlier D.III.*

Right to the end of World War I, the name Albatros could strike fear into the hearts of Allied flyers. The D.V could be a tough adversary and many were flown by the German aces of the day. An Achilles heel of the D.V, however, was a weakness in the wing struts, which was never fully overcome. As Allied air superiority increased, the greatly improved D.Va was introduced and hundreds of examples entered service before November 1918.

ALBATROS D.VA

◄ **Fighter pilot Göring**
Lieutenant Hermann Göring, later the infamous head of the Luftwaffe, led Jasta 27 in an Albatros D.V similar to this, but black with a white nose and tail.

▲ **Proud pilot and his D.I**
A young pilot in the German Imperial Air Service poses next to his Albatros D.I. The positioning of the upper wing on the D.I impaired the pilot's upward forward vision – a problem rectified on the later D.II by lowering the wing. D.IIs also had a modified radiator system.

▲ **Captured Albatros**
The occasional capture of enemy aircraft allowed Allied pilots to test fly and assess the machines they would meet in hostile skies.

▼ **Albatros D.IIIa**
The D.V was developed from the earlier D.III, but with a deeper, more elliptical fuselage and a modified rudder, among other changes.

▲ **Albatros D.I**
The Albatros D.I of 1916 was the earliest ancestor of the D.V, designed to meet the threat of the Allied DH.2s and Nieuports. Note the flat fuselage sides compared to the D.V. Though not very manoeuverable, the D.I was relatively fast.

FACTS AND FIGURES

➤ Total production of the Albatros D.V was 900 aircraft, followed by 1,612 examples of the D.Va.

➤ The D.Va took just 17 minutes to reach a height of 3658 m (12,000 ft.).

➤ The D.Va was the last Albatros design to see action in World War I.

➤ In April 1918, D.V and D.Va aircraft made up more than 54 per cent of the total number of German fighters available for action.

➤ The 'Red Baron', Manfred von Richtofen, was shot down in a D.V on 6 July 1917.

➤ Albatroses of Jasta 21 shot down 41 French aircraft in September 1917.

PROFILE

Imperial Germany's bird of prey

The intended successor to the Albatros D.III, the D.V fighter was something of a compromise design that entered service without adequate testing. German engineers overlooked a dangerous flaw in the wing-fuselage attachment points and one that, despite modifications, was never completely cured.

No less a personality than Baron Manfred von Richtofen was scathing about the flying and fighting qualities of the D.V. In a letter written in July 1917 he called it 'so obsolete and so ridiculously inferior to the English that one can't do anything with this aircraft'. But such was the strength of the opposition on the Western Front at that time that the German air service had little choice.

Timely testing of the suspected weak areas of the

D.V airframe helped save the situation, as did the availability of the Mercedes D.IIIa engine. This powerplant gave back what the D.Va had lost to increased weight as a result of wing and strut modifications.

Albatros D.Va fighters were ordered in quantity and began to reach operational units in October 1917 in time for the Spring Offensive the following year. They soon represented over half the fighters available to the Germans during the last months of the war.

Above: The need for aircraft was so great that the D.V was produced in large numbers despite its inferior performance.

Left: With the success of such aircraft as the Fokker Triplane, Albatros flew an unsuccessful triplane version of the D.V.

D.Va

Type: Single-seat scout fighter.

Powerplant: One 134-kW (180-hp.) Mercedes D.IIIa six-cylinder in-line engine

Maximum speed: 185 km/h (115 m.p.h.)

Service ceiling: 6095 m (20,000 ft.)

Range: 354 km (220 mi.)

Weights: Empty 679 kg (1,496 lb.); loaded 935 kg (2,061 lb.)

Weapons: Two 7.92-mm Maxim LMG 08/15 machine guns in forward fuselage.

Dimensions:
span	9.04 m (29 ft. 8 in.)
length	7.32 m (24 ft.)
height	2.44 m (8 ft. 10 in.)
wing area	20.81 m² (224 sq. ft.)

D.Va

This Albatros D.V flew with Jasta 5, one of the Imperial Air Service's elite fighter units on the Western Front. The multi-point star emblem was the personal marking of its pilot, Lietenant Klein.

Typical of fighters of the period, the aircraft's machine guns fired through the arc of the propeller, with the aid of interrupter gear.

A strong monocoque plywood fuselage and smoothly faired engine made the Albatros one of the most streamlined aircraft of the period.

Many Albatros Scouts in service with the German Air Corps flew with their plywood fuselages largely unpainted.

The large spinner on the Albatros's propeller was designed to reduce drag, increasing performance.

Sustained diving maneuvers resulted in vibrations in the lower wing and its eventual failure. A design flaw was to blame. Strengthened wing struts solved the problem temporarily.

The elliptical fuselage cross-section of the D.V and D.Va contrasted with the flat fuselage sides of the earlier D.I.

ACTION DATA

SPEED

A major area in which the Albatros D.V was deficient compared to the Allied fighters of the closing years of World War I was speed. Aircraft like the SE.5a and Spad VII were capable of speeds in excess of 200 km/h (124 m.p.h.).

SE. 5A	222 km/h (138 m.p.h.)
ALBATROS D.V	185 km/h (115 m.p.h.)
SPAD VII	211 km/h (131 m.p.h.)

WEAPONS

The twin Maxim machine gun armament of the Albatros was introduced first on the D.I of 1916 and took a major toll on Allied aircraft. By 1917, however, guns of this type and caliber were more common, and the advantage became nil.

SE. 5A	2 x 7.7-mm (.303 cal.) MGs
SPAD VII	1 x 7.7-mm (.303 cal.) MG
ALBATROS D.V	2 x 7.92-mm MGs

CEILING

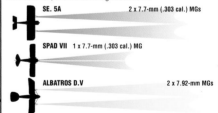

Once again, the dated design of the D.V was reflected by its service ceiling. Wing problems led to pilots being advised not to over-dive their aircraft. This restriction had obvious effects on morale.

SE. 5A	SPAD VII	ALBATROS D.V
6703 m (21,990 ft.)	6553 m (21,500 ft.)	6095 m (20,000 ft.)

Multi-coloured wooden dogfighters

■ **JASTA 4:** In service the yellow tail of this D.V signifies an aircraft of Jasta 4. The plywood fuselage of this aircraft has been varnished to a high degree.

■ **JASTA 5:** With the green fin of Jasta 5, this D.V adorned with a edelweiss symbol was flown by Obltn Paul Baümer (43 kills) and later Lt. Wilhelm Lehmann, Jastafuhrer.

■ **JASTA 5:** This aircraft, with its entire fuselage in green, was seen at Boistrancourt in the summer of 1917. A black chevron was painted on the upper wing.

■ **JASTA 5:** Another Jasta 5 aircraft featuring an elaborate blue and white diamond colour scheme; the upper surfaces of the wings are a more conventional green.

ANTONOV

AN-2 'COLT'

● Biplane utility aircraft ● Post-war design ● More than 18,000 built

▲ *Entering*
service in 1948, the An-2
immediately became the standard utility type for
Aeroflot and the armed forces. More than 10,000,
mainly Polish-built examples, have been delivered.

When the first An-2 flew in
August 1947, nobody could have
predicted that it would become
the best-selling post-war aircraft. Yet it has
remained in production for more than 40
years and at least 18,000 have been
built in Russia, Poland and China. The
biplane configuration that makes it look
so old-fashioned in the jet age gives it
outstanding short take-off performance
and low-speed handling qualities.

ANTONOV AN-2 'COLT'

◄ Sturdy design
Just like the wartime C-47
transport, the An-2 has been
an economical, rugged aircraft.

▼ Fedya, the spotter aircraft
The An-2F Fedya had a new rear
fuselage for a tactical observer
and a 12.7-mm (.50 cal.)
machine-gun in a dorsal cupola.

▼ Soviet colours
Naturally, the Soviet armed forces have
been the biggest users of the An-2 in its
various versions. Since the break-up of
the USSR, Russia operates the largest
fleet of 'Colts', with more than 300
examples in the utility role.

▼ 'Scimitar' blades
Early aircraft were fitted with a 3.6-m (11-ft. 10-
in.) V-509A propeller with four scimitar-like
blades. The usual propeller on later aircraft was
a 3.35-m (11-ft.) example with straight blades.

◄ Atmosphere sampler
An-2ZA had a heated compartment for a scientific
observer, faired into the tailfin and accessed from the
fuselage. The aircraft's ASh-62IR engine was fitted
with a turbocharger to maintain 634 kW (850 hp.) at
its operating ceiling of 9500 metres (31,200 ft.).

FACTS AND FIGURES

➤ Originally, An-2s had a two-man crew: a
pilot and flight engineer. The pilot was not
allowed to touch the engine controls.

➤ 'Anusha' (or 'little Anna') is a common
nickname for the An-2 in Eastern Europe.

➤ Some Chinese Y-5s were built with Pratt &
Whitney PT6A turboprops.

➤ During its design, consideration was
given to a welded tube and fabric
structure to allow local repairs.

➤ An-2s have been fitted with glider tow
hooks; all are easily fitted with skis.

➤ For parachute training, the cargo door
is removed and a static line fitted.

PROFILE

Irreplaceable 'little Anna'

Tasked with designing a replacement for the Po-2 agricultural aircraft, Antonov chose the biplane configuration because it gave the aeroplane manoeuvrability and compactness. The An-2 was soon in production for a host of uses, from airline transport and paratroop training to crop-spraying and ambulance work.

By 1959, around 5,450 An-2s had been built in the Soviet Union, when production was transferred to Poland. Since

then, WSK-PZL has built more than 12,000 (mostly for the USSR), including several locally developed variants.

Meanwhile, Nanchang had flown the first Chinese-built An-2 in 1957 under the designation Y-5. Shijiazhuang took over Chinese production in 1968, bringing the total built in the country to around 1,000, including the Y-5B modified agricultural model.

Thousands of An-2s remain in service around the world.

Fitted with wheels, skis or floats, they are used for water-bombing, aerial survey, glider towing and a host of other military roles, although the majority were completed as agricultural aircraft. A turboprop conversion designated An-3 was flown, but plans to convert large numbers of An-2s were abandoned.

Above: Since 1959, An-2 production has been concentrated at the PZL-Mielec plant in Poland.

Below: Among the many nations, to have received versions of the An-2, Egypt finished their aircraft in appropriate desert colours.

An-2P 'Colt'

Type: biplane utility aircraft

Powerplant: one 746-kW (1,000-hp.) Shvetsov ASh-621R nine-cylinder air-cooled radial engine

Maximum speed: 258 km/h (160 m.p.h.) at 1750 m (5,700 ft.)

Climb rate: 210 m/min (600 f.p.m.) at sea level

Range: 900 km (560 mi.) at 1000 m (3,300 ft.) with 500-kg (1.100-lb.) payload

Service ceiling: 4400 m (14,400 ft.)

Weights: empty 3450 kg (7,590 lb.); maximum take-off 5500 kg (12,100 lb.)

Accommodation: two crew plus 12 passengers or 2140 kg (4,700 lb.) of cargo

Dimensions: span 18.18 m (59 ft. 8 in.)
length 12.74 m (41 ft. 9 in.)
height 6.10 m (20 ft.)
wing area 71.52 m² (770 sq. ft.)

Y-5

Manufactured under Soviet licence, the An-2 was built in China for 30 years for both civil and military duties. The first of 948 examples from Nanchang and Shijiazhuang (SAP) factories flew on 7 December 1957.

A huge area of cockpit glazing gives the pilot an excellent field of view. He is also able to look down, thanks to 0.3 metres (a foot) of window overhang either side of the cockpit.

A light alloy stressed-skin construction was used in the An-2. The tailplane and all control surfaces are fabric-covered.

A centre-of-gravity problem caused by the narrow chord wings required the controls to be pushed fully forward during a full load take-off. To correct this, a larger tailplane was fitted from the 61st aircraft onwards.

The first prototype was fitted with a seven-cylinder Shvetsov ASh-21 rated at 522 kW (700 hp.), and the second with a 746-kW (1,000-hp.) ASh-62IR engine (a design derived from the Wright R-1820 Cyclone). The more powerful engine was chosen for production aircraft as it allowed an extra 800 kg (1,760 lb.) to be carried.

'Colts' are able to lift over 2 tons in their capacious fuselages. However, the An-2 has always had problems with being tail-heavy and this precludes carrying anything in the rear of the fuselage. Take-offs are made tail-down at 90 km/h (56 m.p.h.) with a full load.

A large, upwardly-hinged cargo door dominates the port side of the aircraft. Inset into this is an inward-opening passenger door. In basic passenger configuration, 12 seats may be fitted.

8192

ACTION DATA

ECONOMIC CRUISING SPEED

Speed is not a major consideration in the design of any of these utility aircraft. Short take-off and landing (STOL) performance and load-carrying ability are more important parameters, together with economy of operation.

 An-2P 'COLT' 185 km/h (115 m.p.h.)

 DHC-3 OTTER 195 km/h (121 m.p.h.)

Do 28D-1 SKYSERVANT 230km/h (143 m.p.h.)

PASSENGERS

The An-2 is large for a single-engined aircraft and is equipped with a sizeable fuselage for 12 seats (in standard passenger configuration), or more than 2000 kg (4,400 lb.) of cargo in the freight transport role. A comparable Western design is the de Havilland Canada Otter, although this cannot carry the same payload as the 'Colt'.

An-2P 'COLT' 12 passengers | DHC-3 OTTER 10 passengers | Do 28D-1 SKYSERVANT 12 passengers

RANGE

Where the An-2 has been left behind by some more recent Western designs is in its range performance. The twin-engined Skyservant has a range twice that of the An-2. Recently, DHC-3s have been fitted with the ASh-62 engine to improve performance.

An-2P 'COLT' 900 km (560 mi.)
DHC-3 OTTER 1408 km (873 mi.)
Do 28D-1 SKYSERVANT 1810 km (1,120 mi.)

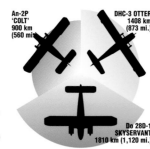

'Colts' in worldwide service

■ **NORTH KOREAN Y-5:** 'Red 44' is finished in the all-over matt black worn by Chinese-built Y-5s involved in night-time covert operations over South Korea.

■ **POLISH An-2V:** Seen in Polish markings, this float-equipped An-2V further illustrates the versatility of the 'Colt'. Floats tended to be fitted at factory or major depot level, rather than in the field.

■ **SOVIET An-2TD:** This parachute training version of the An-2 carries the markings of DOSAAF, the huge paramilitary grouping which organises all sporting aviation in the USSR.

ARADO
AR 68

● Biplane fighter ● Superseded by the Bf 109 ● Combat proven

▲ With its
sleek lines and outstanding
handling, the Ar 68 should be considered, along
with the Polikarpov I-153 and Fiat CR.42, one of
the finest biplane fighters.

When German authorities approved production of the Arado Ar 68 in 1936, they were ordering the Luftwaffe's last biplane fighter. The Ar 68, like so many similar aircraft of its era, was destined to spend only a brief time as a front-line fighter. However, when fitted with early Junkers Jumo engines, the Ar 68 gave excellent performance which was not surpassed until the introduction of the Bf 109 into squadron service.

ARADO AR 68

▼ **Arado's last attempt**
Convinced that the biplane fighter was still viable in 1937, Arado built a single Ar 68H, with an enclosed cockpit and a radial engine.

▲ **Luftwaffe service**
One of the earliest Ar 68Es shows its clean and aerodynamic lines.

▼ **Supercharged Jumo**
With its Jumo 210Da engine, the Ar 68e marked a departure from the BMW engine of the Ar 68d.

▲ **Third prototype**
The second of the Jumo-engined prototypes, the Ar 68c featured a cleaner radiator installation than that of the similarly engined Ar 68b.

Inferior fighter ▶
Problems in supplying the Jumo engine led to an initial order for Ar 68F-1s powered by the BMW VId engine of the Ar 68a and d prototypes. Very poor performance meant that only a few Ar 68F-1s were built.

FACTS AND FIGURES

➤ The Ar 68 followed on from the unsuccessful Arado Ar 67, which had first flown in late 1933.

➤ By the outbreak of World War II only a few Ar 68s were left on the front line.

➤ The Ar 68a prototype made its initial flight early in the summer of 1934.

➤ Arado used the distinctive fin seen on the Ar 68 on all its subsequent single-engined designs.

➤ Arado was producing He 51 fighters while it designed the Ar 68.

➤ Early in 1938 the Ar 68 equipped the majority of German fighter units.

Germany's finest biplane fighter

As the Luftwaffe's principal fighter aircraft in the late 1930s, the Arado Ar 68 was flown by a generation of German aviators who later used their skills in war.

The Ar 68, with its metal airframe covered by plywood skinning and fabric, was very much up to early-1930s standards of advanced biplane design. Some pilots were initially concerned about the Ar 68,

however. Attrition rates of the earlier He 51 had been high because of its comparatively high weight and fast landing speeds, characteristics which were even more pronounced in the Arado fighter. To dispel any doubts, Ernst Udet, who was then Inspector of Fighter and Dive-Bomber Pilots, arranged for a mock combat between himself, in a Jumo-engined Ar 68, and one of the Luftwaffe's top fighter

pilots in an He 51. Udet's decisive victory proved the exceptional manoeuvrability and ruggedness of the Ar 68, which immediately entered squadron service.

A few Ar 68s were in service as night-fighters during the winter of 1939/40, but most saw wartime service as trainers.

Above: Arado initially fitted the Ar 68a with the BMW VI engine, even though it was limited in performance.

Left: This Ar 68F-1 shows the troughs for the twin MG 17 machine-gun installation in the top of the engine cowling. The upper wing ailerons were almost full span.

AR 68E-1

This aircraft was the personal mount of Leutnant Riegel, the Gruppe adjutant of III/JG 141. The unit was based at Fürstenwalde during 1938. Most Ar 68s were operated by fighter pilot training schools by the time war broke out.

This highly distinctive tailfin design became something of an Arado trademark. It was also used on types such as the Ar 95, Ar 96 and Ar 196. Unusually placed vee-struts connected the tailplane to the vertical fin. Like the fuselage, the tail surfaces had a steel framework and metal skinning.

Powered by the excellent Junkers Jumo 210 powerplant, the Ar 68E-1 had an exceptionally neat engine installation. Twin machine-guns were mounted in the upper fuselage.

A small windscreen protected the pilot from the worst of the slipstream. Pilots of early aircraft complained that exhaust fumes entered the cockpit.

A rectangular welded steel-tube framework made up the basic structure of the aircraft. A great deal of the fuselage and wings was plywood covered with some fabric.

Unusually for an aircraft with a spatted undercarriage, the Ar 68E-1 appears to have retained its spats while in service. The cantilever main undercarriage legs were also aerodynamically faired.

The upper wing had large ailerons and the lower wing had flaps fitted. A single set of interplane struts braced the wings on each side. They were of N-type and canted outwards.

Even the tailwheel was faired by a spat. The unit was free swivelling, giving improved ground handling. The landing speed of the Ar 68 was comparatively high.

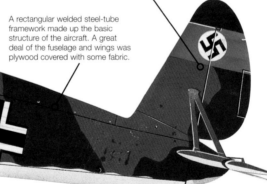

Ar 68E-1

Type: single-seat biplane fighter

Powerplant: one 515-kW (690-hp.) Junkers Jumo 210Da 12-cylinder inverted-vee liquid-cooled piston engine

Maximum speed: 305 km/h (189 m.p.h.) at sea level

Cruising speed: 281 km/h (174 m.p.h.) at sea level

Range: 415 km (260 mi.)

Service ceiling: 8100 m (26,500 ft.)

Weights: empty 1840 kg (4,048 lb.); maximum take-off 2475 kg (5,445 lb.)

Armament: two fixed forward-firing 7.92-mm MG 17 machine-guns with 500 rounds per gun and six 10-kg (22-lb.) SC 10 fragmentation bombs in an optional underfuselage magazine

Dimensions: span 11.00 m (36 ft. 1 in.)
length 9.50 m (31 ft. 2 in.)
height 3.28 m (10 ft. 9 in.)
wing area 27.30 m² (294 sq. ft.)

COMBAT DATA

POWER

In the UK the Gloster Gladiator represented the last service biplane fighter. It had the most powerful engine of these three aircraft, but was only a development of the Gauntlet and represented no real advance in fighter design.

Ar 68E-1 — 515 kW (690 hp.)
GLADIATOR Mk II — 619 kW (830 hp.)
I-15BIS CHAIKA — 578 kW (775 hp.)

RANGE

Again the Gladiator Mk II was the superior aircraft. If a fighter is to be useful on patrol missions during which it is expected to spend some time on station, then range is important. The I-15bis had only marginally shorter range and was probably a better fighter.

Ar 68E-1 415 km (260 mi.)
I-15BIS CHAIKA 550 km (330 mi.)
GLADIATOR Mk II 708 km (440 mi.)

ARMAMENT

In service the Ar 68E-1 rarely carried fragmentation bombs because of the excessive drag associated with the magazine installation. In air-to-air combat the I-15bis has the edge with its four-gun armament and good performance.

Ar 68E-1 2 x 7.92-vmm machine-guns 60-kg (132-lb.) bombload
GLADIATOR Mk II 4 x 7.7-mm (.303 cal.) machine-guns
I-15BIS CHAIKA 4 x 7.62-mm (.30 cal.) machine-guns 150-kg (330-lb.) bombload

Wartime Arados

■ **Ar 95:** Having first flown in 1937, the Ar 95 was combat tested in the Spanish Civil War and served the Luftwaffe early in World War II.

■ **Ar 96:** Although designed by Arado, the majority of these advanced trainers were built by other companies; 11,546 were completed.

■ **Ar 196:** Respected for its excellent sea performance, good flying qualities and heavy armament, the Ar 196 was a classic floatplane.

■ **Ar 234:** Arado pioneered the twin-jet bomber with the Ar 234. Many of them were used on daylight raids and reconnaissance over the UK.

ARADO

AR 95

● Limited service ● Small numbers built ● Biplane floatplane

Designed to fly from Germany's aborted aircraft-carrier, the Ar 95 was a torpedo-bomber with floats or wheeled landing gear. It flew for the first time in 1936 and served briefly in the Spanish Civil War, but the aircraft-carrier was never completed and only a small number of Ar 95s were built. A handful went to Chile and a batch was supplied to the Luftwaffe, while three Ar 95s served with the Spanish air force until 1948.

▲ The Ar 95 served reliably in combat over Spain and in northern Europe. The Luftwaffe only operated the type until 1941, when the BV 138 was introduced.

ARADO AR 95

◄ **Production prototype**
Both the Ar 95 V3 and V5 were finished as three-seat floatplanes and were regarded as prototypes of the production Ar 95A.

▼ **Distinctly Arado**
Arado retained several features of the Ar 95 in later designs, including the Ar 196.

▼ **Torpedo bomber**
In its original form the Ar 95 was to be a carrier-based torpedo aircraft. A 700-kg (1,760-lb.) weapon could be carried between the float struts.

▼ **Trousered undercarriage**
Serving as the Ar 95B prototype, the Ar 95 V4 featured large trouser-type fairings on its main undercarriage. Three aircraft of this type were ordered by the Chilean government.

◄ **Grupo 64**
Based at Pollensa, Majorca, the six Ar 95A-0s were flown by Grupo 64 of the Condor Legion.

FACTS AND FIGURES

➤ Early trials showed that the Ar 95A fell short of the required performance, and the Ar 95B was obsolescent by 1937.

➤ Grupo 64 disbanded in 1939 and passed its Ar 95s to the Spanish Nationalists.

➤ Luftwaffe unit 3./SAGr. 125 gave up its Ar 95s at Constanza, Romania, in 1941.

➤ SAGr. 127 operated both Ar 95s and He 60s; it retained the Arado floatplanes until 1944.

➤ Turkey ordered Ar 95s, but its aircraft were diverted to the Luftwaffe.

➤ Arado built the unsuccessful Ar 195 as a potential replacement for the Ar 95B.

PROFILE

Fighting floatplane from Arado

It was clear that the Ar 95B would be obsolescent by the time Germany's aircraft carrier was completed.

There were both two- and three-seat prototypes of the Ar 95, and one was temporarily fitted with a liquid-cooled Junkers Jumo engine. Production aircraft had three seats under a single, long canopy and used the more powerful BMW 132 radial.

All six pre-production Ar 95A-0s went to Majorca in 1938 as part of a Condor Legion reconnaissance unit supporting the Nationalist forces in the Spanish Civil War. They saw only limited service during the conflict, but three of the aircraft were transferred to the Nationalists in 1939 and served until 1948.

Only 14 production aircraft were built – 11 Ar 95A floatplanes and three Ar 95B landplanes. Three of each were delivered to Chile in 1939 and remained in service until after World War II.

One squadron of the Luftwaffe's 125 maritime reconnaissance wing (3./SAGr. 125) was equipped with eight Ar 95A-1s. This unit was stationed in the Baltic in June 1942, when Germany invaded the Soviet Union. Ar 95s were involved in the occupation of islands off the coast of Estonia in October 1941, before ending their service career in the Gulf of Finland.

AR 95A-1

Luftwaffe Ar 95A-1s served with only two units, the second unit receiving aircraft retired by the first. The aircraft were initially delivered to 3./SAGr. 125, one of whose machines is seen here in the summer of 1941.

Two 7.9-mm machine-guns were fitted as standard. The forward-firing MG 17 was supplied with 500 rounds, while the flexibly-mounted MG 15 in the rear cockpit had 600 rounds stored in eight 75-round ammunition drums.

7R + FL

A reliable and well-tested BMW 132 engine was fitted to the Ar 95. Take-off power was 656 kW (880 hp.), falling to 634 kW (850 hp.) at 2500 metres (8,000 ft.). The performance of the Ar 95 fell short of official expectations.

This four-bomb rack was commonly fitted to the Ar 95. Alternative loads included a 700-kg (1,540-lb.) torpedo or a 375-kg (825-lb.) bomb beneath the fuselage, with six 50-kg (110-lb.) bombs beneath the wings.

The Ar 95 had an all-metal fuselage of semi-monocoque construction and aft folding metal framed wings. The wing upper surfaces were metal-covered, with fabric lower surfaces.

The floats were of light metal, giving buoyancy and stability on the water. A small rudder was attached to the rear of each, providing directional control during taxiing.

COMBAT DATA

ARMAMENT

At the beginning of World War II, the Fairey Seafox was already obsolescent since it was an old design. The Ar 95 was also dated, although it was more heavily armed. Arado produced its best seaplane in the Ar 196, sacrificing bombload for heavy gun armament.

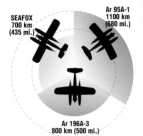

Ar 95A-1	2 x 7.92-mm machine-guns 800-kg (1,760-lb.) bombload
Ar 196A-3	2 x 20-mm cannon 2 x 7.92-mm machine-guns 100-kg (220-lb.) bombload
SEAFOX	1 x 7.7-mm (.303 cal.) machine-gun

RANGE

The Ar 95 had long range, which was particularly important in the torpedo-bombing and reconnaissance roles. It also allowed long coastal patrols and even search and rescue missions to be undertaken. The Ar 196 had shorter range but excellent handling.

SEAFOX 700 km (435 mi.)
Ar 95A-1 1100 km (680 mi.)
Ar 196A-3 800 km (500 mi.)

CRUISING SPEED

Although the Ar 196 used a more powerful BMW 132 engine than the Ar 95, it was only marginally faster. The Seafox was a considerably less powerful aircraft but gave useful service, including confirming the fate of the *Graf Spee*.

Ar 95A-1	255 km/h (158 m.p.h.)
Ar 196A-3	267 km/h (166 m.p.h.)
SEAFOX	171 km/h (106 m.p.h.)

Biplane floatplanes in World War II

■ **DE HAVILLAND DH.82 TIGER MOTH:** Many examples of this ubiquitous trainer were mounted on floats.

■ **FAIREY SWORDFISH:** Usually launched from a ship's catapult, Swordfish floatplanes saw widespread Fleet Air Arm service.

■ **HEINKEL He 59:** Used extensively on search and rescue missions during the Battle of Britain, the He 59 was retired in 1943.

■ **IMAM Ro 44:** Thirty Ro 44s were in service with the Italian navy at the outbreak of World War II. A few survived the Armistice.

ARADO

AR 196

● Catapult-launched reconnaissance floatplane ● Eyes of the fleet

A highly successful design, the little Arado 196 was the eyes of the Kriegsmarine. Not only did it perform the hazardous role of spotting for the guns of the fleet, it performed daring air–sea rescues in the English Channel and lonely coastal patrols over Biscay. The Ar 196 served on Germany's capital ships and cruisers and in all European maritime theatres of war. It was one of the finest floatplane designs of its time.

▲ Most Ar 196 floatplanes served from land bases in occupied Norway, France and Denmark, but the aircraft is best remembered as the catapult-launched light spotter of the German navy.

ARADO AR 196

Trials on the water ▶
The prototypes of the Ar 196 were recognisable by the twin-bladed propeller. This was replaced by a variable-pitch three-bladed type, and the airframe was slightly modified in production aircraft.

Lone patrol ▶
Although designed to spot for the fleet's guns, the Ar 196 was used for many tasks, such as dropping agents and attacking Allied maritime patrol planes.

▲ Seal hunter
One of the Ar 196's great moments was the capture of HMS Seal in 1940. The British submarine had been damaged by a mine during a patrol off the coast of Norway. Two Ar 196s, operating from Aalborg in Denmark, attacked the crippled submarine and managed to inflict enough damage to prevent it submerging. It was then captured by the Kriegsmarine.

▲ Plane sailing
Most Ar 196s had twin floats, as trials of a single-float version with small outrigger floats had proved it to be tricky to operate on water.

◀ On the slipway
This Ar 196 served with 2./SAGr 125, and was moored in Suda Bay, Crete. The unit carried out anti-submarine patrols against the Royal Navy.

FACTS AND FIGURES

➤ The Arado beat a rival Focke-Wulf design in the competition to replace the Heinkel He 50 as the fleet floatplane.

➤ Ar 196s also served in coastal units with Bulgaria, Finland and Romania.

➤ Twin floats were chosen because pilots liked the stability given during taxiing.

➤ The Ar 196 was almost used in a floatplane record-breaking attempt, but the Reich Air Ministry banned it.

➤ Bismarck launched its Ar 196 to drive off a shadowing RAF Catalina in 1941.

➤ Ar 196 operations ranged from the Arctic Circle to the Black Sea.

PROFILE

Eyes of the German fleet

Arado began designing the Ar 196 in 1936, to replace the obsolete Heinkel He 50 reconnaissance floatplanes then in service with the fleet. Unlike the floatplanes of most navies, the Ar 196 was a thoroughly modern design, with metal frame construction for most of the aircraft. It also packed a very powerful punch; two Ar 196s even managed to

capture a Royal Navy submarine in 1940 after blasting it with their cannon and machine-guns.

The Ar 196 completed trials just as the war was beginning. The first warship to take the aircraft to sea was the *Admiral Graf Spee*, and all the other Kriegsmarine capital ships and heavy cruisers subsequently received them, including the

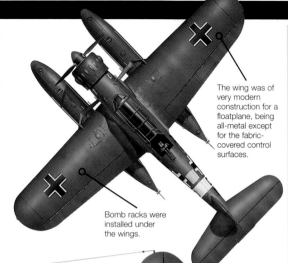

The Arado was the last fighting floatplane to be built in Europe. This example was captured by the Royal Navy and was evaluated by the Marine Aircraft Experimental Establishment.

Bismarck. The Ar 196 was produced in several variants, and was built by Fokker and SNCA for Germany.

The wing was of very modern construction for a floatplane, being all-metal except for the fabric-covered control surfaces.

Bomb racks were installed under the wings.

Ar 196A-3

Type: two-seat shipboard and coastal patrol aircraft

Powerplant: one 716-kW (960-hp.) BMW 123K nine-cylinder radial

Maximum speed: 310 km/h (192 m.p.h.) at 4000 m (13,120 ft.)

Cruising speed: 255 km/h (158 m.p.h.)

Combat radius: 1070 km (663 mi.)

Service ceiling: 7000 m (22,960 ft.)

Weights: empty 2990 kg (6,592 lb.); loaded 3730 kg 8,223 lb.)

Armament: two fixed MG FF 20-mm cannon in the wings; one or two 7.92-mm guns in the rear cockpit and front fuselage; two 50-kg (110-lb.) bombs

Dimensions:
span	12.40 m	(41 ft.)
length	11.00 m	(36 ft.)
height	4.45 m	(15 ft.)
wing area	28.40 m²	(305 sq. ft.)

AR 196A-5

This aircraft served with 2./Seeaufklärungsgruppe 125 which operated from shore bases in the eastern Mediterranean and the Aegean Seas during 1943.

Power was provided by a 716-kW (960-hp.) BMW radial engine. The mounts were one of the aircraft's weak spots – engines were known to break off when moving across choppy water.

The cannon armament was unusually powerful for a floatplane, enabling it to take on RAF Whitley bombers over the Bay of Biscay or shoot up enemy ships.

Final production versions carried two MG 81 machine-guns in the rear cockpit, but most versions carried a single 7.92-mm MG 15.

The Arado had a roomy, modern, enclosed cockpit, in contrast with its British opponents, which were generally open to the elements and far more uncomfortable for their crews.

The Ar 196 had a conventional steel tube frame with a forward metal skin covering and a fabric covering for the rear fuselage. The airframe was a sound design, and was barely changed after completing prototype trials.

To ease handling on the water the floats were equipped with rudders. They also contained fuel tanks, and could store emergency survival kit.

COMBAT DATA

MAXIMUM SPEED

Floatplanes are not very fast, since their huge floats create immense amounts of drag in flight. However, the Arado's clean, modern design meant that it was one of the fastest of its type.

Ar 196	310 km/h (192 m.p.h.)
OS2U KINGFISHER	265 km/h (164 m.p.h.)
SEAFOX	200 km/h (124 m.p.h.)

RANGE

Scout planes were designed to extend the horizon of the mother ship out to 100 or 200 km (50 or 125 mi.). The ability to loiter for long periods was more important than out-and-out range, and the Ar 196 could remain on station for more than four hours.

OS2U KINGFISHER 1300 km (806 mi.)

Ar 196 1070 km (633 mi.)

SEAFOX 700 km (434 mi.)

SERVICE CEILING

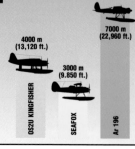

The Arado could climb much higher than either the American Kingfisher or the British Seafox. This was of inestimable advantage when searching for ship-sized targets, as the crew of the German machine could keep watch over a greater area of sea than observers in either of their opponents.

7000 m (22,960 ft.)

4000 m (13,120 ft.)

3000 m (9.850 ft.)

OS2U KINGFISHER

SEAFOX

Ar 196

Prowling the oceans

■ **SCOUTING FOR THE FLEET:** The Arado Ar 196 was designed to scout for raiders like the battlecruiser *Gneisenau*. In effect, it gave the warship's lookouts the ability to search for targets at distances of several hundred kilometres.

■ **COMMERCE RAIDING:** The Kriegsmarine's main task was to interrupt Britain's seaborne trade. Battleships, cruisers and disguised commerce raiders used their Arados to locate Allied convoys or individual merchant ships, checking to see if they were escorted. The location of a target would be transmitted to the mother ship, which would then steam to intercept, sinking the hapless merchantman by gunfire.

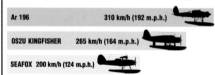

ARMSTRONG WHITWORTH

SISKIN

- ● All-metal fighter ● Highly manoeuvrable ● King's Cup winner

▲ Although it was not beautiful to look at, the Siskin was a delight to fly and had none of the vices that were so apparent in early biplane fighters. The unequal span wings and the uncowled radial engine were distinctive features.

F ighter development slowed almost to a halt after the end of World War I. It was five years before the RAF started to replace its wartime Sopwith Snipes, even though one of its two new fighters, the Siskin, had flown for the first time in early 1919. Despite its slow start, the Siskin developed into a capable combat aircraft and went on to become the RAF's standard fighter of the late 1920s serving with a total of 11 UK-based squadrons.

ARMSTRONG WHITWORTH SISKIN

▼ Canadian service
Canada acquired 12 Siskins, including this IIIA which took part in the 1931 Trans-Canada Air Pageant.

▲ Squadron service
The most famous Siskin squadron was No. 43, which regularly thrilled crowds at the RAF Display, Hendon.

▼ Learning to fight
The RAF operated more than 40 two-seat Siskin IIIDC trainers until their retirement in 1932.

▲ Civilian Siskin
The second Siskin II, G-EBHY, was exported to Sweden where it was equipped with skis.

◀ Ultimate Siskin
By 1931 the 142 Siskin IIIAs were showing their age and the RAF sought a replacement. Armstrong Whitworth submitted the Siskin IIIB, which had better speed and climb performance. However, testing revealed inadequate handling and range and the IIIB was not selected.

FACTS AND FIGURES

- ➤ The Siskin III entered RAF service in May 1924 with No. 41 Squadron based at Northolt aerodrome.

- ➤ The Siskin was designed by Siddeley Deasy and was originally called the S.R.2.

- ➤ Siskins became famous for their tied-together aerobatic routines.

- ➤ S.R.2 test pilot Oliver Stewart said: 'The Siskin was gentle, easy-going, calm and good-tempered.'

- ➤ By June 1931 there were 179 Siskins in service with the RAF.

- ➤ Altogether, 485 Siskins of all marks, including the S.R.2, were built.

PROFILE

Britain's famous inter-war fighter

A Dragonfly engine powered the original Siskin, and one of a pair built as civil aircraft won the 1923 King's Cup air race at an average speed of 240 km/h (149 m.p.h.). The original prototype was rebuilt with a steel fuselage frame and wing spars, and was fitted with a Jaguar radial engine. The result was the Siskin III, which entered service in May 1924 and equipped two squadrons. A dozen of the 62 Mk IIIs were built as two-seat fighter trainers before the first IIIA flew in October 1925.

With its supercharged Jaguar engine, the IIIA was 35 km/h (22 m.p.h.) faster at sea level than the earlier model and had a higher service ceiling. It also had minor airframe changes, and the twin nose guns were enclosed by the forward fuselage. As well as serving with the RAF until 1932, the Siskin became the standard fighter of the Royal Canadian Air Force. Some of the Mk IIIAs supplied to Canada were still in service in 1939. Total production reached 382, including one fitted with a ski undercarriage for the Swedish air force in 1925.

After the failure of the Dragonfly engine subsequent Siskins were powered by the very reliable and powerful Armstrong Siddeley Jaguar radial engine.

Above: The Siskin prototype first flew in 1919 as the Siddeley S.R.2, powered by the ill-fated A.B.C. Dragonfly engine. In 1921 a Jaguar radial was fitted and the Siskin name was adopted.

Above: The Romanian government ordered the Siskin V, but after a fatal accident the order was cancelled.

SISKIN IIIA

This Siskin IIIA is in the markings of No. 43 Squadron in 1929. Famous for their aerobatic displays at the Hendon pageants, the unit operated the type until 1932.

The pilot sat just behind the top wing with his eyes roughly level with the trailing edge; his view upward and forward was therefore good.

The Siskin IIIA had a raised tailplane and did not have the ventral fin that was fitted to earlier marks. The control surfaces were well balanced and gave the aircraft excellent agility.

No. 43 Squadron's black and white checkerboard markings on the fuselage and tail were highly distinctive.

The V-type undercarriage featured telescopic legs consisting of steel tubes forming an oil dashpot which damped the action of the rubber shock-absorber cords.

The short-span, narrow single-spar lower wing contrasted sharply with the broad overhanging top wing. The wings were supported by V-shaped interplane struts and bracing wires.

Although the initial Siskin variants were of wood and fabric construction, the production variants were the first all-metal framed aircraft to be built in quantity for the RAF.

J-8959   J 8959

COMBAT DATA

MAXIMUM SPEED

Aircraft were not a priority during the 1920s and fighters of this period were not much faster than World War I dogfighters. The Siskin is the slowest of the three designs, but is also the earliest.

SISKIN IIIA 251 km/h (156 m.p.h.)

P-1A HAWK 257 km/h (159 m.p.h.)

CR.1 272 km/h (169 m.p.h.)

SERVICE CEILING

The Siskin had excellent performance at altitude, mainly due to its supercharged engine. One RAF squadron even used the Siskin as a specialised high-altitude fighter.

SISKIN IIIA 8260 m (27,100 ft.)

P-1A HAWK 6157 m (20,200 ft.)

CR.1 7450 m (24,450 ft.)

ENGINE POWER

The Siskin's powerful Jaguar engine gave it an excellent service ceiling and an impressive rate of climb. Although the CR.1 had less power, its streamlined shape gave it good performance.

SISKIN IIIA 336 kW (450 hp.)

P-1A HAWK 324 kW (435 hp.)

CR.1 224 kW (300 hp.)

Armstrong Whitworth family

■ **F.K.8:** The excellent F.K.8 reconnaissance aircraft was produced in considerable numbers during the last two years of World War I.

■ **F.K.10:** This amazing quadruplane design first flew in 1917, but it was not successful and only a small number were eventually delivered.

■ **APE:** The ugly Ape had an adjustable incidence tail and was built as an experimental aircraft for the Royal Aircraft Establishment.

■ **STARLING:** Based on the highly successful Siskin, the Starling was intended to be a day- and night-fighter, but was never put into production.

AVIA

B.534

● Biplane fighter ● Outstanding performance ● Ground attack

P roduced by the Czechoslovakian Avia company, the Hispano-Suiza-engined B.534 was widely considered to be the finest biplane fighter of its time and was the most important Czech aircraft built between the two world wars. Production totalled 566 and a number were exported. After the occupation of Czechoslovakia by Germany in 1939, B.534s equipped the Slovak 'puppet' regime and were sold to Bulgaria.

▲ A sturdy and agile machine
with adequate performance, the Avia B.534 also had relatively powerful armament, consisting of four 7.7-mm (.303 cal.) machine-guns.

AVIA B.534

▼ Reliable power
After the failure of the Avia Rr 29 nine-cylinder radial engine, the B.34/2 prototype was re-engined with the 12-cylinder Hispano-Suiza 12Ybrs and became known as the B.534/1 after official trials.

▲ Front-line strength
The majority of B.534s were supplied to the Czechoslovakian air force and by the time of the Munich crisis in September 1938, they equipped 21 front-line fighter squadrons.

Modern replica▶
As a tribute to the B.534 and the airmen who flew it, this full-scale replica, accurately painted with Czechoslovakian markings, was completed in 1975. It is on display at the Air Force and Army Museum in Prague-Kbely.

▼ Fine performance
The B.534 was a sturdy fighter, with outstanding climb and dive capabilities. Its enclosed cockpit was a modern feature for the era.

◀ Winter operations
B.534s were often equipped with skis to cope with the harsh operating conditions of Eastern Europe.

FACTS AND FIGURES

➤ A refinement of the B.34, the B.534 entered service with the Czechoslovakian air force in 1935.

➤ A number of B.534s were exported – six to Greece and 14 to Yugoslavia.

➤ The most-produced version was the B.534-IV, of which 272 were built.

➤ The B.534 proved to be the outstanding biplane fighter at the Zurich international flying meet in July 1937.

➤ Bulgarian B.534s were flown in combat against USAAF B-24 Liberators.

➤ Three Slovak fighter squadrons operated B.534s on the Russian Front in 1941.

PROFILE

Czech biplane warrior

Nearly 500 B.534s were built in four series. The first 100 had two machine-guns, but later models had four guns with the 272 Series IV aircraft also having cockpit canopies and metal propellers. In addition, 54 Bk.534s were built, armed with a 20-mm cannon firing through the propeller, plus two 7.7-mm (.303 cal.) machine-guns.

Some B.534s were used by the Luftwaffe, both as fighter trainers and as tugs for troop-carrying gliders. A few, previously supplied to Greece, were used in combat during the Italian invasion of 1940.

Around 65 were used to equip the Slovak air force. Some were shot down by Hungarian C.R.32s, and one squadron fought alongside the Germans during the invasion of Poland. Three Slovak B.534s even survived to take part in the 1944 uprising against the German occupation.

Below: This was one of several B.534-IVs operated by the Czechoslovakian air police in 1938. The Avia emblem is on the fin next to the national insignia.

Above: Early versions of the B.534 flew without the wheel spats that were later incorporated on the definitive B.534-IV.

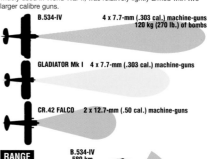

B.534-IV

This aircraft carries the markings of a Slovak air force unit at Zitomir-Kiev, Ukraine, during the invasion of the USSR in 1941/42.

Some 450 B.534s and Bk.534s were on strength with the Czechoslovakian forces when the country was occupied by the Germans in March 1939. Of these, a number were absorbed into the newly created Slovak air force and the Luftwaffe. Five squadrons of the Bulgarian air force also received 78 examples.

B.534-IV

Type: single-seat biplane fighter

Powerplant: one Avia-built 634-kW (850-hp.) Hispano-Suiza HS 12Ydrs in-line piston engine

Maximum speed: 395 km/h (245 m.p.h.) at 4400 m (14,450 ft.)

Initial climb rate: 900 m/min (2,950 f.p.m.)

Range: 580 km (373 mi.)

Service ceiling: 10600 m (37,750 ft.)

Weights: empty 1460 kg 3,219 lb.); maximum take-off 2120 kg 4,764 lb.)

Armament: four fixed 7.7-mm (.303 cal.) synchronised machine-guns in the forward fuselage, plus up to six 20-kg (45-lb.) bombs on underwing racks

Dimensions:
span	9.40 m	(30 ft. 10 in.)
length	8.20 m	(26 ft. 11 in.)
height	3.10 m	(9 ft. 2 in.)
wing area	23.56 m²	(254 sq. ft.)

The B.534 was an unequal-span, staggered-wing biplane, with ailerons on both upper and lower wings. The wings and aft fuselage were fabric covered, with detachable metal panels on the forward fuselage.

B.534-IVs had an aft-sliding cockpit canopy with raised fuselage rear decking. Earlier versions had an open cockpit.

Development of the earlier B.34 fighter led to the B.34/2 prototype being re-engined with a Hispano-Suiza 12Ybrs 12-cylinder Vee liquid-cooled piston engine after the failure of the planned Avia Rr 29 nine-cylinder radial. This became the B.534/1 and the final version, the B.534-IV, was fitted with the 634-kW Avia-built 12Ydrs, giving it a maximum speed of almost 400 km/h (250 m.p.h.).

Four 7.7-mm (.303 cal.) machine-guns armed the B.534 – two in the fuselage and two in the wings – but excessive wing vibration led to all four being fuselage-mounted after the 48th aircraft. The Bk.534 was fitted with an engine-mounted 20-mm Oerlikon cannon and two 7.7-mm guns, but problems with the cannon meant that it was replaced by a third 7.7-mm weapon.

COMBAT DATA

MAXIMUM SPEED

The last biplane fighter designs of the late-1930s were capable of around 400 km/h (250 m.p.h.). This performance was soon surpassed by the new monoplane designs, but biplanes were still able to harass unescorted bombers.

B.534-IV	395 km/h (245 m.p.h.)
GLADIATOR Mk I	407 km/h (252 m.p.h.)
CR.42 FALCO	420 km/h (260 m.p.h.)

ARMAMENT

The Avia B.534-IV had the versatility of a light bombload in addition to its four machine-gun armament. The CR.42, which was widely used in World War II, was relatively lightly armed with two larger calibre guns.

B.534-IV — 4 x 7.7-mm (.303 cal.) machine-guns, 120 kg (270 lb.) of bombs

GLADIATOR Mk I — 4 x 7.7-mm (.303 cal.) machine-guns

CR.42 FALCO — 2 x 12.7-mm (.50 cal.) machine-guns

RANGE

A range of around 600 to 700 km was typical of fighters of this period. The earliest monoplane fighters did not improve on this by a significant amount. The war soon spurred designers to increase range, however.

B.534-IV 580 km (373 mi.)

GLADIATOR Mk I 547 km (439 mi.)

CR.42 FALCO 780 km (484 mi.)

B.534 during World War II

LUFTWAFFE GLIDER TUG: Several B.534s in Luftwaffe service were given raised canopies and were used as glider tugs. Although operational use was limited, they were used extensively for training, usually towing the DFS 230 assault glider.

FIGHTING THE LIBERATOR: Bulgaria operated its B.534s against US Army Air Force B-24 bombers which entered Bulgarian airspace while returning from the 'Tidal Wave' bombing raid against the Ploesti oilfields.

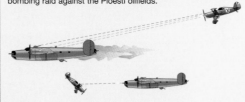

SLOVAK INSURGENTS: During the Slovak national rising of the summer of 1944, three B.534s were flown from Tri Duby airfield by insurgents. The Luftwaffe destroyed two on the ground and the third was eventually burned to prevent it being captured.

BEECH

17 STAGGERWING

● Pre- and post-war production ● Cabin biplane ● Military users

▲ Today the Staggerwing is a highly collectable and valuable classic aircraft. Here, engineers are seen working on the Pratt & Whitney R-985-SB Wasp Junior engine fitted to the D17S version.

Beech's Staggerwing is widely regarded as one of the most beautiful aircraft ever built, and is a true classic. The very first Staggerwing biplane was a hand-crafted work of art, completed in 1932 when Walter Beech's Wichita, Kansas, manufacturing company had only eight employees. The last Staggerwing was built in 1949, but this appealing aircraft can still be found flying, today, in the hands of a few loving, proud owners.

BEECH 17 STAGGERWING

▼ RAF transport
To fill an urgent need for a high-performance light transport aircraft, Britain received 106 Staggerwings. In RAF service they were named Traveller Mk I.

▲ Staggered wings
The Staggerwing gets its name from the arrangement of the wings which has the lower wing situated forward of the upper wing.

▼ Connecting bases
Used by the USAAF both in the USA and abroad, the UC-43 flew diplomatic and military staff between the many military establishments which existed in the 1940s.

▲ Wartime delivery
During World War II, Model 17s were delivered to both the US Navy (GB-1 and GB-2) and US Army Air Force (UC-43). This GB-2 was delivered in 1943.

◄ US Navy service
Flying under the US Navy designation GB-2 Traveller, this example was used as a personal transport by US Navy attachés abroad.

FACTS AND FIGURES

➤ Beechcraft records indicate that 785 Model 17 Staggerwings were built between 1932 and 1949.

➤ In 1935 Capt. H.L. Farquhar successfully flew around the world in a Model B17R.

➤ Dwane L. Wallace, future president of Cessna, helped design the Staggerwing.

➤ A Model B17L was impressed into Republican service during the Spanish Civil War and was used as a bomber.

➤ Of around 225 Staggerwings surviving today, over 200 are on the US register.

➤ Each Staggerwing was a custom-built aircraft manufactured by hand.

PROFILE

High-performance personal transport

At the start of the 1930s, Theodore Wells and Walter Beech designed the Model 17 Staggerwing, the first of tens of thousands of Beechcraft aircraft. The Staggerwing was refined over the years but from the beginning it held a unique place in aviation – a majestic aircraft suited for the job of providing elegant transportation to wealthy owners.

The Staggerwing provided quality service in the 1930s to a few corporate and private customers. Some intrepid aviators, veterans of the 'barnstorming' era of a decade earlier, entered the Staggerwing in racing and endurance events, gaining victory in the Texaco Trophy of 1933 and the Bendix Trophy of 1936 when the successful pilot, Louise Thaden, was voted the outstanding US woman pilot of the year.

The Staggerwing continued to gain fame in races and competitions, but is best remembered as a superb transport carrying passengers in speed and comfort.

It was inevitable that the Staggerwing would be inducted into military service. Many of these aircraft served with a number of armed forces during World War II, and continued to serve both civilian and military customers into the 1950s.

The powerful engine and smooth lines of the Staggerwing helped it establish a number of records. Jacqueline Cochran set new women's speed records over 100 km (62 mi.) and 1000 km (620 mi.).

The cantilever monoplane tail unit had a welded steel framework for the elevators and rudder, and a wooden framework for the tailplane and fin. The entire unit was fabric-covered.

G17S Staggerwing

Type: four/five-seat cabin biplane

Powerplant: one 336-kW (450-hp.) Pratt & Whitney R-985-AN-4 Wasp Junior radial piston engine

Maximum speed: 341 km/h (211 m.p.h.)

Cruising speed: 298 km/h (185 m.p.h.) at 2895 m (9,500 ft.)

Range: 1610 km (1,000 mi.)

Ceiling: 5805 m (19,000 ft.)

Weights: empty 1270 kg (2,794 lb.); maximum take-off 1928 kg (4,240 lb.)

Accommodation: one pilot and four passengers

Dimensions:
span	9.75 m	(32 ft.)
length	8.15 m	(26 ft. 9 in.)
height	2.44 m	(8 ft.)
wing area	27.54 m²	(296 sq. ft.)

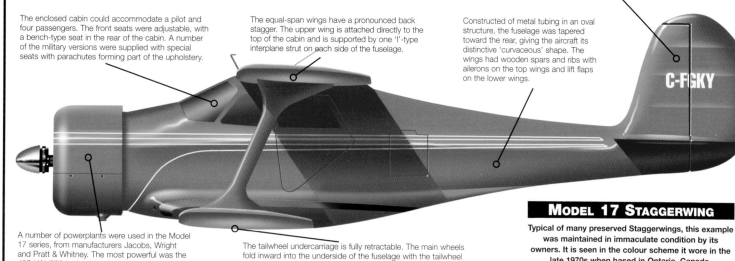

The enclosed cabin could accommodate a pilot and four passengers. The front seats were adjustable, with a bench-type seat in the rear of the cabin. A number of the military versions were supplied with special seats with parachutes forming part of the upholstery.

The equal-span wings have a pronounced back stagger. The upper wing is attached directly to the top of the cabin and is supported by one 'I'-type interplane strut on each side of the fuselage.

Constructed of metal tubing in an oval structure, the fuselage was tapered toward the rear, giving the aircraft its distinctive 'curvaceous' shape. The wings had wooden spars and ribs with ailerons on the top wings and lift flaps on the lower wings.

C-FGKY

A number of powerplants were used in the Model 17 series, from manufacturers Jacobs, Wright and Pratt & Whitney. The most powerful was the 485-kW (650-hp.) engine fitted in the A17F.

The tailwheel undercarriage is fully retractable. The main wheels fold inward into the underside of the fuselage with the tailwheel retracting into the tail. The retraction system is electrical.

MODEL 17 STAGGERWING

Typical of many preserved Staggerwings, this example was maintained in immaculate condition by its owners. It is seen in the colour scheme it wore in the late 1970s when based in Ontario, Canada.

ACTION DATA

POWER

The Staggerwing had by far the biggest engine, which is one of the main reasons for its impressive performance. A larger engine means a higher rate of fuel consumption, and as prices have risen economy has become an important factor.

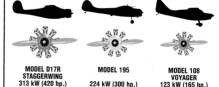

MODEL D17R STAGGERWING	MODEL 195	MODEL 108 VOYAGER
313 kW (420 hp.)	224 kW (300 hp.)	123 kW (165 hp.)

MAXIMUM SPEED

With retractable landing gear and a big engine, combined with its smooth aerodynamics, the Staggerwing outperformed almost all single-engined pre-war lightplanes. The Cessna Model 195 was also quite powerful, with a respectable turn of speed.

MODEL D17R STAGGERWING	339 km/h (210 m.p.h.)
MODEL 195	290 km/h (180 m.p.h.)
MODEL 108	235 km/h (146 m.p.h.)

ACCOMMODATION

As a light single-engined transport a capacity of five is more than sufficient for the intended tasks. The smaller and less powerful Stinson Model 108 Voyager can carry a pilot plus three passengers. When the Staggerwing carries four passengers, it is not able to carry maximum fuel, so restricting the aircraft's range.

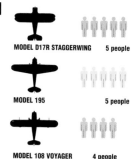

MODEL D17R STAGGERWING	5 people
MODEL 195	5 people
MODEL 108 VOYAGER	4 people

Cabin lightplanes of the 1930s

TAYLORCRAFT SERIES : Starting by building the Cub in the 1930s Taylorcraft went on to produce similar designs throughout the 1940s.

CESSNA MODEL A SERIES: The Type A was Cessna's first production aircraft. This example is a type AW, of which 48 were built.

DE HAVILLAND DH.87B HORNET MOTH: Introduced in 1935, 165 Hornet Moths were produced before the outbreak of World War II.

PIPER CUB: Sales of the Cub in 1936 and 1937 represented about one third of the total aircraft sold in the USA.

BERIEV

BE-6 'MADGE'

● Soviet-designed ● Flying-boat ● Maritime patrol aircraft

A heavy flying-boat intended for the challenging job of stalking submarines and surface warships, the Beriev Be-6 (NATO code name 'Madge') was not well-known even within the Soviet Union, where it served for three decades. The Be-6 carried out the job that was asked of it during the Cold War, without a great deal of recognition, and achieved an enviable record for reliability and durability after entering service in 1950.

▲ *All post-war Soviet flying-boats including the Be-6 'Madge' maritime patrol aircraft were products of the Georgi M. Beriev design bureau at Taganrog.*

BERIEV BE-6 'MADGE'

▼ Patrol radar
The scanner for a search radar was fitted in a retractable radome beneath the step of the hull. Here it is shown in the lowered position.

▲ Flying-boat
Fitted with wingtip floats, a boat hull and no undercarriage, the Be-6 was purely a flying-boat rather than an amphibian. Beaching wheels were used ashore.

▲ 'Stinger' tail
A late-series Be-6 on which a magnetic anomaly detector (MAD) boom has replaced the original tail turret: this was one part of the sophisticated submarine detection equipment installed.

▲ Powerful engines
Two 1790-kW (2,400-hp.) Shvetsov ASh-73 radial piston engines were installed.

Long service ▶
By the late 1950s the Be-6 was the most widely used flying-boat with the Soviet Morskaya Aviatsiya.

FACTS AND FIGURES

➤ 'Madge' was one of many codenames assigned by NATO to Soviet aircraft in the 'M-for-miscellaneous' series.

➤ The Be-6 prototype made its first flight in February 1949, flown by M.I. Tsepilov.

➤ The first production Be-6s were delivered in 1950.

➤ Russian Admiral Petchev said that patrol planes like the Be-6 were 'among our most important weapons'.

➤ In the 1970s, Be-6s were relegated to transport and unarmed patrol duties.

➤ The Be-6 was based on the LL-143 prototype first flown in 1945.

PROFILE

Little-known Soviet sea patroller

Maritime patrol work involves little glory. The pilots rarely achieve fame. There are no best-selling books or blockbuster movies about naval pilots and crews who slog along, day after day, on marathon nautical patrol missions inside machines that fly only slowly and sluggishly. Most of the public in Russia today know almost nothing about the men who flew, maintained and supported the Beriev Be-6 'Madge' between

1950 and 1974. Yet in spite of the routine nature of their work, they had a vital role in the Cold War.

Both sides used submarines and both sides tried to find ways to prevent submarines from being able to hide in the depths of the ocean. The Beriev Be-6, equipped with magnetic anomaly detection (MAD) gear, scoured the seas seeking to locate and counter NATO submarines. Around 200 aircraft were built for the naval aviation fleets. With a crew

ranging in size from four to 10 men, the Be-6 was a big, ungainly machine – it lacked the grace of the Beriev jet-powered flying-boats that came later – but it was a very capable predecessor of the four-engined, land-based maritime patrol aircraft being used around the world today.

Other Be-6s were found in paramilitary and Aeroflot service as utility transports. By the mid-1970s, the last transport conversion examples had all been retired.

This early Be-6 had a total of five 23-mm cannon located in the nose, tail and atop the fuselage. From 1954 aircraft were modified with a MAD boom replacing the rear barbette.

Be-6 'Madge'

Type: maritime reconnaissance and anti-submarine flying-boat

Powerplant: two 1790-kW (2,400-hp.) Shvetsov ASh-73 radial piston engines

Maximum speed: 414 km/h (257 m.p.h.) at 1800 m (5,900 ft.)

Initial climb rate: 20 min to 5000 m (16,400 ft.)

Range: 4800 km (2,975 mi.)

Ceiling: 6100 m (20,000 ft.)

Weights: empty equipped 18,827 kg (41,420 lb.); normal take-off 23,456 kg (51,603 lb.); maximum take-off weight with bombload 29,000 kg (63,800 lb.)

Armament: five 23-mm Nudelmann NR-23 23-mm cannon in nose, dorsal and tail installations, plus offensive load of up to 4400 kg (0,680 lb.) of mines, depth charges, or torpedoes

Dimensions:
span	33.00 m (108 ft. 3 in.)
length	23.56 m (77 ft. 3 in.)
height	7.64 m (25 ft. 1 in.)
wing area	120 m² (1,291 sq. ft.)

BE-6 'MADGE'

'Madge' was a long-range, twin radial-engined flying-boat developed for the post-war Soviet navy. Intended as a maritime patrol and reconnaissance aircraft, it was later used for fishery patrol.

The flying-boat's extended, deep nose provided adequate accommodation for a crew of eight, including radar operators. The 'balcony-style' flight-deck windows gave good downward vision.

Large oval-shaped twin fins and rudders were fitted on the ends of the dihedral tailplanes. They were high-set to be well clear of the water spray during take-off, and in clear air facilitated low-speed control during landing.

Later versions had the Ilyushin tail barbette replaced by a magnetic anomaly detector (MAD) 'stinger' for anti-submarine warfare.

Nose guns were replaced in later aircraft by two different radars – one for surveillance and the other for missile guidance in co-operation with surface warships.

Up to 4400 kg (9,680 lb.) of weapons could be carried, including 16 FAB-100, eight FAB-500 or AMD-500 mines, two FAB-1500 depth charges or two 1100-kg (2,420-lb.) torpedoes.

Be-6s had a fully retractable radar situated in a 'dustbin' in the planing bottom aft of the main hull step. The barbette on top of the rear fuselage was remotely controlled.

A water rudder was fitted to the rear of the planing hull. This was to provide directional control after the aircraft had alighted on the water, and for taxiing.

'Madge' in service

WELL PROTECTED: Equipped with up to five 23-mm cannon, the 'Madge' was well protected, in the style of large Soviet military aircraft of the period. Be-6s are not known to have been engaged in hostile action during their service.

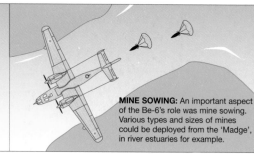

MINE SOWING: An important aspect of the Be-6's role was mine sowing. Various types and sizes of mines could be deployed from the 'Madge', in river estuaries for example.

MISSILE GUIDANCE: Little is known about this aspect of the Be-6's role. The aircraft are believed to have been employed to provide over-the-horizon guidance for ship-launched surface-to-surface missiles.

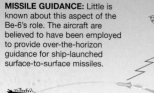

COMBAT DATA

POWER

Compared to its US contemporary, the Martin Marlin, the Be-6 was under-powered. The Beriev Be-12, intended to replace the Be-6, was powered by two turboprops which offered considerably more power for their size.

Be-6 'MADGE' 3580 kW (4,800 hp.)
Be-12 TCHAIKA 'MAIL' 6248 kW (8,378 hp.)
P5M-2 MARLIN 5145 kW (6,900 hp.)

MAXIMUM RANGE

Maritime patrol aircraft such as these are required to fly long distances while patrolling over huge areas. In this respect the 'Madge' performed better than the Martin Marlin, though not as well as the later 'Mail'. Range varied according to the fuel load available once weapons had been stowed.

Be-6 'MADGE' 4800 km (2,975 mi.)
Be-12 Tchaika 'Mail' 7500 km (4,650 mi.)
P5M-2 MARLIN 3300 km (2,050 mi.)

MAXIMUM BOMBLOAD

Neither the Be-6 nor Be-12 had the carrying capacity of the Marlin. However, the Marlin's bombload was achieved at the expense of its range, which was less than half that of the Be-12.

Be-6 'MADGE' 4400 kg (9,680 lb.)
Be-12 TCHAIKA 'MAIL' 5000 kg (11,000 lb.)
P5M-2 MARLIN 7250 kg (15,950 lb.)

BERIEV

BE-12 TCHAIKA 'MAIL'

● Flying-boat ● Anti-submarine warfare ● Search and rescue

The Be-12 served as a combat flying-boat in the Soviet Union long after most nations had given up on this type. Bearing the name of Georgii Beriev, the designer whose bureau produced generations of water-based military aircraft, the Be-12 is an amphibian with narrow-track wheels for land operation. The Be-12 served as an anti-submarine (ASW) aircraft, and was often seen in the Baltic tracking NATO ships. It still flies, although in reduced numbers as helicopters have taken over the ASW role.

▲ *Although large seaplanes have all but gone from the inventories of most nations, they remain in Japan and Russia, where the Beriev Be-12 still serves in some numbers.*

BERIEV BE-12 TCHAIKA 'MAIL'

◄ Baltic patrol
Be-12s operated extensively over the Baltic. This one, spotted by a Draken of the Swedish air force, was probably engaged on a shipping patrol.

Shore base ►
Beriev floatplanes were vital to the Soviet Union in the 1950s, because the country had a weak surface fleet and no shipboard naval air power to attack Western submarines.

Tail sting ►
The MAD boom detects submarines by the effect of their metal hulls on the Earth's magnetic field. It gives the Be-12 crew precise information for targeting.

▼ Search and rescue
Flying-boats are not quite as versatile as helicopters, but their superior speed, range and endurance make them invaluable in the search-and-rescue role.

▼ Wet landing
The Be-12 can touch down in smooth seas to pick up a downed pilot or listen for submarines on its sonar.

FACTS AND FIGURES

➤ The Be-12 made its first flight in 1960 and was codenamed 'Mail' by NATO.

Be-12s operated in the Mediterranean when Egypt was a Soviet ally.

➤ Be-12s probably serve today with the Russian Northern Fleet, Ukraine, Vietnam and Syria.

➤ The 'Mail' broke several speed records for flying-boats in 1970.

Be-12s have been used in trials as water-bombing fire-fighters.

➤ The jet-powered Beriev A-40 Albatross, or 'Mermaid', was developed as a possible replacement for the Be-12.

Sub-hunting with the Tchaika

The Beriev design team produced the Be-12 as a replacement for the radial-engined Be-6, which had a similar layout and was itself a replacement for wartime Catalinas. The Be-12, given the NATO reporting name 'Mail', was built with massive and sturdy landing gear, making it a fully-fledged amphibian and therefore far more versatile than earlier Beriev floatplane designs.

The Be-12 had no gun turrets, but carried MAD (magnetic anomaly detection) equipment in the tail, for detection of submarines. The lifting capability of the Be-12 was demonstrated in a series of class records for amphibians set in 1964, 1968 and 1970, suggesting a weapons load for short distances as high as 5000 kg (11,000 lb.). It could carry a potent mix of mines, torpedoes, bombs and depth charges. The aircraft was designed to load on the water through side hatches in the fuselage, and weapons can be dropped through a watertight hatch in the hull.

Above: With its distinctive front profile, it is easy to see why Soviet naval crews called their Be-12s seagulls.

Be-12s still fly, mostly in the search-and-rescue role in remote areas like Kamchatka and in the Black Sea. This popular aircraft is known as 'Tchaika' (Russian for seagull) to its crews.

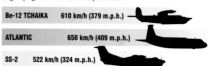

Below: The Be-12 hull has a specially designed spray-suppression system to reduce the risk of engine water ingestion. Tchaikas routinely operate in dangerous sea conditions in the Sea of Japan.

Be-12 Tchaika 'Mail'

Type: five-/six-seat maritime patrol amphibian

Powerplant: two 3125-kW Ivchenko AI-20D turboprop engines

Maximum speed: 610 km/h

Patrol speed: 320 km/h

Range: 7500 km

Service ceiling: 11250 m

Weights: empty 21700 kg; loaded 31000 kg

Armament: up to 5000 kg of bombs, rockets or guided air-to-surface missiles on underwing pylons; depth charges and sonobuoys in fuselage bays

Dimensions: span 29.70 m (97 ft. 5 in.)
length 30.20 m (99 ft. 1 in.)
height 7.00 m (23 ft.)
wing area 105 m² (1,130 sq. ft.)

BE-12 TCHAIKA 'MAIL'

The Beriev Be-12 entered service with the Soviet Naval Air Force in 1964, and about 70 of the aircraft probably remain in use in the search-and-rescue role around Russia's coast.

The crew consists of pilot and co-pilot, navigator, radar operator and MAD operator.

The huge Ivchenko turboprops are high-mounted on the cranked wing to keep the propeller disc clear of the sea. They drive four-bladed metal propellers.

The undercarriage was another new feature that the old Be-6 did not have. It was removed from one Be-12 (to make it a pure flying-boat) for a record attempt in 1968.

Inside the roomy fuselage there is a storage rack for sonobuoys, flares and a life raft. Weapons are carried in the main hull and on two wing pylons.

MAD equipment provides short-range attack information, informing the crew exactly when they are passing over a submerged submarine, so that weapons can be dropped precisely on target.

Surface search radar is fitted in a nose-mounted 'thimble'. The navigator sits below in the glazed nose section.

The rear fuselage is designed with a bend in it to keep the tail clear of the sea. The twin-fin arrangement gives useful stability in rough weather.

COMBAT DATA

MAXIMUM SPEED

Turboprop power makes the 'Mail' one of the fastest propeller-driven seaplanes ever built, with a performance similar to equivalent-sized landplanes such as the Dassault Breguet Atlantic. It is considerably faster than the ShinMaywa SS-2, the only other large flying-boat still in military service.

Be-12 TCHAIKA	610 km/h (379 m.p.h.)	
ATLANTIC	658 km/h (409 m.p.h.)	
SS-2	522 km/h (324 m.p.h.)	

RANGE

Designed as an anti-submarine warfare machine, the Be-12 has a very long range. Although this task has been taken over by helicopters and landplanes, it is ideal for search-and-rescue duties along the immense length of Russia's coastline, especially in the unpopulated wastes of Siberia and the far east.

SS-2 SHINMAYWA 3800 km (2360 mi.)
Be-12 TCHAIKA 'MAIL' 7500 km (4660 mi.)
ATLANTIC 9000 km (5592 mi.)

WEAPONS LOAD

The Be-12 established several payload-to-height records in the late 1960s, and it could carry a significant load of bombs, mines, torpedoes and depth charges. Although no longer armed, its lifting capacity means the 'Mail' is being considered for conversion as a fire-fighting water-bomber.

SS-2 1500 kg (3307 lb.)
ATLANTIC 3500 kg (7716 lb.)
Be-12 5000 kg (11,023 lb.)

Beriev's seaborne tradition

■ **Be-2:** G.M. Beriev began designing seaplanes in 1928. The Be-2 was an early product designed as a shipborne reconnaissance plane.

■ **Be-4:** Originally designated KOR-2, the Be-4 was a sleek single-engined flying-boat which saw service during World War II.

■ **Be-6 'MADGE':** The standard Soviet military flying-boat of the 1950s was a heavily-armed, piston-engined precursor to the Be-12.

■ **Be-10 'MALLOW':** The jet-powered Be-10 set many seaplane speed, height and payload records, but lacked the longevity of the Be-12.

■ **A-40 ALBATROSS:** The Albatross will be known as the Be-42 in rescue form and the Be-44 ASW variant if the Russian navy eventually buys them.

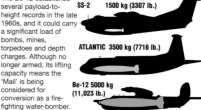

BERIEV

M-10 'MALLOW'

- Jet-powered flying-boat ● Record breaker ● Limited production

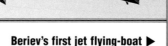

▲ *Throughout the Cold War the Soviet Union was keen to demonstrate the abilities of its designs on an international stage by attempting to break FAI world records, and often succeeding.*

Shrouded in secrecy for many years, the M-10 was the only aircraft in its class to enter operational service. Known to NATO as 'Mallow', the M-10 (or Be-10, as it was known to the Beriev design bureau) was Beriev's second, and latest, jet flying-boat design until the Be-42 appeared in the mid-1980s. Destined to enjoy only a short service life with Soviet Naval Aviation (AV-MF), it was as a record breaker that the M-10 made its name.

BERIEV M-10 'MALLOW'

Wingroot engines ▶
At high speed and low level, the 'Mallow', with its anhedral wings, was an imposing sight. Note the engine nacelles tucked under the wingroots. The engines were attached to the fuselage and front wing spar.

◀ Defensive armament
In common with other large Soviet military designs, including maritime patrol aircraft, bombers and transports, the M-10 featured a rear cannon turret.

Powered rudder ▶
The M-10's large, swept fin was fitted with a powered rudder and could be used to maintain straight flight even with maximum asymmetrical power applied, for example in the event of engine failure.

◀ Porpoising tendency
Although intended for operation in heavy seas, the M-10 was prone to 'porpoising' in bad conditions.

Beriev's first jet flying-boat ▶
Armed with four NR-23 cannon and 1000 kg (2,000 lb.) of bombs, the R-1 was a three-man maritime patrol prototype. Experience with the R-1 was invaluable in the M-10's design.

FACTS AND FIGURES

➤ Four M-10s flew at Tushino during the 1961 Soviet aviation day; US analysts believed it to be in squadron service.

➤ The M-10's design was based broadly on that of the R-1 jet flying-boat of 1952.

➤ The prototype, piloted by V. Kuryachi, first flew on 20 July 1956.

➤ Because of the secrecy of such projects in the Soviet Union, little was known of the M-10 in the West for over 30 years.

➤ Although the M-10 equipped two units, the exact number built is unclear.

➤ The Be-12 turboprop flying-boat met the same requirements and remains in use.

PROFILE

Jet flying-boat record breaker

Beriev had already flown a jet flying-boat, a small, three-seat bomber prototype known as the R-1, in 1953. When the AV-MF requested a waterborne replacement for the Be-6 to fill the maritime reconnaissance, anti-ship and bombing roles, Beriev produced a larger, swept-wing three-seater jet with a 3300-kg (7,260-lb.) weapons load.

Strongly constructed to withstand the rigours of operations in heavy seas (an area in which it subsequently failed to perform adequately in testing), the prototype of the M-10 flew on 20 July 1956. It demonstrated a speed and

ceiling performance twice that of the Be-6 'Madge', and its rate of climb was three times better than the piston-engined design.

A few M-10s joined two units of the AV-MF's Black Sea fleet, but their service use was brief. The high point of the M-10's career was establishing a number of world records for seaplanes in 1961. These included an average speed mark of 875.86 km/h (543 m.p.h.) over a 100-km (62-mile) circuit with a 5000-kg (11,000-lb.) payload, a straight line speed record of 912 km/h (565 m.p.h.) and an altitude record of 14962 metres (49,075 ft.). The last two records still stand – a remarkable achievement.

Beriev M-10s were the only jet-powered flying-boats in service during the Cold War. The US Navy had hopes for its Martin P6M SeaMaster, but it failed to proceed past prototype stage.

M-10 'MALLOW'

Detailed information on the exact number of M-10s built and their service history has yet to emerge from the former Soviet Union.

For a relatively large aircraft the M-10 had a small crew of just three: a pilot and navigator in a pressurised compartment (the former under a fighter-style canopy, and the latter in the bow of the aircraft) and a radio operator/gunner in the tail.

Two Lyul'ka AL-7PB non-afterburning turbojets powered the M-10. The AL-7 was fitted to a number of other types, including the Sukhoi Su-7 'Fitter' fighter. The engines were fed from 14 fuel tanks in the fuselage and wings.

For strength, the fuselage and hull were made up from 77 frames and five massive bulkheads, and were skinned in light alloy. The planing bottom of the hull stretched the entire length of the aircraft.

Defensive armament consisted of a twin NR-23 cannon installation in the tail turret. The radio operator/gunner's cabin was pressurised and equipped with a downward-firing ejection seat.

The wingtip floats required only small pylons, as the wings' anhedral brought them close to the water. The tailplane was constructed with dihedral and featured powered elevators.

The M-10's design was essentially an enlargement of the earlier R-1, with the engines tucked under the wingroots. Beriev conducted extensive testing to ensure that spray did not enter the engine intakes.

The underfloor area was divided into 10 watertight compartments. Immediately aft of the bottom hull 'step' was the bomb-bay with a 3300-kg (7,260-lb.) capacity. Its doors were sealed by a pneumatic tube, which was inflated at a pressure of 3 kg/cm² (42 PSI).

M-10 'Mallow'

Type: twin-jet maritime patrol flying-boat

Powerplant: two 63.75-kN (14,340-lb.-thrust) Lyul'ka AL-7PB turbojets

Maximum speed: 912 km/h (565 m.p.h.) at sea level

Cruising speed: 785 km/h (487 m.p.h.)

Initial climb rate: 7 min to 5000 m (16,400 ft.)

Weights: empty 26,500 kg (58,300 lb.); normal loaded 45,000 kg (99,000 lb.); maximum take-off 48,000 kg (105,600 lb.)

Armament: twin NR-23 23-mm cannon in rear turret, plus up to 3300 kg (7,260 lb.) of weapons, including bombs, mines and depth charges, or four torpedoes totalling 3075 kg (6,765 lb.)

Dimensions:
span   28.60 m (93 ft. 10 in.)
length   30.72 m (100 ft. 9 in.)
wing area   130 m² (1,400 sq. ft.)

COMBAT DATA

MAXIMUM SPEED

In operational guise the M-10 was designated the Be-10, and its jet engines gave it an unbeatable top speed for its type. The more recent A-40 design is not as fast, because it is optimised for range and load capacity rather than speed. Both attributes are more important for a maritime reconnaissance aircraft.

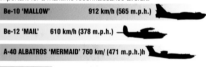

Be-10 'MALLOW'   912 km/h (565 m.p.h.)

Be-12 'MAIL'   610 km/h (378 m.p.h.)

A-40 ALBATROS 'MERMAID' 760 km/ (471 m.p.h.)h

CLIMB RATE

A modern design, the A-40 has a considerably better rate of climb than the two older designs, enabling it to take off with heavier loads and to reach operational heights quickly.

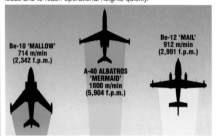

Be-10 'MALLOW' 714 m/min (2,342 f.p.m.)

A-40 ALBATROS 'MERMAID' 1800 m/min (5,904 f.p.m.)

Be-12 'MAIL' 912 m/min (2,991 f.p.m.)

WEAPONS LOAD

The installation of defensive gun armament was a feature of a number of Soviet designs in the 1950s. The Be-10's weapon load capacity was limited by the weight of the strongly-built airframe.

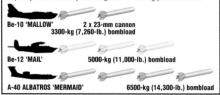

Be-10 'MALLOW'   2 x 23-mm cannon   3300-kg (7,260-lb.) bombload

Be-12 'MAIL'   5000-kg (11,000-lb.) bombload

A-40 ALBATROS 'MERMAID'   6500-kg (14,300-lb.) bombload

Soviet record holders

■ **ANTONOV An-124 'CONDOR':** One of Russia's giant An-124 transport aircraft set a jet-powered landplane closed circuit distance record of 20150.921 km (12,494 mi.) in 1987.

■ **MIKOYAN-GUREVICH E-266 'FOXBAT':** Early variants of the MiG-25 hold several records. In 1977 an E-266M set the current absolute world height record of 37650 metres (123,490 ft.).

■ **MIL Mi-6 'HOOK':** In August 1964 an Mi-6 broke the 100-km (62-mi.) closed-circuit speed record for helicopters. The new record was 340.15 km/h (210.89 m.p.h.) and still stands.

■ **TUPOLEV Tu-114 'CLEAT':** Derived from the Tu-95, the Tu-114 has held the turboprop closed-circuit speed record of 877.212 km/h (543.87 m.p.h.) with a 25-ton load since 1960.

BERIEV

EKRANOPLANE/SEA MONSTER

- Surface skimmer ● Missile cruiser ● Submarine destroyer

Despite the misapprehension that Russian aviation designers are heavily influenced by Western designs, in one area they are recognised as world leaders. Looking like something straight out of a science-fiction film, Ekranoplanes skim over the Earth's surface at high speed, faster than any traditional boat or land vehicle. Equipped with short stubby wings and high-mounted engines, the Ekranoplanes bring unique qualities to the world of flying.

▲ *With its revolutionary ability to skim the surface of the Earth, the Ekranoplane has seen a host of applications. The Russian space shuttle resembled it in its design.*

◀ **Monino mystery**
The Bartini VVA-14 was equipped with one main engine and 14 smaller lift engines. Although it carried Aeroflot colours, it was primarily perceived as a future military aircraft.

Overland, overseas ▶
During trials, the VVA-14 was equipped with the undercarriage from a Tu-22 'Blinder' for land operations, and twin floats for overwater flights.

◀**Flight of fantasy**
A host of designs has been proposed, including large passenger carriers, but few have seen full-scale development.

▼ **Proud heritage**
Within the next few years the VVA-14 will be fully restored by Monino's air museum.

▲ **Space skimmer**
With its blended lower body and small wings, the space shuttle had similar design characteristics to the Ekranoplanes.

FACTS AND FIGURES

- ➤ Ekranoplanes can be designed to any size and are able to travel five times faster than standard large marine craft.

- ➤ A projected civilian transport variant has yet to be completed.

- ➤ Sukhoi intended to develop the S-90 model with seating for 400 passengers.

- ➤ Designed in 1979, the A-90 'Eaglet' was able to operate in sea state 5 and could travel up a beach and over terrain.

- ➤ In 1980 the largest of the Ekranoplanes – the KM-04 – was lost in a crash.

- ➤ The KM-04 was known as the 'Caspian Sea Monster' by Western observers.

PROFILE

Soviet sea monsters

Falling somewhere between a fully-fledged flying aircraft and a hovercraft, Ekranoplanes hold a unique position within the Soviet armed forces. Utilised in the military role as assault transports and cruise missile attack platforms, Ekranoplanes will provide a unique form of commercial passenger transport in civilian applications.

Able to ride on its own cushion of air created by complex aerodynamic forces, Ekranoplanes are able to skim across the water at great speed with very little resistance.

Serious research into military development of the Ekranoplane began in the early 1960s with proposals from a multitude of Russian aviation manufacturers.

Sokolov quickly emerged as the leader in the field with its A-90 'Eaglet', which was used in the largest numbers of any Ekranoplane. Serving as an assault transport with the Soviet navy, it could be equipped with surface-to-surface missiles.

Most outstanding of all was

Above: Lack of funding has seen a host of advanced Russian aviation programmes halted.

the KM-04, known as the 'Caspian Sea Monster'. Weighing 503 tonnes (495 tons) and armed with cruise missiles, it was designed to destroy American submarines.

Above: Cuts in the Soviet air force resulted in Sukhoi's order books being drastically reduced. The company has undertaken Ekranoplane development.

A-90 ORLYONOK

The first large 'wingship' to enter operational service, the A-90 Orlyonok (Eaglet) was designed in 1979. The latest variants proposed by Sokolov are a SAR model and a commercial passenger-carrying example.

Mounted on the upper fuselage was a 76-mm gun turret to provide covering fire during the final stages of the assault. Missile launchers could also be installed to attack surface ships.

Conventional stressed skin was used in the construction of the A-90. After trials, additional strengthening was added to the wings and fuselage.

Propulsion was provided by a large, tail-mounted turboprop fitted with contra-rotating AV-68N propellers. The two balanced rudders gave the A-90 exceptional manoeuvrability.

Used in the assault transport role, the A-90 'Eaglet' was equipped with a side-hinging nose. This allowed the aircraft to carry the latest Soviet main battle tanks.

The wings were mounted low on the fuselage to provide lift at high speed. Smaller skegs (which act in a similar way to tailfins) were fitted at each tip to allow the aircraft to remain stable at high speed.

Naval versions of the A-90 'Eaglet' were equipped with a pylon-mounted surveillance radar and other avionics. The crew of nine provided the Soviet navy with a rapid transport attack and assault team.

A-90 Orlyonok

Type: sea-skimming assault/transport craft

Powerplant: starting, two NK-8-4K; cruise, one NK-12MK turbofan/turboprop engine

Cruise speed: 350-400 km/h (217-250 m.p.h.)

Operational range: 1000 km (621 mi.)

Range: 3000 km (1864 mi.)

Cruise height: 1-4 m

Weights: empty 86.36 tonnes (82 tons)

Armament: six 'SS-N-22 Sunburn' cruise missiles fired from retractable launchers, 76-mm cannon

Accommodation: five crew

Dimensions:
span 31.50 m (103 ft. 4 in.)
length 58.00 m (190 ft. 3 in.)
wing area 304.6 m² (3,279 sq. ft.)

EKRANOPLANE DEVELOPMENT

PRE-1960

1 Quickly realising the future potential in using Ekranoplanes as transports and attack platforms, a host of Russian manufacturers developed small single-seat models to test the validity of their designs.

1960s

1970s — BARTINI, ORLYONOK

2 With unlimited funding available, the 1970s saw rapid development of a host of Ekranoplanes within the AV-MF.

1980s — UTKA, LUN

3 Though intended primarily for a military role, later versions were designed with the civilian passenger market in mind.

1990s

4 The collapse of the Soviet finances has resulted in the current development of Ekranoplane being temporarily suspended.

'CASPIAN SEA MONSTER'

Soviet sea watchers

■ **Be-12 'MAIL':** With its design dating back to 1945, Beriev's Be-12 continues to serve in limited quantities on anti-submarine duties and rescue work.

■ **A-40 'MERMAID':** One of the biggest amphibian aircraft currently flying, the 'Mermaid' is designed to replace the Be-12 in the ASW and maritime reconnaissance role.

■ **Tu-95RT 'BEAR-D':** Following a more conventional design path, the Tupolev Tu-95 operates on extended long-range maritime reconnaissance patrols from coastal land bases.

BLOHM UND VOSS

HA 139

● Long-range mailplane/freighter ● Three built ● Transatlantic flights

T he Ha 139 floatplane was built to a Deutsch Lufthansa specification for a long-range seaplane which was able to take off from, and land on, rough seas. It was also required to carry a 500-kg (1,100-lb.) payload over a distance of 5000 km (3,100 mi.) at 250 km/h (155 m.p.h.). As seaborne bases were envisaged it was realised that the heavy, rugged aircraft would need to be catapult-launched from its depot ship if it was to cross the Atlantic non-stop.

▲ The three Ha 139s were named Nordmeer (North Sea), Nordwind (North Wind) and Nordstern (North Star) and registered D-AMIE, D-AJEY and D-ASTA, respectively.

BLOHM UND VOSS HA 139

◀ Fastest flights
The Ha 139's best transatlantic performances during the 1938 trials were 13 hours 40 minutes east to west by Nordmeer and 11 hours 53 minutes west to east by Nordstern.

▲ Ha 139 V3 at war
The third Ha 139, Nordstern, was modified for the Luftwaffe, first as a maritime reconnaissance aircraft and then as a minesweeper when war broke out.

▲ Rough sea performance
The Ha 139's huge floats gave the aircraft the stability required by the DLH specification.

▲ Third prototype
Among the changes made to the V3 were lower-mounted engines, greater overall dimensions and increased weights.

◀ Jumo diesels
An important factor in the Ha 139's ability to fly the Atlantic was its engines. The two-stroke Jumo diesels had a much lower fuel consumption than equivalent petrol engines.

FACTS AND FIGURES

➤ The 'Ha' in the aircraft's designation stood for Hamburger Flugzeugbau – Blohm und Voss' aircraft design bureau.

➤ During the war the two Ha 139As were modified to Ha 139B standard.

➤ As the war began the Ha 139s' crews were also drafted into the Luftwaffe.

➤ The Ha 139B once left Africa overloaded at 16500 kg after a 90-second take-off run in rough seas.

➤ The BV 142A, a land-based derivative with BMW radial engines, was built for DLH.

➤ A reconnaissance-bomber version was proposed but was not built.

PROFILE

North Wind, Sea and Star

Deutsch Lufthansa's (DLH) specification for a long-range transatlantic mailplane was demanding. Dornier proposed the Do 26 flying-boat based on its proven Wal, while ship-builders Blohm und Voss offered a floatplane design. Both were powered by economical diesel engines developed by Junkers.

Impressed by the Blohm und Voss design, DLH ordered three prototypes. The first two (V1 and V2, later designated Ha 139A) were delivered in 1937 and trials began

immediately between depot ships off the Azores and New York.

Ha 139 V3 (later Ha 139B) was delivered in 1938 and joined the other two for trials. All three entered service on DLH's route between the Gambia and Brazil across the South Atlantic just before World War II began.

During the war the Ha 139s were modified for a maritime reconnaissance role and used as supply aircraft in the Norwegian campaign. All were scrapped in the early 1940s as spare parts became scarce.

Above: Schwabenland *was one of two seaplane depot ships fitted with cranes used to hoist the Ha 139 aboard prior to a catapult launch.*

Below: In the foreground the Ha 139 V1 is seen suspended from a crane, while the V2 is aboard the Friesenland, *from which North Atlantic trials were made in 1937.*

HA 139A

Nordwind (North Wind) was the second Ha 139 to be built and was originally known as Ha 139 V2. It was delivered to Deutsch Lufthansa in 1937 and was engaged in trials from mid-August.

Ha 139A

Type: long-distance mailplane

Powerplant: four 451-kW (605-hp.) Junkers Jumo 205C diesel engines

Maximum speed: 315 km/h (195 m.p.h.)

Normal cruising speed: 260 km/h (211 m.p.h.)

Economic cruising speed: 225 km/h (140 m.p.h.)

Climb rate: 6 min to 1000 m (3,100 ft.)

Range: 5300 km (3,285 mi.)

Service ceiling: 3500 m (11,500 ft.)

Weights: empty 10,360 kg (22,792 lb.); loaded for catapult launch 17,500 kg (38,500 lb.)

Dimensions:
span	27.00 m (88 ft. 7 in.)
length	19.50 m (63 ft. 11 in.)
height	4.80 m (15 ft. 9 in.)
wing area	117 m² (1,259 sq. ft.)

The aircraft's nose featured a mooring compartment and stowage for marine gear. The flight deck seated the two pilots, with positions aft for a flight engineer and radio operator.

The wing's main spar separated the flight deck from the mail and freight compartment. No access between the two was possible in flight. The wing itself was an inverted gull design.

Poor directional stability with the original circular fin and rudder assemblies meant that they were replaced with triangular-shaped fins, the rudders being considerably larger. Other modifications involved the engine cooling system. The float-stub-mounted radiators were prone to corrosion and were removed in favour of a radiator for each engine beneath the wing.

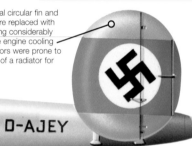

The Ha 139's engines were unusual Junkers Jumo 205C two-stroke diesels with six cylinders and 12 opposed pistons. Initially, radiators were mounted in pairs in the float-stub fairings.

The tubular centre section wing spar was divided into five separate fuel tanks with a total capacity of 6000 litres (1,585 gal.). The wing had a metal-skinned centre section with fabric covering the outer panels.

Modifications for service with the Luftwaffe included a lengthened glazed nose for an observer and a 7.9-mm MG 15 machine-gun. Another machine-gun was fitted in a hatch above the cockpit, with two in mountings either side of the aft fuselage.

ACTION DATA

MAXIMUM SPEED

Designed to the same specification, the Do 16 and Ha 139 had a similar top speed. Range was the most important factor, however. The Fw 200, as a land-based aircraft with a sleeker fuselage and more powerful engines, was capable of higher speeds. As speeds increased seaplanes fell out of the running.

Ha 139 V1	315 km/h (195 m.p.h.)
Do 26 V6	323 km/h (200 m.p.h.)
Fw 200 V1 CONDOR	374 km/h (232 m.p.h.)

RANGE

In its standard configuration the Fw 200 V1 had a much shorter range than the flying-boats. For the record-breaking flight in 1938 it was fitted with extra tanks and carried a minimal load, other than fuel. This range made it the ideal maritime patrol aircraft.

Ha 139 V1	5300 km (3,285 mi.)
Do 26 V6	7097 km (4,400 mi.)
Fw 200 V1 CONDOR	6558 km (4,065 mi.)

Deutsch Lufthansa mailplanes

■ **DORNIER Do 18:** Designed to replace Lufthansa's Wals on their South Atlantic mail service, the Do 18 flew in 1935 with two Jumo 205 diesels. A number saw war service.

■ **DORNIER Do 26:** Built to the same specification as the Ha 139, the graceful Do 26 flew in 1938. It was employed on South Atlantic routes rather than the northern route, however.

■ **FOCKE-WULF Fw 200 CONDOR:** This modified Fw 200 made a record-breaking pre-war transatlantic crossing in 1938, paving the way for passenger services after the war.

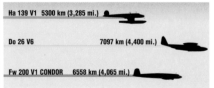

BLOHM UND VOSS

BV 138

- Flying-boat ● Air-sea rescue ● Maritime patrol

The Blohm und Voss BV 138 was crucial to Germany's naval war effort. It was the brainchild of Dr Ing Richard Vogt, and although it suffered from initial structural weaknesses the BV 138 had a successful career as a maritime patrol aircraft and anti-ship bomber. Despite extensive problems with the initial design, the BV 138 eventually proved to be a capable machine and was later adapted for minesweeping.

▲ Although it finally emerged as a useful design, the BV 138 had a problematic start and came close to being abandoned. It served from the Black Sea to the fringes of the Arctic Circle.

BLOHM UND VOSS BV 138

▲ Sweeping circle
With its guns removed, the BV 138MS (nicknamed the mouse-catching aircraft) was used to sweep canals for mines.

▲ Water jump
Early BV 138s had alarming handling on water. Hull drag was excessive, making take off a prolonged business.

▼ First missions
The Luftwaffe was so short of floatplanes that it impressed the first two BV 138s into service for the Norwegian campaign.

▲ Black Sea patrol
BV 138s flew patrols in the Black Sea as late as 1944 from bases in Romania, with protection from Romanian escort fighters.

Back to the drawing board ▶
The Ha 138V2 was the second prototype. With enlarged tail surfaces it handled better than the original aircraft but still suffered from vibration problems. A complete redesign was recommended by the Air Ministry technical office.

FACTS AND FIGURES

- ➤ A BV 138 was one of the last planes to leave Berlin on 1 May 1945, taking off from a lake with wounded troops.

- ➤ In 1941 a BV 138 shot down an RAF Catalina over the North Sea.

- ➤ Convoy PQ-18 was the first to fight off shadowing BV 138s with Sea Hurricanes.

- ➤ This seaplane was nicknamed 'Der Fliegende Holzschuh' (The Flying Clog) when it appeared as a prototype in 1937.

- ➤ The prototype, known then as the Ha 138, first flew on 15 July 1937.

- ➤ As late as the summer of 1944 BV 138s flew anti-ship missions in the Black Sea.

PROFILE

Germany's hunchback

The BV 138 was handicapped by not being strong enough to withstand the battering of prolonged operation on the open seas, and the prototype had to be extensively redesigned after showing severe instability on the water. After major modifications, the aircraft entered squadron service in 1940, initially proving unreliable. However, the aircraft's problems were later solved and it went on to provide good service, flying important naval reconnaissance missions against Allied convoys, especially in the Atlantic and Barents Sea. Two

BV 138s even operated from the frozen wastes of Novaya Zemlya with the support of U-boats.

In addition to shore bases, BV 138s flew from seaplane tenders, some modified with catapults for launch. All BV 138s were able to use assisted take-off rockets and some carried FuG 200 Hohentwiel radar for shadowing convoys. The BV 138 could even fight off Allied fighters, as one crew showed by downing a Blenheim over Norway. The final version was fitted with a giant electromagnetic ring for triggering magnetic mines.

One of the BV 138's main problems was the centrally mounted engine which suffered exhaust blockages.

Although its enclosed cockpit was an improvement on rival designs, the prototype's crew stations were criticised as being inadequate for long patrols.

With the increases in weight caused by structural modifications, the BV 138 was considered somewhat underpowered. This was remedied in the BV 138B-1 by the installation of Jumo 205D engines.

Wing construction was all-metal with a tubular main spar. It was built in three sections.

BV 138C-1

Type: reconnaissance flying-boat

Powerplant: three 656-kW (880-hp.) Junkers Jumo 205D inline piston engines

Maximum speed: 285 km/h (177 m.p.h.) at sea level

Cruising speed: 235 km/h (145 m.p.h.)

Range: 5000 km (3,100 mi.)

Service ceiling: 5000 m (16,400 ft.)

Weights: empty 11,770 kg (25,895 lb.); maximum take-off 17,650 kg (38,830 lb.)

Armament: one 20-mm MG 151 cannon in the bow turret, one 13-mm MG 131 machine-gun at the rear centre engine nacelle and one 7.92-mm MG 15 firing through starboard hatch; three 50-kg bombs under starboard wingroot, or six 50-kg (110-lb.) bombs or four 150-kg (330-lb.) depth charges (BV 138C-1/U1)

Dimensions:
span	27.00 m (89 ft.)
length	19.90 m (65 ft.)
height	5.90 m (19 ft.)
wing area	112 m² (1,205 sq. ft.)

BV 138C-1

The BV 138 equipped the Luftwaffe's See Aufklarungsgruppen, serving in the coastal patrol and reconnaissance role.

One of the BV 138's best features was its flying controls. These were hydraulically operated and fabric covered, making the aircraft easy to fly.

Production aircraft had rectangular section stressed-skin metal tail booms replacing the earlier tubular booms. They suffered from vibration problems, which in turn caused crew fatigue.

Nose armament was especially effective, with a power-operated turret mounting a 20-mm MG FF cannon. The BV 138B-1 used the faster firing MG 151 cannon.

7R RL

The biggest fault was the hull design, which was not sufficiently strong to withstand the stresses imposed by rough seas at maximum load.

COMBAT DATA

ARMAMENT

Cannon armament made attacking a BV 138 a hazardous task, as the nose gunner occupied a powered turret and had an excellent field of fire. In comparison the He 115 and the Walrus were easy targets for a fighter pilot and neither usually carried bombs.

BV 138C-1 — 1 x 20-mm cannon, 1 x 7.92-mm MG, 1 x 13-mm MG, 4 x 150-kg (330-lb.) bombs

He 115 — 2 x 7.92-mm MGs, 2 x 250-kg (550-lb.) bombs

WALRUS — 2 x 7.7-mm MGs, up to 345 kg (760 lb.) of bombs

RANGE

The BV 138 was much larger than the He 115 or the Walrus, and its capacious if ungainly fuselage held a large amount of fuel. The Walrus was a short-range aircraft, used for coastal air-sea rescue duties or for launching from warships for spotting the fall of gunfire. This range was for unladen aircraft; the weight of the minesweeping ring made the BV 138MS version less capable.

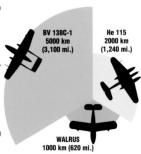

BV 138C-1 5000 km (3,100 mi.)

He 115 2000 km (1,240 mi.)

WALRUS 1000 km (620 mi.)

BV 138 missions

AIR-SEA RESCUE: At the start of the war the Luftwaffe was notably more efficient than the RAF at rescuing its shot-down aircrew. Pilots had excellent survival equipment.

PICK-UP: One of the last BV 138 sorties of the war was to a lake in Berlin. The pilot picked up 10 wounded soldiers and escaped back to Denmark.

CONVOY PATROL: BV 138s spotted the location of Allied convoys, giving position reports to U-boat Wolf Packs. The British replied by using Sea Hurricanes in defence, rocket-launched from ships.

MINE SWEEP: Using a powerful magnetic signal, the BV 138MS could set off enemy mines which were often dropped in canals.

BLOHM UND VOSS

BV 222 WIKING

● Airliner design ● Huge capacity ● Transport and patrol service

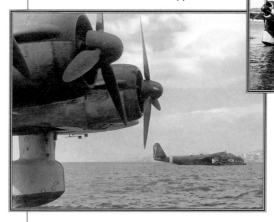

▲ During 1942
BV 222s were engaged on supply missions to North Africa. From Greek and Italian bases the aircraft flew to Tobruk or Derna, and often returned carrying casualties.

Deutsche Lufthansa (DLH) ordered three Blohm und Voss BV 222 Wiking (Viking) aircraft in September 1939 to fill a requirement for a new 24-berth transatlantic airliner. The first of these made its initial flight in September 1940; by then World War II had started and DLH no longer had a use for the type. Possible military roles were investigated and the following July BV 222 V1 made its first supply flight, the first of many sorties for the Luftwaffe.

BLOHM UND VOSS BV 222 WIKING

Responsive controls ▶
Flight tests proved that the BV 222 handled well in flight. The only drawbacks were slight directional instability and a tendency to porpoise whilst taxiing.

▲ Diesel power
The long-range reconnaissance BV 222C was powered by six Jumo 207C diesel engines.

▼ Submarine support
In May 1943 BV 222 V5 was transferred to south-west France for U-boat support duties.

▲ Defensive sting
After two BV 222As were lost to Allied fighters in 1942, the bow gun position (seen here) was removed and more powerful armament installed including unusual wing-mounted turrets.

Diverted to the Luftwaffe ▶
Rolled out in August 1940, the prototype BV 222 carried a civilian registration. The aircraft was acquired by the Luftwaffe and began operations in July 1941.

FACTS AND FIGURES

➤ Production time of a complete BV 222 airframe (less engines and equipment) totalled 35,000 man hours.

➤ Slow and vulnerable, a number of BV 222s were shot down by RAF fighters.

➤ Towards the end of World War II, Wikings reverted solely to transport roles.

➤ By the end of 1942 Wikings had carried more than 1422 tonnes (1,400 tons) of cargo, 17,000 troops and 2,400 casualties in the Mediterranean.

➤ Seven BV 222s survived the war; two were flown to the US for evaluation.

➤ In October 1943 a Wiking shot down an RAF Lancaster bomber over the Atlantic.

PROFILE

Giant German flying boat

Powered by six BMW-Bramo Fafnir 323R radial engines, the giant Wiking was the largest flying-boat to see service during the war.

The first prototype (BV 222 V1) made its first cargo flight to Norway in July 1941 and later flew supplies to the Afrika Korps in North Africa. The subsequent V2 and V3 were armed with machine guns in various positions on the fuselage and wings for defence. By late 1942, five more pre-production Wikings had entered service

and, with the first three aircraft, equipped the specially-formed Luft-Transportstaffel (See) 222.

With interest in the BV 222 as a long-range reconnaissance aircraft growing, a number of the flying-boats were refitted, receiving search and rear-warning radar equipment and powered gun turrets. Soon they were in service from bases in the Bay of Biscay, for Atlantic U-boat co-operation flights.

Meanwhile, in April 1943, BV 222 V7 made its first flight, powered by six Junkers Jumo

207C diesels. This became the prototype for the BV 222C, which entered production at the Blohm und Voss plant near Hamburg. Five were delivered to maritime patrol units in 1943; four others remained uncompleted.

Above: The stabilising floats retracted to lie flush with the outer wing panel. This example has its floats lowered in preparation for landing.

Above: BV 222A-0 V8 is seen here testing its engines on a launching ramp. It was shot down by RAF Beaufighters on 10 December 1942.

BV 222C Wiking

Type: long-range transport and maritime reconnaissance flying boat

Powerplant: six 746-kW (1,000-hp.) Junkers Jumo 207C in-line diesel engines

Maximum speed: 390 km/h (242 m.p.h.) at 5000 m (16,400 ft.)

Range: 6095 km (3,779 mi.)

Service ceiling: 7300 m (24,000 ft.)

Weights: empty 30,650 kg (67,430 lb.); maximum take-off 49,000 kg (107,800 lb.)

Armament: (BV 222C-09) three 20-mm MG 151 cannon and five 13-mm MG 131 machine-guns

Dimensions:

span	46.00 m	(150 ft. 10 in.)
length	37.00 m	(121 ft. 4 in.)
height	10.90 m	(35 ft. 9 in.)
wing area	255 m²	(274 sq. ft.)

The flight crew consisted of two pilots, two flight engineers, a navigator and a wireless operator. To help the pilot on longer missions an autopilot system was fitted to a three-section elevator. The pilot controlled the outer and inner sections with the autopilot controlling the central section.

Armament was upgraded a number of times although, even with its most powerful arrangement, the aircraft was still vulnerable to fighters. Upgraded BV 222As had the unusual arrangement of two turrets mounted in the wings aft of the outer engine nacelle each armed with a single 20-mm cannon.

The main passenger/cargo portion of the hull was very spacious thanks to the lack of bulkheads. The bulkheads were fitted between the keel and the floor.

BV 222A-0 WIKING

This BV 222 flew transport sorties from Petsamo, Finland during the early months of 1943. The yellow bands signify that the aircraft was operating in the Eastern Front theatre.

Of all-metal construction, the two-step hull was covered by corrosion-resisting alloy sheet which varied from 3 mm to 5 mm in thickness. It was divided into two sections, the lower for passengers/cargo and the upper for the flight crew.

The all-metal wings were supported by a single, immensely strong, wing spar measuring 145 cm (57 in.) in diameter. The spar was sub-divided to contain six fuel tanks.

The fin and rudder were large and, after initial problems, provided good directional stability. The rudder was operated by two interconnected tabs driven by the main circuit. The elevator was mounted near the base of the fin.

COMBAT DATA

MAXIMUM SPEED

With six engines, the BV 222 was by far the most powerful of the German World War II seaplanes. This power translated into a healthy maximum speed for an aircraft of this type. It was faster than the RAF's closest equivalent, the Short Sunderland.

BV 222C WIKING	390 km/h (242 m.p.h.)
BV 138B	289 km/h (179 m.p.h.)
Ju 52/3mW	262 km/h (162 m.p.h.)

OPERATIONAL RANGE

Designed for the long-range maritime patrol role, the BV 222C had much greater range than the BV 138 and Ju 52 floatplane which were intended to patrol coastal waters. The BV 222C actually had a shorter range than the BV 222A as fuel capacity was decreased with the installation of the Junkers Jumo diesel-powered engines.

BV 222C WIKING 6095 km (3,779 mi.)

BV 138B 3878 km (2,404 mi.)

Ju 52/3mW 1496 km (928 mi.)

CREW CAPACITY

As the largest flying boat to reach operational status in any country during World War II, the BV 222 was capable of carrying a large crew. Eight of the crew were gunners.

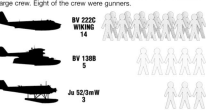

BV 222C WIKING 14

BV 138B 5

Ju 52/3mW 3

Blohm und Voss seaplanes

■ **BV 138:** The first flying-boat design to be built by the company, the BV 138 was used in a variety of roles during World War II including reconnaissance and mine-sweeping.

■ **Ha 139:** Designed to meet a requirement for a transatlantic mailplane, the Ha 139 was pressed into Luftwaffe service late in 1939. Three examples were operated until 1942.

■ **Ha 140:** In 1935 design work began on the Ha 140 which was to compete directly with the Heinkel He 115 as a torpedo and reconnaissance floatplane. It did not win the orders.

■ **BV 238:** The giant BV 238 was to have been built in both sea and landplane versions. Only one example flew and this was sunk at its moorings by USAAF P-51 Mustangs.

BOEING

314 CLIPPER

● 1930s transoceanic flying-boat airliner ● Wartime draftee

BOEING 314 CLIPPER

▲ Double Cyclone power
For minor inflight maintenance the engines could be reached by passageways in the wings.

▲ Three tail configurations
When first built the prototype had a single tailfin, which was later changed to two – one at either end of the tailplane. Production 314s, however, had a triple tail.

Impressed in wartime ▶
Before World War II three 314s had been sold to BOAC. The remaining nine were placed under US Army, then Navy, control.

▼ Hybrid design
The 314's sleek lines belied the fact that its wing was borrowed from the XB-15 bomber, with the hull being a fairly conventional design.

▲ Pan American fleet
Designed to a Pan Am requirement, 12 Clippers were built. NX18601 was the prototype, with the 'NX' prefix indicating an experimental type.

Pan American Airways introduced the Boeing 314 in 1939. The 'Clipper', as it was known, spanned oceans in the golden age of the flying boat when air travel was a luxury for a privileged few. Following the Martin M-130 and Sikorsky S-42 on Atlantic and Pacific routes, the 314 ushered in new standards in range and speed, as well as passenger comfort. However, World War II brought the era to an end and the flying-boats' days were numbered.

▲ By today's standards flying-boat travel was slow – New York to Marseilles via the Azores and Lisbon took 29$^{1}/_{2}$ hours. Compared to a sea crossing, however, it was quick but very expensive.

FACTS AND FIGURES

➤ The four passenger cabins of this flying-boat had different floor levels because of the 314's stepped hull.

➤ The first Boeing 314 Clipper made its maiden flight on 7 June 1938.

➤ Clipper flying-boats used the wing and engine nacelles of the XB-15 bomber.

➤ One 314 caught by the outbreak of war in New Zealand escaped by flying west, completing a round-the-world journey.

➤ In 1939 the Clipper was the largest production aircraft in regular airline use.

➤ In 1942 Churchill flew home from the United States via Bermuda in a BOAC 314.

PROFILE

Transoceanic Boeing airliner

Boeing workers were excited in 1936 when their company won a Pan American contract to build six Model 314s. After successful flight tests, the first of these high-wing, triple-tail, four-engined flying-boats, called 'Clippers' by Pan Am, entered transatlantic air mail service on 20 May 1939.

When it began hauling passengers, the Boeing 314 was the world's largest production airliner. Pan Am used its Clippers on the Pacific route to the Far East and New Zealand, across the North Atlantic and on the southerly routes to Brazil and the West Indies.

A second batch of six, known as 314As, were built for Pan Am in the early 1940s, three of these later going to British Overseas Airways Corporation (BOAC) for use in support of the war effort in North Africa. The other nine also saw war service,

requisitioned by the US Army as the C-98. More suited to a naval role, all were turned over to the US Navy as the B-314.

By 1946, when Pan Am made their last Clipper flight, faster landplanes had rendered the majestic 'boats' obsolete.

Above: The large sponsons fitted either side of the hull meant that wing floats were not necessary.

Above: The second batch of six Clippers, known as 314As, incorporated more powerful engines and increased fuel capacity.

314 Clipper

Type: long-range flying-boat transport

Powerplant: four 1118-kW (1,500-hp.) Wright GR-2600 Cyclone 14 radial piston engines

Maximum speed: 311 km/h (193 m.p.h.) at 3050 m (10,000 ft.)

Cruising speed: 295 km/h (183 m.p.h.)

Range: 5633 km (3,495 mi.)

Service ceiling: 4085 m (13,400 ft.)

Weights: empty 22,801 kg (50,162 lb.); maximum take-off 37,421 kg (82,326 lb.)

Accommodation: flight crew and cabin crew of 10, plus up to 74 passengers in four separate cabins (40 passengers in sleeper configuration)

Dimensions:
span	46.33 m	(151 ft. 11 in.)
length	32.31 m	(106 ft.)
height	8.41 m	(27 ft. 7 in.)
wing area	266 m²	(2,866 sq. ft.)

314 CLIPPER

NC18602 'California Clipper' was the second 314 delivered to Pan American Airways. During World War II it served with the Army Transport Command (ATC) and the US Navy.

Wright R-2600 Cyclone 14 engines powered the Clippers; the same engine was fitted to wartime B-25 Mitchell and A-20 Havoc bombers and the PBM Mariner flying-boat.

Painted silver overall, the top surface of the wing carried a broad 'Dayglo' orange band from wingtip to wingtip. This made the aircraft more conspicuous and therefore easier to find in the event of it ditching.

A crew of six flew the Clipper: pilot, co-pilot, radio operator, flight engineer, navigator and aircraft commander. All were seated in a six-man control cabin.

Clippers had enough space for up to 10 crewmembers and 74 passengers, the exact arrangement varying according to the type of flight. As a sleeper, the 314 was limited to 40 passengers.

The cabin area had two decks. The lower deck was divided into compartments: four with seats or bunks, the others including a galley, cocktail bar and promenade deck. The upper level included the flight deck and luggage storage.

Pan Am's Clippers had 'stars and stripes' on the nose and the airline's logo below the cockpit. On the tail was the aircraft's registration and the Boeing trademark.

ACTION DATA

MAXIMUM SPEED

Kawanishi's H6K was another pre-war flying-boat, but was designed as a military aircraft. Its engines were similar in output to those of the Clipper, but powered an airframe which was a fraction of the weight. The post-war Solent used much more powerful engines.

314 CLIPPER	311 km/h (193 m.p.h.)
SOLENT 3	430 km/h (267 m.p.h.)
H6K 'MAVIS'	385 km/h (239 m.p.h.)

Transatlantic flying-boats

■ **LATÉCOÈRE 521:** The 521 first flew in 1935 before carrying out long-distance flights to South and North America for the Air France Trans-atlantique Company between 1937 and 1939.

■ **SHORT 'G' CLASS:** The S.26 'G' class was ordered by Imperial Airways for transatlantic mail services. Three were built and served in World War II before flying with BOAC in the 1940s.

■ **SIKORSKY VS-44 EXCALIBUR:** Designed to carry passengers and mail between the USA and Europe, the VS-44 flew cargo and troops to the UK during World War II.

■ **SHORT SOLENT 3:** Four of the Hercules-powered Solents were built for Tasman Empire Airways after the end of World War II. They also served with BOAC until 1950.

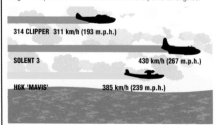

BOEING
F4B/P-12

● Biplane fighter ● Inter-war defender of the US Fleet

S erving the US Navy at the end of the biplane era, the classic F4B was the star of a family of famous Boeing fighters which included the US Army Air Corps' P-12 and the export Model 100. The F4B was a super ship to fly and was the most capable carrier-based fighter of its time. For all its elegance and manoeuvrability, the F4B triumphed successfully for only a brief time before being eclipsed by the arrival of the monoplane in the late 1930s.

▲ Pilots loved the F4B for its superb manoeuvrability, massive strength and impressive performance. But by the end of the 1930s the days of open-cockpit biplane fighters were numbered.

BOEING F4B/P-12

▲ **Last of the line**
A late-model P-12F above Hensley Field, Texas. This model was the equivalent of the Navy's F4B-4, and often had radio fitted.

▲ **Still going strong**
This P-12C is a rare survivor of the 568 built. A Boeing F4B-4 that also survived is on display at the Naval Aviation Museum at NAS Pensacola, Florida.

▲ **Line abreast**
P-12Es of the 27th Pursuit Group practise their immaculate precision formation flying above Selfridge Field, Michigan.

▲ **Fabric fighter**
Early P-12s had a fabric-covered fuselage, but by 1930 Boeing was building P-12Es with a stressed metal skin for better strength.

Streamlining ▶
Early P-12 models had uncowled Wasp engines. The Townend ring cowling fitted to later models streamlined the engine and helped increase speed.

FACTS AND FIGURES

➤ The first F4B-1 went on duty aboard the carrier *Lexington* on 8 August 1929.

➤ A special F4B-1A served as a 'taxi' for Assistant Secretary of the US Navy Douglas Ingalls.

➤ The first protoype in this great fighter series flew on 25 June 1928.

➤ The F4B landed on a carrier deck at about 60 km/h, or about one-third the speed of the modern F-14 Tomcat.

➤ Many F4B-4 fighters served as unmanned target drones during World War II.

➤ The F4B was the favourite aeroplane of stunt pilot hero Frank Tallman.

PROFILE

Boeing's great Navy biplane

In early days of carrier aviation, the F4B was the hottest thing with wings. Boeing's Model 83 and 89 prototypes led to four principal versions of this superb biplane fighter, numbered F4B-1 through F4B-4; the final version is the best remembered among the 200 or so of these aircraft which saw active service with the Navy between 1930 and 1938.

These great fighters were exciting and colourful: most had grey fuselage and wings, a brilliant yellow upper wing surface, and squadron colours on fuselage and cowling.

Part of the success of the F4B belongs to the Wasp engine, or R-1340, which was this period's finest technical achievement. But the real measure of the F4B was its prowess as a fighting plane.

Touchdown landing on the wooden deck of the USS Lexington. Landing and take-off accidents were common.

In the heyday of the biplane, this air-to-air dogfighter could not be defeated. Unfortunately, the romance of this era was all too brief. By the late 1930s, faster monoplane fighters had consigned biplanes to history.

US military aircraft generally sported bright colour schemes in the inter-war period. The vivid yellow wings aided recognition over the sea.

F4B-4

Type: single-seat carrier-based fighter

Powerplant: one 410-kW (550-hp.) Pratt & Whitney R-1340-16 radial piston engine

Maximum speed: 300 km/h (186 m.p.h.) at 1830 m (6,000 ft.)

Range: 600 km (375 mi.)

Service ceiling: 8200 m (29,600 ft.)

Weights: empty 1068 kg (2,350 lb.); loaded 1638 kg (3,600 lb.)

Armament: two 7.62-mm (.30 cal.) fixed forward-firing Browning machine-guns or one 7.62-mm and one 12.7-mm (.50 cal.) Browning machine-guns, five 12-kg (25-lb.) bombs or one 227-kg (500-lb.) bomb or one 208-litre (50-gal.) drop tank

Dimensions:
span	9.14 m	(30 ft.)
length	6.12 m	(20 ft. 1 in.)
height	2.84 m	(9 ft. 4 in.)
wing area	21m²	(228 sq. ft.)

A compartment in the headrest housed a dinghy in case the pilot was forced to crash-land in the sea. This version also had a radio fitted.

F4B-4 9025

NAVY 6-F-10

The 'Felix the Cat' insignia was the squadron badge of fighter squadron VF-6, operating from USS *Saratoga* in 1935. The badge is still being used today on the F-14 Tomcats of VF-31.

F4B-4

This F4B-4 was one of about 200 used by the US Navy between 1929 and 1938. The F4B-4 was similar to the Army's P-12E, with a 410-kW Wasp engine but with the essential arrester hook and wing bomb racks.

The fuselage frame of all F4Bs was built of welded steel tube for strength. Stressed metal skins replaced fabric on the fuselage of the later versions, but all F4Bs retained a fabric-covered wing.

The undercarriage of the F4B needed to be strong. Even with the low speeds of biplane fighters, landings on carrier decks were often very hard.

The nine-cylinder Pratt & Whitney Wasp radial was the forerunner of a family of engines that would power US Navy fighters throughout World War II.

COMBAT DATA

RANGE

Even in the early days of carrier aviation, naval aircraft were expected to operate over greater distances than their land-based equivalents – after all, emergency landing fields are few and far between in the vast ocean spaces – and the F4B comfortably outranged the British Bulldog.

BULLDOG 475 km (295 mi.)

F4B 600 km (375 mi.)

FLYCATCHER 500 km (310 mi.)

MAXIMUM SPEED

BULLDOG	280 km/h (174 m.p.h.)
F4B	300 km/h (186 m.p.h.)
FLYCATCHER	214 km/h (135 m.p.h.)

The F4B was one of the fastest fighters around when it went into service in the late-1920s. It had the edge on land-based machines like the Bristol Bulldog and was much quicker than the Fairey Flycatcher, the standard British carrier fighter of the time.

ARMAMENT

Aircraft armament in the biplane era had not advanced much in the decade since the end of World War I. Two forward-firing machine-guns was the norm for most fighters of the early 1930s. However, the F4B's powerful radial engine meant that it could carry a fairly heavy bombload for a fighter.

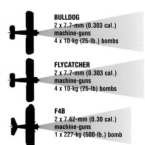

BULLDOG
2 x 7.7-mm (0.303 cal.) machine-guns
4 x 10-kg (25-lb.) bombs

FLYCATCHER
2 x 7.7-mm (0.303 cal.) machine-guns
4 x 10-kg (25-lb) bombs

F4B
2 x 7.62-mm (0.30 cal.) machine-guns
1 x 227-kg (500-lb.) bomb

Carrier Air Power – then and now

■ **USS *KITTYHAWK*** has been in service since 1961 and displaces more than 91,500 tonnes (90,000 tons). It carries an air wing of 85 advanced combat jets, and with its nuclear arsenal deploys more firepower than the entire US Navy of the 1930s, and is able to project power on a global basis.

■ **USS *RANGER*** was laid down in 1931. It displaced only 14,500 tonnes (14,732 tons), but it too could carry more than 80 aircraft. Most were tiny biplanes, however, and five or six could be stored in the space a single modern F-14 Tomcat occupies.

BOULTON-PAUL

SIDESTRAND/OVERSTRAND

- Biplane medium bomber ● Powered turret ● Speed and agility

▼ Outstanding platform
In bombing and gunnery exercises, No. 101 Squadron's Sidestrands broke all RAF records for accuracy. They were limited to a 476-kg (1,050-lb.) bombload.

▲ Exposed to the elements
The Sidestrand's crew were at the mercy of the elements. Yet the Overstrand represented a huge improvement in crew comfort, with its enclosed cockpit and nose turret and shielded mid-upper gun position.

▲ On exercises
On air exercises the Sidestrand demonstrated that it was as fast and agile as a single-engined bomber.

▲ Gunnery training
Superseded as a first-line bomber in 1937, the Overstrand was relegated to gunnery training. It served in this role until 1941.

No. 101 Squadron, RAF ▶
The unit most associated with the Sidestrand Mk III and Overstrand was No. 101, which was based at three different RAF stations while flying the types.

I ntended to complement the Fairey Fox, the Sidestrand was the RAF's first medium bomber. Initially flown in 1926, it served with only one squadron, No. 101, from 1928 until 1936. The Overstrand (both types were named after villages near the Boulton and Paul factory in Norwich) was a developed version of the Sidestrand and replaced it from 1937. The Overstrand was notable as the first RAF aircraft to be equipped with a powered gun turret.

▲ Both types
shared an all-metal structure with fabric covering. Although representing the peak of British biplane bomber design, they were destined for a short service life.

FACTS AND FIGURES

➤ Part of No. 101 Squadron's badge consisted of a castle tower – a reference to the Overstrand's powered turret.

➤ After an Overstrand fell apart in mid-air in 1940 flying was severely curtailed.

➤ The Overstrands of No. 101 Squadron were the last new RAF biplane bombers.

➤ At the outbreak of World War II the RAF had 11 Overstrands on charge, six of which were flying with training units.

➤ At the 1937 RAF display an Overstrand demonstrated air-to-air refuelling.

➤ Although innovative, the Overstrand was reliable and popular with ground crew.

PROFILE

RAF's first medium bombers

Left: J9181 was the fifth production Sidestrand Mk II. The type entered RAF service in 1928.

Like the two prototypes, the 18 production Mk II Sidestrands were powered by 317-kW Jupiter VI engines. These aircraft were later modified with geared Jupiter VIIFs to become Mk IIIs. They had both dorsal and ventral gun mountings, although only a single gunner was carried in the fuselage. The choice of installation was intended to be made according to the individual aircraft's position in the attack formation.

One of the Mk IIIs was re-engined again with Bristol Pegasus IM3s. Originally designated Sidestrand Mk IV, it became the prototype for the Overstrand. The most obvious change introduced by the new type was a powered nose turret, although the structure was also strengthened and the crew's accommodation, protection and the bomb installation were all improved.

The turret itself used pneumatic motors for rotation,

while hydraulic rams helped the gunner to elevate or depress the Lewis machine-gun. Two 227-kg (500-lb.) and two 113-kg (250-lb.) bombs could be carried beneath either the wings or the fuselage.

From 1936 the 24 production Overstrands were used by No. 101 Squadron (which had operated the Sidestrand) and, briefly, by No. 144 Squadron until they were replaced by Blenheims in 1938. A projected development with a retracting undercarriage, the Superstrand, was abandoned.

Above: Originally intended to be fitted with Napier Lion in-line engines, the Sidestrand Mk I was powered by Jupiter VIs.

OVERSTRAND MK I

No. 101 Squadron was one of two squadrons to be equipped with the Overstrand. Production totalled 24, K4546 being the first of the initial batch of 19 aircraft. An overall silver finish was typical of the period.

Sidestrand Mk III

Type: medium day-bomber

Powerplant: two 343-kW (460-hp.) Bristol Jupiter VIIF nine-cylinder air-cooled radial engines

Maximum speed: 225 km/h (140 m.p.h.) at 3050 m (10,000 ft.)

Climb rate: 4572 m (15,000 ft.) in 19 min

Range: 805 km (500 mi.)

Service ceiling: 7300 m (24,000 ft.)

Weights: empty 2726 kg (6,000 lb.); loaded 4627 kg (10,179 lb.)

Armament: three 7.7-mm (.303 cal.) Lewis machine-guns, plus up to 476 kg (1,050 lb.) of bombs

Dimensions: span 21.92 m (71 ft. 11 in.)
length 14.02 m (46 ft.)
height 4.52 m (14 ft. 10 in.)
wing area 91 m² (979 sq. ft.)

ACTION DATA

ARMAMENT

The Overstrand had a more limited bombload than contemporary bombers from France and the USA. Its defensive armament was on a par with other top bombers, but it did not form a successful basis for further bomber development.

OVERSTRAND Mk I — 3 x 7.7-mm machine-guns 726-kg (1,600-lb) bombload

MB.200B.4 — 3 x 7.5-mm machine-guns 1200-kg (2,650-lb) bombload

B-10B — 3 x 7.62-mm (.30 cal.) machine-guns 1025-kg (2,250-lb.) bombload

Overstrands were the first RAF bombers to be fitted with a power-operated gun turret. While later aircraft had electrically-actuated turrets, the Overstrand's used pneumatic rotation. In air-to-air fighting gunners were able to improve their accuracy five-fold.

As well as the powered nose turret, the Overstrand had a more traditional Scarff ring-mounted Lewis gun in the dorsal position. One innovation was a protective windscreen for the gunner.

For a bomber the Overstrand was highly manoeuvrable and immensely strong. This was demonstrated at the 1936 air display at RAF Hendon during which the aircraft performed half-rolls and loops.

Bristol supplied the radial engines for both the Sidestrand and Overstrand; Jupiters in the former and early versions of the Pegasus in the latter.

During the 1930s RAF bomber squadron aircraft often carried their numbers on the fuselage. Individual aircraft were identified by a code letter, in this case 'W' on the aircraft's nose.

A ventral gun position mounted the third 7.7-mm (.303 cal.) machine-gun. A 227-kg (500-lb.) capacity bomb rack was fitted beneath each wing inboard of the engine. Fuselage racks under the cockpit and mid-upper gun position could each carry four 9-kg (20-lb.) bombs.

The Overstrand continued the good reputation of its predecessor. With a top speed of above 240 km/h (150 m.p.h.), it was able to 'hold its own' against many fighters of the day, with its defensive armament covering most 'blind' spots.

SPINNING: Few modern combat aircraft are cleared for regular spinning manoeuvres, but Boulton-Paul's Overstrand accomplished them with ease.

SPIRALLING EARTHWARDS: As the aircraft descends at a shallow angle, the nose revolves slowly around the vertical. At the same time the tail rotates at a faster rate around the nose, causing the aircraft to spin as it slowly spirals down.

Aerobatic Overstrand

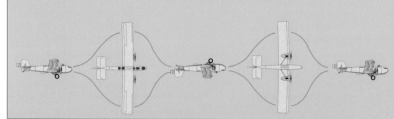

ROLLING: Thanks to the Overstrand's manoeuvrability and structural integrity crews found that it was possible to perform aerobatics in the aircraft. Rolls could be carried out quite easily – an impressive accomplishment for such a large aircraft.

LOOPING: The Overstrand could also perform loops. It was the first, and one of the very few, RAF bombers able to perform such manoeuvres with regularity.

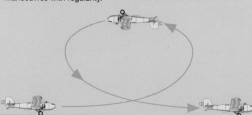

BREGUET

14

● **Famous World War I bomber** ● **Built in large numbers**

Built in greater numbers than any other French aircraft of its vintage, the Breguet 14 flew for the first time, with Louis Breguet himself at the controls, in November 1916. More than 5,500 had been ordered by the end of the war, and production continued until 1926 to bring the total built to more than 8,000. The type was used by the French, Belgian and US air forces during the war itself, and afterwards served with a dozen other countries.

▲ *Not one of the prettiest aircraft to emerge from the Breguet Velizy-Villacoublay works, the model 14 nevertheless became one of the most important types of World War I.*

BREGUET 14

▲ Longevity
A very sound basic design ensured that the Breguet 14 remained in production for many years after World War I. It also spawned a number of successors which shared many components with this excellent aircraft.

▲ Service pioneer
First version to see action was the A2 reconnaissance variant which entered service in 1917.

Exclusive power ▶
Only one engine, a Renault 12 Fe, powered the Breguet 14 series, though others were evaluated.

◀ Sturdy design
Like several other late-war French aircraft, such as the SPAD VII, the Breguet 14 was a sturdy machine and featured ailerons on both the upper and lower wings.

Tending to the injured ▶
In addition to its primary roles as a bomber, reconnaissance and artillery support aircraft, the Breguet 14 was also used by the Armée de l'Air as a flying ambulance, evacuating casualties from the front line.

FACTS AND FIGURES

➤ Known as the Breguet AV (*avant*, or forward), the prototype was the first Breguet biplane with a tractor engine.

➤ In 1923 Breguet 14 air ambulances evacuated 870 casualties in Morocco.

➤ The United States Air Service used model 14s on the Western Front in 1918.

➤ In 1919 French airmen, Captain Coli and Lieutenant Roget, flew a record distance of 1609 km in a Breguet model 14.

➤ A small number of aircraft were built post-war to keep the company in being.

➤ By the end of its production run, at least five firms had built Breguet 14s.

France's famed World War I bomber

The initial production version of the Breguet 14 was the B2 day bomber. In addition to a forward-firing Vickers machine-gun, it carried a pair of Lewis guns on a ring mounting for the observer and some later examples had a third Lewis firing downward to the rear. The B2 was soon joined in service by the A2 reconnaissance bomber, which had wings of reduced span and did not have the B2's rear-cockpit side windows. Other variants included the E2 trainer

and B1 single-seat bomber. Many different engines were also tested. The type was manufactured by at least three other French firms during the war and was later built under licence in Japan and Spain.

The B2 equipped French units in Greece, Macedonia, Morocco and Serbia as well as serving in large numbers on the Western Front. It was also used in smaller numbers by the American Expeditionary Force and two Belgian air force units. Post-war users of the military

Breguet 14 included Brazil, China, Czechoslovakia, Denmark, Finland, Greece, Japan, Poland, Portugal, Romania, Siam (Thailand) and Spain. There was also a passenger transport version called the Salon.

Left: A civil registration and the modern cityscape below betray this particular aircraft as a Breguet 14 replica. Such machines allow the legacy of early aircraft to live on today.

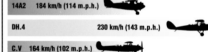

Above: Breguet 14s remained in production after World War I. This is a Bre. 14T bis, identified by the four large cabin windows on each side, which first appeared in 1921.

Bre. 14B2

Type: two-seat bomber and reconnaissance aircraft

Powerplant: one 224-kW (300-hp.) Renault 12 Fe liquid-cooled V-12 engine

Maximum speed: 177 km/h (110 m.p.h.) at 2000 m (6,600 ft.)

Endurance: 2 hr 45 min

Service ceiling: 5750 m (18,850 ft.)

Weights: empty 1040 kg (2,288 lb.); loaded 1765 kg (3,883 lb.)

Armament: three or four 7.7-mm (.303 cal.) machine-guns plus up to 320 kg (704 lb.) of bombs

Dimensions:
span	14.36 m	(47 ft. 2 in.)
length	8.87 m	(29 ft. 1 in.)
height	3.03 m	(9 ft. 11 in.)
wing area	51 m²	(549 sq. ft.)

BREGUET 14A2

This Breguet 14 is in fact a post-war variant, which served with 15e Escadrille, 5e Groupe, 33e Regiment Aerien d'Observation, French air force, during 1920-21. The last of the Bre. 14s was retired in 1932.

Protruding from the top of the engine cowling was the exhaust, which deflected fumes away from the pilot.

Housed under the metal panelling was a 12-cylinder Renault 12 Fe in-line piston engine. Although a fairly bulky powerplant, this engine performed admirably and few problems were encountered. Derivatives of this engine powered later Breguet designs.

An excellent feature of the Bre. 14 was its cockpit layout, with both pilot and gunner/observer in proximity to each other. Twin Lewis 7.7-mm (.303 cal.) machine-guns were mounted in the rear cockpit.

Although the aircraft did not have severe handling vices, horn-balanced elevators were introduced in 1918 to improve control further.

By World War I standards, the Breguet was a relatively large aeroplane with a deep fuselage. On the Bre. 14A2 variant, twin windows were fitted on each side for the reconnaissance role.

In common with the vast majority of aircraft of the time, the Bre. 14 was fitted with a tail skid. A rather crude bungee cord provided suspension for the skid.

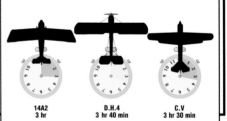
Breguet biplane designs

■ **BREGUET 16:** An enlarged Bre. 14, this aircraft was a two-seat night bomber which served in this role until the mid-1920s.

■ **BREGUET 17:** This was a down-sized version of the Breguet 14 and had a more powerful engine for better performance.

■ **BREGUET 19:** Perhaps even more famous than the Bre. 14, these aircraft were widely exported and were built under licence abroad.

■ **BREGUET 410:** One of the company's last biplane designs, this was a twin-engined machine which entered service in the late 1920s.

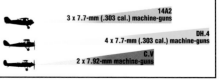

BREGUET

MODEL 19

● Day-bomber ● Reconnaissance ● Long-range record breaker

France introduced the Breguet 19 day-bomber and reconnaissance aircraft in 1922. This practical biplane was built in larger numbers than any other inter-war type and excelled in tough conditions during colonial operations in Africa and Asia. The Breguet was also manufactured abroad and reached users as diverse as Persia and Japan. Pilots greatly admired the two-seat aircraft, which kept pace with advances in aviation during its era.

▲ *Aviation Militaire*
(French air force) personnel pose proudly by a 15ᵉ Escadrille Bre.19 A.2. The type was built in two main variants, the A.2 for reconnaissance and the B.2 bomber.

BREGUET MODEL 19

◄ **Spanish special**
Named Cuatro Vientos, *this was a long-range special built by CASA. It flew from Seville to Cuba non-stop, but was then lost flying on to Mexico.*

▲ **Civil War in Spain**
Breguet 19s were licence-built by CASA in Spain, and both sides used the type during the Spanish Civil War. This aircraft carries Nationalist markings.

French bomber ►
Many French bomber squadrons were equipped with the Bre.19 B.2 between 1926 and 1933. The aircraft served reliably in overseas colonies, seeing action in several small wars.

▲ **Pride of France**
The prototype A.2 version was displayed at the 1921 Paris Air Show before it had flown.

▼ **Balkan warrior**
Greece bought 30 Bre.19s in 1930 and the survivors saw action in World War II, attempting to fend off the Italian invasion.

▲ **Export success**
Large numbers of Breguet 19s were sold overseas. In South America it served with Argentina (illustrated), while Bolivia and Paraguay took their aircraft to war. It also flew with Brazil and Venezuela.

FACTS AND FIGURES

➤ The prototype Breguet 19 first took to the air in March 1922.

➤ Test pilot Pierre Messerli referred to the Breguet 19 as 'a love affair – the way you love your mother'.

➤ More than 1,000 of these fine aircraft were built for the French air arm.

➤ A Breguet 19 flew a record-breaking 7905 km from Paris to Manchuria in 1929.

➤ Spain's CASA completed 203 Breguet 19s, some with Spanish engines.

➤ The last Bre.19s to be completed were 48 Kraljevo-built machines delivered to the Yugoslav air force in 1937.

PROFILE

Backbone of the French air force

Left: The ultimate long-range Breguet 19 was the one-off 'Super Bidon', seen here in 1929, the year of its record-breaking flight.

Breguet's chief engineer Louis Vuillerme put his considerable experience with earlier, successful aircraft into the Breguet 19. The result was a metal warplane with fabric-covered wings of unequal span, fixed landing gear and open cockpits. It had a very long range for the period, and the aircraft was used on many record flights in the 1920s.

The Breguet 19 was one of the best bombers of its time and proved extremely reliable. It was manufactured in huge numbers, with close to 2,500 being built in 15 years of production in Belgium, France, Spain and Yugoslavia.

France used the Breguet 19 against Druze tribesmen in Syria and Riff insurgents in Morocco. Spain became a major operator in its colonial wars of the 1930s. Others went to Belgium, Bolivia, Britain, Italy, Poland and Paraguay. Two were delivered to Japan, where the Japanese Nakajima company eventually decided not to proceed with production plans.

Yugoslavian aircraft saw action against the Wehrmacht in 1941, and were later used by Croat forces. Two survived to be captured by Tito's partisans in 1945.

Right: Named Nungesser-Coli, this Breguet 19 made the first non-stop flight across the South Atlantic on 14/15 October 1927. It flew from St Louis, Senegal, to Port Natal in Brazil.

Breguet 19 B.2

Type: two-seat reconnaissance bomber

Powerplant: one 336-kW (450-hp.) Lorraine 12Ed inline piston engine

Maximum speed: 214 km/h (133 m.p.h.) at sea level

Range: 800 km (500 mi.)

Service ceiling: 7200 m (23,600 ft.)

Weights: empty equipped 1387 kg (3,051 lb.); maximum take-off 2500 kg (5,500 lb.)

Armament: one fixed forward-firing 7.7-mm (.303 cal.) Lewis machine-gun and two Lewis guns mounted in the rear cockpit, plus provision for 30 10-kg (22-lb.), eight 50-kg (110-lb.) or two 200-kg (440-lb.) bombs

Dimensions:
span	14.83 m	(49 ft.)
length	9.61 m	(32 ft.)
height	3.69 m	(12 ft.)
wing area	50 m²	(538 sq. ft.)

The 'Super Bidon' was powered by a Hispano-Suiza 12Lb engine for its distance record-breaking flight. Earlier it had featured a Lorraine-Dietrich 12Db.

The upper wings and the raised forward fuselage severely restricted the pilot's view making taxiing the aircraft especially dangerous. The guns fitted in the rear cockpit were removed to save weight.

The 'GR' on the fin stood for 'Grand Raid' – literally 'long range'. The 'Super Bidon' was the last in a series of special 'GR' aircraft built by Breguet.

A feature of the Breguet 19 was its protruding radiator below the engine cowling.

The 'Super Bidon' special aircraft was given extra fuel tankage in the upper wings, in the lengthened fuselage and in the underwing slipper tanks. The word *bidon* is French for petrol can.

The 'Super Bidon' carried a large question mark and was called the *Point d'Interrogation*. The cigognes (stork) badge was from a famous World War I fighter squadron.

BREGUET 19 'SUPER BIDON'

The most famous of the 'Grand Raid' aircraft, *Point d'Interrogation*, undertook a failed attempt to cross the Atlantic, only reaching the Azores. It was later used to gain the world distance record.

COMBAT DATA

MAXIMUM SPEED

Throughout the 1920s, the speed of warplanes showed no dramatic improvement over those of World War I. The Breguet 19 was not a streamlined design, but did have a powerful engine and its drag was minimised by having a very short lower wing.

BREGUET 19 B.2	214 km/h (133 m.p.h.)
DH.9A	198 km/h (123 m.p.h.)
O-1E	227 km/h (140 m.p.h.)

ARMAMENT

For observation and light bomber aircraft of the 1920s, defensive armament was fairly standard, comprising one forward-firing machine-gun and two on a ring mount in the observer's cockpit. Most used the World War I-vintage Vickers and Lewis guns.

| BREGUET 19 B.2 | DH.9A | O-1E |
| 3 x 7.7-mm MGs | 3 x 7.7-mm MGs | 2 x 7.7-mm MGs 1 x 7.62-mm MG |

RANGE

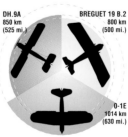

Thanks to its 'Grand Raid' special variants, the Breguet 19 has a reputation for long range, but in its mainstream service versions it was at the lower end of the league compared to its competitors. The range was respectable for its day, and was more than adequate for the tasks it was used for.

DH.9A 850 km (525 mi.)
BREGUET 19 B.2 800 km (500 mi.)
O-1E 1014 km (630 mi.)

Breguet's early dynasty

■ **BREGUET G.3:** The company of Louis Breguet was active before the start of the war. The G.3 was a typical product, with a 97-kW (130-hp.) engine driving a four-bladed propeller.

■ **BREGUET 5:** A handful of Breguet 5s served as fighters during World War I, armed with a 37-mm Hotchkiss cannon. There was also a bomber version armed with six light bombs.

■ **BREGUET 14:** One of France's best-known warplanes, the Bre.14 was built in huge numbers. It served from 1917 until 1932 in many roles, including bomber and air ambulance.

■ **BREGUET 17:** Essentially a scaled-down but up-engined Bre.14, the Breguet 17 was intended as a fighter, and a few saw service in the last months of World War I.

■ **BREGUET XX:** Known as the Léviathan, the Bre.XX was an attempt to provide an early airliner. The Breguet-Bugatti powerplant consisted of four engines driving one propeller.

BRISTOL

F.2B FIGHTER

● Two-seat, twin-gun fighter ● Long service career ● Army co-operation

At a time when the RAF was reducing its forces in the peace following World War I, the Bristol F.2B Fighter became one of post-war Britain's most important and long-serving combat aircraft. Initial wartime losses with the less-developed F.2A led pilots to adopt new fighting tactics for the F.2B, making it one of the Allies' best two-seat fighters. The aircraft went on to serve into the 1930s in army co-operation and light attack roles.

▲ Serving with the RAF and many overseas air arms, the Bristol Fighter operated with distinction in countries as distant as China. It flew on into the early 1930s with No. 20 Squadron.

BRISTOL F.2B FIGHTER

Rear gun defence ▶
Flown at its best, the F.2B used its rear gun for defensive purposes. This heavily retouched photograph shows the Lewis gun installation.

▼ War on the Frontier
For active service on India's North West Frontier, several F.2Bs were given larger rudders and bomb-carrying capabilities and became Bristol Fighter Mk IVs.

▲ Civilian transport
Substituting a Siddeley Puma engine for the Falcon of the Fighter and adding a 'coupé' cover over a modified two-seat rear cockpit produced the 206-km/h (128-m.p.h.) Bristol Tourer.

▲ Historic start
This preserved Bristol Fighter is being started by a Hucks starter.

Jumping for joy ▶
Bristol's Fighter was popular in service. The lower wing of this aircraft shows the shackles for a dozen 9-kg (20-lb.) Cooper bombs.

FACTS AND FIGURES

➤ Falcon I engines were fitted to the first 150 aircraft, Falcon IIs to the next 50 and all other aircraft had the Falcon III.

➤ On 20 June 1917 the F.2B scored its first victory, against an Albatross D.III.

➤ During September and October 1917, 1,600 F.2Bs were ordered.

➤ As an alternative to the Falcon engine, Hispano-Suiza and Sunbeam Arab engines were tried, but without success.

➤ At the end of World War I the RAF had 1,583 F.2Bs in service.

➤ No. 20 Squadron was posted straight to India in 1918, without returning home.

PROFILE

Revolutionary two-seat fighter

Bristol first flew its F.2A two-seat fighter on 9 September 1916. Powered by the 142-kW Rolls-Royce Falcon I, the aircraft was to have a disastrous combat debut.

Experience with the F.2A led to a number of improvements. These changes produced the F.2B Fighter, which first flew on 25 October 1916. With the introduction of the 205-kW

Falcon III engine, the F.2B became one of the greatest fighters of World War I. Pilots soon began using the forward gun for attacks, relying on their rear-seater to defend the aircraft against the enemy above and behind.

After the war many RAF squadrons were disbanded, but there was still important work to be done, especially abroad. British colonial interest

was still strong at this time and the F.2B found itself flying in a 'policing role'. These operations involved light-bombing duties and army co-operation.

Flying in the Middle East and other desert-like areas caused the F.2's engines to overheat as the radiators became clogged with sand. Fitted with new radiators, amongst other changes, the last RAF F.2B served in India until 1932.

This is the only remaining airworthy Bristol Fighter. The Shuttleworth Collection flies the aircraft at air shows throughout the summer in the UK.

F.2B FIGHTER

New Zealand was one of the many countries to receive the Bristol Fighter. This aircraft served with the Royal New Zealand Air Force during 1919. Other users included Australia, Mexico and Spain.

F.2B Fighter

Type: two-seat fighter and army co-operation and reconnaissance aircraft

Powerplant: one 205-kW (275-hp.) Rolls-Royce Falcon III 12-cylinder inline piston engine

Maximum speed: 198 km/h (123 m.p.h.) at 1525 m (5,000 ft.)

Endurance: 3 hours

Climb rate: climb to 3048 m (10,000 ft.) in 11 min 15 sec

Service ceiling: 5485 m (18,000 ft.)

Weights: empty 975 kg (2,145 lb.); maximum take-off 1474 kg (3,243 lb.)

Armament: three 7.7-mm (.303 cal.l) machine-guns, plus a 108-kg (240-lb.) bombload

Dimensions:
span	11.96 m	(39 ft. 3 in.)
length	7.87 m	(25 ft. 10 in.)
height	2.97 m	(9 ft. 9 in.)
wing area	37.62 m²	(405 sq. ft.)

Running through a tunnel in the upper fuselage fuel tank, the forward-firing Vickers machine-gun was fitted beneath the engine cowling.

One or two 7.7-mm (.303 cal.) Lewis machine-guns were mounted on the Scarff ring in the rear cockpit. This mounting allowed the rear crewman to move the guns up or down and from side to side.

H.1557

Tailplane incidence could be adjusted, allowing the aircraft to fly straight and level with the pilot's hands off the controls.

Throughout the production run of 5,329 British-built aircraft, no engine was found to be more suitable than the Rolls-Royce Falcon III. This engine powered all the service aircraft, with other powerplants quickly abandoned.

Most aircraft were fitted with very long exhaust pipes, which prevented noxious exhaust fumes entering the cockpit. Exhausts of this type covered the rear cockpit entry step, forcing the gunner to clamber over the hot exhaust when leaving the aircraft.

External cables linked the elevators to the pilot's control column. The rudder was operated by cables which disappeared into the rear fuselage just forward of the serial number.

All Bristol Fighters had a tailskid. Bomb-carrying aircraft serving in the Middle and Far East had strengthened main units with large 'desert tyres'. Special radiators were also required for desert operations.

COMBAT DATA

MAXIMUM SPEED

In comparison with contemporaries at the time of its initial service entry, the Fighter was a fast machine. The F.2B could dive at speeds of up to 270 km/h (165 m.p.h.), without fear of structural failure. It was not as fast as the German single-seaters, however.

F.2B FIGHTER	198 km/h (123 m.p.h.)
Br.14 A.2	184 km/h (114 m.p.h.)
C.II	165 km/h (102 m.p.h.)

MAXIMUM POWER

The L.F.G. Roland C.II was a low-powered, slow aircraft, but the Breguet 14 A.2 featured considerably more power than the Bristol Fighter and yet, by comparison, had poor performance. The Falcon engine of the F.2B provided a reliable, constant output of power.

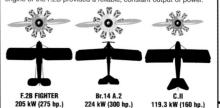

F.2B FIGHTER	**Br.14 A.2**	**C.II**
205 kW (275 hp.)	224 kW (300 hp.)	119.3 kW (160 hp.)

ARMAMENT

Many Bristol Fighters were fitted with twin Lewis guns in the rear cockpit. Attacks were carried out using the forward-firing Vickers machine-gun. A useful bombload could also be carried.

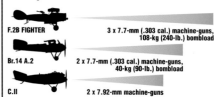

F.2B FIGHTER	3 x 7.7-mm (.303 cal.) machine-guns, 108-kg (240-lb.) bombload
Br.14 A.2	2 x 7.7-mm (.303 cal.) machine-guns, 40-kg (90-lb.) bombload
C.II	2 x 7.92-mm machine-guns

Bristol fighter designs of World War I

■ **SCOUT C:** A Royal Naval Air Service Scout C made the first deck take-off of the type on 3 November 1915.

■ **M.1 MONOPLANE:** Official distrust of the monoplane layout led to the few M.1s built serving away from the front line.

■ **SCOUT F:** Engine problems considerably delayed the first flight of the F until March 1918. No production aircraft were built.

■ **M.R.1:** The M.R.1 was an all-metal development of the F.2A. Only the two prototypes were built.

BRISTOL

BULLDOG

● 1920s design ● Export aircraft in World War II ● Biplane fighter

Britain's reliance on biplane fighters during the 1920s and early 1930s caused it to lag behind other countries in fighter design. Although no successful monoplane fighters were produced, several excellent biplanes were built, including the Bristol Bulldog. Export examples of the Bulldog saw extensive combat during the Spanish Civil War of 1936-39 and the Winter War of 1939-40. A few even survived into World War II.

▲ Finland's Bulldogs saw more combat than most. They served for longer than those operated by the RAF, which were retired in 1939.

BRISTOL **BULLDOG**

▲ **Finnish deliveries**
Finland received Mk IVA aircraft in January 1935. They were the last Bulldogs built at Bristol's Filton plant and were delayed by a dispute between Bristol and Gnome-Rhône over the manufacture of their Mercury engines.

▲ **Denmark's Bulldogs**
Designated Type 105D, the Bulldogs supplied to Denmark were basically Mk IIAs which often operated with skis. Only four were delivered.

▼ **Bulldog at war**
Pictured in 1940, this Finnish Bulldog is a Mk IIA. This type was supplied to Finland by Sweden and was flown in the Winter War.

▲ **Swedish transfer**
Sweden took delivery of 11 Bulldogs in two batches. The second batch, of eight, was flown to Sweden from Filton by Swedish pilots in 1931.

▼ **Estonian line-up**
Estonia first received Bulldogs in 1930. The aircraft were popular with Baltic and Scandinavian air forces.

FACTS AND FIGURES

➤ A second order from Finland, together with an Austrian requirement for 45 Bulldogs, was refused in 1936.

➤ Some RAF Bulldog Mk IIAs served with fighter training schools until 1939.

➤ Only one Bulldog survives, a Finnish example serialled BU-59.

➤ A few RAF senior officers used Bulldogs as personal transports until the start of World War II.

➤ Both Finland and Sweden operated their Bulldogs on skis.

➤ Britain's last airworthy Bulldog was destroyed in a crash in 1964.

PROFILE

Bulldog's Winter War

Latvia received a batch of five Bulldog Mk IIs in 1929. Other export orders followed, most significantly from Sweden in 1930, Denmark in 1931 and Finland in 1933. The Finnish aircraft were the last Bulldogs built and were completed to Mk IVA standard with Mercury VIS.2 engines.

By 1936 second-hand Latvian aircraft were in Spain, flying in support of the Basque cause during the Spanish Civil War. When the Winter War with Russia began in 1939, most of Finland's 17

Bulldog Mk IVAs were still serving with fighter squadron LLv 26. They scored at least five victories. Although the type was replaced by Gloster Gladiators in 1940, one aircraft survived both the Winter War and World War II. One of three Bulldog Mk IIAs supplied to Finland from Swedish stocks served as a

trainer until 1940, together with a few Mk IVAs.

Danish plans to licence-build Bulldogs were abandoned, but the Danish Army Aviation Troop still had three of its four Type 105D Bulldogs in service as fighter trainers when Germany invaded the country in April 1940.

Above: Swedish Bulldogs served faultlessly for several years, enduring the severe conditions of the country's harsh winter.

Left: All of the Bulldogs delivered to Finland direct from Bristol were Mk IVAs. This aircraft is the only surviving Bulldog in the world.

Bulldog Mk IIA

Type: single-seat biplane fighter

Powerplant: one 328-kW (440-hp.) Bristol Jupiter VIIF air-cooled radial piston engine

Maximum speed: 286 km/h (177 m.p.h.) at 3050 m (10,000 ft.)

Climb rate: climb to 6095 m (20,000 ft.) in 14 min 30 sec

Range: 499 km (310 mi.)

Service ceiling: 8230 m (27,000 ft.)

Weights: empty 1008 kg (2,218 lb.); maximum take-off 1660 kg (3,652 lb.)

Armament: two fixed forward-firing synchronised 7.7-mm (.303 cal.) Vickers machine-guns, plus provision for four 9-kg (20-lb.) bombs

Dimensions: span   10.34 m (33 ft. 11 in.)
                  length   7.67 m (25 ft. 2 in.)
                  height   3.00 m (9 ft. 10 in.)
                  wing area 28.47 m² (306 sq. ft.)

In common with the majority of inter-war RAF fighters, the Bulldog carried two forward-firing machine-guns. One was fitted on each side of the forward fuselage, firing through the cowling.

High-tensile steel strips were used in forming the Bulldog's structure. The wings and fuselage were fabric-covered. The Mk IVA represented the pinnacle of Bulldog development, with drag reduced to a minimum.

Bristol was unhappy with the quality of the Mercury engines being supplied under licence by Gnome-Rhône and considerable debate went on before Finland received British-manufactured powerplants.

Finnish Bulldog Mk IVAs had an uprated electrical system for operations in Arctic environments. It could be used for warming of the guns and also for the electrically-heated flying suits worn by the crew.

Unlike the more advanced I-153, against which it fought, the Bulldog had a fixed undercarriage. Here, in common with the main units, the tailwheel has been replaced by a ski.

Several Finnish aircraft, including the Bulldog, flew with skis. This alternative fixture was a common feature even before the Winter War, easing operations in the north of Finland.

BULLDOG MK IVA

Purchased early in 1935, Finland's Bulldog Mk IVAs fought with valour and some survived into the early 1940s. This aircraft is in the colours of TLeLv 35, as worn in the opening months of 1942.

COMBAT DATA

MAXIMUM SPEED

Compared to other types flown during the Winter War, the Bulldog was much slower, especially in its Mk IIA form as donated by Sweden. Even the Gloster Gauntlet biplane had better performance than the Bulldog.

BULLDOG Mk IIA 286 km/h (117 m.p.h.)	
I-16 TYPE 24	490 km/h (288 m.p.h.)
GAUNTLET Mk II	370 km/h (229 m.p.h.)

SERVICE CEILING

The Gauntlet's more powerful engine ensured that its service ceiling was superior to that of its rivals such as the I-16. In spite of its comparatively poor performance, the Bulldog achieved some success against the I-16, thanks to determined piloting.

GAUNTLET Mk II 10210 m (33,500 ft.)

I-16 TYPE 24 9470 m (31,070 ft.)

BULLDOG Mk IIA 8230 m (27,000 ft.)

GUN ARMAMENT

The Bulldog Mk IIA and the Gauntlet Mk II served the Finns well, but both aircraft were handicapped by the standard inter-war RAF fighter armament of two forward-firing guns. Some I-16s carried an additional 12.7-mm (.50 cal.) weapon.

BULLDOG Mk IIA 2 x 7.7-mm (.303 cal.) machine-guns

I-16 TYPE 24 4 x 7.62-mm (.30 cal.) machine-guns

GAUNTLET Mk II 2 x 7.7-mm (.303 cal.) machine-guns

At war in Finland

■ **FOKKER D.XXI:** Two squadrons of Fokker D.XXIs formed the backbone of Finland's Winter War air defence.

■ **GLOSTER GAUNTLET:** Finland flew a number of largely obsolescent biplane fighters, including the Gauntlet.

■ **POLIKARPOV I-153:** Several aircraft were captured by the Finns, including this I-153. The type proved very capable over Finland.

■ **POLIKARPOV I-16:** In the same manner as the I-153, several I-16s fell into Finnish hands. This is a two-seat I-16UTI.

BÜCKER

BÜ 131 JUNGMANN/BÜ 133 JUNGMEISTER

● Two-seat Luftwaffe trainer ● Single-seat aerobatic aircraft

Most of Germany's World War II fighter aces had, at some time, flown Bücker's versatile light trainer, the Bü 131 Jungmann, or its sister aircraft, the single-seat Bü 133 Jungmeister advanced fighter trainer and aerobatic mount. Both of these aircraft were widely exported and production continued after the war. Large numbers of Bü 131s and Bü 133s still remain in airworthy condition.

▲ *Both Jungmann and Jungmeister are docile, yet rugged, aircraft. The Bü 133 Jungmeister has a better performance thanks to its more powerful 119-kW (160-hp.) Siemens radial engine.*

BÜCKER BÜ 131 JUNGMANN/BÜ 133 JUNGMEISTER

▼ **The aerobatic Jungmeister**
Post-war the Bü 133 Jungmeister (Young Champion) has remained a very popular aerobatic aircraft.

▲ **In the Luftwaffe**
Until the arrival of the Bücker Bü 181 Bestmann, the Jungmann was the German Air Force's most important trainer.

Bü 133 stuntplane ▶
Identifiable by its larger engine cowling and single seat, this Jungmeister was used post-war as a stuntplane in the United States.

▼ **Jungmann goes to war**
The Jungmann was used in the war by auxiliary ground-attack squadrons, who were tasked with harassing Soviet forces at night.

▲ **Bückers in Switzerland**
The Swiss air force operated 75 licence-built Bü 131s. Shown here is one of 50 Swiss Dornier-Werke-built Bü 133Bs, which continued in service well into the 1950s.

FACTS AND FIGURES

➤ Armed with light 1-kg and 2-kg bombs, Bü 131s flew night-time nuisance raids on the Eastern Front during 1941/42.

➤ The Bü 131 Jungmann was exported to a total of eight European air forces.

➤ The prototype Bü 131 first flew on 27 April 1934.

➤ The Bü 133B Jungmeister was licence-built in both Switzerland (by Dornier-Werke) and in Spain (by CASA).

➤ The entire Bü 133 series was built in a purpose-made factory at Rangsdorf.

➤ Initially flying with a Hirth inline engine, the Bü 133 later utilised a Siemens radial.

PROFILE

Bücker's biplanes for the Luftwaffe

Bücker Aircraft's first ever product, the successful Bü 131 Jungmann (Youth), first flew in 1934, with the initial production Bü 131A variant serving with both the Luftwaffe and a range of civilian flying clubs. The definitive Bü 131B model, with an uprated Hirth engine, and the experimental prototype Bü 131C, with a 67-kW

(90-hp.) Cirrus Minor powerplant, followed.

Bücker exported the Jungmann to various European nations, the largest customers being Hungary (100) and Romania (150). Licence production was undertaken in both Czechoslovakia and Switzerland. However, the most extensive licence construction took place in Japan, where Kyushu built 1,037 aircraft, known as the Ki-86A, for the army. The same company manufactured a further batch of K9W1s for the

Below: Switzerland was a major Bücker operator and producer. After being retired from the military, airframes were sold to civilian customers.

Above: The Bü 131 Jungmann makes a superb civilian light aircraft. Its military training characteristics make it relatively easy and pleasurable to fly.

navy. The Bü 133 Jungmeister single-seat derivative was equally successful, both with the Luftwaffe, and when built later in Spain and Switzerland.

Bü 131B Jungmann

Type: tandem two-seat biplane light trainer and special operations aircraft

Powerplant: one 78-kW (105-hp.) Hirth HM 504A-2 inline piston engine

Maximum speed: 183 km/h (113 m.p.h.) at sea level

Cruising speed: 170 km/h (105 m.p.h.)

Range: 650 km (400 mi.)

Service ceiling: 3000 m (10,050 ft.)

Weights: maximum take-off 680 kg

Armament: four 1-kg (2-lb.) or 2-kg (4-lb.) fragmentation or anti-personnel bombs on wing racks

Dimensions:
span	7.40 m	(24 ft. 3 in.)
length	6.60 m	(21 ft. 8 in.)
height	2.25 m	(7 ft. 4 in.)
wing area	13.50 m²	(145 sq. ft.)

Bü 131 JUNGMANN

Both Bü 131 and the later Bü 133 served with distinction in the Luftwaffe during World War II, mainly as primary and advanced fighter trainers.

The clean lines of the Bü 131's engine cowling disappeared on the Bü 133, when a larger radial engine was introduced and overall dimensions were reduced. This resulted in a deeper, stubbier appearance.

The Jungmann had two tandem seats, for the instructor (generally behind), and the pupil (ahead). The aerobatic Jungmeister differed in having just one seat.

The Bü 131 was designed by the company's chief designer, Anders Andersson. German Bü 131s were built at Bücker's main Johannisthal factory.

A wire-braced conventional tail was supported underneath on landing by a spring-mounted tailwheel. For winter operations, skis were fitted to all undercarriage units.

The Jungmann was powered by a 78-kW (105-hp.) Hirth 4-cylinder inverted inline piston engine. Surprisingly, the later Jungmeister reverted to an older 119-kW (160-hp.) radial engine.

The fuselage was protected by light alloy around the engine and the crew's compartments.

The pre-war style biplane wings were of wooden construction and covered with fabric. When the aircraft was pressed into special missions operations, light bombs could be carried underwing.

The Jungmann's fuselage was built of welded steel tubing, covered, like the wings, with fabric. This machine carries Luftwaffe markings, but others were operated by civil flying clubs.

ACTION DATA

MAXIMUM SPEED

The Bü 133 Jungmeister was a well-designed aircraft with a relatively powerful inline engine, like the Tiger Moth, and a streamlined fuselage affording good speed. The Americans' radial-engined Ryan PT-22 had a monoplane wing which caused less drag and gave better performance. The Jungmann's speed was one of the factors that led to the development of the Bü 133 single-seater.

Bü 131B JUNGMANN	183 km/h (113 m.p.h.)
PT-22	211 km/h (131 m.p.h.)
DH.82 TIGER MOTH	175 km/h (109 m.p.h.)

RANGE

The Jungmann had better range than the less fuel-efficient Ryan PT-22 and the older British de Havilland Tiger Moth. Its superb endurance led to the Luftwaffe adopting the aircraft as a useful covert reconnaissance platform, special missions aircraft and a counter-insurgency machine.

Bü 131B JUNGMANN 650 km (400 mi.)

PT-22 566 km (350 mi.)

DH.82 TIGER MOTH 486 km (300 mi.)

POWER

Surprisingly, the Jungmann had a less-powerful Hirth inline engine than the similar Tiger Moth and its radial-powered American counterpart. The single-seat Bü 133 Jungmeister, however, introduced a more powerful Siemens engine which, like that of the PT-22, was a radial. The definitive Bü 133C variant was even more powerful.

Bü 131B JUNGMANN	PT-22	DH.82 TIGER MOTH
78 kW (105 hp.)	119 kW (160 hp.)	97 kW (130 hp.)

First-generation trainers of World War II

■ **MORANE-SAULNIER 317:** France's M.S. 317, like the Bü 131, flew long before the war but remained an important part of the air arm.

■ **POLIKARPOV Po-2:** A large Russian trainer, liaison and communications aircraft of the war, the Po-2 later served as a bomber in Korea.

■ **DE HAVILLAND TIGER MOTH:** The Royal Air Force's most important biplane trainer of the war, the Tiger Moth is still widely flown.

■ **BOEING STEARMAN:** The highly successful PT-13/-17 series remained in use until the war's end; the one below still flies in the UK.

CANADAIR

CL-215

● Multi-purpose amphibian ● Aerial firefighter ● 26-place transport

The CL-215 is a fighting machine, but not a military one. It is uniquely designed to combat one of mankind's oldest enemies – fire. From the tinder-dry woods of Quebec to the parched and arid scrub of the Mediterranean, forest fires are a regular feature of the hot summer months. And the big Canadian amphibian is the first line of defence in the struggle to protect lives and property.

▲ A Canadair CL-215 of France's Securité Civile dumps five tons of water on a blazing Provençal forest.

CANADAIR CL-215

Go-anywhere ▶ firefighter
The CL-215, unlike more conventional aircraft, is not restricted to airfields. It can operate from any sufficiently large body of water – lakes, rivers and the sea.

◀ Turbo power
Many CL-215s have been modified with turbine engines, which are smaller, lighter and more economical than the original piston powerplant.

▲ Fire bomber
The centre of the CL-215's fuselage is devoted to two huge water tanks. Their contents are delivered via large doors in the underside of the hull.

Spray instead ▶ of splatter
Some CL-215s have spray pipes under the wings. These are designed to deliver firefighting water in a fine mist over a wide area of fire, rather than in a single cascading deluge in one spot.

▲ Super scooper
Refilling the CL-215 is a superfast process, thanks to twin scoops under the hull. These enable the machine to replenish from any convenient body of water.

FACTS AND FIGURES

➤ CL-215s are very tough. They have to be to withstand dozens or even hundreds of filling cycles per day.

➤ Using scoops, the amphibian can pick up more than 5 tons of water in 10 seconds.

➤ The CL-215 can empty its tanks over a fire in less than a second.

➤ The CL-215 can fill its tanks in any water more than 1.4 metres deep.

➤ In a four-hour cycle, a water bomber will average about 40 drops.

➤ The record performance was by a Yugoslav plane, which made an incredible 225 drops in 24 hours.

PROFILE

Firefighting over the Timberlands

Once a forest fire takes hold, there is little that firefighters on the ground can do to stop it. But all is not lost. A rising engine roar signals the entrance of the CL-215.

Only 30 metres (100 ft.) above the tree tops, the bright-yellow water-bomber flies directly towards the hottest part of the fire. As it passes overhead, long

doors in its boat-like belly open, and five tons of water cascade down. The aircraft immediately turns away to pick up more.

The CL-215 is an amphibian. It can operate from airfields, where its tanks can be pumped full of fire-retardant chemicals in about two minutes. Or it can head for the nearest open water and in a skimming pass can scoop up an

astonishing 5300 litres (1,400 gal.) of water in just 10 seconds.

As soon as its tanks are full, the plane heads back to the fire. This process is repeated tens or even hundreds of times in a day until the fire is eventually brought under control.

The CL-215 is more than a Canadian water bomber. The Thai navy uses the amphibian for coastal patrol and search and rescue.

CL-215
The Canadian provinces are the largest users of the CL-215, with some 49 aircraft in service.

The CL-215 is powered by a World War II-designed piston engine. Although it is reliable, many aircraft are having lighter, more powerful turbo-props retro-fitted.

A shallow hull means that the CL-215 can use its scoop in just over a metre (three feet) of water, although two metres (six feet) is usually the operational minimum.

The CL-215 is immensely strongly built. It has to be, since not only does it have to cope with the corrosive effect of thousands of immersions in water, but it regularly flies through the smoke, heat and turbulence created by the fires it is designed to fight.

The floats positioned at the end of the CL-215's wings mean that the aircraft has great stability when landing on water.

CF-YXG

35

OU 'ERNEMENT
MINISTERE DES TRA

The CL-215 is an amphibian: its retractable undercarriage means it is equally able to fly from land and water.

Large cargo doors mean that the CL-215 is easily convertible to its secondary function as a 26-man or four-ton capacity light general-purpose transport aircraft.

ACTION DATA

FILLING UP
Touching the surface of the water at about 150 km/h (92 m.p.h.), the pilot immediately applies power to counteract the effect of the scoops, which tend to pitch the nose down. The scoops can pick up more than 5000 litres (1,320 gal.) in about 600 metres (2,000 ft.) and in just 10 seconds.

OVERFLOW

FLAP VALVE

RELEASE DOOR

INTAKE

SEA OR LAKE

RELEASE

The CL-215's drop doors are located at the bottom of the boat-shaped hull; early versions have two doors. These can empty the two large tanks in under a second. Later versions have four doors, allowing more flexibility. Whatever the arrangement, the optimum release height is around 30 metres (100 ft.) above the fire.

COVERAGE
A water-bomber pilot has two water delivery options. He can deliver water from both tanks simultaneously, covering a short, wide area of the fire. Or he can empty them in succession, covering a much longer, narrower strip of ground.

145 m (465 ft.)

12 m (40 ft.)

20 m (65 ft.)

85 m (280 ft.)

Water-bombing cycle

3 LOADING: 'Once you are on the water, you wind on the power to keep an indicated airspeed of 85 to 90 knots. The scoops fill the tanks in 10 seconds.'

5 AT THE FIRE: 'We try to bomb from 30 metres (100 ft.) or less. Any higher, especially on really hot days, you lose too much from evaporation. But you don't want to get too low, either – you're flying over a forest, remember. And tough though this plane is, you sure don't want to hit too many trees!'

2 APPROACH: 'You approach like any other water landing. From the cockpit you can't see the surface clearly. We have a couple of retractable probes, about the size of a tea cup, which tell us when we're just a fraction off the right height.'

1 SELECTION: 'Loading up is really straightforward. We can use any piece of water that leaves us enough room to make a touch and go – canals, rivers, lakes, or even the open sea.'

4 CLIMB-OUT: 'Because you're already at flying speed, as soon as the scoops retract you're airborne. Once at safe single-engine climb speed, you're off for the fire as fast as you can.'

CAPRONI

CA.1-CA.5

● Three-engined ● Twin-boom, triple-rudder layout ● Licence production

Italy led the world in establishing an army aviation section in 1884, and in 1911 the first bombing raid in history was carried out by an Italian aviator in Libya during the war with Turkey. The Italian aircraft industry was also one of the first to develop large, multi-engined aircraft. By the time Italy joined World War I in May 1915, its three-engined Caproni Ca.2s were the most advanced heavy bombers used by any national air arm.

▲ *Flown for the first time in late 1914, the ungainly looking Caproni bombers formed an important part of the Italian and French air force inventories into the mid-1920s.*

CAPRONI **CA.1-CA.5**

▼ US production
Two Ca.3s were built by the Standard Aircraft Corporation in the US during 1918. A third was built by Fisher Body Works.

▲ Italian Army Air Service
Having revised its bomber design through the Ca.30 and 31, Caproni went into production with the Ca.32. Known in service as the Ca.1, 164 were delivered to the Italian Army Air Service.

▼ Preserved Caproni
Now a museum piece, this Ca.3 clearly shows the type's characteristic multi-wheel undercarriage, wooden propellers and the mass of struts and bracing.

◀ More power
The Ca.3 (Ca.33) had 112-kW (150-hp.) engines in place of the 75-kW (100-hp.) Fiat units of the Ca.1.

▼ Triplane bomber
Similar in layout to the Ca.1-3, the Ca.4 was actually a new design. This is a Ca.42 variant.

FACTS AND FIGURES

➤ Bombs were stowed vertically on the sides of a nacelle mounted at the centre of the bottom wing of the Ca.4 triplane.

➤ Between 1917 and 1919 Caproni manufactured a total of 299 Ca.3s.

➤ A few Ca.3s were converted to six-seat airliners known as the Ca.56a.

➤ A gunner's position was provided in each of the Ca.4's tailbooms, behind the engines and wing trailing edge.

➤ Following its first flight in 1917, 659 examples of the Ca.5 were built.

➤ US manufacturers would have built 1,500 Ca.5s had World War I continued.

PROFILE

World War I Italian bombers

Using a pusher propeller at the rear of the central nacelle and two tractor propellers mounted in the twin booms, driven via a complex transmission, the Ca.1 of 1914 was known by Caproni as the Ca.30. In the production Ca.2, which entered service in 1915, the tractor engines were moved to the front of the booms and drove the propellers directly.

The 164 Ca.2s which were delivered in 1915/16 were followed by 269 Ca.3s, with more powerful engines. These were used as torpedo-bombers by the Italian navy, and by the French as well as the Italian air arms.

The 38 Ca.4 series bombers delivered in 1917/18 also had three engines, but were triplanes rather than biplanes. The massive Ca.4 had a wingspan of 29.9 metres (98 ft.) and was powered by 149-kW (200-hp.) engines. Even with more powerful engines, the later Ca.4s were too slow for anything but night bombing, although they could carry 1450 kg (3,190 lb.) of bombs. Using all its bomber experience, Caproni completed the series with the improved Ca.5.

Left: Although the Ca.4 triplane was a useful long-range bomber, it was slow and vulnerable. The Ca.5 represented an attempt to overcome these shortcomings.

Right: Ca.3s had positions for defensive gunners at the front and rear of the fuselage.

Ca.5 (Ca.44)

Type: biplane heavy bomber

Powerplant: three 186-kW (250-hp.) Fiat A.12 in-line piston engines

Maximum speed: 150 km/h (93 m.p.h.) at sea level

Endurance: 7 hours

Range: 600 km (375 mi.)

Service ceiling: 4600 m (15,100 ft.)

Weights: empty 3300 kg (7,260 lb.); maximum take-off 5300 kg (11,660 lb.)

Armament: two 7.7-mm (.303 cal.) Revelli machine-guns and 900 kg (1,980 lb.) of bombs

Dimensions:
span	23.40 m	(76 ft. 9 in.)
length	12.60 m	(41 ft. 4 in.)
height	4.48 m	(14 ft. 8 in.)
wing area	150 m²	(1,614 sq. ft.)

CA.3

At least 83 Ca.33s were built in France by Robert Esnault-Pelterie. The aircraft were produced to the same standard as the Italian army's Ca.3s. This aircraft belonged to CEP 115 of the Aéronautique Militaire.

Two pilots sat side-by-side in separate, open cockpits just ahead of the wing leading edge. They had no windscreens or any other form of protection from the elements.

Unusually, the Ca. 3 had no fixed vertical tail surfaces. A full-span tailplane connected the booms and mounted the central rudder. The abbreviation C.E.P. stands for Caproni-Esnault-Pelterie.

An Isotta-Fraschini V.4B engine was mounted at the forward end of each boom. A third engine was fitted in the rear part of the fuselage and drove a pusher propeller.

A substantial tailskid was mounted at the rear of each tailboom. In common with the main undercarriage units, the skid was braced by struts and wires.

Although the Ca.3 was a 'tail-sitting' aircraft, it had a substantial nose undercarriage unit. The nosewheels prevented the aircraft 'nosing-over' on landing.

Construction of the aircraft was conventional, consisting of wood and fabric, but the design was unusual. As well as the twin-boom, triple-rudder layout, the Ca.3 had a multi-wheel landing gear for rough field operations.

COMBAT DATA

MAXIMUM SPEED

Like all World War I bombers the Ca.3 was slow. This made the aircraft vulnerable to enemy fighters, but Caproni was able to produce improved, higher performance designs based on the Ca.3 layout.

Ca.3	140 km/h (87 m.p.h.)
0/400	156 km/h (97 m.p.h.)
R.VI	135 km/h (84 m.p.h.)

SERVICE CEILING

Both the Ca.3 and Handley Page 0/400 had much lower service ceilings than the huge Zeppelin-Staaken R.VI. By flying at high altitude early bombers could avoid interception by fighters, but this did little for bombing accuracy. With its advanced Ca.5 Caproni was able to exceed the service ceiling of the R.VI.

- Ca.3 4100 m (13,450 ft.)
- 0/400 2590 m (8,500 ft.)
- R.VI 4320 m (14,170 ft.)

ARMAMENT

An early bomber design, the Ca.3 was limited in bombload and defensive armament. It was, however, available at the beginning of World War I and allowed Italy to establish a strong bomber force.

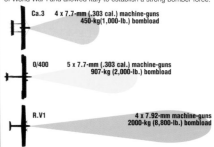

Ca.3	4 x 7.7-mm (.303 cal.) machine-guns 450-kg (1,000-lb.) bombload
0/400	5 x 7.7-mm (.303 cal.) machine-guns 907-kg (2,000-lb.) bombload
R.VI	4 x 7.92-mm machine-guns 2000-kg (8,800-lb.) bombload

Caproni cavalcade

■ Ca.14: Gianni Caproni built and flew this monoplane in 1913. It later became known as the Ca.14 and was powered by a 37-kW (50-hp.) three-cylinder Gnome rotary engine.

■ Ca.82: Originally known as the Ca.73ter, the Ca.82 was a medium bomber powered by two 380-kW (510-hp.) Isotta-Fraschini Asso engines mounted in a push-pull configuration.

■ Ca.90: Powered by six 746-kW engines, this giant heavy bomber was the world's largest landplane from 1929 until the arrival of the Tupolev ANT-20 'Maxim Gorky' in 1934.

■ Ca.97: Used in a variety of roles, which included air ambulance, bomber and reconnaissance, the Ca.97 was available in triple-, twin- and single-engined variants.

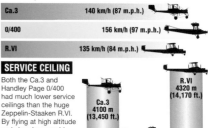

CAUDRON

R/G/C SERIES

● Bomber and reconnaissance aircraft ● Escort fighter ● French service

▲ Caudron
continuously refined its bomber
designs with the aim of improving performance.
A common feature of the G and R series was
unequal span wings.

Caudron's R.11 was a development
of the earlier R.4. Although it proved to
be an outstanding design, it arrived
too late to have much impact on World War I.
While the R.11 was perhaps the most
successful of the Caudron biplane bombers,
the C and G series should not be forgotten,
since they formed an important part of the
French bomber force both before and after
the war. The last of the Caudron biplanes in
service, an R.11, was scrapped in 1922.

CAUDRON R/G/C SERIES

▼ Caudron style
From the R.4 onwards, all the
Caudron bombers were of
similar design. The C.23
introduced wings of equal span.

▲ Late-war night-bomber
In February 1918 Caudron introduced
the C.23 BN.2 night-bomber. Orders for
1,000 aircraft were received, but only
54 had been built by the time of the
Armistice. Heavy and unmanoeuvrable,
they were withdrawn by 1920.

▲ Design by Deville
Having flown as an observer in a G.3, Paul
Deville went on to become technical designer
for Caudron and was responsible for the G.6.

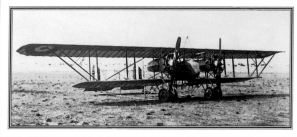

▲ Fighter killer
Escadrille C.46 claimed to have
shot down 34 German aircraft in an
eight-week period flying R.4s.

◀ British bomber
Britain's Royal Naval Air Service
received 55 G.4s for bombing
duties. They were involved in
a number of daring raids.

FACTS AND FIGURES

➤ Caudron produced the G.4 as an
improvement on the G.3, which was
unable to carry adequate armament.

➤ Two versions of the G.4 were built: the
B.2 bomber and the A.2 artillery spotter.

➤ Jules Vedrines, navigating by compass,
flew a G.6 more than 320 km (200 mi.).

➤ In redesigning the structure of the R.4,
Paul Deville also attempted to improve
its performance and created the R.11.

➤ When it first flew in 1917, the R.11 was
considered a reconnaissance-bomber.

➤ C.23s were used post-war on passenger
services between Paris and Brussels.

PROFILE

French wartime bomber family

Caudron's first bomber, the G.4 of 1915, was based on the smaller G.3 trainer and featured twin 60-kW Le Rhône engines. It was followed by the generally similar, but more powerful, G.6 bomber and reconnaissance aircraft, which had an enclosed rear fuselage and tail section.

Gaston Caudron had been largely responsible for the design of the G-series biplanes, but with the R series his brother, René, came to the fore. Breaking away from previous Caudron design trends, the new R.4 featured a completely enclosed, full-length fuselage and a single fin and rudder. In combat during World War I the R.4 acquitted itself well, destroying several enemy fighters before structural problems began to emerge. One of the resulting accidents claimed the life of Gaston Caudron, and the R.4 was withdrawn in 1917.

Unsuccessful prototypes of the R.5 and R.10 followed, before the R.11 appeared in March 1917. Like the R.4, the R.11 was a biplane with unequal span wings. However, the wings were shorter, and more powerful engines enabled

Below: A distinctive feature of the R.4 was the large nosewheel, which helped to prevent 'nosing-over'. The pilot was very vulnerable during such an incident.

Above: The R.11 proved to be a highly capable escort fighter. Armed with five machine-guns and offering good performance, it was regarded as a formidable fighting machine.

it to carry twin Lewis guns in the upper nose and rear cockpits, plus a fifth pointing downwards in the nose. Intended for bombing and reconnaissance, the R.11 served as an escort fighter for the Breguet 14.

R.11

Type: three-seat escort fighter

Powerplant: two 160-kW (215-hp.) Hispano-Suiza 8Bda liquid-cooled V-8 engines

Maximum speed: 190 km/h (118 m.p.h.) at sea level; 183 km/h (113 m.p.h.) at 2000 m (6,500 ft.)

Endurance: 3 hours

Climb rate: 8 min 10 sec to 2000 m (6,500 ft.)

Service ceiling: 5950 m (19,500 ft.)

Weights: empty equipped 1422 kg (3,128 lb.); maximum take-off 2167 kg (4,767 lb.)

Armament: five 7.7-mm (.303 cal.) machine-guns, plus 120 kg (265 lb.) of bombs

Dimensions: span 17.92 m (58 ft. 9 in.)
length 11.25 m (36 ft. 11 in.)
height 2.80 m (9 ft. 2 in.)
wing area 54.25 m² (584 sq. ft.)

Three machine-guns were available to the nose-gunner. Two were fitted on a flexible mount to fire upwards, with a third firing downwards through the floor of the gunner's compartment.

R.11 A.3

R.11s of Escadrille C.46, Aviation Militaire (French air force), flew escort duties for 13e Escadre's bombers between February and November 1918. All surviving R.11s were scrapped in July 1922.

A much larger tail fin was fitted to the R.11 than the R.4. Caudron retained this distinctive tail for several of its R/G and C series aircraft and even used the design in the 1930s, when aircraft such as the C.270 touring biplane featured a tail similar to that of the R.11.

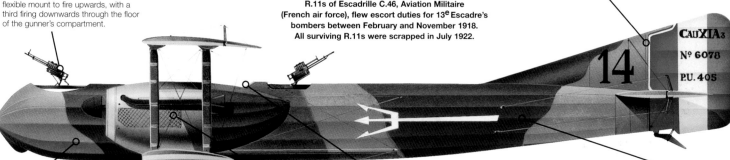

CauXIA₃ Nº 6078 P.U.405

A number of modifications were incorporated into the R.11 when it was developed from the R.4. They included deletion of the auxiliary nose undercarriage.

Each of the R.11's Hispano-Suiza engines was carefully faired and mounted on the lower wing. Many later aircraft had more powerful 175-kW (235-hp.) Hispano-Suiza 8Beb engines.

The R.11 had a simple, open cockpit for the pilot. Having noticed that a number of contemporary aircraft had been lost when the pilot was hit in combat, Caudron fitted a second set of flying controls in the rear gunner's cockpit for emergency recovery of the aircraft.

Although the R.11 and the R.4 which preceded it was generally of conventional construction, the R.11 introduced a one-piece upper wing. This represented a considerable achievement for the time.

COMBAT DATA

MAXIMUM SPEED

The R.11's maximum speed at 2000 m (6,500 ft.) was closely matched with the Breguet 14 B.2 bomber that it escorted. At this altitude the R.11 was faster than the Fokker DR.1.

R.11	183 km/h (113 m.p.h.)
DR.1	165 km/h (102 m.p.h.)
14 B.2	185 km/h (115 m.p.h.)

SERVICE CEILING

The DR.1 could fly at a higher altitude than the French aircraft. This gave the German machine a huge advantage in combat, since it was able to make diving attacks. The R.11 established an excellent record in combat against German fighters, however.

R.11 5950 m (19,500 ft.)
14 B.2 5740 m (18,800 ft.)
DR.1 6095 m (20,000 ft.)

ARMAMENT

With five machine-guns, the R.11 was one of the most heavily armed aircraft of its era. The firepower of the R.11, combined with that of the 14 B.2, could fend off the most determined fighters.

R.11 5 x 7.7-mm (.303 cal.) machine-guns

DR.1 2 x 7.92-mm machine-guns

14 B.2 2 x 7.7-mm (.303 cal.) machine-guns 300-kg (660-lb.) bombload

---

Caudron collection

■ **G.3:** Designed as a two-seat training and reconnaissance aircraft, the G.3 had limited potential because of its low power.

■ **C.449 GOELAND:** Based on the C.440 of 1934, many examples of the C.449 final production variant were built post-war.

■ **C.460:** Designed for the 1934 Coupe Deutsch de la Meurth air race, the C.460 went on to gain a world speed record.

■ **C.630 SIMOUN:** This four-seat cabin monoplane was popular both before and after the war and many were used for long-range flights.

CONSOLIDATED

PBY CATALINA SEARCH AND RESCUE

● Flying-boat and amphibian ● Search-and-rescue aircraft ● War service

N ear the end of WWII, an American Consolidated PBY Catalina flying-boat took off from Okinawa, flew to hostile waters within sight of the Japanese shoreline and rescued seven men from a ditched B-29 bomber. The mission involved flying over a long distance in bad weather, touching down on the water in full view of the enemy and filling the aircraft to capacity. It was a tough challenge, but the PBY Catalina was up to the demand.

▲ The approach of a PBY Catalina was a welcome sight for many Allied sailors or downed airmen as they bobbed on the vast ocean in a dinghy awaiting rescue.

CONSOLIDATED PBY CATALINA

▼ Parasol wing
The Catalina's wing lifted the engines well clear of spray from rough waters.

▲ Navy 'non-specular sea blue'
This matt-blue finish was typical of that applied to US Navy aircraft in 1943. The PBY-5A amphibian was developed from the PBY-5 flying-boat to give the aircraft greater flexibility.

▼ RAF Catalina operations
Towards the end of World War II RAF Coastal Command's No. 240 Squadron carried out air-sea rescue duties in the Far East.

▲ RATO take-off assistance
This OA-10A of the USAF's 10th Rescue Squadron is seen in Alaska. It carries two rocket-assisted take-off (RATO) bottles on each side.

◀ In the Aleutians
At the northernmost extremities of the Pacific Ocean, Catalinas were used for offensive and rescue roles in the campaigns along the Aleutian archipelago.

FACTS AND FIGURES

➤ When landing on open sea, the pilot brought the Catalina to a full stall just before touchdown.

➤ The first PBY flew in 1936 and the type stayed in production until 1945.

➤ Some PBYs carried the AR-8 airborne lifeboat, fitted under the wing.

➤ PBYs for Britain were the first military aircraft delivered by trans-Atlantic flight during the war.

➤ The US Coast Guard used PBYs for rescue duties from World War II until the 1950s.

➤ PBYs saved 161 airmen in the Solomon Islands in the first eight months of 1943.

Search-and-rescue by 'Dumbo Cat'

No one knows how many men were rescued in combat by the courageous pilots who flew the Consolidated PBY Catalina into dangerous situations – but the number is in the thousands.

This twin-engined, parasol-wing flying-boat and amphibian was one of the slowest aircraft of the war; it was said that it was in danger of being struck by birds from behind. But, despite its unimpressive speed, the PBY was a sturdy, well-armed and versatile flying machine that could land in some of the most

difficult conditions to rescue men in peril.

More Catalinas were built than any other flying-boat in history. Designed to a US Navy requirement for a long-range patrol bomber, the PBY proved to be a highly successful anti-shipping and anti-submarine aircraft in a number of theatres, and served with several Allied air forces. PBYs also rescued more survivors from ships and aircraft than any aircraft of the war.

Perhaps the most famous of all Catalinas were the US Navy's 'Black Cats', which operated

against the Japanese in the Pacific in 1942. US Navy and USAAF 'Cats' were used for the search-and-rescue (SAR) role until the late 1940s.

Above: The USAAF received 75 ex-US Navy PBY-6As for the SAR role. These were designated OA-10B (A-10B after 1948) and were distinguished by their taller tails.

Below: After 1945 USAAF OA-10As remained in the Air Rescue Service, along with converted C-47s, B-17s and B-29s.

PBY-5A Catalina

Type: long-range maritime patrol bomber and air-sea rescue aircraft

Powerplant: two 895-kW (1,200-hp.) Pratt & Whitney R-1830-92 Twin Wasp piston engines

Maximum speed: 288 km/h (179 m.p.h.) at 2135 m (7,000 ft.)

Range: 4096 km (2,545 mi.)

Service ceiling: 4480 m (14,700 ft.)

Weights: empty 9485 kg (20,910 lb.); loaded 16,066 kg (35,420 lb.)

Armament: two 7.62-mm (.30 cal.) machine-guns in bow, one 7.62-mm machine-gun firing aft from the hull step and two 12.7-mm machine-guns in beam position, plus air-sea rescue equipment including life rafts

Dimensions: span 31.70 m (104 ft.)
length 19.47 m (63 ft. 11 in.)
height 6.15 m (20 ft. 2 in.)
wing area 130 m² (1,340 sq. ft.)

OA-10A CATALINA

Canadian Vickers built 230 PBY-5A amphibians for the US Navy, and all were transferred to the USAAF as OA-10A search-and-rescue craft. 44-33924 was one of this batch and is seen in post-war markings.

The antennas on the wings are part of the Catalina's ASV (air-to-surface vessel) radar which was developed during World War II for maritime patrol aircraft hunting enemy shipping and submarines. The radar was also useful for finding downed aircraft. The radome above the cockpit contains an additional centimetric-wavelength radar.

With the Catalina's ungainly appearance and performance and in honour of the Walt Disney cartoon character of the 1940s, SAR PBY aircraft were nicknamed 'Dumbo' by USAAF and Navy personnel.

Cupolas on both sides of the fuselage, which each carried a 12.7-mm machine-gun in wartime, were introduced on the PBY-5 and were ideal for observers on the look-out for downed aircraft or personnel awaiting rescue.

High-visibility markings distinguished USAF SAR aircraft, especially after World War II.

Built by Canadian Vickers, the PBY-5A was known as the PBV-1A. The same company built 139 for the Royal Canadian Air Force, which called it the Canso. In RAF service the PBY-5A was known as the Catalina Mk III.

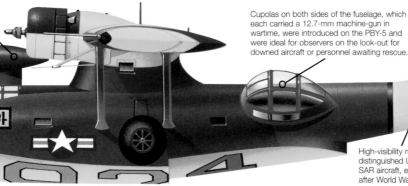

ACTION DATA

CRUISING SPEED

USAAF Catalinas survived in the SAR role after World War II alongside the converted Douglas C-47 transports and B-17 and B-29 bombers of the Air Rescue Service. By the late 1940s, when the USAAF became the USAF and took overall responsibility for SAR, the Catalina was outmoded. The Albatross which replaced it had a higher cruising speed plus other improvements.

OA-10A CATALINA	182 km/h (113 m.p.h.)
SA-16A ALBATROSS	241 km/h (150 m.p.h.)
Do 24T-3	249 km/h (155 m.p.h.)

RANGE

The SA-16A Albatross had only modest range. The Do 24 was a wartime German design which was capable of flying 1000 km (600 mi.) further than the Albatross, although not as far as the OA-10.

OA-10A CATALINA 3782 km (2,350 mi.)
Do 24T-3 2897 km (1,800 mi.)
SA-16A ALBATROSS 1850 km (1,150 mi.)

ENGINE POWER

The Dornier Do 24 had more power than the other two types because of its three engines. Piston engine technology advanced in the years after World War II, and the Albatross had twin engines of appreciably more power than those fitted to the Catalina. Reliability was important for maritime patrol aircraft. Engines tuned to run at less than peak power were less likely to fail in service.

OA-10A CATALINA 1790 kW (1,200 hp.) | SA-16A ALBATROSS 2125 kW (2,850 hp.) | Do 24T-3 2238 kW (3,000 hp.)

Catalina rescue off Japan

29 MAY 1945: An OA-10A on station with a US Navy lifeguard submarine shadowing a B-29 bombing raid on Japan was called to rescue the crew of a ditched aircraft.

CREW LOCATED: Having located the men, the Catalina landed and picked them up. However, on take-off the aircraft slammed into three large swells and the port engine was torn from its mount and smashed into the cockpit. The pilot was badly injured and the co-pilot radioed the rescue submarine.

SAVED BY THE SUB: The following morning the submarine delivered the crews from the B-29 and OA-10 to Iwo Jima. Between November 1944 and 14 August 1945, the 21st Bomber Command lost 3,125 crewmen in attacks on Japan. Of these, 1,424 went down at sea. Air Force and Navy units rescued 687, nearly half of those who ditched.

CONSOLIDATED

PBY CATALINA

● Amphibian and flying-boat ● Long-serving naval patrol bomber

I t was old when World War II began. It was slow and could be very uncomfortable, but the Consolidated PBY Catalina was one of the classic designs; rarely has an aircraft proved so useful to so many people. A deadly adversary to an enemy submarine or warship, the PBY is better remembered as the angel of mercy which performed thousands of maritime rescues in all circumstances throughout the war.

▲ The Catalina operated in every theatre of the Pacific war, from the balmy southern waters to the frozen oceans of the North. This crew is seen in the Aleutians.

CONSOLIDATED PBY CATALINA

◄ Slow but sure
Although slow and cumbersome, the PBY was immensely tough and had a great range, essential for long maritime patrols.

Flight deck ►
On long missions, pilots might be expected to occupy the flight deck for up to 20 hours at a time.

▼ Shipboard operations
Catalinas often operated from seaplane tenders, being hoisted aboard by cranes for maintenance and restocking.

▲ Observation blisters ►
The large 'greenhouses' on each side of the rear fuselage could mount heavy machine-guns and were perfect for rear observation.

◄ Assisted take-off
The Catalina had good take-off performance, but for launching at high weights or in tight spots it could use strap-on rockets for extra boost.

FACTS AND FIGURES

➤ In October 1935 the Catalina prototype made a non-stop flight of 5633 km from Coco Solo to San Francisco.

➤ In the 1930s, civil PBYs were used for scientific exploration of New Guinea and later the Indian Ocean.

➤ Over 1,000 Catalinas were manufactured in Russia.

➤ The 'Black Cats' squadron hunted Japanese ships at night; in addition to bombs and depth charges they unleashed empty beer bottles, which made an eerie whistling descent.

➤ The Catalina was so slow that critics joked that its navigator needed a calendar rather than a stopwatch.

'Black Cats' over the Pacific

Here was aviation at its essence. The high-wing, twin-engine Catalina was not speedy, not flashy, not graceful, but it was more practical than anyone realised when the first ship took to the skies on 28 March 1935. With its braced parasol wing and seagoing hull, the PBY Catalina became famous and was built in larger numbers than any other flying-boat in aviation history.

The PBY revolutionised long-range patrol in the US Navy. The well-loved 'Cat' ranged outward at great distance to stalk the enemy's fleet or to attack his submarines, and British Catalinas ferreted out the elusive German warship *Bismarck*. A PBY spotted the periscope of a Japanese submarine at Pearl Harbor. On all the world's oceans, Catalinas fought valiantly. Some were among the first American aircraft to carry radar. They were amphibians, flying from land or sea.

Also produced in Canada and Russia, the Catalina often became a peacetime Samaritan, bringing salvation to those in peril.

Ranging far and wide, the Catalina was instrumental in denying Axis forces the use of the sea. It was a Catalina which tracked down the Bismarck *during the hunt for the battleship, which ended in its sinking.*

The large unobstructed plank-like wing gave the Catalina excellent endurance and benign handling. The outrigger stabilising floats hinged upwards to form the wingtip fairing in flight.

PBY-5A Catalina

Type: seven-/nine-seat long-range maritime patrol bomber

Powerplant: two 895-kW (1,200-hp.) Pratt & Whitney R1830-92 Twin Wasp radial engines

Maximum speed: 288 km/h (175 m.p.h.) at 2000 m (6,500 ft.)

Range: 4900 km

Service ceiling: 4480 m (18,100 ft.)

Weights: empty 9485 kg (21,000 lb.); loaded 16,066 kg (35,420 lb.)

Armament: two 7.62-mm (.30 cal.) machine-guns in bow, one 7.62-mm machine-gun firing aft from the hull step, and two 12.7-mm (.50 cal.) machine-guns in beam position; up to 1814 kg (4,000 lb.) of bombs or depth charges

Dimensions:
span	31.70 m	(104 ft.)
length	19.47 m	(63 ft. 10 in.)
height	6.15 m	(20 ft. 2 in.)
wing area	130 m²	(1,400 sq. ft.)

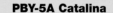

OA-10 CATALINA

During the war the US Air Force took over a large number of Catalinas for use in the air-sea rescue role, designated OA-10. These gave valuable service long after the end of the conflict.

Most late-production PBYs had search radar, with an antenna in a teardrop fairing above the flight deck. Other aerials were carried under the wings.

Catalinas were powered by a pair of Pratt & Whitney Twin Wasp radial piston engines. Sturdy and reliable, the Twin Wasp's output was boosted from 615 kW (820 hp.) in early examples to nearly 900 kW (1,200 hp.) in the final production PBY-5s.

The basic crew of the Catalina comprised eight. In the extreme nose was an observer/bomb aimer, behind which sat the two pilots. Behind them was a compartment for the radio operator and navigator.

Catalinas were built either as pure flying-boats or, as here, as amphibians, with a retractable tricycle undercarriage. The main wheels pulled up into wells above the hull line, and were left exposed.

The flight engineer's station was in the centre of the aircraft beneath the wing, while the aft cabin usually housed two gunner/observers. Weapons were carried under the wing.

OB-924
433924

COMBAT DATA

CRUISING SPEED

The Catalina was old, noisy and slow, especially when compared with its contemporaries. But it was tough and reliable, and could land and take off in anything short of a hurricane.

H6K 'MAVIS'	339 km/h (211 m.p.h.)
PBY Catalina	281 km/h (175 m.p.h.)
BV 138	275 km/h (171 m.p.h.)

RANGE

The big patrol 'boats' may not have been fast, but they could cover a lot of ocean. A typical flying-boat at the beginning of World War II could stay aloft for up to 24 hours, and often crew fatigue was the limiting factor on mission length.

PBY CATALINA 4900 km (2,350 mi.)
H6K 'MAVIS' 6700 km (4,200 mi.)
BV 138 5000 km (3,100 mi.)

World War II maritime patrollers

■ **KAWANISHI H6K 'MAVIS':** The H6K was Japan's main long-range flying-boat at the start of World War II. Based on a Sikorsky design, it was very tough and seaworthy.

■ **SHORT SUNDERLAND:** Much larger than the PBY, the Sunderland was Britain's main maritime patrol machine. It was adapted from a civil design, and first flew in 1937.

■ **CANT Z.506:** Italy specialised in floatplanes rather than flying-boats, and the three-engined Cant was one of the largest of its kind. It held numerous pre-war seaplane speed records.

■ **BLOHM UND VOSS BV 138:** Known as 'Die fliegende Holzschuh', the twin-boom three-engined BV 138, or 'Flying Clog', saw action from the Mediterranean to the Arctic.

CONSOLIDATED

PB2Y CORONADO

● Maritime reconnaissance ● Anti-shipping ● Transport

▲ This PB2Y
has had its armament removed
and was used in the transport role. The specialist
PB2Y-5H was used as a casualty evacuation aircraft
with accommodation for 25 stretchers.

Soon after Consolidated's famous PBY Catalina had flown, plans were drawn up to build a larger maritime patrol flying-boat with a greater weapons capacity and higher speed. The resulting XPB2Y-1 competed successfully against the Sikorsky XPBS-1 and after a number of modifications it entered production as the PB2Y Coronado. The type saw limited service in World War II with the US Navy and 10 examples were used by the RAF, mainly as transports.

CONSOLIDATED PB2Y CORONADO

▼ **Experimental squadron**
All six PB4Y-2s built were operated by VP-13 Squadron, US Navy, for experimental duties. Each could carry 5443 kg (11,975 lb.) of bombs.

◄ **Principal production version**
The US Navy procured a total of 210 PBY-3s which were used in the Pacific theatre. These are early examples without radar.

Single-fin prototype ►
In competition with the Sikorsky XPBS-1, the XPB2Y-1 first flew in December 1937 and was regarded as the more suitable aircraft for production. A lack of lateral stability was rectified by replacing the single fin with two endplates.

▼ **Lend-lease Coronado**
Ten PB2Y-3Bs were diverted to the RAF as Coronado GR.Mk Is. After brief service with Coastal Command they were used as transports with No. 231 Squadron.

▲ **Searching for ships**
Later-model PB2Ys were fitted with a dorsal Air to Surface Vessel (ASV) radar. This could detect targets in bad weather or at night.

FACTS AND FIGURES

➤ Named XPB2Y-1, the Coronado prototype first flew on 17 December 1937, powered by Pratt & Whitney XR-1830-72 engines.

➤ With five defensive gun positions, a crew of nine was needed to man the PB2Y.

➤ The PB2Y-3R transport version featured faired-over turrets and R-1830-88 engines.

➤ The first squadron to operate the Coronado was VP-13, which received its first PB2Y-2 on 31 December 1940.

➤ The PB2Y-3 featured self-sealing fuel tanks and protective armour.

➤ Production PB2Ys had a much deeper hull than the prototype to improve handling.

PROFILE

Patrol boat from San Diego

Left: A number of PB2Y-3s were converted to PB2Y-5 standard. Alterations included fitting more powerful R-1830-92 engines, increased fuel capacity and provision for RATO (rocket-assisted take-off) gear.

With heavy defensive armament, long range and a large weapons load the PB2Y had the potential to be one of the US Navy's most important patrol flying-boats of World War II. However, production preference was given to the twin-engined PBY Catalina of which thousands were built compared to a mere 226 production PB2Ys.

The prototype, designated XPB2Y-1, underwent evaluation in early 1938 and was selected over the XPBS-1, but a number of shortcomings needed to be addressed before production could begin. The most serious problem was lateral instability which was solved by modifying the tail unit. The tailplane was given significant dihedral, and endplates similar to those on the B-24 bomber were fitted. The nose profile was also changed to a more rounded appearance.

The main production version was the PB2Y-3, which saw little operational service during the War. Ten PB2Y-3Bs supplied to the RAF as Coronado GR.Mk Is were mostly used for hauling freight across the Atlantic.

Later versions were fitted with air to surface vessel (ASV) radar and other variants included the PB2Y-3R transport and the PB2Y-5H casevac aircraft. All Coronados had been withdrawn from service by VJ Day.

Above: This photograph shows the sharp dihedral of the Coronado's tailplane and its associated endplates. The aircraft were wheeled to the water using a trolley system.

PB2Y-3 Coronado

Type: long-range flying-boat patrol bomber

Powerplant: four 895-kW (1,200-hp.) Pratt & Whitney R-1830-88 Twin Wasp radial piston engines

Maximum speed: 359 km/h (223 m.p.h.) at 6095 m (20,000 ft)

Range: 3814 km (2,365 mi.)

Service ceiling: 6250 m (20,500 ft.)

Weights: empty 18,568 kg (40,850 lb.); maximum take-off 30,844 kg (67,857 lb.)

Armament: two 12.7-mm (.50 cal.) machine-guns in each of bow, dorsal and tail turrets, and one 12.7-mm machine-gun in each of two beam positions, plus up to 5443 kg (11,975 lb.) of bombs, depth bombs or torpedoes in bomb bays

Dimensions:
span	35.05 m	(115 ft.)
length	24.16 m	(79 ft. 3 in.)
height	8.38 m	(27 ft. 6 in.)
wing area	165 m²	(1,779 sq. ft.)

To protect the PB2Y from enemy fighter attack the aircraft was equipped with nose, dorsal and tail turrets each with a pair of 12.7-mm (.50 cal.) machine-guns. Single 12.7-mm machine-guns were also fitted to the fuselage sides on flexible mounts.

The PB2Y-5 was fitted with more powerful R-1830-92 engines giving the aircraft much improved performance at low altitudes. The fuel capacity was also increased.

PB2Y-5 CORONADO

Little use was made of the PB2Y Coronado in World War II. This example was used mostly for transport purposes before it was retired along with the rest of the fleet in 1944–45.

After the single fin arrangement on the XPB2Y-1 was found to be inadequate, a new tail unit with rounded endplate fins was fitted. The fins and rudders were similar to the units fitted to the B-24 Liberator.

R51

This PB2Y-5 shows a mixture of darker non-specular sea blue merging into pale grey-blue with white undersurfaces, the camouflage scheme carried by PB2Y-5s in the later stages of World War II.

A two-step hull provided the aircraft with good handling in water. The stabilising wingtip floats retracted to form the wingtips in flight.

COMBAT DATA

MAXIMUM SPEED

Although the H6K was an earlier design than the other two types it had the edge in speed. Speed was less important than endurance and to increase fuel economy all three types generally operated at a speed of about 250 km/h (155 m.p.h.).

PB2Y-3 CORONADO	359 km/h (223 m.p.h.)
H6K5 'MAVIS'	385 km/h (238 m.p.h.)
SUNDERLAND Mk V	343 km/h (213 m.p.h.)

ARMAMENT

The Coronado had a massive bombload compared to the other two types, making it capable of attacking more than one target. All three types had formidable defensive armament.

PB2Y-3 CORONADO	H6K5 'MAVIS'	SUNDERLAND Mk V
8 x 12.7-mm (.50 cal.) machine-guns 5443-kg (11,975-lb.) bombload	4 x 7.7-mm (.303 cal.) machine-guns 1 x 20-mm cannon 1600-kg (3,520-lb.) bombload	8 x 7.7-mm (.303 cal.) and 2 x 12.7-mm (.50 cal.) machine-guns 907-kg (2,000-lb.) bombload

RANGE

As the best flying-boat of the early years of World War II, the H6K had exceptional range, allowing it to operate deep into the Pacific Ocean on reconnaissance and anti-shipping missions. Both the Sunderland and the Coronado had modest range in comparison but could still operate 10-hour missions.

PB2Y-3 CORONADO 3814 km (2,365 mi.)

H6K5 'MAVIS' 6775 km (4,200 mi.)

SUNDERLAND Mk V 4329 km (2,684 mi.)

World War II maritime patrol aircraft

■ **CONSOLIDATED LIBERATOR:** Operated by both RAF Coastal Command and the US Navy, the Liberator helped close the 'U-boat gap' in the middle of the Atlantic Ocean.

■ **FOCKE-WULF Fw 200 CONDOR:** With unprecedented range, the Fw 200 was a major threat to Allied shipping in the early years of World War II.

■ **LOCKHEED HUDSON:** As the first US-built aircraft to be used operationally by the RAF in World War II, the Hudson filled an urgent requirement for a maritime patrol bomber.

■ **SHORT SUNDERLAND:** Operating in the Atlantic and the Pacific, the Sunderland flew reconnaissance sorties as well as anti-shipping and anti-submarine missions.

CONVAIR

R3Y TRADEWIND

● Turboprop flying-boat ● Transport tanker ● Limited US Navy service

▲ Starting life
as a maritime patrol aircraft, the
P5Y always had potential as a transport.
However, engine problems continued to
plague the design and ultimately proved
to be its downfall.

Convair's last flying-boat and the world's first turboprop seaplane was a giant that began life as a patrol aircraft, evolved into a transport and served briefly with the US Navy as both a transport and air-to-air refuelling tanker. Only one squadron operated the Tradewind, as it became known. Although the aircraft had considerable potential, it suffered from being powered by untried engines at a time when the trend was towards land-based naval aircraft.

CONVAIR R3Y TRADEWIND

▲ Solitary P5Y
The only XP5Y-1 to take to the air
flew in 1950. It was the world's first
turboprop-powered flying-boat.

▲ R3Y-1 maiden flight
Lacking the nose door of the
R3Y-2, early Tradewinds had
a large hatch in the fuselage,
aft of the wing.

▼ Tanking Tradewind
In 1956 four aircraft were fitted
with in-flight refuelling
equipment. Fuel was carried in
the wings, which left the fuselage
available for cargo.

▲ Special beaching cradle
When on land P5Ys/R3Ys used an enormous 10-ton,
self-propelled cradle. Once the aircraft was
in the water, the cradle was 'sailed' back to shore.

'Flying LST' ▶
The R3Y-2 was able to land Marine Corps vehicles
and men at a beach head, although it was never
intended that they do so under fire.

FACTS AND FIGURES

➤ In October 1955 an R3Y flew between Hawaii and California in six hours 45 minutes and at a speed of 579 km/h (360 m.p.h.).

➤ An R3Y flew across the United States at an average speed of 649 km/h (403 m.p.h.) in 1955.

➤ The entire R3Y fleet flew a total of less than 3,300 hours; one flew only 40 hours.

➤ $262 million was spent on the P5Y/R3Y; retired R3Ys had their tails cut off so that they could be hidden away from the public.

➤ The R3Y's main cabin was sound-proofed, air-conditioned and pressurised.

PROFILE

Convair's last – the first with turbines

Between its first flight in 1950 and the crash that ended the P5Y programme in 1953, the world's first turbine-powered seaplane became a low-altitude reconnaissance aircraft, then an anti-submarine platform and finally a mine-layer.

However, the trend towards land-based naval aircraft, plus the problems associated with the T40 twin-turbine engine and the crash of the sole XP5Y-1 stopped development. From the outset, a transport version of the Tradewind was contemplated. The start of the Korean War in 1950 brought plans to reality. The US Navy ordered six R3Y-1 Tradewinds, which were based on the P5Y but fitted with improved, and supposedly more reliable, T40 engines.

The R3Y established several long-distance flight records. Eventually, 11 were delivered, including five of the 'Flying LST' (Landing Ship, Tank) R3Y-2 with a front-loading bow door. All of these aircraft entered service with Transport Squadron Two (VR-2), performing transport duties between California and Hawaii from 1956 until 1958.

Four R3Ys were retro-fitted with four-point in-flight refuelling gear, which further improved their versatility. Despite plans to convert the rest of the fleet, engine problems continued, culminating in an accident in January 1958 that prompted the US Navy to ground the Tradewind fleet. By March 1958, R3Y development had ceased and within 12 months all the aircraft had been retired.

Left: Everything about the Tradewind was big. It's propellers were 4.6 metres in diameter and its underwing floats 6.4 metres (21 ft.) long. The R3Y-1's gross weight was more than 79 tons.

Above: The R3Y-2's T40-A-10 turboprops continued to be problematic and engine failures were routine. The Navy's VR-2 Squadron could change an engine in under 15 man-hours.

R3Y-1 Tradewind

Type: heavy transport flying-boat

Powerplant: four 4362-kW (5,850-hp.) Allison T40-A-10 turboprop engines

Maximum speed: above 579 km/h (359 m.p.h.)

Maximum range: 6437 km (3,990 mi.)

Service ceiling: 7700 m (25,250 ft.)

Weights: normal take-off 74,843 kg (164,655 lb.); maximum take-off 79,379 kg (174,634 lb.)

Dimensions:
span	44.42 m (145 ft. 8 in.)
length	42.57 m (139 ft. 7 in.)
height	13.67 m (44 ft. 9 in.)
wing area	195 m² (2,100 sq. ft.)

R3Y-2 TRADEWIND

South Pacific Tradewind was the 11th and last R3Y built. Here it carries the 'RA' tailcode of Navy Transport Squadron Two (VR-2), the only unit to operate the type. This example was scrapped in 1959.

The 'bridge' structure above the nose of the aircraft held the entire crew of five: two pilots, a navigator, a flight engineer and a radio operator. An extra engineer and radio operator were sometimes carried. The R3Y-2 differed primarily from the R3Y-1 in having an upward-opening bow door and hydraulic ramps for loading/unloading.

The Tradewind's very powerful, but highly unreliable, Allison T40 turboprop engines were its downfall. Each T40 was in fact two turbines driving a common gearbox and contra-rotating propellers. The gearbox was troublesome throughout the P5Y/R3Y's career, with the turbines being prone to vibration and excessive fuel consumption.

VR-2 Squadron used its 11 R3Ys to replace the Martin JRM-2 Mars flying-boats.

The P5Y's immensely strong hull was designed to leave the main deck free of obstruction and was therefore suitable for adaptation for transport roles. The main cabin could hold 103 seats or 92 stretchers, or more than 21 tons of cargo.

In order to prevent the aircraft's tail swinging during, for example, a beach landing, an anchor was deployed from the rear of the aircraft.

VR-2'S OTHER BIG 'BOAT'

MARTIN JRM MARS: In its role on the resupply routes across the western Pacific, VR-2 at NAS Alameda, California, was chosen as the sole operator of the small fleet of JRM Mars transports. Like the Tradewind, the Mars, with its 75-ton maximum take-off weight, was developed from a patrol aircraft, the XPB2M of 1943. Six JRMs were built, and the last was delivered in 1947. Two aircraft were lost in accidents, but the remaining four served until 1956.

Convair's seaplane family

■ **P4Y CORREGIDOR:** Designed in the late-1930s, the P4Y maritime patrol aircraft did not proceed past the prototype stage. Shortages of the R-3350 Cyclone resulted in its cancellation.

■ **PBY CATALINA:** The most widely-used Allied seaplane of World War II, the 'Cat' was built at four plants in the US and Canada. It served with several air forces in offensive and rescue roles.

■ **PB2Y CORONADO:** This four-engined, long-range patrol-bomber suffered early handling problems, but more than 200 were built. They were not widely used operationally in World War II.

■ **F2Y SEA DART:** This experimental delta-winged fighter seaplane employed retractable hydroskis. It was the first seaplane to exceed Mach 1, but did not enter service.

CONVAIR
XF2Y SEA DART

● Experimental water-based fighter ● First supersonic seaplane

O ne of the strangest aircraft ever to fly, the Convair XF2Y Sea Dart was the abortive result of what, on the face of it, was a practical notion: if a jet fighter could operate from water, it would be able to fly and fight almost anywhere in the world. The delta-winged Sea Dart used retractable 'water skis' to lift the hull clear of the water on take-off, skimming across the surface before powering into the air.

▲ The Sea Dart was a bold attempt to incorporate a host of new technologies into a unique airframe. The fastest seaplane ever, it was a great aviation pioneer even though it was never operational.

PHOTO FILE
CONVAIR XF2Y SEA DART

▼ Promising early tests
In its early development stages the Sea Dart concept was known as the Convair Skate. Here a scale model is shown undergoing spray tests.

▲ Hydroplanes
The Sea Dart's hydrofoil was pushed to the surface by hydrodynamic forces as the aircraft got under way, skimming across the water like a water-skier.

Flying-boat ▶
The aircraft had no conventional floats; the watertight hull and wings provided sufficient buoyancy and stability when the aircraft was in the water.

▲ Boat-shaped hull
The underside of the Sea Dart had a shallow 'V'-section profile, like a high-speed motor boat. On take-off, this was lifted clear of the water.

▲ The shaking take-off
Powering over the water on its hydroskis, the Sea Dart made for spectacular viewing. But the vibration caused by skimming across anything more than a mirror-smooth surface became almost unbearable for the pilot.

FACTS AND FIGURES

➤ The prototype Sea Dart made its initial flight on 9 May 1953.

➤ On 3 August 1954, a Sea Dart became the first supersonic seaplane, exceeding Mach 1.0 in a shallow dive.

➤ An order for 12 production F2Y Sea Dart fighters was cancelled when the test programme ran into trouble.

➤ The XF2Y was redesignated F-7A in 1962, even though no Sea Darts were still flying.

➤ The Sea Dart did not enter service, but Convair used its data in the successful F-102 and F-106 delta-winged fighters.

➤ The US Navy also tested a jet-powered patrol seaplane, the Martin P6M Seamaster.

PROFILE

Supersonic water-skier

In 1951, the US Navy assigned Consolidated Vultee (Convair) an exciting project based on advanced aerodynamic and hydrodynamic research – the waterborne XF2Y Sea Dart.

With an eye to the post-war American role as worldwide policeman, the US Navy was looking into the possibility of using water-based fighters.

These had the potential advantage of being able to operate from any sufficiently clear stretch of water almost anywhere in the world, without the need for the long runways which so restricted land-based aircraft.

While the concept of a flying-boat fighter was reasonably practical, the Sea Dart was not the answer to the problem. It used a unique retractable hydroski system in place of floats. Taking off from the sea posed unprecedented challenges, since the hydroskis vibrated badly enough to shake the entire aircraft like a cement-mixer making control almost impossible.

There were also problems with the Westinghouse engines fitted to most Navy tactical aircraft of the period. Flown with J34 and J46 jets, the Sea Dart never had quite enough

Below: Once aloft, the Sea Dart handled well. It might have been a failure as a seaplane, but it contributed a great deal to Convair's widening database on high-performance delta-wing aircraft.

Above: Although the Sea Dart was a failure in its main aim of becoming a practical combat aircraft, it has the distinction of being the first and only supersonic flying-boat.

power for its weight, although it performed well when aloft.

Pilots had a roomy cockpit, fair forward visibility and handy controls, but the vibration problems were insurmountable, and the Sea Dart programme had to be abandoned in 1956.

The Convair company was a pioneer in exploring the properties of tailless aircraft with delta-shaped wings and control surfaces. The Sea Dart was one of the earliest aircraft to fly with this planform, and provided designers of later supersonic aircraft with a great deal of useful data.

XF2Y Sea Dart

Type: experimental seaplane fighter

Powerplant: two 26.69-kN (6000lb) Westinghouse J46-WE-2 turbojets

Maximum speed: 1118 km/h (695 m.p.h.) at 2440 m (8,000 ft.)

Range: 825 km (512 mi.)

Service ceiling: 16,700 m (54,800 ft.)

Weights: empty 5739 kg (12,652 lb.); loaded 7495 kg (16,524 lb.)

Armament: production versions would have had up to four 20-mm cannon and two air-to-air missiles

Dimensions:
span	10.26 m	(33 ft. 8 in.)
length	16.03 m	(52 ft. 7 in.)
height	6.32 m	(20 ft. 9 in.)
wing area	52.3 m²	(563 sq. ft.)

XF2Y SEA DART

In addition to its unique method of operation, the XF2Y Sea Dart incorporated advances in construction, propulsion and aerodynamic design. It was a great technological leap forward – perhaps a leap too far.

The Sea Dart had a fairly conventional cockpit, roomy and with well-thought-out controls. Pilots found it easy to work in.

The main engine intakes were mounted above the wing on top of the fuselage. This prevented water ingestion on take-off or landing which would destroy the powerplant.

The XF2Y was originally powered by two Westinghouse J34 jets, but these never delivered their promised performance. Even with more powerful J46s, the Sea Dart was not as fast as had been expected.

The underside of the hull had a shallow boat-like section, which aided low-speed handling in the water.

Twin hydroplanes extended for beaching and for take-off, retracting into the fuselage for maximum aerodynamic efficiency.

At rest, the wings of the Sea Dart rest on the water, serving as floats to provide some measure of stability.

COMBAT DATA

MAXIMUM SPEED

XF2Y SEA DART	1118 km/h (695 m.p.h.)
F-102 DELTA DAGGER	1328 km/h (825 m.p.h.)
SRA.1	825 km/h (512 m.p.h.)

The Sea Dart's continuing engine problems meant that it never achieved the speed it might have done. Given more power, and a redesigned fuselage as had been applied to Convair's F-102 fighter, there is no reason to suppose that it might not have matched the landplane's performance. The British SRA.1 could not achieve the supersonic speeds thought necessary for a jet fighter.

ARMAMENT

Designed as a fighter, the Sea Dart would have had an effective air-to-air armament by the standards of the early 1950s, incorporating two of the newly-developed AIM-4 Falcon missiles or later AIM-9 Sidewinders, fitted inside a weapons bay in the lower fuselage.

SRA.1
4 x 20-mm cannon
2 x 1000-kg (2,200-lb.) bombs

XF2Y SEA DART
4 x 20-mm cannon
2 x short-range air-to-air missiles

F-102 DELTA DAGGER
6 x AIM-4 air-to-air missiles
12 x folding-fin unguided rockets

RANGE

The Sea Dart was an experimental aircraft, so its range was not as great as might have been expected in an operational version. It could not match the larger and slower British SRA.1 of 1947, the only other jet-powered flying-boat fighter to take to the air.

XF2Y SEA DART	F-102 DELTA DAGGER	SRA.1
825 km (512 mi.)	2175 km (1,350 mi.)	1500 km (932 mi.)

Fighters from the sea

■ **HANSA BRANDENBURG:** The German C-1 monoplane was one of the most successful fighters of World War I.

■ **CURTISS SC-1:** This single-seat scout was entering service as World War II ended. It could carry bombs in a bay in the main float.

■ **KAWANISHI N1K:** The N1K was a superb performer, but high-drag floats meant that it could not match more aerodynamic landplanes.

■ **SAUNDERS-ROE SRA.1:** Lack of airstrips in the Pacific prompted post-war Royal Navy interest in this experimental flying-boat.

CURTISS

CONDOR II

● **1930s biplane airliner** ● **Overseas service** ● **Antarctic pioneer**

A t first sight the T-32 Condor II appeared to be an anachronism – a new biplane transport at a time, in the early-1930s, when the all-metal monoplane was the way of the future. Curtiss-Wright, however, had seen a niche in the market for a 'stop-gap' aircraft that offered performance improvements over contemporary designs, pending the arrival of the truly advanced Boeing 247 and Douglas DC-2, then under development.

▲ *Condor IIs*
were destined to have a very short history in US airline service. However, overseas airlines and Antarctic explorers soon put the aircraft to work elsewhere.

CURTISS **CONDOR II**

▼ On floats in Colombia
Seen here on floats prior to delivery, this BT-32 operated as a transport from rivers in Colombia and flew Atlantic anti-submarine patrols during World War II.

▲ Design advances
Although cheap to produce, the Condor II introduced new features, including zip-fastened panels for easy maintenance. The batteries could also be changed in less than a minute.

▼ Military sales
There were just four T-32s in US military service. Overseas sales, however, were made in Colombia (below) and Argentina.

▲ Chinese bomber
This, the first military Condor II, flew in 1934 and was immediately demonstrated to the Chinese. After repairs following a landing accident it became the personal transport of Chiang Kai-shek (the head of Chinese central government).

Airline service in America ▶
The Condor II's use as an airliner in the US was shortlived as more advanced types like the Douglas DC-2 became available. Many then served overseas.

FACTS AND FIGURES

➤ In all, only 45 Condor IIs were built, including a prototype, 28 airliners, 15 military aircraft and one survey machine.

➤ Swissair's sole AT-32 was the first airliner in Europe to carry a stewardess.

➤ The three Condor IIs used in the Antarctic were fitted with floats or skis.

➤ In the late 1930s a Canadian railroad company used a Condor based in Alaska to reach isolated Yukon communities.

➤ The last operational Condor II was used by the Peruvian air force until 1956.

➤ Four ex-Eastern Air Transport T-32s served as cargo aircraft in England in 1937/38.

PROFILE

Last of the US biplane airliners

Curtiss-Wright's St Louis factory had been closed for two years by the great depression and the company needed an aircraft with which to resume production. It had to be developed cheaply and quickly.

The result was the XT-32 (Experimental Transport to carry a payload of 7055 kg (3,200 lb.)), the first of which flew on 30 January 1933. The name Condor II was adopted to cash in on

the solid reputation of the earlier Model 18 Condor, which it resembled in basic layout.

Among the T-32's innovative features was an electrically-retracted undercarriage, flexible engine mounts (to reduce vibration) and even hot and cold running water in the toilet.

Eastern Air Transport and American Airways placed orders. By the end of 1935, however, the Condor II was

being replaced with DC-2s. Ultimately, Condor IIs saw a great deal more service overseas. Bomber (BT-32) and transport (CT-32) versions were sold in South America and US civil and Navy examples made pioneering survey flights over the Antarctic.

Two Condor IIs were purchased by the US Navy in 1934 for transport duties. Both were lost in the Antarctic.

AT-32-B CONDOR II

American Airways bought Condor IIs to replace the smaller Ford Trimotor. However, the Trimotor was to outlive the Condor IIs, the last of which was retired by AA in 1937. NC12394 was destroyed in a hangar fire in July 1937.

AT-32-A Condor II

Type: twin-engined biplane airliner

Powerplant: two 529-kW (710-hp.) Wright SGR-1820-F3 Cyclone radial engines

Maximum speed: 306 km/h (190 m.p.h.) at 2438 m (8,000 ft.)

Cruising speed: 245 km/h (152 m.p.h.) at 2438 m (8,000 ft.)

Climb rate: 366 m/min (1,200 f.p.m.)

Range: 1152 km (715 mi.) at 2438 m (8,000 ft.)

Service ceiling: 7010 m (23,000 ft.)

Weights: empty 5550 kg (12,210 lb.); loaded 7938 kg (17,464 lb.)

Accommodation: 12 passengers

Dimensions: span 24.99 m (82 ft.)
length 14.81 m (48 ft. 7 in.)
height 4.98 m (16 ft. 4 in.)
wing area 112.2 m² (1,207 sq. ft.)

The T-32's simple design and Curtiss-Wright's efficient management allowed the company to offer the aircraft to US airlines at a comparatively cheap price, quoted as 'less than $60,000'.

The AT-32-A was a convertible dayplane/sleeper aircraft with capacity for 12 passengers. The AT-32-C carried 15 passengers in a dayplane-only configuration; other models had engines of varying horsepower ratings. American Airlines was the biggest customer for the A-model with 10 examples.

The engines were mounted on rubber bushes to reduce vibration. To ease maintenance Condor IIs had no less than 125 access panels, closed with zip fasteners.

Passenger comfort was an important selling point for the T-32. The cabin was soundproofed and each seat was provided with individual hot and cold air outlets. Cabin furnishings were composed of a combination of fabric and leather.

Two Wright SGR-1820 Cyclone geared radial engines powered early T-32s. The improved AT-32 used a supercharged variant driving a variable-pitch propeller.

The electrically-retracted undercarriage was the first to be used on a twin-engined airliner and was among a number of innovations that set the Condor apart from other airliners of the period. The airframe, however, retained a metal structure and fabric skin.

ACTION DATA

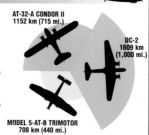

CRUISING SPEED

Despite being a twin-engined biplane, the AT-32 had almost a 50-km/h advantage over the three-engined Trimotor monoplane. The DC-2 showed an even better turn of speed, setting new standards in airliner performance.

AT-32-A CONDOR II	245 km/h (152 m.p.h.)
TRIMOTOR	198 km/h (123 m.p.h.)
DC-2	306 km/h (190 m.p.h.)

RANGE

The Condor II's range was also an improvement over that of the Trimotor, despite being considerably heavier. This was largely due to its twin engines, which used less fuel than the Ford's three powerplants. Once again, the DC-2 set new standards.

AT-32-A CONDOR II 1152 km (715 mi.)
DC-2 1609 km (1,000 mi.)
MODEL 5-AT-B TRIMOTOR 708 km (440 mi.)

ACCOMMODATION

Early model Condor IIs carried fewer passengers than the Trimotor, but could be flown in a sleeper/dayplane configuration. Later AT-32 variants could carry 15 passengers, more than the first DC-2s.

AT-32-A CONDOR II 12
MODEL 5-AT-B TRIMOTOR 15
DOUGLAS DC-2 14

From the Americas to Antarctica

ANTARCTIC PIONEER: The first Condor II on the southern continent accompanied Admiral Byrd's second expedition.

ARMY TRANSPORT: There were just two USAAC Condor IIs. Designated YC-30 and fitted out as VIP transports, they were retired in 1938.

SWISSAIR'S SOLE EXAMPLE: A few T-32s saw service in Europe. Swissair's was the last civil Condor II built, but it crashed after four months.

BT-32 BOMBER IN CHINA: The turret- and bomb rack-equipped BT-32 appeared in February 1934. This, the first, went to China.

CURTISS

R3C

● Navy floatplane racers ● Schneider Trophy winners ● Seven built

Sleek Curtiss biplane racers will forever be linked with the prestigious 1920s Schneider Trophy races and with America's best-known military racing pilot, James H. Doolittle. Beginning with the CR-1 and CR-2, Curtiss produced seven aircraft, mainly for the US Navy. As well as taking part in the Schneider Trophy races, these aircraft also participated successfully in the Pulitzer Trophy races, helping to establish Curtiss as a builder of fighter aircraft.

▲ *Air races were seen by the*
US armed services as valuable proving grounds for new engines and equipment. To obtain funding, the aircraft were given spurious designations – the CR-1 was known as the CF-1 fighter.

CURTISS R3C

The magnificent Schneider Trophy ▶
Presented by Jacques Schneider, this coveted prize for a dozen races between 1913 and 1931 is now on display at London's Science Museum.

▲ Pulitzer-winning R2C-1
After the Army won the 1922 Pulitzer Trophy Race in its Curtiss R-6 racers, the Navy ordered two R2C-1s, which won the 1923 races.

▲ Army R3C-1 on wheels
Of the three R3C-1s, two were built for the Navy and one for the Army. All were landplanes.

▲ Second place at Cowes
A6080 was the second CR-3 (originally a CR-1) and was placed second in the 1923 Schneider Trophy Race, in the hands of Navy Lieutenant Paul Irvin.

Curtiss 12-cylinder powerplants ▶
While the CR and R2C used the D-12 engine, the R3C introduced the V-1400 of 421 kW (565 hp.).

FACTS AND FIGURES

➤ The predecessor of the R3C, Curtiss's R2C, was a world-class racer but was plagued by a series of accidents.

➤ With a bigger engine, the sole R3C-3 reached 410.37 km/h (255 m.p.h.).

➤ US Army R3C-2 A6979 is preserved at the National Air and Space Museum.

➤ After the 1923 Pulitzer race, R2C-1 A6691 was sold to the Army for $1.00 and redesignated R-8. It crashed in 1924.

➤ Each successive racer type used a new aerofoil section wing to improve speed.

➤ A6878, as an R3C-4, crashed before the 1926 Schneider Trophy race.

PROFILE

World-beating racers from Long Island

Curtiss was chosen as the builder of two aircraft for the US Navy in 1921. These aircraft, the CR-1 and CR-2, were to be raced for the Pulitzer Trophy which had been won by the Army in 1920. The Navy withdrew shortly before the race, leaving Curtiss to enter the CR-2 and win the event.

In 1922, victory eluded both machines, but in 1923, after the aircraft were rebuilt to CR-3 floatplane standard, they were entered in the prestigious Schneider Trophy event, taking first and second places.

Meanwhile, for racing in the US, Curtiss had produced an improved design, the R2C. Again a landplane in its original form, the R2C had wing surface radiators to reduce drag. After winning the Pulitzer event in 1923, one aircraft was fitted with floats for the cancelled 1924 Schneider Trophy races. Next came the R3C, with a new V-1400 engine, of which were built, two for the Navy and one for the Army. Once again, the Pulitzer

Army pilot, Lieutenant James H. Doolittle, stands on the float of the R3C-2 in which he won the 1925 Schneider Trophy at a speed of 374.289 km/h (232.572 m.p.h.).

and Schneider Trophies were the targets, the Army R3C-1 winning the Pulitzer Trophy and, rebuilt as a float-equipped R3C-2, taking the Schneider Trophy as well, with James Doolittle at the controls.

In order to provide cooling for the engine, without bulky, drag-inducing radiators, the CR-2 and subsequent designs employed wing surface radiators.

CR-3

Type: single-seat racing seaplane

Powerplant: one 336-kW (450-hp.) Curtiss D-12 5DL Vee-configuration liquid-cooled piston engine

Maximum speed: 312 km/h (194 m.p.h.) at sea level

Initial climb rate: 6 mins to 1524 m (5,000 ft.)

Range: 840 km (522 mi.)

Service ceiling: 5852 m (19,200 ft.)

Weights: empty 961 kg (2,119 lb.); gross 1246 kg (2,747 lb.)

Dimensions:
span	6.93 m (22 ft. 9 in.)
length	7.63 m (25 ft.)
height	3.27 m (10 ft. 9 in.)
wing area	15.61 m² (168 sq. ft.)

The CR-3's pilot was snugly enclosed in a cramped cockpit, surrounded by a 'horsecollar' coaming to reduce drag.

At the heart of the CR-3 was a 336-kW (450-hp.) Curtiss D-12 5DL 12-cylinder, Vee-configuration engine driving a Reed fixed-pitch, two-bladed forged aluminium propeller. This replaced the original wooden airscrew and allowed higher engine speeds.

The two CR-3s were originally built as a CR-1 and CR-2, each with wheeled undercarriage. Floats were fitted for the 1923 Schneider Trophy races.

Curtiss's established laminated wood veneer construction technique was used for these naval racers. It provided a strong yet relatively lightweight airframe.

After the 1924 Schneider Trophy races were cancelled, A6081 went on to set a closed-circuit seaplane speed record of 302.681 km/h (188.077 m.p.h.). It was fitted with a later version of the D-12 engine and redesignated CR-4.

The streamlining of the flying wires was one of various measures introduced to reduce drag. Also, the wing N-struts were cross-laminated to produce a more aerodynamic form, and the original Lamblin radiators fitted to the CR-1 and CR-2 were replaced with wing surface radiators.

CR-3

Bearing the race number '4', CR-3 A6081 was flown by David Rittenhouse during the 1923 Schneider Race at Cowes. In 1924, it set 100-km (60-mi.), 200-km (120-mi.) and 500-km (300-mi.) closed-circuit world speed records.

ACTION DATA

MAXIMUM SPEED

Unfortunately, the Supermarine S.4 did not get a chance to demonstrate its top speed, as it crashed before the 1925 race. The Curtiss R3C-2 was some 30 km/h faster than the S.4 and Gloster III. Cornering performance was good in all three.

R3C-2   394 km/h (245 m.p.h.)

IIIA   362 km/h (225 m.p.h.)

S.4   365 km/h (227 m.p.h.)

MAXIMUM TAKE-OFF WEIGHT

The S.4 was the heaviest of the three designs, by some 200 kg (440 lb.), but had a less powerful engine than the Gloster III. However, as a more streamlined monoplane design, the S.4 suffered far less from drag and was capable of higher speeds.

R3C-2
1242 kg (2,738 lb.)

IIIA
1218 kg (2,685 lb.)

S.4
1447 kg (3,190 lb.)

POWER

The Schneider Trophy Races were an ideal testing ground for new technology, like engines, destined for fighter aircraft. This was reflected in the sponsorship of teams by military services such as the US Army and Navy. Most engines were liquid-cooled, in-line types, like the Curtiss D-12 and Napier Lion, which minimised frontal area and therefore reduced drag.

R3C-2
421 kW (565 hp.)

IIIA
522 kW (700 hp.)

S.4
507 kW (680 hp.)

The 1925 Schneider Trophy Race

REPEAT PERFORMANCE: The 1924 Schneider Trophy meeting, planned for Baltimore, Maryland in the US, had been cancelled after the French and Italian teams pulled out, Supermarine produced no design and Gloster's aircraft crashed. Foreign attendance was assured for 1925. The Curtiss CR-3s had won the 1923 event; with the improved R3C, the US Army/Navy team was poised for further glory. As the race date neared, Supermarine's S.4 suffered a crash, leaving Gloster and Macchi to challenge the Americans. On the day (26 October), the R3C's superior speed was telling. The British Gloster III took second place, the Macchi M.33 third.

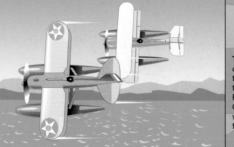

THE VENUE: The site of the 1925 race was the sheltered mouth of the Susquehanna River, near Baltimore. Good water conditions were an important feature.

Start & Finish

CHESAPEAKE BAY

THE COURSE: From a start/finish line at Bay Shore, the aircraft turned at a pylon and lighthouse on the triangular course.

CURTISS

R-6

- US Army racer and record breaker ● Inspired by Navy CR floatplane

D uring the 1920s Curtiss was America's leading builder of racing aircraft. Its first successful machine was the CR, built for the US Navy so they could compete for the annual Pulitzer Trophy. The US Army had won this race in 1920, inter-service rivalry spurring the Navy to compete again the following year. Entered by Curtiss, the Navy-owned CR won the 1921 event. Thus, with pride at stake, the Army asked Curtiss to build the R-6.

▲ *Air racing became steadily more popular during the inter-war years, especially in the United States where a number of contests were held each year. Success at home was followed by success abroad as landplane designs were adapted for seaplane racing.*

CURTISS R-6

▼ **Second-placed Curtiss Cox**
Cox triplane Cactus Kitten *took second place in the 1921 Pulitzer Trophy race.*

▲ **Unstable Texas Wildcat**
This early Curtiss design proved highly unstable at high speeds. Rebuilt with new biplane wings, it crashed on a cross-country flight.

R-6 descendent ▶
After successes with the CR and R-6 aircraft, Curtiss continued to develop the basic design. It built three R3C-1s, powered by a 421-kW (565-hp.) V-1400 engine, two for the US Navy and one for the Army.

▼ **Pulitzer success in 1925**
Army flyers were again successful in 1925, racing the latest Curtiss racer, the R3C-1, to victory.

▲ **Lieutenant Maitland and his R-6**
Lester Maitland flew the R-6 for the first time on 27 September 1922. He took it to second place in the following month's Pulitzer race.

FACTS AND FIGURES

➤ The Pulitzer Trophy for air racing was presented annually by American newspaper owners the Pulitzer brothers.

➤ Two R-6 racers cost the Army $71,000, plus $5,000 for spare parts.

➤ R-6 A.S. 68564 was lost in a fatal crash during the 1924 Pulitzer Trophy race.

➤ Brigadier General 'Billy' Mitchell allegedly 'pulled rank' in order to make the October 1922 record-breaking flight.

➤ During speed trials in April 1923, A.S. 68563 was damaged in two accidents.

➤ Both R-6s were later fitted with large-bore D-12A engines rated at 373 kW (500 hp.).

PROFILE

Army racer and record breaker

Service interest in air races arose largely because they were recognised as a valuable proving ground for new designs.

Curtiss cut their racing 'teeth' on two racers built for a Texan oil millionaire, S. E. J. Cox – *Texas Wildcat* and *Cactus Kitten* – the latter finishing second behind the CR in the 1921 Pulitzer race.

Determined to beat the Navy in 1922, the Army ordered two racers from Curtiss. The R-6 was a development of the CR series but introduced a new Curtiss D-12 engine rated at 343 kW.

So it was that on 14 October Lieutenant Russell Maughan took the second of the two machines (A.S. 68564) to victory at a speed of 331.19 km/h (205.79 m.p.h.) – an unofficial world speed record. Lieutenant Lester Maitland in the other aircraft, A.S. 68563, gained second place.

Having achieved their goal and shattered the world speed mark, the Army then set about gaining official recognition. Just four days later Brigadier General William Mitchell took the race winning aircraft to 358.923 km/h (223.024 m.p.h.) before official observers.

The following February a French flyer pushed the world mark to 375 km/h (233 m.p.h.). Not to be outdone, Maughan managed 380.751 km/h (236.588 m.p.h.) on 19 March – a record that lasted seven months.

Inside the Curtiss factory, three of the company's racing designs are seen in various states of repair. In the foreground is an R-6, to its right the US Navy's CR-2, and behind is the Cox Racer Cactus Kitten.

The R-6 was essentially an all-wood aircraft comprising a stressed-skin, all-wood monocoque weighing 57.6 kg (127 lb.) with a two-ply veneer skin covered with doped linen. The wings were also wooden with plywood skinning and fabric-covered ailerons.

R-6

Type: single-seat biplane racer

Powerplant: one 343-kW (460-hp.) Curtiss D-12 v-configuration liquid-cooled piston engine

Maximum speed: 380 km/h (237 m.p.h.)

Landing speed: 121 km/h (75 m.p.h.)

Range: 455 km (283 m.p.h.) at full throttle

Weights: empty 659 kg (1,453 lb.); gross 884.5 kg (1,950 lb.)

Dimensions:
span	5.79 m (18 ft. 10 in.)
length	5.76 m (18 ft. 11 in.)
height	2.41 m (7 ft. 11 in.)
wing area	12.82 m² (138 sq. ft.)

ACTION DATA

POWER

Crucial to a racing aircraft's success was its engine. Curtiss was heavily involved in engine as well as airframe development and introduced various engines for racing, culminating in the D-12, which powered the R-6 and the Navy's CR-3. The Curtiss Cox racer *Texas Wildcat* was fitted with the earlier geared-drive C-12 engine. Gearing was required to reduce engine revolutions because of the strength limitations of wooden propellers used at the time.

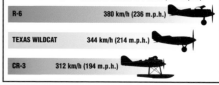

R-6 343 kW (460 hp.)	TEXAS WILDCAT 318 kW (426 hp.)	CR-3 336 kW (450 hp.)

MAXIMUM SPEED

The maximum speeds achievable by racing aircraft between the wars leapt ahead at an astonishing rate. Though the R-6 was the fastest aircraft in the world during 1922–23 it was outclassed within 12 months by the Navy's R2C which, at the end of 1923, had set a new world record of over 428 km/h (266 m.p.h.). Not until 1932 did the United States again hold a world record, when the Granville Brothers' Gee Bee R-1 achieved almost 474 km/h (295 m.p.h.).

R-6	380 km/h (236 m.p.h.)
TEXAS WILDCAT	344 km/h (214 m.p.h.)
CR-3	312 km/h (194 m.p.h.)

After the success of their geared-drive C-12 and direct-drive CD-12 engines, Curtiss developed the all-new D-12 liquid-cooled, vee-configuration 12-cylinder powerplant. The engine's full potential was not realised until 1923 when metal propellers were employed for racing.

A breakthrough in airframe drag reduction introduced on the R-6 was the use of wing-mounted radiators on both surfaces of the upper wings; these replaced the French Lamblin units attached to the undercarriage legs of earlier designs. Surface radiators subsequently became standard on racing aircraft.

R-6 Army racers carried the Air Service bald eagle insignia. The ribbon carried in the eagle's beak read 'US Army Air Service'. The aircraft's fuselage was black overall with gold wings.

R-6

A.S. 68563 was the first of the two R-6s built to contest the 1922 Pulitzer Trophy race, for which it carried the race number '44'. It finished second in the hands of Lieutenant Lester Maitland. In the 1923 event it finished fifth and then second in 1924. The following year it was written off during static testing.

Curtiss racing landplanes

CURTISS COX *TEXAS WILDCAT*: Built as a monoplane for the 1920 Gordon Bennett race in France, the *Wildcat* proved unstable and was rebuilt as a biplane, only to crash.

CURTISS COX *CACTUS KITTEN*: The second of the Cox racers was shipped to France but was not assembled. A triplane, it came second in the 1921 Pulitzer race.

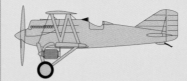

CR-1/CR-2: The US Navy's CRs employed a wheeled undercarriage for the Pulitzer races. Both were fitted with floats for the Schneider Trophy racing and seaplane record breaking.

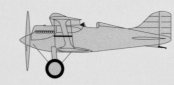

R-6: The R-6's resemblance to the CR racers was readily apparent. A major change was the use of evaporative engine cooling for the new Curtiss D-12 powerplant.

R2C-1/R-8: The 1923 Pulitzer race was won by the Navy in their improved R2C-1 aircraft. One of the two built was then sold to the Army as the R-8, crashing in 1924.

CURTISS
SBC HELLDIVER

● Dive bomber ● Combat trainer ● Complex development

▲ Although the SBC was a strong aircraft with very good handling characteristics, it was totally outclassed by new monoplanes by the time World War II started in Europe.

As the second of three aircraft named Helldiver by the Curtiss company, the SBC was probably the least successful. Originally a parasol-winged fighter, the SBC went through major changes in design and role before becoming a carrier-based scout-bomber. The outbreak of World War II saw the Helldiver exported to France and Great Britain, but its only combat service was with the US Navy aboard the aircraft carrier USS Hornet.

CURTISS SBC HELLDIVER

Staggered wings ▶
After the failure of the initial parasol design, it was realised that a much stronger wing unit was needed to withstand the stresses of dive-bombing. The solution was a strong biplane arrangement with the upper wing further forward than the lower wing and a single sturdy interplane strut.

▼ Improved version
The last SBC-3 on the production line became the XSBC-4, with a more powerful Wright R-1820 engine and the ability to carry a 454-kg (1,000-lb.) bomb.

▲ Capable trainer
Although intended as a front-line aircraft, the SBC made a vital contribution to the US war effort as a combat trainer.

▼ French deliveries
In 1940 the US diverted 50 SBC-4s to beleaguered France although they arrived too late to be used in combat. This example is seen at the factory prior to delivery.

Diverted to Britain ▶
After the fall of France in 1940, five SBC-4s were acquired by the RAF as instructional airframes and were named Clevelands.

FACTS AND FIGURES

➤ The prototype XSBC-1 crashed in September 1934 when the wing folding mechanism failed in flight.

➤ British Clevelands differed from standard SBC-4s in having self-sealing fuel tanks.

➤ The SBC-4 was the last biplane combat aircraft ever ordered by the USA.

➤ In 1940, SBC-4s aboard a French aircraft carrier were diverted to Martinique where they were eventually scrapped.

➤ The SBC was the second of three Curtiss bomber types named Helldiver.

➤ US Marine Corps SBC-4s remained in service until June 1943.

PROFILE

Last American combat biplane

In 1932 the US Navy ordered a new two-seat fighter prototype from Curtiss. Designated XF12C-1 and fitted with a parasol wing, the aircraft proved to be unsuitable in this role. However, it was decided to use the design as a scout aircraft and the XSBC-1 prototype was constructed. More problems followed as the aircraft suffered a structural wing failure during tests, and the parasol wing layout was abandoned.

The resulting XSBC-2 biplane was a far better aircraft and went into production for the US Navy with an uprated Pratt & Whitney Twin Wasp Junior engine as the SBC-3 Helldiver.

Entering service in 1936, 83 SBC-3s were delivered before production switched to the SBC-4 fitted with a more powerful engine. The US Navy ordered 174 of this new model, but 50 were diverted to France as the situation in Europe worsened.

The type saw brief wartime service with the US Navy and Marines before being withdrawn to second-line duties.

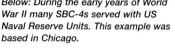

Below: During the early years of World War II many SBC-4s served with US Naval Reserve Units. This example was based in Chicago.

Above: SBC-4s of VS-8 and VB-8 from USS Hornet are seen engaged in manoeuvres days before the Japanese attack at Pearl Harbor.

SBC-4 Helldiver

Type: two-seat carrier-based scout-bomber

Powerplant: one 708-kW (950-hp.) Wright R-1820-34 Cyclone 9 radial piston engine

Maximum speed: 381 km/h (236 m.p.h.) at 4635 m (15,000 ft.)

Initial climb rate: 497 m/min (1,630 f.p.m.)

Range: 950 km (590 mi.) with 227-kg (500-lb.) bombload

Service ceiling: 8320 m (27,900 ft.)

Weights: empty 2196 kg (4,831 lb.); maximum take-off 3462 kg (7,616 lb.)

Armament: two 7.62-mm (.30 cal.) machine-guns plus up to 454 kg (1,000 lb.) of bombs

Dimensions: span 10.36 m (34 ft.)
length 8.64 m (28 ft. 4 in.)
height 3.84 m (12 ft. 7 in.)
wing area 29.45 m² (317 sq. ft.)

SBC-3 HELLDIVER

The brightly painted red tail is the marking carried by aircraft from USS *Yorktown* in 1937. The black 'Man O'War Bird' emblem denotes that this aircraft is from VS-5.

After the failure of the parasol wing design a biplane unit was introduced. The wings were of metal frame covered with metal skin on the upper wing and fabric on the lower wing.

A forward-firing 7.62-mm machine-gun was aimed by the pilot using a sight attached to the windshield. A second 7.62-mm (.30 cal.) machine-gun could be fitted on a flexible mounting in the rear cockpit.

A large 'greenhouse'-type cockpit covered both crew members. It was situated behind the top wing and so gave the pilot poor vision above and forward.

The SBC-3 was fitted with a 615-kW (825-hp.) Pratt & Whitney R-1535-82 Twin Wasp Junior piston engine.

5-S-7   U.S.NAVY

The landing gear retracted into the all-metal monocoque fuselage in a similar fashion to the Grumman F2F and F3F. An arrester hook was fitted for aircraft carrier operations.

COMBAT DATA

MAXIMUM SPEED

Although the Skua was a more modern monoplane design, it was slower than the biplane SBC-4. A lack of speed with all early war scout bombers resulted in heavy losses to enemy fighters.

SBC-4 HELLDIVER   381 km/h (236 m.p.h.)
SKUA Mk II   362 km/h (224 m.p.h.)
SB2U-3 VINDICATOR   391 km/h (242 m.p.h.)

BOMBLOAD

Although the SB2U-3 Vindicator was a significantly more powerful aircraft, it could only match the earlier SBC-4 in bomb-carrying capacity. The Skua was less capable than either American design.

SBC-4 HELLDIVER   454-kg (1,000-lb.) bombload
SKUA Mk II   227-kg (500-lb.) bombload
SB2U-3 VINDICATOR   454-kg (1,000-lb.) bombload

RANGE

With the large areas covered by a carrier group, long range is essential for naval aircraft. Again the Vindicator was far superior, allowing it to strike at targets beyond the range of most carrier-based bombers. The Skua had the shortest range but generally operated in the smaller North and Mediterranean Seas.

SBC-4 HELLDIVER 950 km (590 mi.)
SKUA Mk II 760 km (471 mi.)
SB2U-3 VINDICATOR 1802 km (1,117 mi.)

US Navy carrier aircraft of 1939

■ **DOUGLAS TBD DEVASTATOR:** Entering service in 1937, the TBD remained the US Navy's primary torpedo aircraft until 1942.

■ **GRUMMAN F3F:** Following on from the successful FF and F2F biplane fighters, the F3F served with both the US Navy and US Marines.

■ **GRUMMAN JF/J2F DUCK:** Being of amphibious design, the Duck was very versatile and was used in patrol, survey and rescue roles.

■ **VOUGHT SB2U VINDICATOR:** Operated as a scout and a bomber, the SB2U served with front-line units for six years from 1936.

CURTISS

SOC SEAGULL

● Scout aircraft ● Operated from battleships ● Seaplane

The Curtiss SOC Seagull was the US Navy's top observation aircraft in the years just before World War II. The battleship was still thought to be the most important 'war wagon' on the high seas, and the Seagull was the 'eyes' of the fleet's battleships and cruisers. The pilot and observer aboard were expected to spot targets and direct the big guns of the huge ships. Obsolete by the time war arrived, the SOC was still in service in 1945.

▲ One of the last biplanes to serve with the US Navy, the SOC Seagull flew extensively from battleships and cruisers during World War II. It actually outlasted its replacement.

CURTISS SOC SEAGULL

◄ On dry land
When operating from shore bases, Seagulls were fitted with a wheeled undercarriage.

▼ Boss bird
Painted overall dark blue, this aircraft was assigned to the Commander of the Fleet.

◄ Use over North Africa
Although famous for their involvement in the Pacific war, these aircraft also gave valiant service in other theatres, flying in support of the Allied landings in North Africa in 1942 during Operation Torch, for example.

▲ Recovery
Seaplanes landed alongside their parent ships and were hoisted aboard by cranes.

Start of a patrol ►
Catapulted from a US Navy cruiser, an SOC sets out on a mission during the Pacific war.

FACTS AND FIGURES

➤ In original configuration, the prototype SOC was an amphibian that had wheels incorporated into the floats.

➤ The 64 aircraft built by the Naval Aircraft Factory were designated SON-1.

➤ Production of the SOC Seagull began in 1935 and ended in 1938.

➤ A proposed successor, the SO3C Seamew, was unsatisfactory and was replaced in service by Seagulls!

➤ SOCs featured prominently in most of the major battles of the Pacific war.

➤ When the SOCs were finally withdrawn, the era of the combat seaplane ended.

PROFILE

Long-serving naval scout

In the late 1930s, few aviation experts would have envisaged that this biplane scout would outlast several monoplanes in service.

The last of the Curtiss biplanes to be used operationally by the US Navy, the SOC Seagull originated in 1933. It was out of date by the time America entered World War II in 1941, but remained on duty until the war was over.

The SOC Seagull had folding wings and tail structure made of fabric-covered light metal alloy, and a welded, steel-tube fuselage. The pilot and observer/gunner were accommodated in tandem cockpits, enclosed by a continuous transparent canopy with sliding panels for access.

Very much a product of 1930s' technology, the Seagull appeared outmoded by rapid changes occurring in aviation as the war loomed; nevertheless, it performed admirably during World War II and was well loved by those who flew it.

Production Seagull floatplanes began to reach the fleet in 1935. In due course, about three dozen naval scouting squadrons were equipped with the type. A decade later, in 1945, when American Marines were landing on Iwo Jima in one of the final actions of the war, SOCs were still in front-line service.

Being a biplane, the SOC was blessed with remarkable agility, and in wheeled configuration could out-turn many faster monoplanes. To facilitate stowage in tight spaces on board battleships or aircraft carriers, the wings could be folded back.

SOC-3 SEAGULL

US aircraft operating in support of Operation Torch in North Africa had a distinctive yellow circle added outboard of their national insignia. This SOC-3 Seagull is quite unusual in that it carries no unit markings.

Powering the SOC-3 was a Pratt & Whitney R-1340 engine, which churned out 447 kW. It provided more than adequate performance for a seaplane, though the Seagull remained vulnerable to fighter attack.

In the SOC, the standard crew consisted of a pilot and observer. A 7.62-mm (.30 cal.) MG was fitted in each cockpit and provided some defence. For take-off and landing, the canopies were often left in the open position.

In seaplane configuration, the SOC-3 was fitted with a single large centreline float. When the parent ship was in port, the aircraft were assigned to land bases and the floats were exchanged for a spatted wheeled undercarriage.

Construction of this aeronautical anachronism consisted of a welded tubular steel fuselage with aluminum framed wings and tail surfaces, all covered in fabric.

A pair of small outrigger floats was fitted to the lower wings. Their purpose was only to provide stability for the aircraft while on the water.

SOC-3 Seagull

Type: two-seat scout/observation aircraft

Powerplant: one 447-kW (600-hp.) Pratt & Whitney R-1340-18 Wasp radial engine

Maximum speed: 266 km/h (165 m.p.h.)

Cruising speed: 214 km/h (133 m.p.h.)

Initial climb rate: 321 m/min (1,050 f.p.m.)

Range: 1086 km (673 mi.)

Service ceiling: 4540 m (14,900 ft.)

Weights: empty 1648 kg (3,626 lb.); loaded 2492 kg (5,482 lb.)

Armament: two 7.62-mm (.30 cal.) machine-guns, plus external racks for two 147-kg (325-lb.) bombs

Dimensions:
span 10.97 m (36 ft.)
length 9.47 m (31 ft. 1 in.)
height 4.44 m (14 ft. 7 in.)
wing area 31.77 m² (328 sq. ft.)

COMBAT DATA

MAXIMUM SPEED

Dismissed as an anachronism at the start of the war, the SOC was slower than the two main rival enemy types, although, as a biplane, it had much greater agility and was a more flexible aircraft. The 'Jake' was its primary opponent in the Pacific war.

SOC-1 SEAGULL	266 km/h (165 m.p.h.)
ARADO AR 196	310 km/h (192 m.p.h.)
AICHI E13A 'JAKE'	375 km/h (233 m.p.h.)

RANGE

An important criterion for naval seaplanes was an ability to range far from the parent ship to observe enemy activity. In the Pacific, the Seagull could roam extensively. The Japanese E13A could range even further and was one of the best scouts of World War II.

SOC-1 SEAGULL 1086 km (673 mi.)
ARADO AR 196 1070 km (663 mi.)
AICHI E13A 'JAKE' 2090 km (1,296 mi.)

BOMBLOAD

Scout aircraft were sometimes called upon to drop bombs, and here the Seagull received top marks, being able to carry a greater load than either of its main rivals. Bombs were mainly used to attack smaller warships, while leaving more specialised aircraft to attack larger capital ships.

SOC-1 SEAGULL 295 kg (650 lb.) **ARADO AR 196 100 kg (220 lb.)** **AICHI E13A 'JAKE' 250 kg (550 lb.)**

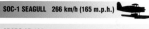

Curtiss naval aircraft in World War II

■ **SBC HELLDIVER:** This early dive-bomber was obsolete at the start of the war, though some remained in service until late 1942.

■ **SB2C HELLDIVER:** Also named Helldiver, this monoplane dive-bomber replaced the Douglas Dauntless from 1943 onwards.

■ **SC SEAHAWK:** Designed in 1942, the Seahawk was really too late to see service; only 66 examples were delivered before VJ-Day.

■ **SO3C SEAMEW:** Intended as a successor to the SOC, these aircraft proved unsuccessful and had short careers in the Navy.

CURTISS

JN-4 'JENNY'

● Two-seat World War I trainer ● Barnstorming aircraft

T he JN-4 'Jenny' had a double career. It was America's universal aircraft of the 1920s, having been developed as a military trainer early in the Great War and then becoming the machine of post-war flying instructors and barnstormers. An open field, a nice day and a few heads cranked upwards in curiosity were all that were needed for the JN-4 to bring the thrill of aviation to ordinary people. Many of them learned about aircraft by watching the 'Jenny' perform.

▲ From 1919 to the late-1920s thousands of 'Jennys' were flown in what was known as the 'barnstorming era', introducing many Americans to aircraft for the first time. Surplus JN-4s were bought from the US Army for as little as $50 each.

CURTISS JN-4 'JENNY'

▲ JN-3 collision
The JN-4 was developed from the interim JN-3, 91 of which were sold to Britain and two were purchased by the US Army.

▲ Wartime Army JN-4D
Between November 1917 and January 1919 over 2,800 JN-4Ds were built. To speed up delivery, six manufacturers built the D model.

Barnstorming in the 1920s ▶
Unhampered by regulations governing their use, post-war pilots used JN-4s for stunt flying.

▼ Half-scale Jenny
In 1961, F. A. Murray of Rockford, Illinois, built this half-scale replica of a JN-4D-2, and called it the JN-2D-1 'Jennette'. Power was supplied by a converted Ford Model 'A' 37-kW (50-hp.) car engine.

▲ In the Navy
Most of the US Navy's JN-4s were H models powered by 112-kW (150-hp.) engines. Thirty were purchased for advanced pilot training in 1918 and were followed by 90 JN-4HG gunnery trainers.

FACTS AND FIGURES

➤ The contract to build 1,400 JN-4Ds for the US Army was worth $4,417,337 for the Curtiss Corporation.

➤ Approximately 7,280 JN-4s were built, including 4,800 for the US Army.

➤ Of American and Canadian pilots in the World War I, 95 per cent trained on JN-4s.

➤ The 'Jenny' first appeared in July 1916 when an initial batch of planes was sold to Britain and the US Army.

➤ After more than a decade, the last US Army JN-4s were retired in 1927.

➤ As well as pilot training, JN-4s were used for observation and bomber training.

PROFILE

From training to 'barnstorming'

A development of the 1915 JN-3 that flew combat reconnaissance with General Pershing during the US Army's expedition against Pancho Villa on the Mexican border, the Curtiss JN-4 'Jenny' was conceived to replace the antiquated pusher-type, open-to-the-wind trainers that had served the military until that time.

The military JN-4, a two-seater made of fabric, wood and wire, became the standard US Army trainer during World War I and for about seven years after. In the air, the 'Jenny' seemed to have no vices. Even for the beginner it was an easy machine to fly.

After the war, 'Jennys' had a lively time in the civil world. Many pilots-turned-barnstormers purchased JN-4s from the government for very little and set out to earn their fortunes flying for fun, giving joy rides and displays. Stuntmen like Ormer Locklear were called the 'Flying Fools' for their wild antics in the air – indeed, crashes were not infrequent.

The JN-4 gained immortality as a trainer aircraft and as a machine that brought aviation to the people.

Below: Wearing Army JN-4H markings, this 'Jenny' was preserved in the US. As with the de Havilland Moth family, the numbers built ensured that examples still survive.

Above: This preserved 'Jenny' clearly shows the unequal-span wings. It carries the markings applied to US Army aircraft at the end of World War I.

JN-4D 'Jenny'

Type: two-seat military trainer

Powerplant: one 67-kW (90-hp.) Curtiss OX-5 inline piston engine

Maximum speed: 121 km/h (75 m.p.h.)

Cruising speed: 97 km/h (60 m.p.h.)

Service ceiling: 1980 m (6,500 ft.)

Weights: empty 630 kg (1,386 lb.); maximum take-off 871 kg (1,916 lb.)

Accommodation: two pilots in tandem open cockpits

Dimensions:
span	13.30 m	(43 ft. 8 in.)
length	8.33 m	(27 ft. 4 in.)
height	3.01 m	(9 ft. 10 in.)
wing area	32.70 m²	(352 sq. ft.)

The Curtiss OX-5 inline piston engine drove a two-bladed wooden propeller on the JN-4Can. Later variants had a Wright-built Hispano-Suiza engine.

Privately owned, Canadian-built JN-4s remained in use into the 1930s. A few were built as late as 1927, using reconditioned parts. Some had a third cockpit and were known as the Ericson Special Three.

The JN-4 had a larger tailfin and tailplane than earlier members of the JN family.

JN-4CAN

The School of Aerial Fighting in Canada was equipped with the JN-4Can (for 'Canadian'). This was built by the Canadian Aeroplane Corporation of Toronto and known as the 'Canuck'.

CITY OF TORONTO

C368

Behind the wheel covers were the spokes and wheel-rim, to which a rubber tyre was fitted. The undercarriage was of the cross-axle type.

Underwing skids near the wingtip prevented the wing from touching the ground during a rough landing.

The two-seat trainer aircraft was arranged to have an instructor in the rear seat and the pupil in the front. In civil aircraft the latter position was used for joy riders.

Control wires on aircraft of this era were often exposed, taking the shortest route between cockpit and the control surface.

The airframe structure was almost entirely wooden with a doped fabric covering.

ACTION DATA

MAXIMUM SPEED

The Avro 504 used a more powerful engine than the early JN-4s, giving the aircraft improved performance; it was also more aerodynamically streamlined. The Albatros B.IIa was primarily an observation aircraft that was used for a secondary training role.

JN-4D 'JENNY'	121 km/h (75 m.p.h.)	
504K	153 km/h (95 m.p.h.)	
B.IIa	120 km/h (74 m.p.h.)	

RANGE

Designed originally as a reconnaissance aircraft, the Albatros had a marginally better range than the 'Jenny' and 504K. Range figures for these machines tend to be converted into endurance – the time the aircraft can spend in the air, on a training flight for example. An endurance of three to four hours is typical for all three types.

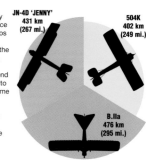

JN-4D 'JENNY' 431 km (267 mi.)

504K 402 km (249 mi.)

B.IIa 476 km (295 mi.)

ENGINE POWER

The 504's rotary engine was the most powerful of those fitted to these three types; later versions of the JN-4 had bigger powerplants. The extra power of the 504 is reflected in its shorter range due to higher fuel consumption. All three aircraft had two-bladed propellers.

JN-4D 'JENNY' 67 kW (90 hp.)

504K 82 kW (110 hp.)

B.IIa 75 kW (100 hp.)

Two-seaters of the inter-war years

■ **AVRO 504:** Famous as a trainer from World War I until the mid-1920s, the 504 started life as a bomber and reconnaissance aircraft.

■ **DE HAVILLAND DH.60 MOTH:** The first of the famous Moth family that ended with the Tiger Moth, DH.60s appeared in the early 1920s.

■ **HANDLEY PAGE GUGNUNC:** Designed for a US competition to find an aircraft that was 'safe' to fly, only one Gugnunc was built.

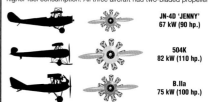

■ **HANRIOT H.433:** A dual-role observation and training aircraft of the late 1920s, the H.433 shared the JN-4's unequal-span wing layout.

CURTISS

P-1 & P-6 HAWK

● Interwar biplane fighter ● Classic US design ● Air racing heritage

▲ Over a 10-year period, Curtiss developed a series of increasingly capable Hawk biplanes. Together with the Boeing P-12 they formed the backbone of the US Army's fighter force until the mid-1930s.

Flying Curtiss biplane fighters was one of the great adventures in aviation. Powerful and nimble, the Curtiss P-1 and P-6 were the flagships of a family of great warplanes that equipped the US Army in the 1920s. The decade was called the 'Roaring Twenties' by Americans who celebrated the end of the Great War and the dawn of a new age of progress. Advances in aviation were happening quickly, with Hawk fighters at the forefront.

CURTISS P-1 & P-6 HAWK

▼ Six-gun fighter
One P-6E had two additional 7.62-mm (.30 cal.) machine-guns installed in each wing by the manufactuer; it was designated the XP-6H.

▲ Ice-bound Hawk
Aircraft belonging to the 1st Pursuit Group, home-based in Michigan, often used a ski undercarriage for Arctic operations.

▼ Aerobatics over Washington
With higher weights, larger landing wheels, an improved radiator and V-1150-3 engine, the P-1B was an improved, although slightly slower, development of the P-1A. Twenty-three P-1B Hawks were delivered from October 1926 and served alongside earlier aircraft.

▲ Skis on P-1Cs
Curtiss received its first large Hawk order for the P-1C model. The aircraft was heavier and slower than earlier variants, but 33 were delivered. Some flew with this optional ski undercarriage.

Prestone-cooled Conqueror ▶
Some of the original water-cooled YP-6 Hawks were re-engined with a Prestone cooling system and were designated P-6As. The system used much smaller radiators.

FACTS AND FIGURES

➤ A P-6 prototype, actually a converted P-1, won the 1927 National Air Races trophy at a speed of 320 km/h (198 m.p.h.).

➤ A US Army air pioneer, Lt Frank Tyndall, died in a P-1 crash on 15 July 1930.

➤ Curtiss manufactured a total of 239 Hawk biplane fighters.

➤ Curtiss Hawk biplanes served for exactly 10 years before giving way to the Boeing P-26 monoplane.

➤ Some Hawks had turbo superchargers for high-altitude performance.

➤ A single export Hawk was sold to Japan in the late 1920s.

PROFILE

End of the biplane era

Arriving at McCook Field, Dayton, Ohio, in August 1925, the Curtiss P-1 Hawk was the first aircraft in the US Army's 'P' for 'Pursuit' category, which later included immortals like the P-47 and P-51. A standard, single-seater biplane of the type which was popular in the 1920s, the P-1 was widely used. It was joined in 1928 by the P-6 Hawk, which had the same basic airframe but

many improvements. These included better all-round performance, spats on the wheels and machine-guns mounted on the fuselage sides, rather than on top, to provide better visibility.

The P-1 and P-6 were the greatest fighters of their brief moment in history, between the Great War and the Depression. Army pilots used them in aerobatic displays and entered

them in races, but the Curtiss Hawk never went to war.

The best-known fighter in this series, the P-6E, began to reach the 17th Pursuit Squadron in 1932. But, by then, an era had ended: the first monoplane fighters were beginning to appear, and the biplane fighter soon disappeared for ever.

Eight P-6Es, in the flamboyant markings of the 17th Pursuit Squadron, demonstrate their highly polished formation flying skills. These formations were of no practical use in combat.

P-6E Hawk

Type: single-seat pursuit biplane

Powerplant: one 522-kW (700-hp.) Curtiss V-1750C Conqueror inline piston engine

Maximum speed: 317 km/h (198 m.p.h.)

Service ceiling: 7285 m (24,700 ft.)

Range: 459 km (285 mi.)

Weights: empty equipped 1224 kg (2,693 lb.); maximum take-off 1559 kg (3,430 lb.)

Armament: two synchronised fuselage-mounted 7.62-mm (.30 cal.) machine-guns

Dimensions:
span	9.60 m	(31 ft. 6 in.)
length	7.06 m	(23 ft. 2 in.)
height	2.72 m	(8 ft. 11 in.)
wing area	23.41 m²	(252 sq. ft.)

Most P-6Es were fitted with three-bladed, variable-pitch propellers. The two machine-guns fired through the propeller arc.

Curtiss studied the effects of wing flutter after one of its racers lost its wings. This research allowed them to use only two sets of main wing struts.

Moving the radiator back from its former chin position to a location just forward of the undercarriage legs, improved the aerodynamics of the P-6E. In addition, single-strut main landing gear units, with spatted wheels, were installed. The machine-guns were moved from high on the nose to low on the fuselage sides.

P-6E HAWK

Wearing the distinctive black and white markings of the 17th Pursuit Squadron of the 1st Pursuit Group, this aircraft was delivered in 1932.

The most colourful of all Hawk markings were applied by the 17th Pursuit Squadron. The overall paint scheme was based on the Arctic snow owl which was the unit insignia.

On the P-6E the tailskid was replaced with a fixed tailwheel. This, together with other improvements, produced a 13 km/h (8 m.p.h.) speed increase over the P-6A.

COMBAT DATA

MAXIMUM SPEED

With its racing heritage and refined design, the P-6E was better than both of its contemporaries in terms of speed. British fighters had advanced little since World War I, hence the poor speed of the Siskin.

P-6E HAWK	317 km/h (198 m.p.h.)
P-12	272 km/h (169 m.p.h.)
SISKIN IIIA	251 km/h (156 m.p.h.)

ARMAMENT

Boeing's P-12 was the US Army Air Corps' second fighter. It was more heavily armed than the P-6E but could not match its performance. The Siskin retained World War I standard armament.

P-6E HAWK	**P-12**	**SISKIN IIIA**
2 x 7.62-mm (.30 cal.) machine-guns	1 x 12.7-mm (.50 cal.) machine-gun 1 x 7.62-mm (.30 cal.) machine-gun 1 x 227-kg (500-lb.) bomb	2 x 7.7-mm (.303 cal.) machine-guns 4 x 9-kg (20-lb.) bombs

SERVICE CEILING

While the Armstrong Whitworth Siskin lagged behind in other areas, it did offer a good service ceiling. Without engine superchargers, however, none of these aircraft was capable of exceptional performance at high altitudes. The open cockpits of these machines also made flying at altitude very uncomfortable.

7285 m (24,700 ft.)	8199 m (26,900 ft.)	8230 m (27,000 ft.)
P-6E HAWK	**P-12**	**SISKIN IIIA**

Curtiss Hawk evolution

■ R-6: This specialist air racing machine set a new world speed record in 1922, and inspired the Hawk fighter designs.

■ P-2 HAWK: Curtiss' own V-1400 engine powered the P-2, but it proved disappointing. The aircraft were therefore converted back to P-1As.

■ EXPORT HAWK: Powered by Pratt & Whitney R-1340 radials, 16 of these aircraft were delivered.

■ HAWK P-3: Only five production P-3A Hawks were built. This experimental aircraft has a retractable undercarriage.

91

DE HAVILLAND

DH.18/34

● Commercial airliner ● European flights ● Wooden construction

A irco's first commercial aircraft designed as such from the outset, the DH.18 achieved considerable savings for its operators compared to the ex-military types commonly in use after World War I. Only six were built, but they gave reliable service, mainly on routes between London and the Continent. The DH.18's successor, the DH.34, addressed the main weaknesses of the DH.18 by carrying a greater payload at a higher speed.

▲ For the privileged
passengers who could afford the fare,
the DH.18 and DH.34 allowed weekend trips to
Paris without the need for a long sea crossing.

DE HAVILLAND DH.18/34

Luggage space ▶
Passengers were accommodated in the forward section of the fuselage, with their luggage stored under the pilot's seat. The traditional triangular shaped hatch was used throughout the series.

▲ Airport operations
This DH.34 is fitted with larger mainwheels, which allowed it to operate from less well-equipped airports.

▲ Landing run
An unusually tall undercarriage was installed on the DH.34, which enabled it to make short landing runs. Traditional bungee shock absorbers were replaced with a rubber cord system and offered better performance during rough landings.

▲ Wider horizons
Passengers board an Instone Airline's DH.18 for a flight to the Continent during the 1920s.

Continental service ▶
The first scheduled flights were between Croydon and Paris and took less than 2 hours 40 minutes.

FACTS AND FIGURES

➤ The first de Havilland aircraft to be built at its Stag Lane, Middlesex, factory were the two DH.18Bs.

➤ DH.18s boasted an operating cost of just two shillings and sixpence per ton-mile.

➤ G-EARO, the first DH.18A, flew 144840 km during its airline career.

➤ After its retirement, G-EARO was used for fuel consumption tests by the Royal Aircraft Establishment at Farnborough.

➤ One DH.34 was exported to Russia for service with the airline Dobrolet.

➤ DH.34 G-EAWW was deliberately ditched during flotation tests by the Air Ministry.

PROFILE

Airliners for an expanding industry

Powered by a 336-kW Napier Lion engine, the DH.18 had a standard de Havilland rear fuselage of fabric-covered, wire-braced wooden construction. However, the plywood-covered cabin was revolutionary, with a watertight door in case of a forced landing, and seating for eight people. With seats removed there was room for 7.25 m³ (265 cu. ft.) of cargo, weighing 998 kg (2,195 lb.). The pilot sat in an open cockpit behind the cabin.

The first aircraft flew from Airco's Hendon factory in 1920 and after testing entered service with Aircraft Transport & Travel Ltd flying between Croydon and Paris.

Five DH.18As and Bs (the latter with a higher all-up weight and inertia engine starting) followed, and were operated by Daimler Hire and the Instone Airline. Most were withdrawn from airline use by 1923.

The DH.34 (built by Geoffrey de Havilland's new company, bearing his name) differed from the DH.18 in having a larger fuselage (from the DH.29 10-seater monoplane) and the cockpit was positioned behind the engine. The prototype flew on 22 March 1922 and entered service on the cross-Channel route in April. Eleven were built, 10 of which eventually served with Imperial Airways until 1926. Two were converted to DH.34B standard in 1924/5 by increasing their wing area to reduce their stalling speed.

Left: The large dimensions of the DH.18 allowed a replacement engine to be installed from inside the fuselage

Above: Awaiting its next flight from Croydon Aerodrome, this DH.34 was capable of reaching Paris, Brussels and Cologne on the first regular commercial flights. These aircraft pioneered passenger flights to Europe.

DH.34

Type: early commercial biplane

Powerplant: one 336-kW (450-hp.) Napier Lion in-line piston engine

Maximum speed: 206 km/h (128 m.p.h.)

Maximum cruising speed: 169 km/h (105 m.p.h.)

Landing speed: 112 km/h (70 m.p.h.)

Range: 587 km (364 mi.)

Service ceiling: 4876 m (16,000 ft.)

Weights: empty 2075 kg (4,565 lb.); maximum take-off 3266 kg (7,185 lb.)

Accommodation: 10 passengers and one pilot

Dimensions:
span	15.65 m (51 ft. 4 in.)
length	11.89 m (39 ft.)
height	3.66 m (12 ft.)
wing area	54.81 m² (590 sq. ft.)

Constructed from wood, the two mainplanes were fitted with ailerons operated by an effective differential gear mechanism.

Passengers were seated underneath the pilot away from the noise of the engine. The cabin was accessed via a small triangular door on the starboard side.

The rear fuselage followed de Havilland's established method of construction and consisted of wire bracing around a strengthened wooden box structure.

DH.34

Building on experience gained from the DH.18, de Havilland's DH.34 offered benefits to both travellers and airlines, and began a new era in passenger travel.

Hinged platforms were fitted around either side of the nose to allow the engine to be serviced.

The pilot was seated in an open cockpit above the fuselage. To keep him warm during long overseas flights, hot air was drawn from a muff which surrounded the exhaust pipe.

Rubber cord shock absorbers were installed on each undercarriage leg to allow the aircraft to operate from rough airfields.

With most major airports still in their infancy, flights were often made from grass runways so a tailwheel was rarely installed. Most DH.34s were fitted with a skid.

G-EBBQ DAIMLER HIRE LONDON

ACTION DATA

MAXIMUM SPEED

Many early airliners were ex-military types with low full-load speeds. With the introduction of pure civil designs there was an overall improvement in performance. The DH.34 was faster despite being single engined.

DH.34	206 km/h (128 m.p.h.)
H.P.42	160 km/h (99 m.p.h.)
DH.9C	185 km/h (115 m.p.h.)

RANGE

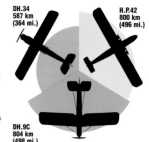

For the expanding market of air travel an aircraft's range was particularly important. As larger designs capable of carrying greater loads and with longer ranges entered service, the less sophisticated types such as the DH.34 and DH.9C were replaced.

DH.34 587 km (364 mi.)

H.P.42 800 km (496 mi.)

DH.9C 804 km (498 mi.)

PASSENGERS

Although still restricted to the rich, a new era of air travel saw larger aircraft carrying increased passenger loads. Compared to the converted DH.9C, the DH.34 offered a respectable lifting capability, but it was a lot smaller than the later H.P.42.

DH.34 10

H.P.42 38

DH.9C 2

Imperial Airways: the early years

■ **A.W. ARGOSY:** Banking over London, an Argosy returns from Paris on one of the first scheduled flights between the two capital cities.

■ **SUPERMARINE SEA EAGLE:** One of the first flying-boats used by Imperial Airways, the Sea Eagle flew to the Channel Islands.

■ **DE HAVILLAND DH.66:** The three engines improved safety margins and increased the lifting capacity of the DH.66.

■ **HANDLEY PAGE W.10:** Awaiting passengers at Croydon in the 1920s, the W.10 offered a much improved capability to Imperial Airways.

DE HAVILLAND

DH.51

● Rare biplane ● Pleasure flights ● Oldest airworthy de Havilland

▲ In the early
1920s, the de Havilland
Company unveiled its DH.51.
A real effort was made to produce an
aircraft for the masses powered by a war
surplus engine. Only three were built.

T his touring biplane could be described
as the aircraft that launched de
Havilland's highly successful Moth
family, the most successful member of
which was the DH.82 Tiger Moth. Using
proven, conventional construction methods,
de Havilland aimed to produce a cheap,
practical, two- or three-seat aircraft and
although only three were built, they helped
prove the concept of 'affordable flying for
the masses' in the 1920s.

DE HAVILLAND DH.51

▼ de Havilland trademark
*Many de Havilland aircraft from the inter-war period
displayed the distinctive tail profile and wing-mounted
fuel tank. This example is operated by the Shuttleworth
Trust alongside* Miss Kenya, *the sole surviving DH.51.*

▲ Grounded
*Initially powered by a surplus
RAF 1A engine, the DH.51
was denied a certificate of
airworthiness because of its
single ignition system.*

Fathering success ▶
*The design of the DH.51 was
unmistakably de Havilland and,
although the aircraft was not a
great commercial success, it led to
the famous Moth series of classic
British biplanes of the late 1920s.*

▼ Flying antique
Since 1965, G-EBIR Miss Kenya, *has been part
of the Shuttleworth Collection in Bedfordshire,
where it is still flown regularly.*

▲ New engine, greater cost
*Ending the prospect of a low-cost DH.51 was the
adoption of a war surplus Renault engine with
redesigned cylinder heads and valve gear.*

FACTS AND FIGURES

➤ The third DH.51, G-EBIR *Miss Kenya*, was
flown after restoration in 1973; it
currently flies with the Shuttleworth
Trust.

➤ Registered G-KAA, *Miss Kenya* was the
first aircraft registered in Kenya.

➤ War surplus RAF 1A engines reputedly
cost 14s 6d (72.5 pence) each.

➤ The first DH.51 was rebuilt in 1924 as a
DH.51A with short-span wings and
automatic camber-changing flaps.

➤ After being sold in Australia, the first
DH.51 was fitted with floats, as a DH.51B.

➤ G-EBIR was restored by apprentices from
Rolls-Royce and Hawker Siddeley.

Forerunner of the Moths

A two-bay biplane with all the hallmarks of a de Havilland design, the DH.51 had a plywood-covered fuselage and was powered by a war surplus, 67-kW (90-hp.) Royal Aircraft Factory (RAF) 1A, air-cooled, eight-cylinder engine, which drove a large, four-bladed, wooden propeller.

This latter feature allowed the DH.51 to climb easily from small fields, an ability that de Havilland felt a small touring aircraft should be able to demonstrate.

With a cruising speed of 140 km/h (84 m.p.h.), the prototype flew for the first time in July 1924, but immediately struck certification problems. The Air Ministry refused to grant the design a Certificate of Airworthiness without changes to the RAF engine. Unwilling to bear the cost, de Havilland instead re-engined the aircraft with an Airdisco engine (itself a Renault wartime design, reworked by the Aircraft Disposal Company to produce 89 kW

(120 hp.). However, this change pushed up the cost of the type; only two more were built.

The first of these took part, along with the prototype, in the 1925 King's Cup Race; both failed to finish. Also in 1925, the third machine flew to Kenya where it remained airworthy until 1937. Stored during World War II, the aircraft was shipped to the UK in 1965 and subsequently restored to flying condition.

Above: Second of the three DH.51s was G-EBIM, which participated in the 1925 King's Cup air race, but did not finish.

Above: Today, the sole airworthy DH.51 remains the oldest de Havilland aircraft still capable of flight. It looks set to continue flying for many years to come.

DH.51

This was the last of the three DH.51s built and also had the most interesting career. It was shipped out to Kenya in late 1925 and was the first aircraft to be registered in the African state. It still flies today.

In late 1924, the DH.51 prototype was retrofitted with new short-span single bay wings. These featured automatic camber altering flaps and proved so successful, that they were retained. Atop the upper wing was the fuel tank, a characteristic of de Havilland designs of the mid- to late 1920s.

The tail unit was a typical de Havilland design and covered in fabric. To keep things as simple as possible, the rudder did not incorporate a trim tab, but made use of a spring actuated elevator.

Intended primarily for pleasure flights, the DH.51 was designed as a three seater, with the pilot sitting at the rear for a clear and unobstructed view.

Originally powering the DH.51 was a 67-kW (90-hp.) RAF 1A eight-cylinder engine. The Air Ministry's dislike of its single ignition prompted the installation of a more powerful Airdisco engine.

Low unit cost was the order of the day and the DH.51 made extensive use of abundant materials, including balsa wood.

MISS KENYA

G-EBIR

G

DH.51

Type: three-seat touring biplane

Powerplant: one 89-kW (120-hp.) Airdisco V8 in-line piston engine

Maximum speed: 174 km/h (108 m.p.h.)

Stalling speed: 69 km/h (43 m.p.h.)

Initial climb rate: 292 m/min (960 f.p.m.)

Range: 579 km (360 mi.)

Service ceiling: 4572 m (15,000 ft.)

Weights: empty 609 kg (1,340 lb.); loaded 1016 kg (2,235 lb.)

Accommodation: one pilot, sitting to the rear, and two passengers

Dimensions:
span	11.28 m (37 ft.)
length	8.08 m (26 ft. 6 in.)
height	2.97 m (9 ft. 9 in.)
wing area	40.32 m² (434 sq. ft.)

ACTION DATA

MAXIMUM SPEED

Once fitted with the Airdisco engine, the DH.51 became a great performer and had the edge on many other contemporary biplanes in terms of speed. It was faster than both the Avro Avian and the Russian Polikarpov Po-2 in level flight.

DH.51	174 km/h (108 m.p.h.)
AVIAN Mk IIIA	164 km/h (102 m.p.h.)
PO-2/U-2	156 km/h (97 m.p.h.)

RANGE

Tailored as it was for long distance flying, it was no surprise that the Avro Avian had a greater range than the other aircraft. The DH.51 had a slightly greater endurance than the Po-2, though the latter was adaptable for military use.

DH.51 579 km (360 mi.)

AVIAN Mk IIIA 643 km (399 mi.)

PO-2/U-2 400 km (248 mi.)

SERVICE CEILING

Compared to the DH.51 and the Po-2, the Avian also had the edge in service ceiling, able to climb to around 5000 m. Compared to the two British designs, the Polikarpov had a poor ceiling, though it was most often flown on low level sorties.

D.H.51 4572 m (15,000 ft.)

AVIAN Mk IIIA 5486 m (18,000 ft.)

PO-2/U-2 4000 m (13,100 ft.)

de Havilland biplanes of the mid-1920s

■ **DH.37:** This aircraft has the significance of being the first private aircraft built by de Havilland. Only two were built.

■ **DH 42:** Developed in response to an Air Ministry requirement for a fighter/reconnaissance aircraft, it did not enter service.

■ **DH.50:** Much larger than the DH.51 these four-seat airliners were used on long-range survey flights to Australia.

DE HAVILLAND

DH.60G GIPSY MOTH 'JASON'

● Record-breaking craft ● Amy Johnson's epic flight ● Preserved today

▲ Amy Johnson took part in a triumphant procession through London on 8 August 1930, with enormous crowds turning out to see her. Pioneer aviators, especially female ones, were extremely popular.

May 1930 was at the height of the era of trail-blazing long-distance flights, but this one was different. Twenty-six-year-old Amy Johnson was planning to fly from England to Australia. Amy had less than one year of solo experience, but as she set off single-handed in her fragile de Havilland Gipsy Moth biplane 'Jason', she faced one of the longest and most adventurous flights ever attempted.

DE HAVILLAND DH.60G GIPSY MOTH 'JASON'

▲ Engine checks
Amy Johnson had to complete all her own maintenance and repairs during her epic flights. Luckily, the small Gipsy engine was a simple one to fix. Johnson was also a talented navigator, plotting her position by means of 'dead reckoning' and a simple compass.

▲ Return from the Cape
Amy Johnson snatched from her husband Jim Mollison the record for flying to the South African Cape in 1932.

▼ A warm welcome
On landing at Darwin, Australia, Amy was greeted by the Australian Government's chief medical officer, who found her fit but tired.

◄ Moth skeleton
The fuselage frame of a Moth was simple, but very strong. The central section of the upper wing contained a fuel tank. The engine installation consisted of a bolted steel tube framework.

Ready to go ►
Amy Johnson waves goodbye just before setting off. She survived fuel shortages, ferocious headwinds, primitive landing strips and a monsoon, She died in a mysterious accident over England in 1941.

FACTS AND FIGURES

➤ Amy Johnson's target was to beat the 15-day record set by Bert Hinkler in 1928.

➤ Her six-day flight to Karachi knocked two days off the previous best time from England to India.

➤ Maintaining her aircraft by night, she averaged only three hours of sleep.

➤ Returning to Britain by Imperial Airways, Amy found herself a national heroine.

➤ Up to one million people lined the streets as her motorcade made its way from Croydon to central London.

➤ King George V made Amy a Commander of the Order of the British Empire (CBE).

PROFILE

Solo to the far side of the world

Amy Johnson set off from Croydon aerodrome on the morning of 5 May 1930. The first day, leaking petrol fumes almost suffocated the intrepid aviatrix. In cloud over Turkey, she almost hit a mountain, and later a sandstorm forced her to land in the desert outside Baghdad. Covering the engine, she stood guard, revolver in hand, in case she was attacked by wild dogs. She reached Karachi on 10 May.

Continuing via Jhansi – where she was forced down by a petrol shortage – Allahabad and Calcutta, she crossed the Bay of Bengal to Burma, where 'Jason' was damaged, putting paid to any chance of the record. It took two days for locals to help her repair the wheels and propellers, but she pressed on – only to disappear over the Timor Sea.

Amy had been forced down on East Timor, but resourceful as ever she managed to persuade a priest and local tribesmen to clear a runway. The last stage of the flight saw her making the 800-km (500-mi.) overwater passage to Port Darwin, which she reached on 24 May after 19 days.

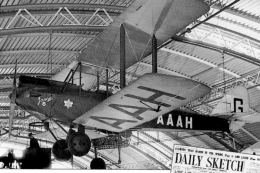

Amy Johnson's valiant little Moth can still be seen today, preserved with other famous aircraft in the aviation hall at London's Science Museum.

SPECIFICATION
DH.60G Gipsy Moth

Type: one-/two-seat light aircraft

Powerplant: one 75-kW (60 hp.) de Havilland Gipsy I four-cylinder piston engine

Maximum speed: 160 km/h (100 km/h)

Cruising speed: 135 km/h (84 m.p.h.)

Range: 520 km (323 mi.) (Amy Johnson's aircraft had extra tanks for a range of about 1100 km (680 mi.))

Service ceiling: 4500 m (14,764 ft.)

Weights: empty 417 kg (919 lb.); loaded 750 kg (1,653 lb.)

Dimensions:
span	9.14 m	(30 ft.)
length	7.29 m	(23 ft. 11 in.)
height	2.68 m	(8 ft. 10 in.)
wing area	22.57 m²	(243 sq. ft.)

The de Havilland company was unusual in building its own engines. The Gipsy series were built because of a shortage of the Cirrus engines previously used in Moths. The Gipsy was extremely reliable – some RAF Chipmunks used 40-year-old Gipsy Majors until 1995.

To extend the range of the standard Gipsy Moth, 'Jason' was fitted with extra fuel tanks. This fuel had to be manually pumped to the top wing tank. Fumes from this tank caused problems for Amy Johnson on several occasions.

The tail profile of the Moth was retained throughout the family, and is still seen in the sky on the many remaining Tiger Moths. The rudder had no trim, requiring constant attention from the pilot to make accurately balanced turns.

AMY JOHNSON

AN ADVENTUROUS LIFE

Born in the English provincial city of Hull, Amy Johnson moved to London in her early 20s. There, she was introduced to flying by a friend and took a job as a typist to help pay for flying lessons. A year after going solo for the first time, she set off on her epoch-making flight to Australia. Hailed as a heroine, she was feted in Australia and on her return to England. Amy, known as 'Johnnie' to her friends, carried on flying and in 1931 made a record breaking flight to Tokyo in another de Havilland Moth. A year later she married fellow aviator Jim Mollison and celebrated by taking 10 hours off his record time to South Africa. In 1936, with her marriage breaking up, she set another record time for the flight to Cape Town, pioneering the route down the West African coast in the process. She then retired from public life. As an experienced pilot and a first-class navigator, she volunteered to join the Air Transport Auxiliary at the outbreak of war in 1939 and ferried combat aircraft from the factories to RAF bases around Britain. In January 1941, at the age of 37, she was flying an Airspeed Oxford, like the one below, which ran out of fuel in thick cloud over the Thames Estuary. Amy's body was never found, but she is thought to have baled out of her stricken aircraft and then died of exposure in the freezing winter waters.

G-AAAH

Jason

The Moth used a fixed-pitch twin-bladed wooden propeller. Only when the Chipmunk arrived in the 1950s did de Havilland trainers use metal propellers.

The wing was built entirely of wood, with a doped fabric covering. This was very strong and light. The control forces on Moths were exceptionally light, and they were very responsive to the controls.

The fuselage structure consisted of a wooden frame with fabric covering. When flying in remote areas this was susceptible to damage, so the DH.60G introduced a metal-tube frame in 1928.

DH.60G GIPSY MOTH 'JASON'

This was the aircraft used by Amy Johnson on her 19-day pioneering flight from England to Australia. The Gipsy Moth was an improved and re-engined version of the original DH.60 of 1925, and began its career by winning the 1928 King's Cup Air Race and setting a new altitude record of 6090 metres.

Blazing the Australian trail

ROSS AND KEITH SMITH: Flying a Vickers Vimy, the Smith brothers reached Australia in December 1919, after a 27-day flight from London.

ALAN COBHAM: Long-range specialist Cobham flew a Giant Moth from London to Melbourne and back between June and October 1926.

BERT HINKLER: The Australian officer made the first lightplane solo flight to Australia in 1928. He was killed on a second attempt in 1933.

MacROBERTSON RACE: Won by Scott and Campbell-Black, whose de Havilland Comet took under three days to reach Melbourne.

NON-STOP: A Qantas Boeing 747 made the first non-stop flight from England to Australia, taking 20 hours on its 1989 delivery flight.

DE HAVILLAND

DH.66 HERCULES

● 1920s mailplane ● Middle East service ● Three engines

E stablishing air mail services to India, and ultimately Australia, was a major goal for Britain in the 1920s. The existing British airlines were amalgamated to form Imperial Airways in 1924, and in 1927 Imperial took over the RAF's route from Cairo to Karachi. A new aircraft was required, and the DH.66 Hercules was selected for the task. The first of five Hercules flew to Egypt in December 1926, ready to start the service the following month.

▲ From 1921
the RAF used DH.9As for the Cairo to Baghdad mail service. When Imperial Airways took it over, they received £87,000 ($130,000) per annum for a fortnightly service.

◀ **Cockpit open to elements**
The first DH.66s had open cockpits. The four machines built for Australia introduced an enclosed cockpit, which was later fitted to earlier machines.

▼ **More than 10 years' service**
Although G-EBMY was withdrawn in 1935, the last South African aircraft served until 1943.

▲ **Joy-rides**
At an air pageant held in Perth in October 1932, a Hercules of West Australian Airways was used for joy-rides at a price of five shillings.

◀ **Imperial's first**
G-EBMW was the first DH.66 to enter service, in January 1927, and was later named City of Cairo by King Faud of Egypt.

G-EBMX arrives in India ▶
Soon after the first Hercules had left for Egypt, the second aircraft arrived in Delhi on 8 January 1927. Two days later the wife of the Viceroy officially named this DH.66 the City of Delhi. Imperial Airways received a subsidy to run a mail service between Cairo and Karachi.

FACTS AND FIGURES

➤ Three engines were specified to minimise the risk of power loss on take-off and during forced landings.

➤ The name 'Hercules' was chosen in a magazine competition run in 1926.

➤ An Australian aircraft in New Guinea was destroyed by Japanese forces in 1942.

➤ South African DH.66s flew courier services throughout Africa during the early days of World War II.

➤ In all, 11 DH.66s were built at de Havilland's Stag Lane, Middlesex, plant.

➤ All 11 Hercules were named after cities in Australia, India and the Middle East.

Imperial's Middle Eastern mailplane

Designed specifically for the Cairo to Karachi route, which Imperial Airways took over from the RAF, the DH.66 entered service in January 1927.

The service from Cairo reached only as far as Basra, in Iraq, until April 1929, when it was extended to Karachi. Later that year it was extended to Delhi. Air mail services had reached Cape Town by January 1932, with DH.66s being used for the journey south of Nairobi.

West Australian Airways

ordered four DH.66s, modified to carry 14 passengers, for use on the Perth to Adelaide route from June 1929. Two of these aircraft were later sold to Imperial Airways, which by this time already had seven aircraft. These two DH.66s were used to establish an air service in New Guinea.

By 1935 four of the Imperial DH.66s had been lost, one of them during a trial mail service to Australia in April 1931. Two more were scrapped, and the remaining three went to the South

Below: West Australian Airways used four DH.66s for its Perth to Adelaide passenger and mail service, which had an express train connection to Melbourne. G-AUJO City of Perth (later VH-UJO) was its first aircraft.

Above: The DH.66 prototype crashed in 1931 while flying between Karachi and Darwin, on an England to Australia mail service.

African air force. In mid-1935 one of these aircraft was used to drop arsenical dust on locust swarms – a far cry from the glory days at Imperial Airways.

DH.66 Hercules

Type: medium-range airliner

Powerplant: three 313-kW (420-hp.) Bristol Jupiter VI nine-cylinder air-cooled radial engines

Maximum speed: 206 km/h (128 m.p.h.)

Cruising speed: 177 km/h (110 m.p.h.)

Initial climb rate: 233 m/min (764 f.p.m.)

Service ceiling: 3962 m (13,000 ft.)

Weights: empty 4110 kg (3,040 lb.); maximum take-off 7103 kg (15,630 lb.)

Accommodation: (Imperial Airways aircraft) three crew, seven passengers and up to 13.2 m³ (466 cu. ft.) of mail

Dimensions: span 24.23 m (79 ft. 6 in.)
length 16.92 m (55 ft. 6 in.)
height 5.56 m (18 ft. 3 in.)
wing area 143.7 m² (1,547 sq. ft.)

Mainplane construction followed standard practice at the time with two wooden box main spars and spruce ribs. After initial flights revealed deficiencies in lateral control, ailerons were fitted to all four wings.

In light of experience in hotter climates, Imperial Airways' standard colour scheme was changed from dark blue to a less heat-absorbent all-over silver dope finish.

DH.66 HERCULES

G-AAJH *City of Basra* was the penultimate Imperial Airways DH.66 and was delivered in late 1929. It was sold to the South African Air Force for £775 ($1,662) in 1934 and was finally scrapped in 1943.

G-AAJH

All 11 Hercules were fitted with three of the reliable Bristol Jupiter nine-cylinder air-cooled radials. These were also used on other Imperial Airways aircraft, like the Handley Page HP.42E.

Two pilots flew the Hercules, and the cabin could hold a wireless operator, seven passengers and up to 13.2 m³ (466 cu. ft.) of mail. Australian DH.66s had sufficient seating for 14 passengers and more mail.

The fuselage was of tubular steel construction with two large plywood boxes suspended inside to form the cabin and luggage compartment. A wooden structure had been abandoned because of the risk of deterioration in tropical conditions.

The DH.66 had a large biplane tail with three fins. Below this, a skid supported the rear fuselage. The aircraft built for West Australian Airways had a tailwheel, but this did not survive rough handling and was removed in service.

ACTION DATA

ENGINE POWER

The Vickers Vanguard was a 20-seat biplane derived from the Vimy bomber and had a slight power advantage over the DH.66. The Argosy, which was also used by Imperial Airways, was built to fill a need for a Middle East transport aircraft, but served in Europe.

DH.66 HERCULES	VANGUARD	ARGOSY II
939 kW (1,260 hp.)	969 kW (1,300 hp.)	917 kW (1,230 hp.)

CRUISING SPEED

Slower than the Vanguard in cruising configuration, the DH.66 had a similar performance to the Argosy, which was also a tri-motored aircraft. All three types were slow even by the standards of the 1930s.

DH.66 HERCULES	177 km/h (110 m.p.h.)
VANGUARD	180 km/h (112 m.p.h.)
ARGOSY II	177 km/h (110 m.p.h.)

PASSENGERS

A contemporary of the DH.66, the Argosy had an impressive passenger cabin capacity. This guaranteed a long service life as the mainstay of Imperial Airways' European fleet until the HP.42 was introduced in 1931. The earlier Vanguard was a one-off design.

DH.66 HERCULES
7 passengers

VANGUARD
20 passengers

ARGOSY II
20 passengers

In Imperial Airways service

■ **AVRO TEN:** Avro's Type 618 was, in fact, a licence-built Fokker F.VIIb-3m. The aircraft was so successful that Imperial bought a number of these eight-seater transports.

■ **HANDLEY PAGE HP.42:** A larger airliner, with specific versions for Imperial's European (HP.42W) and eastern Empire (HP.42E) air routes, this four-engined biplane first flew in 1930.

■ **HANDLEY PAGE W.8B:** Modelled on wartime bombers and powered by two Rolls-Royce Eagle engines, three W.8Bs served on Imperial Airways' London to Paris route from 1924.

DE HAVILLAND

DH.80A PUSS MOTH

● Late 1920s cabin monoplane ● Long-range flights by Jim Mollison

Having designed a cabin monoplane in traditional wood and plywood (the DH.80), de Havilland knew that to gain overseas sales a metal fuselage structure would be necessary. Thus, the DH.80A was flown in 1930. Although marred by early crashes, the Puss Moth's career was notable for worldwide sales and a series of ground-breaking, long-distance flights, some of the most notable being flown by well known aviator, Jim Mollison.

▲ *As private*
flying flourished after 1918 and pilots ventured further afield, aircraft with enclosed cabins became popular. In this respect, the DH.80A was a trend-setter.

PHOTO FILE

DE HAVILLAND **DH.80A PUSS MOTH**

▼ First in Ceylon
Flown by Neville Vincent, G-AAXJ (the sixth production aircraft) became the first aircraft to visit Ceylon (now Sri Lanka) when it arrived there in early 1931. Note the long exhaust pipe under the aircraft's fuselage.

▲ Puss Moth on floats
G-AAVB, the third production Puss Moth, was temporarily fitted with Short floats. It flew the 1674 km (1,040 mi.) from London to the Stockholm Aero Show in 12 hours on 4 September 1930.

Commemorative flight ▶
In 1984, this aircraft was flown from Mildenhall, England to Melbourne, Australia to mark the 50th anniversary of the MacRobertson Air Race, in which a DH.80A took part.

▼ Preserved in Canada
Built in 1931 for the US Naval Air Attaché in London, this aircraft found its way to Canada, where it now resides as a museum exhibit.

▲ Folding wings
The Puss Moth's folding wings were built in two halves and shoulder-mounted to cut down centre-section drag. Shock-absorbing legs on the main undercarriage were attached to the front wingroot fittings.

FACTS AND FIGURES

➤ A Puss Moth in the 1934 MacRobertson Air Race from England to Australia finished third on handicap.

➤ In all, 260 DH.80As were built in England; another 30 were assembled in Canada.

➤ The first trans-Canada return flight was made by a DH.80A.

➤ Amy Mollison (née Johnson) broke her husband's England to South Africa record in a time of 4 days 6 hours 54 mins.

➤ Airworthy DH.80s exist today in the UK and New Zealand.

➤ Several DH.80As were impressed by the RAF in 1939 for communications duties.

PROFILE

Mollison's long-distance Moth

Left: De Havilland designed the DH.80A with a view to improving cabin comfort on long-distance flights.

With private flying flourishing during the 1920s, pilots demanded more cabin comfort as they began to fly longer distances. De Havilland answered the call with the DH.80, a high-wing, wooden monoplane resembling a scaled-down DH.75 Hawk Moth. The Gipsy II engine was modified to run inverted (as the Gipsy III), which improved the pilot's forward view, and the cabin seated two passengers behind the pilot. Only one DH.80 was built. Subsequent production aircraft, known as DH.80A Puss Moths, used a welded steel fuselage structure.

Almost half of the total production run went overseas, initial deliveries going as far afield as Argentina, Japan and New Zealand. Early structural problems (that had resulted in several fatal crashes) were remedied and a second production line was established in Canada. Among notable DH.80A flights were those by Jim Mollison in G-ABXY *The Hearts Content* (fitted with a 727-litre (160-gal.) fuel tank, giving a 5800-km (3,600-mi.) (range) in 1932. After flying from Britain to South Africa (in G-ABKG), he made the first solo east–west crossing of the North Atlantic. In 1933, Mollison flew G-ABXY to South America from England, completing the first solo east–west South Atlantic crossing.

Above: Jim Mollison crosses the Irish coast near Portmarnock Strand on 18 August 1932, bound for the US. Thirty-one hours and 20 minutes later, he arrived in New Brunswick, having made the first solo east-west Atlantic crossing.

DH.80A Puss Moth

Type: three-seat cabin monoplane

Powerplant: one 89.5-kW (120-hp.) de Havilland Gipsy III air-cooled in-line piston engine

Maximum speed: 206 km/h (128 m.p.h.)

Cruising speed: 174 km/h (108 m.p.h.)

Initial climb rate: 186 m/min (610 f.p.m.)

Range: 482 km (300 mi.)

Service ceiling: 5334 m

Weights: empty 574 kg (1,265 lb.); maximum take-off 930 kg (2,050 lb.)

Dimensions:
span	11.20 m	(36 ft. 9 in.)
length	7.85 m	(25 ft. 9 in.)
height	2.52 m	(8 ft. 3 in.)
wing area	20.62 m²	(222 sq. ft.)

A key to the Puss Moth's design was modifying the de Havilland Gipsy II engine to operate inverted, so that its cylinder heads were no longer in the pilot's line of view. This improved the pilot's visibility and allowed a shortened undercarriage design.

A series of fatal crashes in the early 1930s were traced to wing failure during high-speed flight in turbulent weather conditions. A mass-balanced rudder and ailerons helped to cure the problem.

Using what was essentially a scaled-down version of the Hawk Moth's fuselage, the DH.80 Moth Three was of traditional wooden construction with a plywood covering. Experience with the DH.60M biplane convinced de Havilland that metal construction was essential for overseas sales success. The metal design was designated DH.80A and named Puss Moth.

The Hearts Content

G-ABXY

De Havilland's air-cooled, four-cylinder, 89.5-kW (120-hp.) Gipsy III was fitted to production Puss Moths. For a flight from England to South Africa, Amy Mollison had G-ACAB fitted with a 97-kW (130-hp.) Gipsy Major.

For the long-distance flights made by Jim Mollison, G-ABXY was modified with a large 727-litre (160-gal.) fuel tank in the cabin, allowing a 5794-km (3,600-mi.) range. To make room for the tank, the pilot's seat was moved back and the controls suitably modified. The standard cabin doors were removed and a smaller door fitted below the trailing edge of the wing.

DH.80A PUSS MOTH

G-ABXY *The Hearts Content* was Jim Mollison's specially built, long-range DH.80A in which he made a number of landmark transoceanic and transcontinental flights between 1932 and 1933.

Mollison's Puss Moth flights

ENGLAND TO SOUTH AFRICA: On 24 March 1932 Jim Mollison left Lympne, Kent in G-ABKG, en route to South Africa via the Sahara and the west coast of Africa. Cape Town was reached four days, 17 hours and 19 minutes later.

SOLO ACROSS THE ATLANTIC: Taking off on 18 August 1932 in G-ABXY, Mollison made the first solo east-west crossing of the Atlantic Ocean, from Portmarnock, Ireland to Pennfield, New Brunswick, Canada in 31 hours and 20 minutes.

FIRST ENGLAND TO SOUTH AMERICA FLIGHT: Arriving in Port Natal, Brazil on 9 February 1933 – three days, 10 hours and eight minutes after leaving Lympne – Mollison became the first man to fly from England to South America, the first to make a solo east-west crossing of the South Atlantic and the first to cross the North and South Atlantic Oceans. Long-distance Puss Moth G-ABXY was, once again, the record-setting aircraft.

ACTION DATA

CRUISING SPEED

Successive de Havilland designs boasted increased speeds as engine power increased. The basic Moth biplane design was developed in a number of directions during the 1920s and 1930s. To provide a cabin version of the Tiger Moth, the Fox Moth was produced.

DH.80A PUSS MOTH	174 km/h (108 m.p.h.)
DH.60G GYPSY MOTH	137 km/h (85 m.p.h.)
DH.83 FOX MOTH	154 km/h (96 m.p.h.)

RANGE

In standard configuration, the Puss Moth had a modest range performance, in part because of the extra weight of an additional passenger. For long-distance flights, extra fuel tankage was required. The Fox Moth combined passenger accommodation with extra fuel tankage in order to maintain range.

DH.80A PUSS MOTH 482 km (300 mi.)

DH.60G GYPSY MOTH 515 km (320 mi.)

DH.83 FOX MOTH 579 km (360 mi.)

PASSENGERS

As the Puss Moth was, in effect, a scaled-down version of the Hawk Moth, so the Fox Moth was a small version of the Giant Moth, with capacity for four passengers in an enclosed cabin and the pilot in an open cockpit aft. The design was largely made up of standard de Havilland parts, including DH.82 Tiger Moth wings and the DH.80A's nose section.

DH.80A PUSS MOTH	**DH.60G GYPSY MOTH**	**DH.83 FOX MOTH**
2 PASSENGERS	1 PASSENGER	4 PASSENGERS

DE HAVILLAND

DH.82 TIGER MOTH

● Primary trainer ● Overseas service ● Over 8000 built

First flown in October 1931, the DH.82 Tiger Moth was the RAF's standard basic trainer for 15 years. It was based on the earlier Gipsy Moth, but with an inverted engine to improve the forward view and swept-back wings to give it better flying characteristics. Production started soon after the first flight, and the type entered service in February 1932. In 1934 the Mk II replaced the original 89.5-kW (120-hp.) Gipsy engine with the more powerful Gipsy Major.

▲ Thousands of Allied pilots learned their trade on the Tiger Moth. Many flew overseas within the Commonwealth Air Training Plan, while others flew with civilian Elementary and Reserve Flying Training Schools whose aircraft had been impressed into the RAF.

DE HAVILLAND DH.82 TIGER MOTH

▼ de Havilland, Hatfield
Responsibility for Tiger Moth production initially fell to de Havilland, whose Hatfield plant eventually produced 3065 aircraft. In 1941 production at Hatfield was turned over to the Mosquito, with Morris Motors taking over the DH.82.

◄ DH.82B Queen Bee
Sharing wings and undercarriage with the Tiger Moth, the DH.82B featured an all-wood Moth fuselage and was flown remotely as a target aircraft.

▼ Training colours
Wearing Dark Earth/Dark Green camouflage over RAF Trainer Yellow, this preserved Tiger Moth is flown at UK air shows.

◄ Aerobatic trainer
This early DH.82 is seen without the anti-spin strakes which were fitted ahead of the tailplanes on later aircraft. All Tiger Moths were cleared for aerobatics at a maximum weight of 794 kg (1,750 lb.).

Landing the Tiger ►
In the UK the majority of Tiger Moths were flown with wheeled landing gear; Canadian aircraft also used floats or skis.

FACTS AND FIGURES

➤ During 1939–40 a number of Tiger Moths were fitted with bomb racks for use as anti-submarine aircraft.

➤ Canadian aircraft had large, glazed cockpit covers for cold-weather flying.

➤ Seven Tiger Moths were converted to Queen Bee standard early in the war.

➤ Five DH.82 Tiger Moths gave a display of inverted formation flying at the 1932 Hendon Air Display.

➤ The redesigned Canadian aircraft were known as DH.82C Tiger Moths.

➤ Many Canadian aircraft were powered by Menasco Pirate engines.

PROFILE

Tiger Moth – training the Empire

There were more than 1000 Tiger Moths in service by the start of World War II and the demand for pilot training led to another 4200 being produced in Britain during the course of the conflict.

Nearly 3000 more were built in Australia, Canada and New Zealand under the terms of the Commonwealth Air Training Plan (CATP), and some of the Canadian-built machines were used by the US Army Air force with the designation PT-24. As the war progressed, most RAF pilot training under the CATP was carried out overseas, but large numbers of Tiger Moths were used in Britain for screening volunteers. There were 28 elementary flying schools, each with about 100 Tiger Moths, where would-be pilots received 12 hours of instruction to see if they were suitable candidates for further, expensive training.

It was not until 1948 that the Tiger Moth's replacement entered service in the form of the Percival Prentice. The Tiger Moth remained in service with reserve squadrons until its replacement by the de Havilland Canada Chipmunk. Many of the surplus aircraft were sold subsequently to flying clubs and civilian flying schools all over the world.

Above: When piloted solo, the Tiger Moth was flown from the rear cockpit, normally occupied by the student.

Below: A number of aircraft flew with the Royal Australian Air Force. This Australian-built DH.82A clearly shows the blind flying hood retracted behind the rear cockpit.

For the DH.82A, de Havilland replaced the traditional fabric-and-stringers construction of the rear fuselage with plywood. The older method was retained on the rudder.

DH.82A Tiger Moth Mk II

Type: elementary trainer

Powerplant: one 97-kW 130-hp. de Havilland Gipsy Major four-cylinder, air-cooled in-line piston engine

Maximum speed: 175 km/h (109 m.p.h.) at 305 m (1,000 ft.)

Initial climb rate: 194 m/min (636 f.p.m.) at sea level

Range: 486 km (302 mi.)

Service ceiling: 4145 m (13,600 ft.)

Weights: empty 506 kg (1,116 lb.); maximum take-off 803 kg (1,770 lb.)

Accommodation: two: student in rear cockpit with blind flying hood and instructor forwards

Dimensions:
span	8.94 m	(29 ft. 4 in.)
length	7.29 m	(23 ft. 11 in.)
height	2.68 m	(8 ft. 10 in.)
wing area	22.20 m²	(239 sq. ft.)

An 86.4-litre (19-gal.) fuel tank was fitted above the centre-section of the upper wing. The Queen Bee used a 114-litre (25-gal.) tank for extra endurance, which was fitted to several war-surplus DH.82As.

De Havilland moved all of the centre-section struts forward of the front cockpit to clear the instructor's escape route in the event of an in-flight emergency.

DH.82A TIGER MOTH MK II

This aircraft wears colours typical of any of the RAF's Elementary Flying Training Schools. Some 4668 Tiger Moths were built in Britain for the RAF, 3433 of them by Morris Motors at Cowley near Oxford.

R-5130

Canadian aircraft featured a modified undercarriage, which was moved further forwards to prevent nosing-over when the wheel brakes, specific to Canada's Tiger Moths, were applied.

Sweeping back the wings obviated handling problems caused by large movements in centre of gravity position. This gave the Tiger Moth excellent flying characteristics and made it one of the world's greatest training aircraft.

By the time of its retirement in the mid-to-late 1950s, the Tiger Moth was a relic from another era. Control wires ran from the control surfaces and along the fuselage sides, just as they had done on the previous generation of military biplanes. The DH.82A was the RAF's last biplane trainer.

Most Tiger Moths were fitted with a simple tail skid, but DH.82Cs had a substantial tail wheel. It improved ground handling and was easily replaced by a ski. Training in Canada continued all year round.

ACTION DATA

POWER

By far the least powerful of these aircraft, the DH.82A was in fact more powerful than the earlier DH.82. As evidenced by the many DH.82As still flying, the aircraft had more than adequate power.

DH.82A TIGER MOTH	PT-17 KAYDET	Ar 66C
97 kW (130 hp.)	164 kW (220 hp.)	179 kW (240 hp.)

SERVICE CEILING

Despite its low power, the DH.82A had a greater service ceiling than the Stearman PT-17. Arado's Ar 66C seems to have been unnecessarily powerful for the primary training role.

DH.82A TIGER MOTH
4145 m (13,600 ft.)

PT-17 KAYDET
4023 m (13,200 ft.)

Ar 66C
4500 m (14,760 ft.)

RANGE

Range was of only minor importance, especially for Tiger Moth pilots flying from vast Canadian bases when almost all training could be carried out within the base perimeter. Many Tiger Moths received larger fuel tanks post-war.

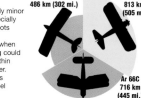

DH.82A TIGER MOTH
486 km (302 mi.)

PT-17 KAYDET
813 km (505 mi.)

Ar 66C
716 km (445 mi.)

World War II biplane trainers

■ **ARADO AR 66:** Initially delivered in only limited numbers, the Ar 66C version of Arado's 1932 design saw extensive Luftwaffe service as a trainer.

■ **BÜCKER BÜ 131 JUNGMANN:** Entering service during 1935, the Bü 131 was an excellent basic trainer. Later, some Bü 131s joined Ar 66s in night harassment units.

■ **FOCKE-WULF FW 44 STIEGLITZ:** Work on the Stieglitz (Goldfinch) began under the leadership of Kurt Tank during 1931. Fw 44Cs served the Luftwaffe throughout the war.

■ **STEARMAN PT-17 KAYDET:** One of the most important US elementary trainers, 2942 examples of the PT-17 were built for the US Army Air Force alone.

DE HAVILLAND

DH.89 DRAGON RAPIDE

● Pocket airliner ● Vintage design ● Fabric and fretwork

Designed in the 1930s, the de Havilland DH.89 Dragon Rapide was one of many reasonably successful light commercial transports of the era. But the outbreak of war was to see production soar to keep pace with demand for communications and navigation trainers. After the war, hundreds of ex-service aircraft came onto the market, and the faithful old biplane was to become an important part of the post-war boom in commercial aviation, flying in a multitude of roles from scheduled airliner to fun flier.

▲ The Rapide was a versatile machine capable of many tasks. RAF versions flew as ambulances with two stretchers in a modified fuselage, and others fought local tribesmen in Iraq.

DE HAVILLAND DH.89 DRAGON RAPIDE

▲ Best of British
The Dragon Rapide served with British Airways after the airline bought up many small regional airlines.

Ancient cockpit ▶
Although the Rapide and its relatives served into the 1960s, the spartan cockpit was an ever-present reminder of the biplane's true age.

Gipsy power ▲
The little Gipsy Major was a four cylinder inline air-cooled engine, delivering about 97 kW (130 hp.). The later Gipsy Six delivered 149 kW (200 hp.), and with the extra power allied to a certain amount of streamlining late-model DH.89As could reach a speed of 253 km/h (157 m.p.h.).

▼ Navigator trainer
Military navigation and communication trainers were known as Dominies. These were almost the same as civil models, except for the loop aerial and green paint.

▲ In the Navy
The Royal Navy used Dominies for training duties, and they could still be found as station flight communications aircraft into the 1960s, when they were replaced by Devons.

FACTS AND FIGURES

➤ The prototype DH.84 flew for the first time on 24 November 1932.

➤ The Rapide was proposed as a coastal patrol aircraft, and saw combat as a light bomber in the Spanish Civil War.

➤ Float- and ski-equipped Rapides could be found in Canada, Chile and New Zealand.

➤ The very first Rapide was sold to Switzerland, where for 30 years it flew skiers from Zürich to St Moritz.

➤ During World War II more than 180 DH.89s were produced each year.

➤ The Royal Navy used DH.89s into the 1960s, mainly for cadet training.

PROFILE

The fretwork airliner

The DH.89A was a twin-engined development of the high-performance DH.84 Dragon. First flying in April 1934, its reliability and economy proved popular with small airlines. Officially called the Dragon Rapide but known to most of its users simply as the Rapide, it was soon in world-wide use with operators from the tropics to the high Arctic, and by the outbreak of war

more than 200 had been built.

World War II increased demand for the aircraft, and 521 were completed as de Havilland Dominie navigation trainers. After the war, several hundred surplus machines were supplied to overseas air forces and, stripped of military equipment, to civil buyers.

After the war Rapides could be found working for major government and commercial

organisations, small charter airlines and air taxi companies. They shipped freight in the South American interior, flew businessmen to important meetings around Europe, took tourists on pleasure trips over the Florida Everglades, and maintained island-hopping commercial services in areas as diverse as Scotland's outer isles and the volcanic chains of French Polynesia.

The reason the Rapide remained in service for so long is that many examples were bought at bargain prices after the war, and they proved very economical in operation.

DH.89A Dragon Rapide

Type: six-/eight-seat commercial transport

Powerplant: two 149-kW (200-hp.) de Havilland Gipsy Queen inline piston engines

Cruising speed: 217 km/h (132 m.p.h.)

Range: 950 km (578 mi.)

Service ceiling: 5950 m (19,500 ft.)

Weights: empty 1485 kg (3,267 lb.); loaded 2500 kg (5,500 lb.)

Accommodation: one or two crew, six to eight passengers

Dimensions:
span	14.63 m	(48 ft.)
length	10.52 m	(34 ft. 6 in.)
height	3.12 m	(10 ft. 3 in.)
wing area	31.2 m²	(336 sq. ft.)

DH.89A DRAGON RAPIDE

The de Havilland Rapide served with British European Airways after the war, with 45 examples in service from 1947. They served on British domestic routes, notably around the Scottish Highlands and Islands.

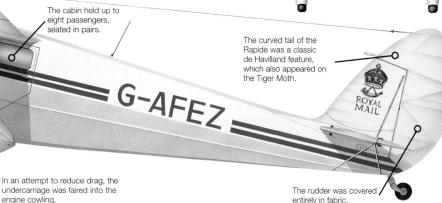

Cockpits were generally of single-pilot configuration, with a very basic standard of instruments and controls.

Rapides were driven by two-blade fixed-pitch wooden propellers. The rear of each engine nacelle contained a 273-litre (72-gal.) fuel tank.

The main structure of the Dragon Rapide was a spruce and birch framework with light alloy and fabric skin.

The cabin held up to eight passengers, seated in pairs.

The curved tail of the Rapide was a classic de Havilland feature, which also appeared on the Tiger Moth.

BRITISH EUROPEAN AIRWAYS

G-AFEZ

ROYAL MAIL

The Rapides used Gipsy Six and Gipsy Major engines. The Gipsy Major engine was also used in the post-war de Havilland Chipmunk trainer.

In an attempt to reduce drag, the undercarriage was faired into the engine cowling.

The rudder was covered entirely in fabric.

ACTION DATA

MAXIMUM SPEED

The Rapide was in many ways an anachronism, since all-metal monoplane airliners like the Boeing 247 had been flying in America since 1930. But the Rapide was simple to fly, easy to maintain and had excellent short-field capability.

DH.89A DRAGON RAPIDE	217 km/h (132 m.p.h.)
MODEL 247	304 km/h (188 m.p.h.)
LOCKHEED 10	325 km/h (201 m.p.h.)

RANGE

Unlike its bigger DH.86 cousin, the Rapide was designed for short-haul operations. Its range could not match more advanced designs, but it was enough for domestic flights in Britain and around the world, and it was very economical to run.

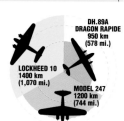

DH.89A DRAGON RAPIDE 950 km (578 mi.)

LOCKHEED 10 1400 km (1,070 mi.)

MODEL 247 1200 km (744 mi.)

PAYLOAD

Early air travel was expensive, and few could afford it. As a result, small airliners of the 1930s could only carry as many passengers as business aircraft of today.

DH.89A DRAGON RAPIDE 8 passengers

MODEL 247 10 passengers

LOCKHEED 10 10 passengers

---

de Havilland airliners of the 1930s

■ **DH.84 DRAGON:** First flown in 1932, the Dragon was a simple wood-and-fabric biplane identifiable from later aircraft by its exposed wheels.

■ **DH.86 EXPRESS AIR LINER:** Basically an enlarged four-engined Dragon, the D.H.86 entered service from Singapore to Brisbane in 1934.

■ **DH.90 DRAGONFLY:** A smaller version of the Rapide, the four-passenger Dragonfly flew in 1936. It had a wooden monocoque fuselage.

■ **DH.91 ALBATROSS:** Designed as a luxurious high-speed inter-continental transport, the graceful Albatross took to the air in 1937.

■ **DH.95 FLAMINGO:** The company's first all-metal design, the 18-seater D.H.95 was completed just before the start of World War II.

DE HAVILLAND CANADA

DHC-2 BEAVER

● Rugged dependability ● Short take-off and landing

F lying in the frozen north presents a real challenge. It takes a very special aircraft to slip into narrow fjords on floats, or to take off from a glacier using skis. Whether you are a cargo hauler delivering people and supplies to remote communities or a policeman enforcing the law over thousands of square kilometres of trackless wilderness, you need an aircraft like the remarkable Canadian de Havilland Beaver to do the job.

▲ The Beaver is a classic wild-country floatplane. It has an immensely tough high-wing airframe with a capacious cabin, and is powered by a rugged and dependable radial engine.

DE HAVILLAND CANADA **DHC-2 BEAVER**

Fishing trip ▶
The annual salmon season brings thousands of well-heeled anglers to the rivers and lakes of Canada. Very often, the only way to the best waters is by Beaver.

▼ On the water
New rules apply when you fly from water. Apart from the obvious like avoiding floating debris on take-off, pilots have to learn tricks such as using the propeller thrust and water rudder to prevent the aircraft 'weather cocking' into wind.

▲ Flying in the wilderness
The Beaver has been plying its trade over the lakes, forests and mountains of Canada's northern wilderness and other countries for nearly 50 years.

◀ Forest fire
The basic concept of the Beaver as a high-wing, STOL-capable transport has been expanded to produce the larger DHC-3 Otter. Both designs have been adapted as fire-bombers, using specially modified floats to scoop up water from lakes.

▲ Amphibian
Deploying wheels within its floats, the versatile Beaver can land on runways. Landing on lakes is actually easier than using a normal runway.

FACTS AND FIGURES

➤ The prototype Beaver made its first flight on 16 August 1947.

➤ Its five-hour endurance makes the slow-flying Beaver ideal for wilderness search-and-rescue missions.

➤ Sixty enlarged, 10-passenger turboprop-powered Beaver IIIs were produced.

➤ The Beaver inspired a larger cousin, the 14-passenger DHC-3 Otter, also widely used for bush flying in the Arctic.

➤ Civil and military DHC-2s have been operated by 65 countries.

➤ More than 1700 Beavers were produced between 1947 and 1965.

PROFILE

Flying in grizzly bear country

The Royal Canadian Mounted Police set an example for all when they carry out bush flying missions with the sturdy DHC-2 Beaver. Designed in 1946-47, the Beaver was tailor-made for adventurous flying under harsh conditions.

With its ability to use wheels, skis, floats or amphibious pontoons, the Beaver can go just about everywhere. Bush pilots use the DHC-2 to haul provisions to remote locations, both in summer and in winter, when temperatures in northern Canada can be as low as minus 40°C (-40°F).

At the height of its career, the Beaver could be found hard at work in every continent, including Antarctica. Superb short take-off ability means that it can operate in remote locations that other aircraft would find impossible.

It is that quality which even now, half a century after its first flight, makes the DHC-2 Beaver a highly effective bush transport.

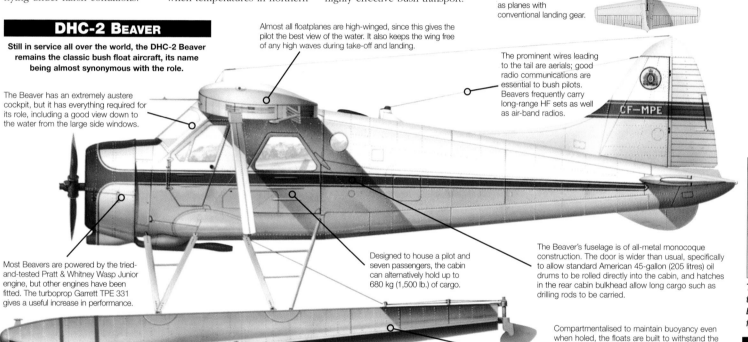

The Beaver's long, straight wing configuration gives it a good short take-off capability. This design feature was retained for its larger brother, the DHC-3 Otter.

In plan view, the huge area of the twin floats is immediately apparent. While essential for water operations, they cause a lot of drag in flight. This is why floatplanes are never as fast or as economical as planes with conventional landing gear.

DHC-2 BEAVER

Still in service all over the world, the DHC-2 Beaver remains the classic bush float aircraft, its name being almost synonymous with the role.

The Beaver has an extremely austere cockpit, but it has everything required for its role, including a good view down to the water from the large side windows.

Almost all floatplanes are high-winged, since this gives the pilot the best view of the water. It also keeps the wing free of any high waves during take-off and landing.

The prominent wires leading to the tail are aerials; good radio communications are essential to bush pilots. Beavers frequently carry long-range HF sets as well as air-band radios.

Most Beavers are powered by the tried-and-tested Pratt & Whitney Wasp Junior engine, but other engines have been fitted. The turboprop Garrett TPE 331 gives a useful increase in performance.

Designed to house a pilot and seven passengers, the cabin can alternatively hold up to 680 kg (1,500 lb.) of cargo.

The Beaver's fuselage is of all-metal monocoque construction. The door is wider than usual, specifically to allow standard American 45-gallon (205 litres) oil drums to be rolled directly into the cabin, and hatches in the rear cabin bulkhead allow long cargo such as drilling rods to be carried.

Compartmentalised to maintain buoyancy even when holed, the floats are built to withstand the severe pounding they get on take-off and landing. They have small retractable rudders, and are fitted with bilge pumps to flush out the water that inevitably finds its way through joints and seams.

DHC-2 Beaver

Type: light utility transport

Powerplant: one 936-kW (1.255-hp.) Pratt & Whitney R-985 Wasp Junior radial piston engine

Maximum speed: 262 km/h (163 m.p.h.) at 1524 m (5000 ft.)

Range: 1180 km (733 mi.)

Service ceiling: 5485 m (18,000 ft.)

Weights: empty 1923 kg (4,240 lb.); loaded 2313 kg (5,100 lb.)

Accommodation: pilot and up to seven passengers, or 680 kg (1,500 lb.) of freight on strengthened cabin floor

Dimensions:
span	14.63 m (48 ft.)	
length	9.22 m (30 ft. 3 in.)	
height	2.74 m (9 ft.)	
wing area	23.22 m² (250 sq. ft.)	

The Royal New Zealand Air Force, one of more than 20 air arms to use the type, used ski-fitted Beavers to patrol the snow-covered peaks and fjords of the country's South Island.

ACTION DATA

PAYLOAD

Light aircraft are a key to communications in wilderness areas, and the most successful aircraft are those that can be modified to carry cargo as well as passengers. The popular aircraft of the Cessna 180 series are, like the Beaver, landplanes which can be fitted with floats. The Buccaneer is by contrast a flying-boat, whose hull provides the buoyancy in water.

DHC-2 BEAVER
7 passengers or 680 kg (1,500 lb.) of cargo

CESSNA 185
5 passengers or 360 kg (794 lb.) of cargo

LA-4 BUCCANEER
5 passengers plus baggage

Water manoeuvres

PLOUGH TURN:
Floatplanes, like sailboats, will turn into the wind if left to themselves. To turn across the wind, you need to use a lot of engine power. This pulls the nose high, digging the rudders deep into the water. A small turn to the right allows the rudders to have more effect.

SAILING FLOATPLANES:
In strong wind, you can use two methods to manoeuvre from A to B:
1 Use engine power to taxi across the wind, then trim and cut power and sail backwards.
2 Drift backwards and then use power in combination with the wind to travel sideways.

METHOD 1
Use power and wind to travel sideways

A

Sail backwards

Sail backwards

METHOD 2
Use power and wind to travel sideways

B

STRONG WIND

DORNIER

DO J WAL

● Flying-boat ● Transatlantic aircraft ● Deutsche Luft-Hansa mailplane

Dornier's Wal was a superb flying-boat that was probably the most important aircraft designed by Dornier in the 1920s. This big craft established a flying-boat configuration of classic lines that was to endure, in refined form, for many years. With its broad, metal, two-step hull the Wal was also one of the most advanced flying-boats in the world in its era, operating on long-distance flights as far afield as South America and Africa.

▲ With its tandem engines, open cockpit and broad wing, the Wal was an instantly recognisable design. Despite being clumsy and heavy, it set several range, payload and distance records in the 1930s and was exported to several countries, including Argentina.

DORNIER DO J WAL

▲ Arctic Wal
In the hands of intrepid pilots like Wolfgang von Gronau and Roald Amundsen, Wals ranged across the world's vast oceans. von Gronau's 1932 record flight to New York took him over the North Atlantic and the Arctic Circle.

Taifun take-off ▶
Like ships or modern airliners, Wals were given individual names. This Deutsche Luft-Hansa Wal, 'Taifun', is ready for deck launch.

▲ Wal on the stocks
Although most Wals were built in Italy, 56 examples were produced by Dornier at its factory in Friedrichsafen.

▼ Ship launch
Wals were even carried and launched from civil liners. This Deutsche Luft-Hansa aircraft was launched from the Schlebenland.

▲ Lion heart
This aircraft is a Wal 40, powered by British Napier Lion engines. Power for the series ranged from 223.6-kW (300-hp.) to 559-kW (750-hp.) engines.

FACTS AND FIGURES

➤ On 18 August 1930, Wolfgang von Gronau flew a Wal from List to New York in 44 hours 25 minutes.

➤ The Italian-built prototype Wal made its first flight on 6 November 1922.

➤ About 300 Wals were manufactured before production stopped in the 1930s.

➤ One aircraft downed on the ice in the Arctic was rebuilt under difficult conditions and reflown.

➤ Wal services from Stuttgart to Buenos Aires began on 3 February 1934.

➤ The Wal was used in the Spanish Civil War by the Nationalist forces.

Dornier's whale takes to the sea

Built in Italy to get around restrictions placed on Germany after World War I, the Dornier Do J Wal flying-boat soon proved a commercial success and was used on European and international civil routes. Some were built in Japan, Netherlands, Spain and Switzerland before German production began at Friedrichshafen in 1933.

The Wal's star status as a heavy lifter was demonstrated in February 1925 when it set 20 world-class records with payloads of 250 to 2000 kg (550 to 4,400 lb.). That year, explorer Roald Amundsen took two Wals to the North Pole. Wals also featured in a round-the-world flight during 1932, and a record-breaking flight from Germany to New York. In 1934, Do Js began a mail service from Germany to South America.

By the mid-1930s, the Wal was supplemented by the Do R SuperWal, with greater wing span and a longer fuselage. In addition to production by

Dornier, Super Wals were built in several countries. They gave valuable service to a number of airlines, including Deutsche Luft-Hansa, predecessor of today's Lufthansa. In this capacity they were launched from specially fitted-out ships, which served as refuelling bases.

The Wal was succeeded by the Do R2 SuperWal with four engines and which could accommodate more passengers.

Above: This Wal 1 was produced in Italy, with a BMW licence-built Rolls-Royce Eagle engine. The Wal was manufactured by SCMP and its successor CMASA, a Fiat subsidiary.

Left: The 10-ton Wal of 1933 was used by Deutsche Luft-Hansa. Flying from the depot ships Westfalen and Schlebenland, they made 328 crossings of the South Atlantic on regular long-distance mail flights.

Do R2 SuperWal

Type: four-engined commercial flying-boat

Powerplant: four 391-kW (525-hp.) Siemens built Bristol Jupiter radial piston engines (Do R4); four 268-kW (360-hp.) Rolls-Royce Eagle IX engines (Spanish Navy Wals)

Maximum speed: 210 km/h (130 m.p.h.)

Cruising speed: 161 km/h (100 m.p.h.)

Range: 1000 km (620 mi.) with maximum payload

Weights: empty 9850 kg (21,670 lb.); maximum take-off 14,000 kg (30,800 lb.)

Accommodation: two pilots, nine to 19 passengers

Dimensions:
span	28.60 m	(93 ft. 10 in.)
length	24.60 m	(80 ft. 8 in.)
height	6.00 m	(19 ft. 8 in.)
wing area	137 m²	(1,474 sq. ft.)

Do R2 SuperWal

Dornier built 16 of the four-engined SuperWals, this one (D-1337 'Pottwal') being the only one powered by Napier Lion engines. The others had Siemens-built Bristol Jupiter air-cooled radial engines.

One of the imperfections of the Wal design was the very broad wingtip which caused high induced drag. This inhibited its impressive range.

The aerofoil-shaped float sponsons gave the Wal extra stability on water.

Flying the first Wals in cold weather required a lot of determination. The later models at least had an enclosed cockpit.

The tandem engine configuration was most unusual. Although it offered lower drag than separate engines, the rear propeller often felt the strain of the airstream from the forward engine. Various engines were fitted to Wals, including Hispano Suiza 42, Rolls-Royce Eagle, Liberty 42, Napier Lion, BMW VI, Jupiter IV, Lorraine Dietrich, Isotta Fraschini and Fiat R.22.

LUFT HANSA POTTWAL

D-1337

Deutsche Luft-Hansa Wals always had the aircraft's name painted on the front of the hull.

Dornier had a reputation for building very seaworthy flying-boat hulls and the Wals were no exception, as pilot Wolfgang von Gronau proved when landing on rough seas in Greenland.

The cabin was very luxurious and had boat-style portholes.

The long rear fuselage and triangular tail shape was a distinct Dornier trademark. This was retained on the later Do 18 flying-boat used in World War II.

ACTION DATA

MAXIMUM SPEED

Speed was not an outstanding feature of bulky and underpowered flying-boats. Wals at least had more powerful engines to offset this, as did the Beriev MP-1.

Do R2 SUPERWAL 210 km/h (130 m.p.h.)

SEA EAGLE 149 km/h (92 m.p.h.)

MP-1 214 km/h (133 m.p.h.)

PASSENGER CAPACITY

Little could compare with the mighty Wals; even the earlier versions could carry up to nine passengers compared to six in the Sea Eagle and MP-1.

Do R2 SUPERWAL 19 PASSENGERS

SEA EAGLE 6 PASSENGERS

MP-1 6 PASSENGERS

RANGE

The Superwals had very impressive range. The Beriev MP-1 was a similar configuration aircraft, with a powerful engine. The Sea Eagle was a much smaller aircraft and had shorter range.

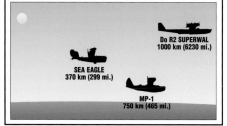

Do R2 SUPERWAL 1000 km (6230 mi.)

SEA EAGLE 370 km (299 mi.)

MP-1 750 km (465 mi.)

Transatlantic record flight

In July 1932 a Wal piloted by von Gronau broke the Transatlantic record. He subsequently made the first round-the-world flight in a flying-boat, taking 111 days.

1 LIST-SYLT: Wolfgang von Gronau set out from List-Sylt on 22 July 1932. He made his first stop in the Faroe Islands, refuelled and set off for Iceland.

2 FROZEN NORTH: He stopped again in Iceland's Seydis Fjord, after flying across the North Sea. The next stop was Ivitgut Fjord in Greenland.

3 NEW YORK: Finally sighting the coast of Newfoundland, von Gronau landed in Labrador and after refuelling he set off for New York, landing just over 44 hours after leaving Germany.

DORNIER

Do X

● Pioneering flying-boat ● Largest aircraft of its time

T oday, it is the haunt of holidaying sailors and windsurfers. But in 1929 Lake Constance was the home of the world's largest aeroplane. Created by the legendary designer Dr Claudius Dornier as a trans-Atlantic passenger carrier, the huge 12-engined Dornier Do X was a marginal performer which was never to be a commercial proposition. But it pushed back the boundaries of aviation.

▲ The appropriately-named Richard Wagner, Dornier's chief test pilot, was behind the huge control wheel of the titanic flying-boat for its first flight.

DORNIER Do X

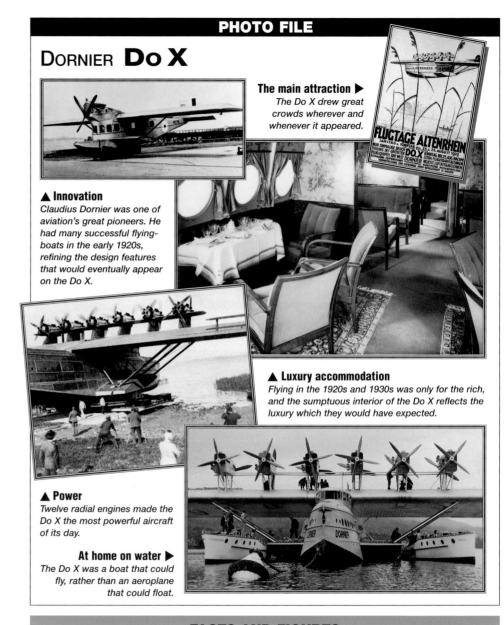

The main attraction ▶
The Do X drew great crowds wherever and whenever it appeared.

▲ Innovation
Claudius Dornier was one of aviation's great pioneers. He had many successful flying-boats in the early 1920s, refining the design features that would eventually appear on the Do X.

▲ Luxury accommodation
Flying in the 1920s and 1930s was only for the rich, and the sumptuous interior of the Do X reflects the luxury which they would have expected.

▲ Power
Twelve radial engines made the Do X the most powerful aircraft of its day.

At home on water ▶
The Do X was a boat that could fly, rather than an aeroplane that could float.

FACTS AND FIGURES

➤ The Do X's record passenger load stood at a crew of 10, 150 invited passengers, and nine stowaways.

➤ In its initial form, the Do X took a snail-like 20 minutes to reach a height of 600 metres (2,000 ft.).

➤ The wings were thick enough to allow an engineer access to the engines.

➤ On one attempted flight, the Do X ran for 13 km (8 miles) without being able to lift off.

➤ Even with more powerful engines, the Do X cruised at a leisurely 175 km/h (110 m.p.h.).

➤ The Do X was in the air for a total of 211 hours on its maiden transatlantic voyage – spread over a period of 19 months!

Transatlantic Titan

The only revolutionary thing about the massive Dornier Do X was its size. But this alone represented a huge leap into the unknown.

At 56 tons all-up weight, it was by far the largest aircraft in the world. But in spite of having more power than any aircraft of its time, the Do X was never more than a marginal performer. The huge flying-boat was painfully slow, and took an age to reach its meagre operating height of less than 1250 metres (3,300 ft.).

But the Do X represented Germany's reappearance on the world aviation stage, only a decade after its industry had been dismantled at the end of World War I. And that rebirth was celebrated by an epoch-making maiden voyage, from Europe to Africa, across the Atlantic to South America, and on to New York and back.

The Do X lifts majestically from the surface of Lake Constance on the morning of 12 July 1929.

The huge machine was eventually handed over to Lufthansa, but the airliner was not commercially viable, and never took any fare-paying passengers. It was to end its days in a Berlin museum and was destroyed in an air raid in 1945.

The Do X's successful, if delayed, flight to New York gave a great boost to the German aircraft industry, which was recovering from the crippling blow of World War I.

Do X

Type: experimental passenger flying-boat

Powerplant: 12 450-kW (660-hp.) Curtiss Conqueror nine-cylinder radial engines

Maximum speed: 210 km/h (130 m.p.h.); cruising speed 175 km/h (110 m.p.h.)

Time to height: 14 minutes to 1000 m (3,280 ft.)

Maximum range: 2200 km (1,370 mi.)

Service ceiling: 1250 m (4,100 ft.)

Weights: empty 32,675 kg (72,040 lb.); loaded 56,000 kg (123,406 lb.)

Payload: 15,325 kg (33,790 lb.), comprising 14 crew, 66 passengers; record flight from Lake Constance, 10 crew, 150 passengers and nine stowaways – a total of 169 people

Dimensions:
span	48.00 m	(157 ft. 5 in.)
length	40.05 m	(131 ft. 2 in.)
height	10.10 m	(33 ft. 1 in.)
wing area	250 m²	(2,690 sq. ft.)

DO X 'MONSTER OF THE SEA'

Dornier's huge flying-boat was an attempt to revolutionise air transport. Unfortunately ambition outstripped available technology, and it was not a success.

The pilot of the Do X sat at the front of the upper deck, behind a large steering-wheel. Smaller wheels controlled trim in flight and the rudder in the water.

The Do X had 12 engines in six nacelles above the wing. The wing was thick enough for a crawlspace, which led to ladders up to each nacelle, allowing engineers free access to the engines, even in flight.

The upper deck was occupied by the flight engineer, navigators, maintenance technicians and radio operators.

The Do X was originally powered by 12 British-designed Bristol Jupiter radial engines, but for the Atlantic crossing they were replaced by 12 slightly more powerful Curtiss Conquerors.

D-1929

Passengers were carried in two cabins fore and aft of the wing leading edge. The bar and smoking room were in the bow, and the galley was at the rear. Baggage was stowed aft of the galley.

The Do X was fitted with a rudder at the rear of the keel to enable the aircraft to be steered while on the water.

The hull and wing of the Do X was of all-metal construction, but the heavy weight and lack of power meant that it could never reach its designed operating altitude.

Large tail surfaces gave the Do X fair stability. For added control, an extra horizontal tailplane was attached to the fuselage.

With the Do X across the Atlantic

■ **DEPARTURE:** The trip was made in easy stages, with calls at seaplane bases at Amsterdam (left) and Calshott in the south of England. Wherever the Do X went, it drew sightseeing crowds.

■ **WEST AFRICA:** In spite of its huge fuel load the Do X had limited range, so the Atlantic crossing had to be made at its narrowest point. On 3 June 1931 the Do X set off from Portuguese Guinea.

■ **FLYING DOWN TO RIO:** Seventeen days later, the Do X reached Rio de Janeiro. The widest part of the crossing, from the Cape Verde Islands to Fernando Noronha, took 13 hours.

■ **WELCOME TO NEW YORK:** Over the next eight weeks, the Do X worked its way up South and North America via the Caribbean. The huge plane caused a sensation on reaching New York.

■ **HOME AGAIN:** After wintering in America, the Do X crossed the North Atlantic via Newfoundland and the Azores. On 24 May 1932 it landed on Berlin's Müggelsee to a tumultuous welcome.

FAIREY

III

● Inter-war general-purpose aircraft ● RAF, FAA and foreign use

▲ One of the best known British military aircraft of the 1920s and 1930s, the Fairey III was developed over several years as a landplane and seaplane for both the RAF and FAA. Most of the type's operational service was spent overseas, in the Middle East, Far East and Africa. The IIIF variant served for some 14 years in a number of roles.

With its origins in a floatplane prototype known as the N10 by the Royal Naval Air Service, the Fairey Series III family comprised three major variants – the IIIC, IIID and IIIF – that between them were used for over 23 years by the services that became the Fleet Air Arm and the RAF. Starting life as a bomber and mine spotter, the Fairey III developed into a general-purpose type in shore-based and ship-board use with the Royal Navy.

FAIREY III

▲ From Cairo to the Cape
In 1926 the RAF's Cape Flight made a long-distance formation flight to South Africa to 'show the flag'. S1105 was among the four IIIDs involved.

▲ No. 481 Flight, FAA
Fairey IIID seaplanes of No. 481 Flight, Fleet Air Arm, were based in Malta for sea search operations around the island. In 1929 the flight was renumbered No. 202 Squadron, RAF, and re-equipped with float-equipped IIIFs.

▲ Portuguese floatplane
Eleven Fairey IIIDs ordered for the Portuguese navy had either Rolls-Royce Eagle or Napier Lion engines.

▲ Fairey IIIFs of 202 Sqdn
Malta-based No. 202 Squadron, RAF was equipped with longer-range IIIFs until 1935.

Napier Lion engine ▶
In the IIIF, the Lion engine was enclosed in a redesigned cowling of more streamlined appearance.

FACTS AND FIGURES

➤ The last RAF and FAA IIIFs in service are believed to have been several used as target tugs until 1941.

➤ Fairey IIIFs were the Fleet Air Arm's most widely-used inter-war type.

➤ Fairey IIIAs and Bs were built in small numbers toward the end of World War I.

➤ A radio-controlled gunnery training version of the IIIF was called the Fairey Queen; three were built.

➤ Fairey's Gordon and Seal were both developments of the IIIF.

➤ Two RAF IIIFs were configured as VIP communications aircraft.

PROFILE

Long-serving inter-war biplane

Combining the bombing capability of the IIIB floatplane with the IIIA's ship-board reconnaissance role, the IIIC was just too late to see service in World War I, though a small number took part in bombing operations with the North Russian Expeditionary Force based at Archangel. Including aircraft converted from IIIB production, 36 were built.

In 1920 the first flight of a IIID took place. Another bomber/reconnaissance type, this IIIC development served widely overseas, both as a landplane and as a seaplane catapulted from warships. By 1926, 207 had been built for the RAF, FAA and various foreign customers, including Portugal and Australia.

Perhaps the best known of the Fairey IIIs was the IIIF. Built in greater numbers than any other inter-war British military aircraft (other than Hawker Hart variants), the IIIF first entered service as a two-seat general-purpose aircraft with the RAF in Egypt in 1927. As the largest user of the type, the FAA employed more than 330 IIIF three-seat reconnaissance aircraft. They operated from every aircraft carrier, land bases and as catapult floatplanes.

Above: A Fairey IIID leaves its launching trolley and the deck of HMS Argus *in August 1922.*

Below: Among a number of civil-registered IIIs was this Jaguar radial-engined IIIF used for survey work in Sudan from 1930 until it crashed in 1934.

IIIF Mk IV

Type: two-seat general-purpose aircraft

Powerplant: one 339-kW (455-hp.) Napier Lion XIA liquid-cooled engine

Maximum speed: 193 km/h (120 m.p.h.) at 3048 m (10,000 ft.)

Initial climb rate: 6 min to 1524 m (5,000 ft.)

Range: 644 km (400 mi.) with 364 litres (96 gal.) of fuel; 2446 km (1,520 mi.) with 1077 litres (285 gal.) of fuel and no bomb load

Weights: empty 1764 kg (3,380 lb.); loaded 2741 kg (6,030 lb.)

Armament: one Vickers 7.7-mm (.303 cal.) machine-gun and one Lewis 7.7-mm machine-gun, plus up to 227 kg (500 lb.) of bombs

Dimensions:
span	13.94 m	(45 ft. 9 in.)
length	11.20 m	(36 ft. 9 in.)
height	4.42 m	(14 ft. 6 in.)
wing area	40.8 m²	(439 sq. ft.)

Australian IIIDs were equipped with Rolls-Royce Eagle VIII 12-cylinder liquid-cooled engines rated at 280 kW (375 hp.). This drove a two-bladed, fixed-pitch wooden propeller.

A10-3 was among six Fairey IIID seaplanes ordered by the Australian government, the first of which was delivered in August 1921. The first, then serialled ANA.1, was 'launched' by the wife of the Australian Prime Minister, W.M. Hughes.

The all-wooden fuselage structure was fabric-covered. The forward fuselage, the engine and its steel bearers, could be removed as a single unit.

Though standard IIIDs, the Australian examples were finished in a special aluminium dope and had white-painted floats to keep internal temperatures down in the Australian heat.

In naval service, the IIID was operated as a three-seater, with an observer and gunner positioned behind the pilot.

By far the most common powerplant fitted to Fairey IIIs was the unusual Napier Lion 'broad arrow', liquid-cooled, 12-cylinder engine.

Armament for general-purpose aircraft consisted of a forward-firing 7.7-mm (.303 cal.) Vickers machine-gun, a Scarff ring-mounted 7.7-mm Lewis in the gunner's position and a small bomb load on external racks.

For stowage aboard naval vessels the IIID had folding wings, hinged either side of the centre-section. One IIID was built with a metal wing structure and metal floats.

Fairey IIIFs introduced major improvements over the IIID. An all-metal fuselage, and later an all-metal wing, were used, as well as a metal propeller and a simplified undercarriage design.

IIID

Originally serialled ANA.3 (Australian Naval Aircraft No. 3), this aircraft was flown on the Britannia Trophy-winning flight round the entire Australian coastline in 1924.

BRITANNIA TROPHY WINNERS

Australian Navy Fairey IIID A10-3, crewed by Wing Commander S.J. Goble and Flying Officer I.E. McIntyre, was flown around Australia's 13,789-km (8,550-mi.) coastline over a period of 44 days between 6 April and 19 May 1924. Flying time was 90 hours. For this achievement they were awarded the 1924 Britannia Trophy. Setting out from the RAAF base at Point Cook, near Melbourne, the aircraft headed north. Bad weather and equipment failure dogged the trip; a new engine and floats were fitted at different points en route. The leg between Thursday Island and Elcho Island, across the open sea of the Gulf of Carpentaria, was one of the most difficult.

Wartime and inter-war Fairey types

■ **CAMPANIA:** The first aircraft intended from the outset to operate from a carrier vessel, this was Fairey's second design. The first example flew from a converted liner, *Campania*, in 1917.

■ **FAWN:** A landplane derivative of the Pintail amphibian, the Fawn was the RAF's first post-war light bomber to enter service. Replacing DH.9As, 70 production examples were built.

■ **FLYCATCHER:** Though clumsy looking, the Flycatcher fighter handled well and was thus popular with FAA pilots. Between 1922 and 1930, 195 were built, including amphibians.

■ **HENDON:** With an all-metal structure and a cantilever wing, the Hendon night bomber was advanced for its day. First flown in 1931, the type was built in small numbers (14) for the RAF.

FAIREY

Fox

- Day bomber designs ● RAF and foreign forces ● High speed

A ny account of the development and career of the Fairey Fox needs to consider two different aircraft designed to fill the same role. The RAF's Fox Mk I of 1925 was faster than any other day bomber of the period, thanks in no small part to its powerful American engine. It was also faster than most fighters! Fairey's later design proposal for a Mk I replacement, the Fox Mk II, was rejected by the RAF, but it found favour overseas, especially in Belgium.

▲ Clean lines,
an especially small frontal area
and a powerful Curtiss D-12 engine were the
keys to the Fox's speed. Despite its performance,
the type was destined to equip just one RAF unit.

FAIREY **Fox**

Clean lines of the Mk I ▶
Compared with its contemporaries, the Fox Mk I, with its single-bay wing and small frontal area, was an exceptionally aerodynamic machine.

▼ Fox Mk VI at Evère, 1936
Fox Mk VIs were built at the Avions Fairey factory as late as 1939. Most were either Mk VIR reconnaissance or Mk VIC combat machines. Two were sold in Switzerland.

▲ Fox Mk IV on floats
For Peru, Fairey produced the Fox Mk IV with floats. The aircraft were shipped from London Docks in 1933.

▼ Enclosed cockpit
This Belgian-built aircraft was the first Fox VI, powered by a 641-kW (860-hp.) Hispano-Suiza 12Ybrs engine. This was the most-produced Fox Mk II variant, with about 85 built.

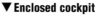

▲ First Mk IIs
Belgium's first 12 Fox Mk IIs were built in Britain. One of these took first prize in the 1932 International Circuit of the Alps race, averaging 258 km/h (160 m.p.h.).

FACTS AND FIGURES

➤ An RAF Fox Mk IA was landed aboard and flown from HMS *Furious* in April 1926.

➤ Though just over 200 kg (440 lb.) heavier than the Fox Mk I, the Mk IA was 6 km/h (4 m.p.h.) faster.

➤ The first RAF crews to be saved by parachutes bailed out from two Foxes after a collision in 1925.

➤ Two single-seat fighter variants of the Mk VI (the Mk VII Mono-Fox) were built.

➤ Dual-control versions of both the Fox Mk I and Mk II family were built.

Faster than the fighters of the day

Built as a private venture by Fairey, the Fox changed the RAF's thinking about performance levels and specification requirements. With a top speed some 80 km/h (50 m.p.h.) faster than that of the then-current Fairey Fawn, the Fox was able to carry the same bomb load and was faster than most fighters.

First flown on 3 January 1925, the prototype was described by its test pilot as one of the easiest and most viceless aircraft he had ever flown.

Financial constraints limited the size of the RAF's Fox fleet to just 23 service examples. That the Fox Mk I was powered by an American engine was controversial; the final four examples were fitted with Rolls-Royce F.XIIAs, as Fox Mk IAs, and the D-12's reliability problems led to others being re-engined.

Fairey was unsuccessful with its entry in the competition to find a replacement for the Fox. The Fox Mk II, a new, Kestrel-engined design with an all-metal structure employing the

Mk I's layout, was instead offered to foreign operators. Belgium became the largest user, and Fairey established an assembly line for the type at Gosselies.

Below: The last four Mk Is were built with Rolls-Royce F.XIIA engines (later known as Kestrel IIAs) and designated Mk IAs. Other Curtiss-engined Mk Is were also re-engined.

Above: Though it retained the Fox Mk I's basic layout, the Mk II was an entirely new design with an all-metal fuselage structure.

The Fox's American engine powered a Curtiss-Reed all-metal propeller which was licence-built.

For self-protection, the Fox Mk I carried a 7.7-mm (.303 cal.) Lewis machine-gun on a high-speed mounting in the rear cockpit and a forward-firing 7.7-mm Vickers on the port side of the forward fuselage. Offensive stores totalled 209 kg of bombs.

FOX MK I

No. 12 (Bomber) Squadron, RAF was the only unit to receive production Foxes. J7943 was the third aircraft in the first order for 18 aircraft. Only 23 were built; by 1931 they had been replaced by Hawker Harts.

In recognition of its association with the Fairey Fox, No. 12 Squadron incorporated a fox's mask into its unit crest with the motto 'Leads the Field', both of which the unit retains to this day.

Though relatively untried, the Curtiss D-12 was chosen to power the Fox because there was no equivalent British design of sufficient power. The D-12 had powered a Curtiss CR-3 racing floatplane to victory in the 1923 Schneider Trophy Race. Plagued by unreliability, the D-12s were later replaced by Rolls-Royce Kestrels.

Wood was used in the construction of the Fox's wings, rear fuselage and empennage, while the load-bearing forward fuselage was of steel tube.

COMBAT DATA

POWER

While the power produced by the Curtiss D-12 engine was only slightly more than that of the Napier Lion in the Fairey Fawn III, the Fox's design allowed higher top speeds. The Rolls-Royce Kestrel in the Hawker Hart offered an extra 41 kW (45 hp.) over the Lion engine.

FOX Mk I 358 kW (480 hp.)	FAWN Mk III 350 kW (470 hp.)	HART SEDB 391 kW (525 hp.)

MAXIMUM SPEED

Fairey designed the Fox to make better use of its engine's power and produced an aircraft that was faster than some fighters of the day. Hawker's Hart was faster still, at almost 300 km/h (170 m.p.h.), having been designed with a view to producing a fast bomber like the Fox that it was intended to replace.

FOX Mk I	252 km/h (156 m.p.h.)
FAWN Mk III	183 km/h (113 m.p.h.)
HART SEDB	296 km/h (167 m.p.h.)

RANGE

Hawker's Hart SEDB (Single-Engined Day Bomber) was fast, but lacked the range of both the Fox and the Fawn. Both of these aircraft were supported by wings designed not so much for speed as long range at lower speed. While the Hart and the Fawn were able to carry comparable bombloads, the Fox was limited to about 200 kg (400 lb.).

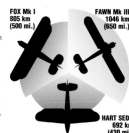

FOX Mk I 805 km (500 mi.)
FAWN Mk III 1046 km (650 mi.)
HART SEDB 692 km (430 mi.)

RAF inter-war day bombers

■ **DE HAVILLAND DH.9A:** Entering service in 1918, the DH.9A was the RAF's standard home-based bomber until the Fawn was introduced.

■ **FAIREY FAWN:** The RAF's first new bomber type, the Fawn Mk II was produced from 1924 and had a top speed of 183 km/h (114 m.p.h.).

■ **HAWKER HART:** Replacing the Fox Mk I, the 296-km/h (184-m.p.h.) Hart joined RAF units in 1930. Small numbers served as late as 1939.

■ **HAWKER HIND:** A development of the Hart, the Hind was an interim type before Battles and Blenheims entered service in the late 1930s.

FAIREY

FLYCATCHER

● 1920s carrier-borne fighter ● Popular with pilots ● Floatplane

A distinctive aircraft with a curious name; this is one way of describing the Fairey Flycatcher of the 1920s. It was an aircraft of odd appearance, and with a long roster of good and bad points. With the fuselage looking as though it was sagging in the middle, it was not good looking from any angle. The Flycatcher was not particularly fast either, but it was a valuable warplane with great maneuverability and the flexibility afforded by both floats and wheels.

▲ *Flight from aircraft carriers has always been hazardous, especially at night. A Fairey Flycatcher performed the first night-time carrier landing by a UK fighter in 1929.*

FAIREY FLYCATCHER

◀ **Fleet fighter**
The Flycatcher was the Royal Navy's standard fighter for over 10 years; in fact it was their only Fleet fighter for the period 1924 to 1932. Here an example flies over one of the Royal Navy's carriers.

Worldwide bases ▶
The Royal Navy's deployments around the globe during the 1920s meant that Flycatchers could be seen from Malta to Hong Kong.

◀ **Ship protection**
As well as flying from aircraft carriers, Flycatchers were deployed from turret platforms aboard selected battleships.

Carrier-borne ▶
No. 403 Flight flew the Flycatcher Mk I from 1924 until 1934. No. 403 was based at Leuchars and served aboard the aircraft carrier HMS Hermes.

▲ **Flycatcher amphibian**
N9678 was the first production amphibian and flew for the first time in October 1925.

FACTS AND FIGURES

➤ The Flycatcher Mk II was an advanced carrier-fighter, first flown in October 1926. It bore little resemblance to the Mk I.

➤ Production of Flycatchers added up to 196 aircraft, including four test aircraft.

➤ The prototype Fairey Flycatcher made its initial flight in November 1922.

➤ Flycatchers operated with the British Fleet until 1934 when the last floatplane versions were retired.

➤ The Flycatcher replaced the Nieuport Nightjar just after World War I.

➤ The second prototype Flycatcher, flown in May 1923, was the first to use floats.

Fly in the Queen's fleet

This remarkable specimen from the vintage years of aviation went into action with Britain's Fleet Air Arm in 1923. It was ugly, unusual, but much-loved by the pilots who flew it. With its short span, the Flycatcher could be raised or lowered on the elevator of an aircraft carrier without the need for wing folding. Apart from its

ability to be equipped with floats or wheels, another unusual feature of the Flycatcher's construction was that the airframe was designed to be dismantled easily with no section more than 4 m (13 ft.) long.

Although not exactly a spectacular performer, the Flycatcher was comparable to most other

fighters of its era and would have acquitted itself well in battle. Its popularity with its pilots was due to its responsiveness and strength in spite of its mixed wood and metal construction with fabric covering. It could be dived vertically at full throttle. As a floatplane, it was even capable of the full range of aerobatic manoeuvers.

Left: On some carriers, Flycatchers took off directly over the bows from a forward hangar below the main deck.

Below: A Flycatcher was the first FAA aircraft fitted with hydraulic wheel-brakes, a standard feature from 1933.

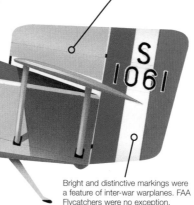

Flycatcher Mk I

Type: Single-seat Fleet fighter

Powerplant: One 298-kW (400-hp.) Armstrong Siddeley Jaguar III or IV 14-cylinder radial piston engine

Maximum speed: 214 km/h (133 m.p.h.)

Initial climb rate: 372 m/min (1,222 f.p.m.)

Range: 500 km (310 mi.)

Service ceiling: 5,790 m (19,000 ft.)

Weapons: Twin fixed, forward-firing 7.7-mm (.303 cal.) Vickers machine guns on fuselage; plus up to four 9-kg (20-lb.) bombs carried beneath the wings

Weights: Empty 2,032 lb.; max takeoff 3,018 lb.

Dimensions:
span	8.84 m	(29 ft.)
length	7.01 m	(23 ft.)
height	3.66 m	(12 ft.)
wing area	26.76 m²	(288 sq. ft.)

FLYCATCHER MK I

S1061 was one of 14 Flycatchers (S1060-1073) ordered in August 1925. A total of 192 was delivered to the Fleet Air Arm.

The pilot had two machine guns at his disposal; a pair of 7.7-mm (.303 cal.) Vickers guns mounted on the forward fuselage and firing through the propeller arc.

Among the type's distinctive features were the dihedral (upward bend) of the top wing and the apparent kink in the rear fuselage, which combined to give an ungainly overall appearance.

A distinctive fin shape was a feature of the Flycatcher. Float-equipped aircraft generally had a taller fin and rudder to maintain directional stability.

Flycatchers were powered by an Armstrong Siddeley Jaguar engine like those equipping the RAF's Armstrong Whitworth Siskin of the same period. This engine drove a two-blade propeller.

Wheeled landing gear was readily interchangeable with floats, as fitted to Flycatchers deployed aboard battleships. Amphibious landing gear could also be fitted, though this did not perform well on water.

Though principally a fighter, the Flycatcher had a limited bombing capability, with wing racks for four 9-kg (20-lb.) bombs. This allowed them to attack surface ships, but only at close range and considerable risk.

Bright and distinctive markings were a feature of inter-war warplanes. FAA Flycatchers were no exception.

ACTION DATA

SPEED

Compared to the Vought FU fighter and the later Boeing FB of the mid 1920s, the Flycatcher compared fairly well in terms of its speed. The FB differed from the other two types in having an inline engine. A version of the FU was equipped with floats.

FLYCATCHER Mk I	214 km/h (133 m.p.h.)
FB-1	256 km/h (159 m.p.h.)
FU-1	196 km/h (122 m.p.h.)

RANGE

Both the American types boasted a better range performance than the Flycatcher, by more than 60 miles. Range translated to endurance when operating from a carrier deck, which governed how long an aircraft could remain on patrol. US types operated in the Pacific and Atlantic Oceans and required extra range.

FU-1 660 km (410 mi.)

FB-1 628 km (390 mi.)

FLYCATCHER Mk I 500 km (310 mi.)

POWER

As engine manufacturers began to produce reliable, more powerful engines, these engines were fitted to new aircraft. This increase is mirrored in the dates that these three aircraft entered service, the Flycatcher being the second of the three.

FU-1	FLYCATCHER Mk I	FB-1
164 kW (220 hp.)	298 kW (400 hp.)	324 kW (435 hp.)

Fairey aircraft between the wars

■ FIREFLY: Built as a private venture, the Firefly fighter competed with and lost to the Hawker Fury in the competition for RAF orders.

■ SEAL: The equivalent of the RAF's Fairey Gordon, the Navy's Seal was an armed carrier-borne spotter-reconnaissance aircraft.

■ FOX: When this day-bomber entered RAF service in the mid 1920s, it was faster than the fighters of the period. Only 28 were delivered.

■ FERRET: Fairey's first aircraft with an all-metal structure, it was intended for FAA use. Despite good performance, none were ordered.

FAIREY

SWORDFISH

● Carrier-based torpedo-bomber ● Anti-submarine ● Taranto attacker

▲ Swordfish crews
carried out some of the most
devastating attacks of the war and achieved
many firsts, including the first torpedo attack
on a fleet in home port at Taranto in 1940.

It was a most unlikely warplane. A fabric
and wire biplane in an age of high-speed
monoplanes, the Fairey Swordfish was
obsolete before it even entered service.
But although it was lumbering and slow,
this classic warplane was no anachronism.
As a carrier-based torpedo-bomber it
amassed a combat record second to none,
from the historic attack on the Italian fleet at
Taranto to its final years as a radar- and
rocket-equipped anti-submarine patroller.

FAIREY SWORDFISH

▲ Floatplane Swordfish
The floatplane version of the Swordfish
was an effective aircraft, but the drag
from the floats and weight of a torpedo
limited its speed quite drastically.

▲ Strike mission
Swordfish from HMS Courageous
begin an anti-shipping strike. Torpedo
attacks required enormous nerve, as
the weapon had to be released at close
range in the face of heavy gunfire.

▲ Memorial flight
Swordfish still fly with the Royal
Navy's Historic Flight, and are star
attractions at air shows.

▲ Sub-chaser
Equipped with radar and rockets, the Swordfish was a lethal foe
to U-boats, especially when flying from small escort carriers.

Slow mover ▶
A loaded Swordfish could
barely make 180 km/h
(112 m.p.h.). But it was very
stable, and could deliver a
torpedo accurately.

▲ Open cockpit
With little weather protection Swordfish
crews were prone to the elements.

FACTS AND FIGURES

➤ The prototype Swordfish flew on 17 April
1934, when it was known as the T.S.R.II.

➤ At the outbreak of World War II, the
Royal Navy's Fleet Air Arm had 13
Swordfish squadrons.

➤ On 13 April 1940 a Swordfish made the
Fleet Air Arm's first U-boat kill.

➤ The Swordfish Mk III carried an
airborne radar scanner between its
mainwheels.

➤ 2,391 Swordfishes were built between
1934 and 1944, 1,699 by Blackburn.

➤ The last front-line Swordfish squadron
disbanded on 21 May 1945.

PROFILE

The victor of Taranto

On 11 November 1940, 21 Swordfish torpedo-bombers from the carrier HMS *Illustrious* ripped the heart out of the Italian fleet at Taranto, sending two battleships, a cruiser and a destroyer to the harbour bottom and effectively taking Italy's navy out of the war.

The Swordfish entered service with Britain's Fleet Air Arm (FAA) in 1936, where it became known as the 'Stringbag'. It was originally used with great success as a torpedo-bomber, making the crucial hit on the *Bismarck*, among other feats; but by 1942 it was simply too slow for the job. In an heroic but futile attack on the battlecruisers *Gneisenau* and *Scharnhorst*, five out of six Swordfishes were downed and the flight leader posthumously awarded the Victoria Cross.

But the big biplane still had plenty to offer, and remained in production until 1944. Assigned instead to anti-submarine, mine-laying, bombing and reconnaissance duties, the Swordfish also tested, and used, the FAA's first air-to-ground rocket projectiles.

SWORDFISH MK II

The Fairey Swordfish was the most successful British torpedo-bomber of the war, sinking more ships than all the Royal Navy's battleships put together.

A large notch was cut out of the upper wing to increase crew visibility upwards.

Most Swordfish wore a grey-green sea camouflage scheme, but some were painted white for Arctic operations.

The radio operator/air gunner was not always carried. He enjoyed an excellent field of fire, but the single Vickers 'K' 7.7-mm (.303 cal.) machine-gun would have deterred very few enemy fighter pilots.

A single forward-firing 7.7-mm (.303 cal.) Vickers gun was fitted in the upper fuselage, synchronised to fire through the propeller disc.

The structure of the Swordfish was from an earlier age, with fabric covering and wire bracing. But it was surprisingly strong, and could tolerate a rocket-assisted take-off.

The pilot communicated with his crew by a very primitive but effective system of voice pipes, known as 'Gosport tubes'.

The Pegasus radial engine proved extremely reliable, and was known to keep running even when one cylinder head was blown away by gunfire.

The Swordfish carried standard 457-mm (18-mm) torpedoes. A hit by one of these weapons was enough to fatally damage the steering gear of the *Bismarck*.

A large arrester hook was standard fit in all Swordfish.

Swordfish Mk II

Type: two-/three-seat torpedo-bomber/reconnaissance biplane

Powerplant: one 559-kW (750-hp.) Bristol Pegasus XXX nine-cylinder radial piston engine

Maximum speed: 222 km/h (138 m.p.h.)

Range: 1658 km (1,028 mi.)

Service ceiling: 3260 m (10,690 ft.)

Weights: empty 2132 kg (4,690 lb.); loaded 3406 kg (7,493 lb.)

Armament: one forward-firing 7.7-mm (.303 cal.) Vickers machine-gun in fuselage and one 7.7-mm Lewis or Vickers 'K' gun mounted in rear cockpit; one 730-kg (1,600 lb.) torpedo, or depth charges, mines or bombs up to 680 kg (1,500 lb.), or eight rocket projectiles

Dimensions:
span	13.87 m	(45 ft.)
length	10.87 m	(36 ft.)
height	3.76 m	(12 ft.)
wing area	56.39 m² (607 sq. ft.)	

COMBAT DATA

MAXIMUM SPEED

Roughly contemporary with the Swordfish, the US Navy's Devastator was a modern low-wing monoplane, as was the Imperial Japanese Navy's 'Kate', which flew some two years after the British 'Stringbag'. Both the other bombers were very much faster than the Swordfish.

SWORDFISH	222 km/h (138 m.p.h.)
TBD DEVASTATOR	330 km/h (205 m.p.h.)
B5N 'KATE'	378 km/h (234 m.p.h.)

RANGE

In spite of its size, the Swordfish's slow speed and light weight did not place much demand on the engine, and the archaic biplane had a very good range. This was to stand in its favour late in its career, when aircraft based on light carriers could mount anti-submarine patrols over convoys for hours at a time.

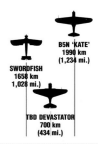

B5N 'KATE' 1990 km (1,234 mi.)

SWORDFISH 1658 km (1,028 mi.)

TBD DEVASTATOR 700 km (434 mi.)

WARLOAD

SWORDFISH	TBD DEVASTATOR	B5N 'KATE'
one torpedo or 680 kg (1,600 lb.) of bombs	one torpedo or one 454-kg (1,000 lb.) bomb	one torpedo or 800 kg (1,760 lb.) of bombs

High lift from its biplane wings and sturdy construction meant that the Swordfish could carry almost 30 per cent of its empty weight in weapons. It could hold its own with the much more advanced Japanese 'Kate', and could carry a heavier load than the USA's surprisingly ineffective Devastator.

Torpedo attackers of World War II

■ **DOUGLAS TBD DEVASTATOR:** The Devastator was a much more advanced aircraft than the Swordfish but was much less successful.

■ **NAKAJIMA B5N 'KATE':** The best torpedo bomber of the early years of World War II, the B5N ripped the heart out of the US Navy at Pearl Harbor.

■ **FAIREY ALBACORE:** Designed to replace the Swordfish, the Albacore was a more modern aircraft built on the same general principles.

■ **GRUMMAN TBF AVENGER:** Tough and very versatile, the highly successful Avenger's combat debut took place at Midway in June 1942.

■ **FAIREY BARRACUDA:** Never performing as well as expected, the ugly Barracuda was nevertheless an effective torpedo- and dive-bomber.

FAIREY
ALBACORE

● Biplane torpedo-bomber ● Designed to replace the Swordfish

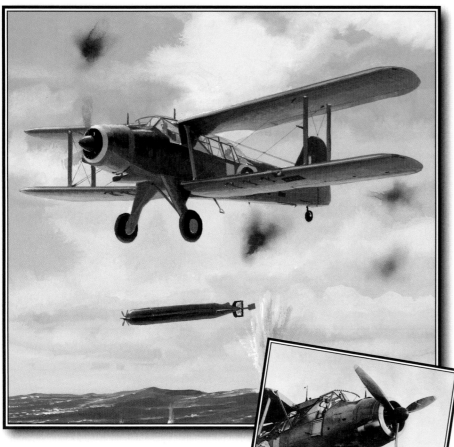

▲ *The outdated nature of the Albacore meant that it did not replace the Swordfish as planned. The last Albacores served with an RAF squadron until January 1945.*

By 1945 there were still nine FAA squadrons equipped with the Fairey Swordfish. The Albacore, 800 of which had been built to replace the old 'Stringbag', was serving with just one unit – and this was an air force squadron.

As a development of an already out-dated design, the Albacore represented an insufficient improvement over the old, but reliable, Swordfish. However, the type was useful, often flying from land bases.

FAIREY **ALBACORE**

▲ **Final days with the RAF**
The last operational Albacores served with No. 415 Squadron, Royal Canadian Air Force, later No.119 Squadron of the RAF, flying night anti-shipping sorties over the English Channel and the North Sea.

▲ **Over Malta**
Albacores in the Mediterranean flew bombing operations in the Western Desert and marked targets for RAF bombers.

▲ **Departing HMS Illustrious**
The Albacores of No. 829 Squadron were stationed aboard HMS Illustrious between June 1940 and June 1941.

◄ **Torpedo away!**
The Albacore's principal anti-ship weapon was a 730-kg (1.600-lb.) torpedo. Bombs and depth charges were also used.

▲ **Convoy escorts**
The first carrierborne operations for the 'Applecore' came at the end of 1940, with a convoy escort to Cape Town aboard HMS Formidable.

FACTS AND FIGURES

➤ No. 826 Squadron, the first unit to equip with the type in March 1940, attacked E-boats off Zeebrugge later in the year.

➤ During the D-Day landings of June 1944, Albacores patrolled the English Channel.

➤ The last carrier-borne Albacores flew during the invasion of Sicily.

➤ Last operations involving Albacores were carried out by the RAF's No. 119 Squadron against Dutch-based E-boats in 1945.

➤ All 800 Albacores were built at Fairey's factory in Hayes, Middlesex.

➤ Aircraft from *Victorious* sank German submarine U-517 on 21 November 1942.

PROFILE

Torpedo-bombing 'Applecore'

D ue to the improvements over its predecessor, the Albacore was described as the 'gentleman's Swordfish'. However, it was a development of an already obsolete idea.

Produced to a 1937 specification for a Swordfish replacement, this was one of a number of Fairey designs submitted. The Fleet Air Arm saw the monoplane as an 'unknown quantity' for the maritime role and so opted for an aircraft that, in the event, represented little advance over

the 'Stringbag', as the Swordfish was known.

Inevitably known as the 'Applecore' by its crews, 800 Albacores were built between 1938 and 1943. The type's first carrier operations were convoy escorts aboard HMS *Formidable*, and one of its notable actions was a fruitless attack on the battleship *Tirpitz* in 1942.

As Barracudas re-equipped FAA units from 1942, British-based Albacores defended the Channel, with the last examples flying with a Belgium-based RAF

Above: During tests the Albacore did not receive good marks for its handling, although it was steady in a dive and recovered well from a torpedo run.

Right: The pilot's view was excellent, but the cockpit was hot in summer; the rear was cold and draughty.

unit in this role. Others, based in North Africa, patrolled the Mediterranean and flew bombing and target-marking sorties for the RAF.

Albacore

Type: carrier- or shore-based torpedo-bomber

Powerplant: one 794-kW (1,065-hp.) Bristol Taurus II or 843-kW (1,130-hp.) Taurus XII radial piston engine

Maximum speed: 259 km/h (160 m.p.h.) at 2135 m (7,000 ft.)

Initial climb rate: 8 minutes to 1829 m (6,000 ft.)

Range: 1319 km (820 mi.)

Service ceiling: 6310 m (20,700 ft.)

Weights: empty 3266 kg (7,185 lb.); maximum take-off 5715 kg (12,757 lb.)

Armament: two 7.7-mm (.303 cal.) Vickers machine-guns

Dimensions: span 15.24 m (50 ft.)
length 12.13 m (39 ft. 9 in.)
height 4.65 m (15 ft. 3 in.)
wing area 57.9 m² (623 sq. ft.)

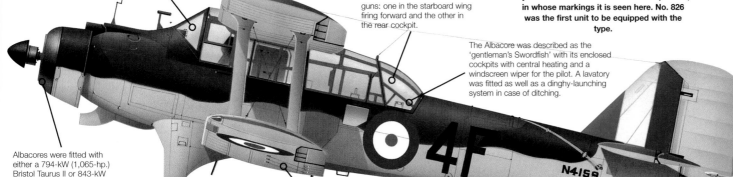

The aircraft had a variable-pitch propeller and hydraulically operated flaps.

Albacores were fitted with either a 794-kW (1,065-hp.) Bristol Taurus II or 843-kW (1,130-hp.) Taurus XII 14-cylinder two-row radial engine. This was the only change made to the aircraft during the production run.

For self-defence the Albacore carried two Vickers 'K' machine-guns: one in the starboard wing firing forward and the other in the rear cockpit.

The Albacore was described as the 'gentleman's Swordfish' with its enclosed cockpits with central heating and a windscreen wiper for the pilot. A lavatory was fitted as well as a dinghy-launching system in case of ditching.

As an alternative to a Mk XIIA torpedo, the aircraft could carry six 113-kg (250-lb.) or four 227-kg (500-lb.) bombs beneath the wings. Other stores included mines and flares. In late 1940 land-based Albacores flew mine-laying missions along the north coast of France.

ALBACORE

N4159 was delivered to No. 827 Squadron, based at Yeovilton, in September 1940. By March 1942 it was with No. 826 Squadron, in whose markings it is seen here. No. 826 was the first unit to be equipped with the type.

COMBAT DATA

MAXIMUM SPEED

The Albacore's top speed was an improvement over that of the Swordfish, but it was still more than 100 km/h (60 m.p.h.) slower than the Barracuda torpedo- and dive-bomber.

ALBACORE	259 km/h (160 m.p.h.)
SWORDFISH Mk II	222 km/h (138 m.p.h.)
BARRACUDA Mk II	367 km/h (228 m.p.h.)

ARMAMENT

The gun- and bomb-carrying capabilities of these three Fleet Air Arm aircraft did not vary greatly. However, the biplanes were considerably deficient in speed and range.

ALBACORE 2 x 7.7-mm (.303 cal.) machine-guns 907 kg (2,000 lb.) of bombs or torpedoes

SWORDFISH Mk II 2 x 7.7-mm (.303 cal.) machine-guns 731 kg (1,600 lb.) of bombs or torpedoes

BARRACUDA Mk II 2 x 7.7-mm (.303 cal.) machine-guns 816 kg (1,800 lb.) of bombs or torpedoes

RANGE

The Albacore and Barracuda both had much longer ranges than earlier types. The Barracuda combined this with improved speed and little reduction in load-carrying capacity, whereas the Albacore's design was merely a development of the outmoded Swordfish and its inherent weaknesses.

SWORDFISH Mk II 879 km (545 mi.)

ALBACORE 1319 km (820 mi.)

BARRACUDA Mk II 1850 km (1,150 mi.)

Fairey's carrier-borne warplanes

 **SWORDFISH:** Known as the 'Stringbag', the Swordfish torpedo-bomber first flew in 1934. Despite its inferior performance it was preferred to its intended replacement, the Albacore.

 **FULMAR:** As the first Fairey-built FAA fighter since the Flycatcher, the Fulmar entered service in 1940. Its lack of speed compared to single-seaters was a handicap, however.

 **BARRACUDA:** These aircraft were given a range of duties from torpedo reconnaissance to dive-bombing. Operational from 1943, the type made attacks on the battleship *Tirpitz* in 1944.

FIREFLY: A fighter reconnaissance aircraft that was later adapted for a strike role, the Rolls-Royce Griffon-powered and cannon-armed Firefly entered FAA service in 1943.

FARMAN

F.60 GOLIATH

● Twin-engine biplane bomber ● Pioneer European airliner

D esigned as a heavy bomber but completed too late to see service during World War I, the Farman F.60 became one of the world's first airliners. During the 1920s it was built in both military and commercial versions, equipping French air force and navy bomber units as well as helping pioneer airline services. Later military models with more powerful engines and the ability to carry bomb loads of up to 1500 kg (3,300 lb.) remained in service into the early 1930s.

▲ In August 1919
Frenchman Lucien Bossoutrot set a long-distance record, flying a Goliath with seven others aboard the 2044 km (1,270 mi.) from Paris to Casablanca in 18 hours 23 minutes.

FARMAN F.60 GOLIATH

▼ Early airliner
This aircraft started life with Belgian airline SNETA in April 1921, on services between Brussels and London. SNETA ceased operations in August after a crash and hangar fire. Its aircraft went to SABENA.

▲ Farman Line to Brussels
On 1 July 1920, Farman Line inaugurated a Paris to Brussels service, which was later extended to Amsterdam and Berlin.

At Le Bourget ▶
Two of Air Unions' Goliaths are seen here at Paris main airport in the 1920s. The other aircraft are an Air Union Blériot Spad 33 (rear) and a Fokker F.III belonging to Dutch airline KLM.

▼ F.60 F-FHMU
The Farman Line, operated by the company that built the Goliath, liked to incorporate the initials of its founders, Henri and Maurice Farman, in its aircraft's registrations.

▲ On the tarmac at Croydon
Air Union and Imperial Airways aircraft meet outside Croydon airport's terminal. Goliaths helped establish air services across the English Channel.

FACTS AND FIGURES

➤ A CGEA F.60 and a British DH.18 were involved in the first mid-air collision between two airliners on 7 April 1922.

➤ A Goliath was priced at the equivalent of $7055 in 1919.

➤ The fuselage, fin and rudder of an Air Union Goliath is preserved in France.

➤ A large number of F.60 airliners were re-engined with 300-hp. Salmson 9Az engines as the F.63bis.

➤ Bomber F.60s were built from 1922; the French army equipped six squadrons.

➤ After the 1930 crash of the first F.140, the French air force scrapped its last Goliaths.

PROFILE

Pioneer airliner from a French pioneer

Designed as a two-seat night bomber, the original Goliath proved readily adaptable to passenger transport. The original passenger conversion involved the creation of two cabins, one for four passengers in the nose and the other for eight behind and below the open cockpit.

On 8 February 1919, the aircraft carried 11 passengers plus a mechanic from Paris to London, returning the next day and flying to Brussels three days later. By the following year there were regular services linking the British, French and Belgian capitals.

Dozens of F.60s were used by fledgling French airlines during the 1920s. Others were operated in Belgium, Japan, Rumania and South America, and six aircraft were built in Czechoslovakia by Avia and Letov. Various engines were used, with the airplane's designation changing accordingly.

Farman also built 20 three-seat F.60M bombers for the French air force and 24 for the navy. Italy used the F.62 and Poland the F.68. In 1928 an improved F.160 series appeared of which there were nine separate variations. They included new floatplane torpedo bomber and transport variants.

Above: French airline Cie des Grands Express Aériens (CGEA) began a Paris to London service with F.60s on March 29, 1920. Flights were irregular at first.

Left: Another of Air Union's Goliaths, F-AEFC was named Provence. The last Goliaths in airline service were Farman Line aircraft in 1933.

F.60 GOLIATH

F-AECU *Normandie* was one of at least 15 aircraft operated by Air Union from 1923. Air Union flew aircraft inherited from CMA and Grands Express, airlines that flew the type on the London and Paris route.

Air Union named its Goliaths after regions in France, including *Normandie*. Other names included *Languedoc*, *Alsace*, *Lorraine*, *Auvergne*, *Provence*, *Flandre* and *Gascogne*.

In their 1.32-m (4-ft. 4-in.) wide fuselage, commercial Goliath variants had a nose cabin for four passengers and a rear cabin for up to eight. These were separated by the raised open cockpit for the two pilots.

Avia and Letov built a number of Goliaths in Czechoslovakia; five for the national airline CSA and one for VIP use by the air force. French-built aircraft served worldwide. Examples were sold in the USSR, Italy and Japan.

Early bomber variants were able to deliver 1043 kg (2,300 lb.) of bombs and carried a crew of three and three defensive 7.7-mm (.303 cal.) machine guns. The later F.140 Super Goliath could haul 1497 kg (3,300 lb.) of bombs.

The various commercial Goliaths were fitted with a variety of engines, the civil F.60 having two 172-kw (230-hp.) Salmson Z.9 radials. Other versions had powerplants by different makers, including Renault, Lorraine, Farman, Armstrong Siddeley and Gnome-Rhône.

The Goliath's sturdy undercarriage was fitted with trousered fairings and were supported by twin main wheels. Its structure was combined with that of the engine nacelle above the leg. The untapered wings with squared tips led to the rumor that they were built by the mile and cut to size.

F.60 Goliath

Type: Passenger transport.

Powerplant: Two 194-kW (260-hp.) Salmson CM.9 nine-cylinder air-cooled radial engines

Maximum speed: 140 km/h (87 m.p.h.)

Cruising speed: 119 km/h (74 m.p.h.)

Range: 402 km (250 mi.)

Service ceiling: 4008 m (13,150 ft.)

Weights: Empty equipped 2495 kg (5,500 lb.); max take-off 4760 kg (10,494 lb.)

Fuel load: 467 kg (1,030 lb.)

Accommodation: 2 crew plus up to 12 passengers (max useful load 1597 kg (3,520 lb.))

Dimensions:
span	26.49 m	(86 ft. 11 in.)
length	13.89 m	(45 ft. 7 in.)
height	5.59 m	(18 ft. 4 in.)
wing area	160.91 m²	(1,732 sq. ft.)

ACTION DATA

SPEED

Compared to airliner types that began to enter service in the late 1920s, the Goliath was short on top speed. It was soon outpaced by types such as the Handley Page W.8 and Vimy Commercial. The latter was another airliner developed from a bomber design.

F.60 GOLIATH	140 km/h (87 m.p.h.)
W.8	195 km/h (115 m.p.h.)
VIMY COMMERCIAL	158 km/h (98 m.p.h.)

RANGE

The Vimy had, albeit in modified form, demonstrated its ability to fly considerable distances in a series of long-distance route proving flights. Companies like Imperial Airways were able to pioneer services over longer routes than those flown by the F.60.

F.60 GOLIATH 402 km (250 mi.)
VIMY COMMERCIAL 724 km (450 mi.)
W.8 805 km (500 mi.)

WEIGHT

In the 1920s, manufacturers were more interested in providing their airliner designs with longer range than with increasing carrying. Thus, the W.8 and Vimy weighed in at less than one ton more than the Goliath. Most of the extra weight would have been fuel.

F.60 GOLIATH	4760 kg (10,494 lb.)
W.8	5598 kg (12,342 lb.)
VIMY COMMERCIAL	5658 kg (12,474 lb.)

Military Goliaths in action

TRAINING: After being declared obsolete as a bomber in Polish service, the Goliath found new roles as a parachute trainer and undertook crew familiarization flights.

1920s BOMBER: Despite obsolescence in the bomber role in Europe, France operated army F.60s and navy F.65s against Rif tribesmen in Morocco between 1925 and 1927.

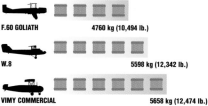

FLOATPLANE TORPEDO BOMBER: The F.168 was a Jupiter-engined development which served with a number of units of the French Aéronautique Maritime from 1928 to 1936. The fuselage was modified to improve the pilot's view. About 60 entered service.

FIAT

CR.1

● Italian fighter design ● Inverted sesquiplane ● Exported to Latvia

▲ *With its distinctive engine installation and unusual wing layout, the CR.1 was a highly successful inter-war fighter which inspired a generation of Fiat designs.*

Designed in 1922 by Ing Celestino Rosatelli to take part in a Regia Aeronautica competition for a new single-seat fighter, the CR.1 was the first of a successful line of biplane fighters built by the Fiat company. Although never seeing combat, the CR.1 was undoubtedly a capable aircraft and was the Italian air force's primary fighter of the late 1920s. The CR.1 was so enduring and popular that the final examples were not retired until 1937.

FIAT CR.1

▲ **Frontal radiator**
A radiator mounted above the propeller hub cooled the eight-cylinder Hispano-Suiza engine. A number of engines were tested.

▲ **Fiat fighter, Fiat engine**
Equipping the CR.1 with a Fiat A.20 engine transformed it into the CR.10. The distinctive radiator installation was lost in this form. Instead, two Lamblin radiators were used, mounted on the undercarriage struts.

▲ **Balanced ailerons**
Small aerofoil surfaces, mounted on the ailerons of the CR.1 and CR.10, acted as aerodynamic balances.

◀ **Minimum bracing**
With its Warren-truss rigid wing-bracing struts, the CR.1 required the minimum of wire rigging.

Sesquiplane layout ▶
Fiat remained faithful to the sesquiplane layout for its biplane fighters, although it abandoned the inverted configuration employed on the CR.1.

FACTS AND FIGURES

➤ The CR.1 prototypes, MM.1 and MM.2, were the first aircraft designated under the current Italian numbering system.

➤ Belgium and Poland tested the CR.1, but did not place production orders.

➤ Modified from the CR.1, the CR.10 was capable of 300 km/h (185 m.p.h.).

➤ The CR.1 was the first of a famous line of successful Fiat biplane fighters that culminated in the CR.42.

➤ The first production CR.1s were delivered to the Regia Aeronautica in 1925.

➤ A single CR.2 was built, fitted with a British Armstrong Siddeley Lynx engine.

PROFILE

Fiat's faithful inter-war fighter

Eclipsing its rival the SIAI S.52 biplane, in the competition for a new Italian fighter, the CR.1 was a fast and highly manoeuvrable biplane which entered squadron service in 1925.

Featuring an unusual inverted sesquiplane layout, the CR.1 was meticulously developed at prototype stage. Minor handling problems were ironed out and the design was adapted to fit the requirements. Initial trials were followed by a production order for 109, built by Fiat. Licence-production was subsequently carried out by OFM (later IMAM-Meridionali) with 40 examples, and by SIAI with another 100.

After serving with up to eight Italian front-line squadrons, a number of CR.1s were modified in the early 1930s to take a more powerful Isotta Fraschini engine, which improved performance.

The only export order received was that for nine examples for the Latvian navy. Other variants included the CR.2, CR.5 and CR.10 with various powerplants, but none of them proceeded past prototype stage.

Above: Fiat tested a single example of the CR.1 with an Armstrong Siddeley Lynx radial, as the CR.2. Belgium, Poland and Latvia tested the CR.1, but only the Baltic state placed an order.

Below: Various refinements were incorporated into the CR.1 in regular service. Several aircraft had their spoked wheels faired over.

Built mostly of wood, the CR.1 gained a reputation in service for strength and reliability. The aircraft beat off a challenge from the rival SIAI S.52 to win its initial production orders.

For the CR.1, Fiat produced one of the cleanest engine installations of any 1920s fighter. Some aircraft were re-engined later in their lives, with the 328-kW Isotta Fraschini Asso Caccia engine giving a considerable performance improvement.

Taken literally, the sesquiplane arrangement requires the lower biplane wing to have half the area of the upper wing. This comparatively rare layout was made all the more unusual by Fiat's use of it in an inverted form.

Another unusual feature of the CR.1 was its Warren-truss struts. From the front, they formed a 'W' shape and appeared to be in two sections which ran in parallel along the forward and aft edges of the wing.

With the canvas skinning of the rudder pulled tight over the ribs beneath, the trailing edge appeared to be scalloped. This feature was retained on the CR.20, but discarded thereafter.

CR.1

Wearing the typical colours and markings of the 1920s, this CR.1 is depicted in the service of the Regia Aeronautica (Italian air force).

ACTION DATA

MAXIMUM SPEED

A comparison of mid- to late 1920s biplane fighters shows the Fiat CR.1 to be considerably faster than either the British Gloster Grebe Mk II or the American Boeing PW-9D. None of these types was to see combat, but all served their countries well.

CR.1	272 km/h (169 m.p.h.)
GREBE Mk II	245 km/h (152 m.p.h.)
PW-9D	249 km/h (154 m.p.h.)

ENDURANCE

Although both the Grebe Mk II and PW-9D were at least 75 kW (100 hp.) more powerful than the CR.1, all had similar endurance. The British and American machines were heavier aircraft with a larger fuel load, but their more powerful, heavier engines consumed fuel at a higher rate and gave them little advantage over the CR.1.

CR.1	**GREBE Mk II**	**PW-9D**
2 hours 35 minutes	2 hours 45 minutes	2 hours 50 minutes

SERVICE CEILING

Altitude performance was another of the CR.1's qualities. It easily outperformed the Gloster and Boeing aircraft, and was one of the finest fighters of its day.

CR.1	**GREBE Mk II**	**PW-9D**
7450 m (24,400 ft.)	7010 m (23,000 ft.)	5557 m (18,000 ft.)

Fiat's fighter family

■ **CR.20:** Retaining a considerable resemblance to the CR.1, the CR.20 served until 1936 as a fighter trainer. This CR.20bis belonged to the Paraguayan national army air force.

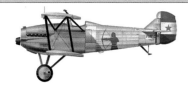

■ **CR.32:** First flown in 1932, the CR.32 was exported widely and served successfully with the Regia Aeronautica. It is best remembered for its service in the Spanish Civil War.

■ **CR.42:** Perhaps the greatest biplane fighter ever, the CR.42 served in great numbers at home and abroad. It saw service in both the Spanish Civil War and World War II.

FIAT

CR.32

● **Thoroughbred fighter** ● **Highly aerobatic** ● **Multi-role aircraft**

O ne of the most agile biplanes, the Fiat CR.32 fought many air battles over Spain during the civil war but it actually made its combat debut over China against the invading Japanese. Highly regarded by Italian fighter pilots, who loved its superb aerobatic qualities, the little Fiat was strongly built and did well in combat. It was equipped with two 12.7-mm (.50 cal.) guns, which had a better range than the smaller calibre weapons of its opponents.

▲ *In August*
1936 Italian CR.32s were flown to Spain to fight for the Spanish Nationalists. It became the chief fighter aircraft of the Aviacion Legionaria and was built by Hispano.

FIAT CR.32

▲ **Spanish squadron**
Spanish Nationalists received a full squadron of CR.32s from Italy.

▲ **Sturdy fighter**
Smaller than the CR.30, the fighter was much stronger and able to withstand the most violent manoeuvres.

Braced biplane ▶
The CR.32 had 'W'-type Warren strut bracing between the unequal span wings, giving it considerable strength.

▼ **Built in Spain**
The Spanish Nationalists were extremely impressed with the Fiat CR.32 and they decided to build their own version, the Chirri, in Spain. At least 380 took part in air battles against Republican Polikarpov I-15s and I-16s.

▲ **Chinese combat**
The first 24 CR.32s were ordered by China, but in the event just nine were delivered in 1935 and were used to fly against the invading Japanese.

FACTS AND FIGURES

➤ Export models of the CR.32 served with the air arms of Austria, Chile, China, Hungary, Paraguay and Spain.

➤ Fiat built over 1,000 CR.32s for the Regia Aeronautica before production ended.

➤ The biplane fighter had outstanding manoeuvrability and was very strong.

➤ During World War II, Spain built its own CR.32s under a licence agreement covering 100 examples made by Hispano.

➤ The CR.32 was obsolete by 1939, but some saw service in World War II.

➤ The final CR.32 was fitted with exhaust shrouds for night flying.

PROFILE

Fiat's sturdy dogfighter

Flying for the first time on 28 April 1933, the Fiat CR.32 represented a peak of aeronautical design evolution which had begun in the 1920s with the CR.1. Fiat's fabric-covered, light alloy and steel construction resulted in a strong structure and an excellent power-to-weight ratio making the CR.32 an outstanding aerobatic aircraft and a very able dogfighter.

Armed with four machine-guns, the Fiat CR.32 made its combat debut in China. Further action was achieved by Italian pilots in the Spanish civil war, who fought for Franco's Nationalist cause. This 'force within a force' operated in every campaign of the war.

The Fiat's 12.7-mm guns outranged the weapons carried by its opponents, and in dogfights this became a considerable advantage. The CR.32 was also able to absorb a considerable degree of battle damage and gained a legendary reputation for bringing its pilots home safely.

Above: With its 12.7-mm (.50 cal.) Breda-SAFAT machine-guns, the CR.32 was a formidable fighter with Franco's forces.

Above: When Italy entered the war some 400 CR.32s out of a total of over 1200 single-seat biplane fighters on strength were still in front-line service with the Regia Aeronautica.

CR.32

Type: single-seat interceptor fighter

Powerplant: one 447-kW (560-hp.) Fiat R.A.30 R.A.bis liquid-cooled piston engine

Maximum speed: 330 km/h (204 m.p.h.) at sea level; 354 km/h (219 m.p.h.) at 3000 m (10,000 ft.)

Range: 780 km (484 mi.) at 315 km/h (195 m.p.h.)

Service ceiling: 8800 m (28,865 ft.)

Weights: empty 1454 kg (3,205 lb.); loaded 1914 kg (4,220 lb.)

Armament: two 12.7-mm and two 7.7-mm (.303 cal.) Breda-SAFAT machine-guns; rack under fuselage for one 100-kg (220-lb.) or two 50-kg (110-lb.) bombs

Dimensions: span 9.50 m (31 ft.)
length 7.45 m (24 ft.)
height 2.63 m (9 ft.)
wing area 22.1 m² (238 sq. ft.)

Armament normally comprised two 12.7-mm (.50 cal.) Breda-SAFAT machine-guns housed in the upper cowling and firing through the propeller. Two 7.7-mm Breda machine-guns could be carried in the lower wings.

The CR.32 was very much a pilot's aircraft, with a pleasant cockpit and excellent controls. The similar CR.40 had the top wing attached to the top of the fuselage.

The aircraft had all-metal tail construction with fabric-covered rudder and elevators. The tailplane was braced to the base of the rear fuselage and the tailwheel was spatted to reduce drag.

V.137

The CR.32's engine was a 447-kW (560-hp.) Fiat R.A.30 R.A.bis inverted, in-line piston engine, driving a two-blade propeller.

CR.32

First flown on 28 April 1933, the CR.32 was one of the top single-seat fighters of the early 1930s. A total of 1,312 aircraft were built in Italy and Spain up until 1943. Most were flown by the Regia Aeronautica (Italian air force), although the Spanish air force was the last to fly them.

The fuselage and wings were of conventional steel framing with light-alloy formers and, in the main, covered by fabric. The unequal span wings were substantially braced in 'W' form with additional wire bracing in between for added strength.

This CR.32 is in the Hungarian air force colours of 1939. A total of 90 CR.32s were flown by the Hungarians, including 38 originally delivered to Austria.

ACTION DATA

MAXIMUM SPEED

The CR.32's Fiat RA.30 engine gave it a top speed of 354 km/h (219 m.p.h.) at 3000 metres (10,000 ft.), which was good for the early 1930s. It was not as fast as the cleaner-designed Gladiator, but had comparable performance to the bulky Polikarpov I-15.

CR.32	354 km/h (219 m.p.h.)
GLADIATOR	414 km/h (257 m.p.h.)
I-15	367 km/h (228 m.p.h.)

SERVICE CEILING

Although the CR.32 had good manoeuvrability it did not have the Gladiator's power to climb to high altitude, its ceiling being some 2770 metres (9,000 ft.) less than the RAF fighter. The Wright-Cyclone-powered I-15 also had a better service ceiling than the CR.32.

CR.32	GLADIATOR	I-15
8800 m (28,865 ft.)	11,570 m (37,950 ft.)	9800 m (32,144 ft.)

RANGE

With its large fuel tanks, the CR.32 had a maximum range of 780 km (484 mi.) at a constant speed of 315 km/h (195 m.p.h.). This was 10 per cent better than the Gladiator's range and appreciably more than the short-range Polikarpov I-15.

CR.32	780 km (484 mi.)
GLADIATOR	706 km (438 mi.)
I-15	510 km (316 mi.)

Fiat biplane fighter aircraft

■ **CR.1:** Equipping the newly reformed Regia Aeronautica in the 1920s, 240 CR.1s were built. The type was modified with more powerful Isotta-Fraschini engines in the 1930s, and the type soldiered on until 1937 before being retired.

■ **CR.20:** Used extensively in the campaigns in Abyssinia and Libya, the Fiat-engine-powered CR.20 was also exported to Lithuania and Hungary. In the early 1930s the type was the mainstay of the Regia Aeronautica fighter strength.

■ **CR.42 'FALCO':** Used widely in Libya in World War II, the CR.42 was a very good biplane fighter but was totally outclassed by the RAF's Hurricanes and Gladiators. The Luftwaffe also used the CR.42 during the war for night-attack duties.

FIAT

CR.42

● Italian fighter ● Manoeuvrable biplane ● Unequal-span wings

By the late 1930s most of the leading warplane producers were abandoning open-cockpit, fabric-covered biplane designs in favour of stressed-skin monoplanes with a retractable landing gear. But in Italy, Celestino Rosatelli of Fiat believed there was still a role for a highly manoeuvrable biplane fighter. Fiat thus produced the CR.42 Falco, the best fighter available to either side in North Africa from the start of the war until the arrival of the RAF's Hawker Hurricane.

▲ *An ignominious end for a CR.42 of 95ª Squadriglia of the Corpo Aereo Italiani. Poor training and a lack of support equipment had contributed to low CR.42 availability.*

FIAT CR.42

Effective camouflage ▶
The Italian air force adopted a new dappled, two-tone brown camouflage for its Fiat CR.42s operating in North Africa.

▼ Foreign sales
Sixty-eight CR.42s were ordered by the Hungarian air force in 1941. Falcos took part in the campaign against Yugoslavia.

With the Swedish air force ▶
One of Sweden's 72 CR.42s of J 11/3 Division, operating from Save in 1942.

▼ Aegean theatre
Italian CR.42s operated in 1941 from the Isle of Scarpanto.

Hungarian Fast Corps ▶
Flying in the Soviet Union during late 1941, this CR.42 was flown by 1/3 Sqn, 1/II Group of the Hungarian Fast Corps.

FACTS AND FIGURES

➤ Although the prototype CR.42 did not fly until January 1939, it entered service with the Italian air force the following November.

➤ A robust, clean and fast design, it was already obsolete when it entered service.

➤ The CR.42 was the last biplane fighter produced by Fiat.

➤ Fifty CR.42s provided the Italian fighter element operating from Belgium against England during 1940/41.

➤ Overall production of all CR.42 versions totalled 1,784.

➤ One CR.42 was built in 1940 as a twin-float seaplane.

PROFILE

Last of the Fiat biplane fighters

After World War I, the Fiat company commenced production of a series of biplane fighters. These aircraft became the mainstay of the Italian air force's fighter squadrons. By the early 1930s, the CR.32 was in service. This was to be the main fighter in Franco's forces during the Spanish Civil War in 1936.

By the late 1930s, most of the world's major air forces were gradually re-equipping with low-wing monoplane fighters. Fiat still believed that there was a place for the biplane and designed the CR.42, with the prototype making its maiden flight in January 1939. It was instantly ordered into production for the Italian air force. With a number of export orders following, some 1,784 had been built by 1943.

In service with the Regia Aeronautica, CR.42s were used as day fighters and escort fighters in the Mediterranean theatre and as night-fighters for home defence.

By 1942, Fiat had managed to raise the top speed to 518 km/h (321 m.p.h.) but the design still fell short in other respects. Biplane fighter production was at an end.

Below: A standard Italian air force fighter in the markings of 95ª Squadriglia, 18º Gruppo. It had a bright yellow engine cowling and spinner on the three-bladed propeller.

Above: A converted two-seat trainer version of the CR.42, painted overall silver with the markings of the post-war Sezione Autonoma Collegiamenti.

CR.42 Falco

This CR.42 carries the markings of the 97ª Squadriglia, 9º Gruppo 'Caccia Terrestre', of the Regia Aeronautica's 4º Stormo based at Benina in Libya during 1940.

The wing was manufactured from light alloy and steel, with a fabric covering. Ailerons were fitted only to the top wings.

The pilot's open cockpit was situated aft of the cut-out in the trailing edge of the upper wing to give better all-round vision.

CR.42s were powered by a Fiat A.74R1C.38 radial air-cooled, geared and supercharged engine.

CR.42s featured a sesquiplane with rigidly-braced wings constructed in two sections, joined at the centreline and supported above the fuselage.

The steel-tube fuselage structure was welded and faired to an oval section and covered with metal panels from the cockpit forwards. The rear section was fabric-covered.

A faired, non-retractable tailwheel was situated at the end of the lower fuselage. A fuel tank was situated in the rear fuselage behind a fireproof bulkhead.

The fixed main landing gear had two oleo-pneumatic legs.

CR.42 Falco

Type: single-seat biplane fighter

Powerplant: one 626-kW (840-hp.) Fiat A.74 R1C.38 14-cylinder, two-row radial piston engine

Maximum speed: 420 km/h (267 m.p.h.)

Initial climb rate: 732 m/min (2,400 f.p.m.)

Combat range: 775 km (480 mi.)

Service ceiling: 10,500 m (33,500 ft.)

Weights: empty 1782 kg (3,929 lb.); maximum take-off 2295 kg (5,060 lb.)

Armament: two fixed forward-firing Breda-SAFAT 12.7-mm (.50 cal.) machine-guns, plus up to 198 kg (440 lb.) of bombs

Dimensions:
span	9.70 m	(31 ft. 10 in.)
length	8.27 m	(27 ft. 1 in.)
height	3.59 m	(11 ft. 9 in.)
wing area	22.4 m²	(241 sq. ft.)

COMBAT DATA

MAXIMUM SPEED

Clearly, in terms of its speed performance the biplane had had its day by 1940. Hawker's Hurricane, which equipped RAF fighter squadrons in large numbers, was a full 100 km/h (60 m.p.h.) faster. The Luftwaffe's Messerschmitt Bf 109 was faster still.

CR.42 FALCO	420 km/h (267 m.p.h.)
HURRICANE Mk I	520 km/h (322 m.p.h.)
Bf 109E-7	578 km/h (358 m.p.h.)

ARMAMENT

With only two machine-guns, the CR.42 was also out-gunned by the monoplane fighters of the day. However, as a biplane the Fiat was a comparatively manoeuvrable machine.

CR.42 FALCO 2 x 12.7-mm (.50 cal.) machine-guns

HURRICANE Mk I 8 x 7.7-mm (.303 cal.) machine-guns

Bf 109E-7 1 x 20-mm cannon, 4 x 7.9-mm machine-guns

RANGE

The range advantage enjoyed by the German Messerschmitt Bf 109 was useful in the type's escort role during the Battle of Britain. The Fiat's range was much less but actually slightly superior to that of early models of the RAF's Hurricane.

CR.42 FALCO 775 km (480 mi.)

Bf 109E-7 1094 km (680 mi.)

HURRICANE Mk I 740 km (460 mi.)

CR.42s in three liveries

■ **BELGIUM:** Serving with the Belgian air force in May 1940, this CR.42, one of 15 in service, had Italian-style camouflage markings but a Belgian roundel and white cocette.

■ **NORTH AFRICA:** This Italian air force CR.42 carries the colours of the 20ª Squadriglia, 46º Gruppo Assolto, 15º Stormo that served in North Africa in the summer of 1942.

■ **BATTLE OF BRITAIN:** An Italian air force CR.42 from the 18º Gruppo 'Caccia Terrestre', based in Belgium and operating over southern England during the Battle of Britain in 1940.

FIESELER

FI 167

- Ship-based design ● Torpedo bomber ● Reconnaissance aircraft

Very few prototypes equal their target specification without further modification and development. Even fewer exceed all expectations, but the Fi 167 can rightfully claim a place in this elite group. Designed as a torpedo bomber and general reconnaissance aircraft for Germany's aircraft carrier, the *Graf Zeppelin*, Fiesler's Fi 167 was to play only a minor role in World War II after construction of the carrier ceased.

▲ *Erprobungsstaffel 167 received 12 Fi 167s for service trials. Some aircraft went on to perform undercarriage tests, while the remainder were sold to Rumania.*

FIESELER FI 167

▲**Folding for the Graf**
Folding wings allowed the Fi 167 to take up minimum deck space.

▲ **Naval features**
Jettisonable main undercarriage units increased the Fi 167A-0's chances of a successful ditching.

▼ **Purposeful design**
Large flaps and slats gave the Fi 167 exceptional flying qualities. None ever flew from a ship.

▲ **Pre-production batch**
Fi 167s entered service in the second half of 1940 and flew a range of service evaluations and trials, until their withdrawal from the Netherlands in 1943.

Tall and angular ▶
The unusually stalky and awkward appearance of the Fi 167 resulted in an aircraft that was exceptionally well suited to its design role.

FACTS AND FIGURES

➤ Fiesler was so pleased with initial trials that it completed only the Fi 167V1 and V2 prototypes, abandoning V3.

➤ Reinhold Mewes designed the Fi 167 for maximum maintainability.

➤ Fi 167s carried out tests to find the best camouflage for maritime operations.

➤ Erprobungsstaffel 167 returned to Germany to disband. Three of its aircraft then went on to undercarriage trials.

➤ Trials were flown with the Fi 167 as a heavily loaded sesqui (wing-and-a-half) plane.

➤ Daimler-Benz used the 11th Fi 167A-0 as an engine testbed.

PROFILE

Striking from the *Graf Zeppelin*

Launched in December 1938, the *Graf Zeppelin* was to be the pride of the German navy's fleet.

A considerable force of aircraft would be required to arm the new ship and in 1937 a specification was issued for a two-seat general-purpose machine, capable of flying in the torpedo-bombing role.

Two companies submitted prototypes, but Arado's Ar 195 was little more than a redesigned Ar 95 and it failed to meet the requirements of the specification.

Conversely, the Fi 167 was a superb aircraft that exceeded all requirements and exhibited stunning slow-speed performance. With the engine throttled right back and the elevators deflected fully upward, the aircraft would sink almost vertically. Gerhard Fiesler once climbed the aircraft 3050 m (10,000 ft.) over the same spot on the ground!

With the cancellation of the *Graf Zeppelin*, 12 Fi 167A-0 aircraft briefly entered service, flying from Dutch land bases.

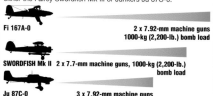

Below: If Graf Zeppelin had been completed, the Fi 167 might never have flown from it. In 1942, it was decided that the Ju 87E could adequately fulfill the torpedo bomber and reconnaissance role.

Above: By removing a number of light-weight metal panels, access was gained to the whole powerplant unit.

Fi 167A-0

Type: Two-seat ship-based general-purpose reconnaissance/torpedo bomber biplane.

Powerplant: One 820-kW (1,100-hp.) Daimler-Benz DB601B 12-cylinder inverted-Vee

Maximum speed: 325 km/h (202 m.p.h.) in the recon role

Climb rate: 2.7 min. to 1000 m (3,280 ft.)

Range: 1545 km (930 mi.) on a recon mission with a 364-litre (80-gal.) drop tank.

Service ceiling: 8200 m (26,900 ft.)

Weights: Empty 2974 kg (6,160 lb.); max take-off 4840 kg (10,670 lb.)

Weapons: One 7.92-mm MG 15 machine gun in the rear cockpit; one fixed forward-firing 7.92-mm MG 17 machine gun; and 1000 kg (2,200 lb.) of bombs or one 765-kg (1,686-lb.) torpedo.

Dimensions:
span	13.51 m	(44 ft. 4 in.)
length	11.41 m	(37 ft. 5 in.)
height	4.76 m	(15 ft. 8 in.)
wing area	48.50 m²	(522 sq. ft.)

Fi 167A-0

The aircraft shown was based in the Netherlands with Erprobungsstaffel 167 during 1942. Several camouflage schemes were worn.

Automatic leading-edge slats were fitted to both upper and lower wings, helping to give the Fi 167 its incredible handling qualities. The aircraft was also faster than required by the original specification.

Designed not only for ease of manufacture as well as maintenance, the center fuselage was covered with light alloy sheet and the rear fuselage was a stressed-skin monocoque.

Mounted on a pivot-mount, the rear machine gun could defend the rear upper area of the airplane. Remarkably, the Fi 167 carried twice the required bomb load.

Compared to the prototypes, the Fi 167A-0 pre-production aircraft had modified flame-damping exhausts and improved inlets and outlets for the DB601B's supercharger.

Large fairings covered the long undercarriage legs. Strong shock-absorbers were fitted to withstand the force of a heavy carrier landing. Larger low-pressure tires were also included on the Fi 167A-0s.

Large trailing-edge flaps were mounted on the lower wing only. The wings were designed to fold at a point just outboard of the main undercarriage attachment points.

As a specialized naval aircraft, the Fi 167 was fitted with an arrester hook from the outset. A combination of the *Graf Zeppelin's* cancellation and Ju 87 developments denied the Fi 167 any opportunity to fly from a carrier.

Warplanes of the German fleet

■ **ARADO Ar 195:** Unsuccessful in competition with the Fi 167, the Ar 195 suffered from excessive drag.

■ **ARADO Ar 197:** In 1936, Germany had no experience with carrier aircraft, hence Arado's decision to build a simple biplane fighter.

■ **JUNKERS Ju 87:** Although represented here by the Ju 87B, two naval variants of the Ju 87 were proposed: the Ju 87C and Ju 87E.

■ **MESSERSCHMITT Bf 109T:** Based on the Bf 109E, the Bf 109T-1 had a larger wing area, arrester hook and other modifications.

ACTION DATA

SPEED

For maximum effectiveness, especially in the reconnaissance role, a reasonably high cruising speed with economical fuel burn is essential. The Fi 167A-0 greatly outperforms the Swordfish in this respect, but falls short of the navalized Ju 87C-0.

Fi 167A-0	269 km/h (167 m.p.h.)
SWORDFISH Mk II	208 km/h (129 m.p.h.)
Ju 87C-0	335 km/h (208 m.p.h.)

WEAPONS

Using its rear, pivot-mounted machine gun for defence while attacking with its forward gun and 1000 kg) (2,200-lb.) ordnance load, the Fi 167 would have packed a much harder punch than either the Fairey Swordfish Mk III or Junkers Ju 87C-0.

Fi 167A-0	2 x 7.92-mm machine guns 1000-kg (2,200-lb.) bomb load
SWORDFISH Mk II	2 x 7.7-mm machine guns, 1000-kg (2,200-lb.) bomb load
Ju 87C-0	3 x 7.92-mm machine guns 500-kg (1,100-lb.) bomb load

RANGE

Junkers proposed the Ju 87C-0 as a naval aircraft capable of reconnaissance, dive bombing, and general duties. As such, it took over much of the Fi 167's role. In reconnaissance configuration, however, it could not match the Fi 167 in range.

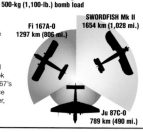

Fi 167A-0	1297 km (806 mi.)
SWORDFISH Mk II	1654 km (1,028 mi.)
Ju 87C-0	789 km (490 mi.)

FOKKER

C.V

● Inter-war design ● Light reconnaissance bomber ● Licence built

O ne of the most successful aircraft of its era in terms of numbers built, the C.V originated in the mid-1920s. Its performance was not very distinguished, but most of the 1000-plus examples assembled subsequently in seven other countries were still in service at the start of World War II. It was offered with a series of wings and a wide range of engines, which helped the type to meet the requirements of a dozen different countries in various roles.

▲ Built in sizeable numbers in a number of factories throughout Western Europe, the C.V was a very important inter-war design. Engine interchangeability was an important feature.

FOKKER C.V

▲ Easily distinguished
Inter-plane 'V' struts distinguished the C.V-D from the later C.V-E, which had 'N' struts.

▲ Kestrel-powered C.VI
Not a new type as its designation suggests, the C.VI was a version of the C.V-D for the Dutch Air Division. To prolong their service life they were re-engined with Rolls-Royce Kestrel engines in 1936.

Inter-war export success ▶
First flying in May 1924 the C.V was, in its different variants, a versatile and popular multi-role machine.

◀ Swedish S.6A
Sweden's State Aircraft Factory built Jupiter-engined C.V-Es under licence, designating them J.3s and then S.6s.

Finnish Fives ▶
Finland purchased an unknown number of C.Vs, some of which were licence-built. The first was a Jupiter-powered C.V-E, like this one; later examples had Pegasus radials. Skis were fitted in winter.

FACTS AND FIGURES

➤ Fokker complained that the C.V was so reliable that none needed overhaul, causing work shortages at the factory.

➤ A C.V-E has been restored to airworthy condition at Malmen, Sweden.

➤ Norwegian C.V-Ds saw action against German forces during the 1940 invasion.

➤ As well as in the Netherlands, C.Vs were built in Denmark, Finland, Hungary, Italy, Norway, Sweden and Switzerland.

➤ Record-breaking flights by Italian C.Vs included a Naples – Tripoli flight in 1927.

➤ C.Vs are believed to have been built with engines from eight different builders.

PROFILE

Fokker's versatile sesquiplane

Fokker's first C.V flew for the first time in May 1924, and around 90 A, B and C models with different wing areas and liquid-cooled in-line engines were built in the following two years. Some were built under licence in Denmark, and the total included C.V-W floatplanes.

In 1926 production switched to the D and E models, which could use either in-line or radial engines, the C.V-E having an increased wing area over the D-model. The latter, with their much smaller lower wings, were generally used as two-seat fighters, while the C.V-Es were bombers; both were used for other missions including battlefield reconnaissance.

Over 1000 Ds and Es were built in Hungary, Italy, Norway, Sweden and Switzerland, and by Fokker in the Netherlands. Versatile and easy to maintain, they followed traditional Fokker construction practice with their fabric-covered steel-tube fuselages and wooden wings. Later aircraft had more powerful engines; 544-kW (730-hp.) Bristol Pegasus were used by Dutch, Danish and Swedish forces, while aircraft built in Switzerland by EKW and Dornier until 1936 used Hispano powerplants.

Above: As well as float-equipped C.V-Cs, the Dutch Naval Air Service flew C.V-Es with wheeled landing gear.

Below: Of the 10 C.V-Es that survived in Danish service until 1940, two were taken over by the Luftwaffe, including 3W+OD, formerly R-42. After the war this aircraft was returned to Denmark, having survived hostilities.

C.V-D

Type: two-seat light fighter and reconnaissance aircraft

Powerplant: one 455-kW (610-hp.) Bristol Jupiter VI nine-cylinder, air-cooled radial engine

Maximum speed: 245 km/h (152 m.p.h.)

Climb rate: 1 min 54 sec to 1000 m (3,300 ft.)

Range: 770 km (480 mi.)

Service ceiling: 7300 m (24,000 ft.)

Weights: empty 1125 kg (2,475 lb.); loaded 1725 kg (3,795 lb.)

Armament: one or two fixed forward-firing machine-guns and one or two machine-guns in a flexible mounting in the rear cockpit

Dimensions:
span	12.50 m (41 ft.)
length	9.46 m (31 ft. 1 in.)
height	3.30 m (10 ft. 10 in.)
wing area	28.8 m² (310 sq. ft.)

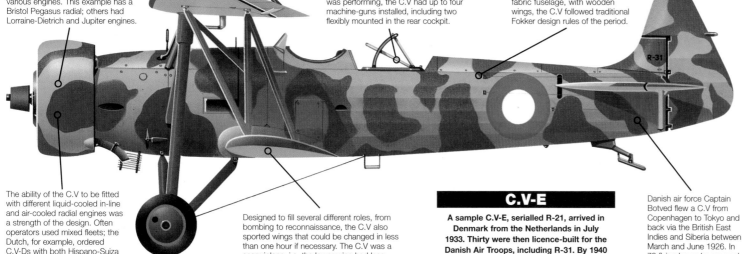

Denmark's C.V-Es were powered by various engines. This example has a Bristol Pegasus radial; others had Lorraine-Dietrich and Jupiter engines.

Depending on the role this versatile aircraft was performing, the C.V had up to four machine-guns installed, including two flexibly mounted in the rear cockpit.

Having a welded steel tube and fabric fuselage, with wooden wings, the C.V followed traditional Fokker design rules of the period.

The ability of the C.V to be fitted with different liquid-cooled in-line and air-cooled radial engines was a strength of the design. Often operators used mixed fleets; the Dutch, for example, ordered C.V-Ds with both Hispano-Suiza and Jaguar engines.

Designed to fill several different roles, from bombing to reconnaissance, the C.V also sported wings that could be changed in less than one hour if necessary. The C.V was a sesquiplane, i.e. the lower wing had less than half the area of the upper.

C.V-E

A sample C.V-E, serialled R-21, arrived in Denmark from the Netherlands in July 1933. Thirty were then licence-built for the Danish Air Troops, including R-31. By 1940 only 10 were still in service.

Danish air force Captain Botved flew a C.V from Copenhagen to Tokyo and back via the British East Indies and Siberia between March and June 1926. In 72 flying hours he covered 10,395 km (6,445 mi.).

COMBAT DATA

POWER

The C.V's power rating depended on its engine and could vary between 186 kW (250 hp.) and 544 kW (730 hp.). The Fairey had a comparable power rating to the -D; the DH.9A was less powerful.

C.V-D	Fairey IIIF Mk IV	DH.9A
455 kW (610 hp.)	425 kW (570 hp.)	298 kW (400 hp.)

ARMAMENT

Once again, the C.V's armament fit was dependent upon the role assigned to the aircraft. Twice as many machine-guns as those carried by its competitors could be fitted if required.

C.V-D	4 x 7.9-mm machine-guns 200-kg (400-lb.) bombload
IIIF Mk IV	2 x 7.7-mm machine-guns 227-kg (500-lb.) bombload
DH.9A	2 x 7.7-mm (.303 cal.) machine-guns 299-kg (660-lb.) bombload

RANGE

De Havilland's DH.9A had good range, in the order of 850 km (530 mi.). The Fokker C.V-D was not far behind, both types easily better than the Fairey IIIF. The DH.9A and IIIF filled light bombing and reconnaissance roles, mainly overseas, for the RAF in the 1920s.

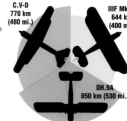

C.V-D 770 km (480 mi.)	IIIF Mk IV 644 km (400 mi.)
	DH.9A 850 km (530 mi.)

Fokker's inter-war combat designs

■ **D.XI:** This fighter design of 1923 had a 225-km/h top speed, but was unable to generate orders from the Dutch air force.

■ **D.XIII:** First flown in September 1924, the D.XIII was a single-seat fighter derived from the D.VII. Power came from a Napier Lion.

■ **D.XVII:** Able to achieve 376 km/h in level flight, the sleek D.XVII fighter was an enlarged development of the D.XVI with twin machine-guns.

■ **C.X:** Designed to replace the C.V, this Pegasus-powered light bomber and fighter-reconnaissance type served from the late 1930s.

FOKKER

D.VII

● Scout fighter ● Flown by fighter ace Ernst Udet ● Best of its time

Iain Wyllie

PHOTO FILE

FOKKER **D.VII**

▲ Fokker heritage
The D.VII was not a totally new design, inheriting features from previous Fokkers. But the Fokker D.VII's performance was unprecedented.

▲ Powerful engine
Much of the D.VII's success was due to its efficient engines, which were far more powerful and reliable than those used by fighters in the early years. The additional power also compensated for the extra weight of the twin machine-guns.

◄ Survivors
Few D.VIIs survived the war and only a handful of the original aircraft remain in museums; one is owned by the RAF Museum. Many more replica aircraft exist than real examples.

▼ Fokker fragments
The remnants of this D.VII show just how strong the aircraft's tubular steel structure was, with the main fuselage still intact after being shot down.

▲ Dutch service post-war
The Armistice at the end of World War I specifically mentioned the D.VII among items to be handed over to the Allies. Anthony Fokker took some dismantled aircraft to Holland and more were built there, some serving with the Dutch air force until the late 1920s.

Fokker's D.VII was the greatest single-seat scout used by Germany in World War I, and possibly the best flown by any nation. It took a courageous pilot to do battle with the West's greatest planes and pilots. The D.VII gave German airmen the chance to fight on more than equal terms with the Sopwith Camel, Spad XIII and other fine fighters which had swung the balance of the air war to the Allies after the disasters of April 1917.

▲ The combination of skilled pilots and the superb D.VII gave the Imperial German air service a new breath of life in 1918, with the capability of matching any other fighter in the world.

FACTS AND FIGURES

➤ By November 1918, 700 D.VIIs had been delivered to the German air arm.

➤ The cost of one of today's European Fighter Aircraft (EFA) would pay for 30,000 Fokker D.VIIs.

➤ The D.VII strongly influenced the Fokker C.I, which appeared in the post-war era.

➤ Almost 43 groups of D.VIIs were in service when the war ended.

➤ The D.VII was specifically singled out for confiscation in the terms of the Versailles Peace Treaty.

➤ Three replicas of the D.VII fly at air shows in the United States.

PROFILE

Fokker's finest biplane fighter

First flown in January 1918, designer Reinhold Platz's Fokker D.VII was an immensely strong yet simple aircraft. Built around a steel tube frame, it performed superbly yet was easy to build and maintain.

It was immediately evident that this was a top-performing warplane. The D.VII was so much better than the Albatros D.V. series that Albatros Werke GmbH was ordered to build the fighter under sub-contract at both of its factories. The Fokker D.VII was termed a 'major threat' by an Allied pilot who flew against it.

It combined speed, agility and firepower with a strong prospect of surviving any fight. So strong was the combat capability of this famous aircraft that the Versailles Treaty which brought the war to an end specified that all planes of this type must be handed over to the Allies. The D.VII and the Zeppelin airships were the only German aircraft singled out for confiscation.

Left: Among the D.VII's many virtues was its power, which allowed the aircraft to maintain a climbing attitude when other fighters would have stalled.

Right: In the late- and post-war periods pilots applied personal markings to the sides of their aircraft. This Swiss machine was one of many export D.VIIs.

D.VII

Type: single-seat fighter/scout

Powerplant: one 138-kW (185-hp.) BMW 6-cylinder in-line piston engine

Maximum speed: 200 km/h (124 m.p.h.) at 1000 m (3,300 ft.)

Climb rate: 1000 m (3,300 ft.) in 2½ min

Service ceiling: 7000 m (22,965 ft.)

Weights: empty 735 kg (1,620 lb.); max take-off 880 kg (1,940 lb.)

Armament: two fixed forward-firing 7.92-mm LMG 08/15 machine-guns

Dimensions:
span	8.90 m (29 ft.)
length	6.95 m (23 ft.)
height	2.75 m (9 ft.)
wing area	20.5 m² (221 sq. ft.)

The armament consisted of a pair of air-cooled LMG 7.92-mm machine-guns.

The pilot sat in an open cockpit, typical of aircraft of the day. He was close enough to his gun breeches to clear any jams by hand, and many pilots carried hammers or chisels for the job.

The main part of the airframe was a metal tube frame with a doped fabric covering.

The first D.VIIs used Mercedes engines, but later versions used BMW engines, all of the inline type.

Later D.VIIs had a small fuel tank in the fairing between the undercarriage wheels, giving much needed endurance.

The strange 'lozenge' pattern on German aircraft was the result of using pre-printed fabric. Many pilots added their own artwork.

A round tailfin was another distinctive feature of many Fokker aircraft. A simple tail skid protected the fin on the ground.

D.VII

The Fokker D.VII served on the Western Front with distinction, and became the most feared German fighter scout of World War I.

COMBAT DATA

MAXIMUM SPEED

The fastest fighters in World War I could reach around 200 km/h (125 m.p.h.), with the heavy and powerful French Spads being among the fastest. But pilots valued other features just as highly. Rate of climb was considered vital, and agility was especially desirable. The D.VII combined all of these qualities in one aircraft.

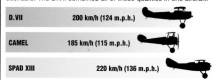

D.VII	200 km/h (124 m.p.h.)
CAMEL	185 km/h (115 m.p.h.)
SPAD XIII	220 km/h (136 m.p.h.)

ENDURANCE

Scout fighters were required to make standing patrols over the battlefield to prevent opposing aircraft crossing their territory. The heavier Spad and Camel carried more fuel than the D.VII, and could stay on patrol for a longer period.

D.VII 1½ hours	CAMEL 2 hours	SPAD XIII 2 hours

SERVICE CEILING

The D.VII had a high power-to-weight ratio, giving excellent climb performance and a high service ceiling. In practice, flying at such altitudes without oxygen equipment in open cockpits was extremely tough on the pilots, many of whom suffered from anoxia or frostbite. Patrols were usually carried out at about 5000 metres (16,500 ft.).

D.VII	CAMEL	SPAD XIII
7000 m (22,960 ft.)	5790 m (19,000 ft.)	6650 m (21,810 ft.)

Finest fighters of the Great War

■ **SOPWITH CAMEL:** Sopwith's finest scout fighter, the Camel featured superb manoeuvrability and speed, but was not an easy aircraft to fly, being prone to flick into spins when mishandled.

■ **SPAD XIII:** The French Spad XIII was a fast and rugged fighter used by several Allied fighter aces such as Rickenbacker and Fonck. It was also used by the fledgling US Army Air Corps.

■ **FOKKER DR.1:** The legendary Fokker Triplane was flown by many German air aces, including Baron Manfred von Richthofen. It was highly agile and possessed an excellent rate of climb.

FOKKER

D.VII STUNT FLYER

● Ace maker ● Film star fighter ● World War I veteran

Spinning and spiralling, twisting and diving biplanes fill the sky at an assortment of angles and altitudes. A pilot hastily looks over his shoulder to search for the enemy fighter looming up on his tail. A flash of guns, and smoke billows from the engine cowling as the enemy dives away. Time and again Hollywood war movies featured such performing aircraft and valiant heroes, and prominent amongst the melées was the Fokker D.VII.

▲ *Once left derelict, the few remaining Fokker D.VIIs are now highly prized possessions. This example was restored to flying condition for exhibition at airshows in Europe.*

FOKKER D.VII

▼ Air pirate
Restored to former wartime markings, this Fokker D.VII is painted with a skull and crossbones on its fuselage. During the war Fokkers wore some of the most elaborate colour schemes.

▲ Everlasting design
By using steel tubes for the fuselage and tailplane structure the Fokker designers produced a fighter that was strong and able to withstand extraordinary stunts, qualities that were not wasted in front of the movie cameras.

Elite units, elite fighter ▶
The exceptional capabilities of the Fokker design allowed the aircraft to be the chosen mount for Germany's fighter aces in 1918.

▼ Revered past
These Fokkers of World War I are displayed here next to a former enemy.

Superior scout ▶
If the Fokker D.VII was not battling with British fighters it was being used as a fast scout. Prominent on most machines were large German crosses on the wheels.

FACTS AND FIGURES

➤ The Fokker D.VII was ordered into production having won Germany's January 1918 fighter competition.

➤ Its performance was matched in combat only by that of the British Sopwith Snipe.

➤ By the end of World War I, some 700 examples had been built.

➤ A number of Fokker D.VIIs were lost when the phosphorous ammunition carried in the aircraft ignited.

➤ During manoeuvres the centre-section fuselage often became over stressed.

➤ Hollywood stunt pilots praised the aircraft for its superb handling.

PROFILE

Silver screen fighter

Hollywood developed as the world centre for the film industry during the Roaring Twenties, with film stars and directors flocking to propose and produce numerous action films.

Having already captured the public's imagination in war, pilots and their aircraft were soon appearing in front of

An important feature of the the Fokker fighter was its ability to 'hang' on its propeller at high altitude. This allowed pilots to fire upwards when other fighters would spin away.

the cameras to thrill the film-going population.

One of the most ambitious movies involving massive aerial dogfights was *Hell's Angels*, directed by Howard Hughes. The success of this film led studios to produce a host of thrilling aerial productions.

With huge numbers of surplus fighter aircraft from World War I being sold for just a few dollars, highly elaborate and complex aerial

Below: A pilot looks over his shoulder to the chase aircraft in anticipation of beginning another dogfight for the cameras.

Above: Though lacking the graceful lines of the Albatros and Pfalz scouts, the Fokker D.VII proved to be a startling surprise to RFC pilots.

battles could be staged. The participating aircraft were often destroyed to add to the overall dramatic effect.

A leading star among these ex-military aircraft was the Fokker D.VII.

Because of the immense strength of the fuselage and wing construction, the Fokker fighter could be manoeuvred vigorously in aerial combat. This sparkling performance allowed Hollywood producers to direct enormous and elaborate dogfights to thrill and excite movie audiences.

As with most fighters of the period a tail-skid was positioned at the rear of the fuselage. Handling of the aircraft was praised by both German and British pilots. With such performance capabilities the Fokker D.VII became a star aircraft in Hollywood.

Early series Fokker D.VIIs were equipped with a Mercedes D.III powerplant. This low-powered engine limited the type's performance. Later models were fitted with a much improved and more powerful BMW engine.

The reputation of the Fokker fighter allowed the aircraft to become the chosen mount of a host of Germany's World War I aces. After the war civilian pilots were equally as keen to obtain an example.

D.VII

Fokker D.VII aces wore a succession of elaborate colour schemes during World War I. After the war these were often faithfully reproduced by Hollywood producers to add realism to their war movies. This particular example wears a black and white colour scheme along its fuselage.

D.VII

Type: single-seat fighter/scout

Powerplant: one 138-kW (185-hp.) BMW III six-cylinder in-line piston engine

Maximum speed: 200 km/h (124 m.p.h.)

Endurance: 1 hr 30 min

Initial climb rate: 321 m/min (1053 f.p.m.)

Service ceiling: 7000 m (22,970 ft.)

Weights: empty 735 kg (1,620 lb.); maximum take-off 880 kg (1,940 lb.)

Armament: two fixed forward-firing 7.92-mm LMG 08/15 machine guns

Dimensions:
span	8.90 m	(29 ft. 2 in.)
length	6.95 m	(22 ft. 10 in.)
height	2.75 m	(9 ft.)
wing area	20.50 m²	(221 sq. ft.)

ACTION DATA

POWER

A steady increase in engine performance allowed the Fokker company to develop a highly powerful fighter in the Fokker D.VII. With the power available the fighter was able to perform the complex manoeuvres which were vital during aerial combat.

D.VII	E.III	D.V
138 kW (185 hp.)	75 kW (100 hp.)	149 kW (197 hp.)

ENDURANCE

Because of the practice of mounting standing aerial patrols, long endurance was a particularly important quality in World War I fighters. Despite the advantages that the Fokker D.VII offered in many areas, its endurance was no more than comparable to that of other fighters of the period.

D.VII	E.III	D.V
1 hr 30 min	1 hr 30 min	2 hr

MAXIMUM SPEED

Speed and manoeuvrability were the key design requirements for fighters of World War I. Light in weight and equipped with a high-powered engine, the Fokker D.VII proved to have exceptional speed, a capability not lost on Hollywood's movie makers.

D.VII	200 km/h (124 m.p.h.)
E.III	140 km/h (87 m.p.h.)
D.V	186 km/h (116 m.p.h.)

Fantastic Fokkers

■ **A DOPED 'D MODEL':** Serving as a two-seat trainer this particular example wore an overall fabric-dope colour scheme. The forward-firing guns were removed from this aircraft.

■ **'BLUEBIRD':** Using a mixture of pre-printed fabric on its fuselage and 'lozenge' pattern for both wings, this particular D.VII was flown by Lieutenant Piel of Jasta 13.

■ **CLOUD COLOURS:** An overall light grey colour was adopted late in the service life of the Fokker D.VII in order to conceal the aircraft at high altitude during scouting missions.

FOKKER

DR.1

● Agile hunter of the skies ● Von Richthofen's fighter

Supremely agile, the Fokker Dr.1 was a powerful tool in the hands of Baron von Richthofen's Flying Circus in the last two years of World War I. The Dr.1 overcame serious manufacturing flaws to become the scourge of Allied aces on the Western Front, weaving a pattern of destruction with its twin machine-guns. A ferocious adversary, this potent fighter was for a brief period the monarch of the skies.

▲ A Fokker Triplane gets a push across muddy ground on the Western Front. The middle wing and steep fuselage angle made it a bit of a handful on the ground.

FOKKER DR.1

▲ Horned wings
Ailerons were on the upper wing only. They were fitted with large 'horns', making the aircraft roll at an unbelievable rate. The large tailplane allowed the pilot to hold the turn better than Allied fighters.

▲ Lightweight fighter
Like other World War I fighters, the Dr.1 was so light that the best way to move it was to pick it up and carry it!

Ace machine ▲
The Dr.1 had plenty of vices and was not for the novice airman. Only the best pilots could handle this tricky little fighter.

▲ Modern triplane
Few aviation stories have achieved the notoriety of that of Baron von Richthofen, making the Fokker Dr.1 a popular subject for replica-builders.

Movie star ▶
Many of the replicas of Dr.1s have been spurred by the requirements of Hollywood; the Red Baron legend is an enduring one.

FACTS AND FIGURES

➤ The Dr.1 was the fastest-climbing and most manoeuvrable fighter of its day.

➤ Triplanes had weak wings, which often collapsed in combat.

➤ Despite its sensational performance, the Fokker was grounded in 1917 while its wings were redesigned.

➤ A Luftwaffe F-4 Phantom today weighs 98 times as much as a Dr.1.

➤ More than 300 Fokker Dr.1s were built and the type remained in service until the end of World War I.

➤ Triplanes were flown by many aces, the most notable being von Richthofen.

PROFILE

Triplanes over the Western Front

Anthony Fokker, the Dutch planemaker working in Germany, joined the triplane craze started by Britain's Sopwith and created the splendid three-winged Dr.1 in 1917. Air ace Baron Manfred von Richthofen told pilots that Fokker Dr.1s 'are manoeuvrable as the Devil and climb like monkeys'. Richthofen was killed

flying a blood-red Dr.1 after scoring many of his 80 aerial conquests in the triplane.

The Fokker Dr.1 moved aviation design forward with wings that needed no bracing struts. At first the design was unreliable; two aces were killed when their wings tore apart in mid-air. Fokker solved construction problems and the

Dr.1 became a superb aircraft to fly, and by 1918 it was a terror to British airmen who faced it in combat.

The Fokker Dr.1 won glory and wreaked havoc amongst its opponents until newer biplane fighters matched its spectacular performance, closing the short but brilliant career of this truly great fighting machine.

The Dr.1 earned a reputation that far outweighed the numbers produced. At no time did the number in service exceed 171 (in May 1918), and by the summer it had virtually disappeared from the front line.

Dr.1 Triplane

Type: single-seat fighter/scout

Powerplant: one 108-kW Thulin-built Le Rhône or Oberursel Ur.II nine-cylinder rotary piston engine

Maximum speed: 185 km/h (115 m.p.h.) at 4000 m (13,100 ft.)

Endurance: 1 hr 30 min

Rate of climb: 1000 m (3,300 ft.) in 2 min 54 sec; time to 3000 m (10,000 ft.) 7 min 6 sec

Service ceiling: 6100 m (20,000 ft.)

Weights: empty 430 kg (948 lb.); loaded 610 kg (1345 lb.)

Armament: two 7.92-mm LMG 08/15 air-cooled machine-guns

Dimensions:
span	7.20 m (23 ft. 8 in.)
length	5.77 m (18 ft. 11 in.)
height	2.95 m (9 ft. 8 in.)
wing area	18.7 m² (201 sq. ft.)

DR.1 TRIPLANE

Arguably the most famous fighter of all time, the Fokker Dr.1 achieved this position through the achievements of just one man, Rittmeister Manfred, Freiherr von Richthofen, better known as the Red Baron. He was flying this type when he was finally brought down.

Armament of the Dr.1 was the standard German fit of two LMG 08/15 guns mounted on top of the fuselage.

There is much controversy surrounding the death of Manfred von Richthofen on 21 April 1918. The official RAF version is that he was shot down by Canadian Camel pilot Captain A.R. Brown. But examination of his wounds when he was found slumped in the cockpit of his crashed Dreidecker would suggest that he was actually killed by Australian troops firing from the ground.

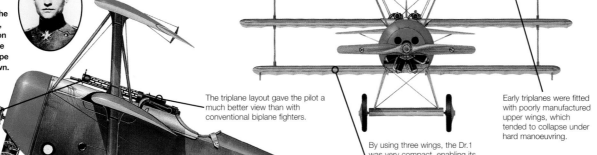

The triplane layout gave the pilot a much better view than with conventional biplane fighters.

By using three wings, the Dr.1 was very compact, enabling its pilots to perform astonishing aerial manoeuvres.

Early triplanes were fitted with poorly manufactured upper wings, which tended to collapse under hard manoeuvring.

The origins of the Fokker Dr.1 lay in the Sopwith Triplane, which greatly impressed the Germans. When one crashed behind enemy lines Anthony Fokker managed to steal it away from the authorities to his own factory, and rapidly set to work copying many of its features.

As with all aircraft of the period, the triplane was fitted with a simple tail skid rather than the heavier and more complex castoring wheel which was to appear on later machines.

COMBAT DATA

MAXIMUM SPEED

Extremely agile machines such as the Dr.1 or the Camel were not known for their great speed, but their light construction meant that they had good acceleration, and could out-turn and outfight faster machines.

DR.1 TRIPLANE	185 km/h (115 m.p.h.)
CAMEL	187 km/h (116 m.p.h.)
SPAD VII	192 km/h (119 m.p.h.)

ENDURANCE

German scouts generally fought over their own lines. Allied fighters, on the other hand, needed longer endurance since they often patrolled aggressively over German-occupied territory.

DR.1 TRIPLANE 1 hour 30 minutes	CAMEL 2 hours 30 minutes	SPAD VII 2 hours 15 minutes

'The Fokker Scourge'

■ FOKKER E.III
The 'Eindecker' was the first scoutplane with a machine-gun which fired between the propeller blades. It created havoc over the skies of France in 1915 and 1916, downing hundreds of Allied aircraft and helped create the Fokker legend.

■ FOKKER DR.1
Its three wings gave the Triplane phenomenal lift, and for a time in 1917 it was as dominant as its monoplane ancestor had been two years before. However, it was tricky to fly and the three wings severely restricted ground visibility.

■ FOKKER D.VII
The D.VII was the pinnacle of Imperial German fighter design. Fast, tough, and with all the agility of the triplane, it was perhaps the first fighter of World War I, although it appeared too late to influence the air war.

FOKKER

DR.1: JG 1

● JG 1's most famous fighter ● von Richthofen's final aircraft

▲ Jasta 11's pilots included Manfred von Richthofen's brother Lothar (seated, cross-legged), who joined the unit in March 1917. He was to amass 40 victories and was credited with the SE.5 of Captain Albert Ball, No. 56 Squadron, RFC – Britain's most famous fighter pilot of the time.

F or brave pilots who flew with Baron Manfred von Richthofen, the 'Flying Circus' meant high risks and no safety net. Richthofen was Germany's top ace and the Dr.I was one of its best fighters. But climbing into a fragile, fabric-covered Fokker and going aloft often meant an appointment with peril. Meeting Allied pilots in battle was the greatest challenge of all. This was the cutting edge of fighter aviation during the Great War.

FOKKER DR.I

▲ First 'Dreideckers' arrive
von Richthofen (right) looks on as a pilot is introduced to the new Fokker. Aircraft 102/17, later flown by von Richthofen himself, carries the early F.I designation.

▲ Highly manoeuvrable
While von Richthofen appreciated the Dr.I's handling, he was not the fan of the type that the press portrayed. The greatest exponent of the Dr.I was Werner Voss, who gained 48 victories in the Dr.I.

▲ Albatros D.III
Richthofen's Jagdgeschwader 1 used a number of types, including the Albatros D.III.

▼ Jasta 11 aces
von Richthofen is seen here with two other aces: Scholz (seven victories) and Mohnicke (nine victories).

▲ von Richthofen's first Dr.I
This aircraft was the second production Fokker F.I (later Dr.I) and was the first machine assigned to von Richthofen. While flying it he scored his 60th kill, and Kurt Wolff of Jasta 11 later met his end in it.

FACTS AND FIGURES

➤ JG 1's third and final commander was Oberleutnant Hermann Göring, World War II Luftwaffe commander-in-chief.

➤ The exact cause of Richthofen's death is unclear, although ground fire seems likely.

➤ Jasta 10's aircraft were yellow; Jastas 4 and 6 wore black and white spirals.

➤ One of JG 1's greatest rivals was the Royal Flying Corps' No. 56 Squadron, led by British ace Captain James McCudden.

➤ von Richthofen's Albatros D.III was known to RFC pilots as 'le petit rouge'.

➤ 'Jagdgeschwader Richthofen' was reborn twice – in 1936 (JG 2) and 1959 (JG 71).

PROFILE

JG 1: the world's first fighter wing

April 1917 – 'Bloody April' – saw Imperial Germany's Army Air Service, the Luftstreikräfte, in virtual control of the skies over the Western Front. To maintain this hard-won position, a decision was taken in June to formally amalgamate four Jagdstaffeln (Jastas) that had been flying together experimentally against enemy fighter patrols. Jagdgeschwader Nr.1 was the result. Jasta

11's commander, the 25-year-old Rittmeister Manfred von Richthofen, the 'Red Baron', was to be its first leader. Each Jasta had its own distinctive colour scheme (Jasta 11's was red) and pilots often had their

own personal markings; JG 1 soon became known as 'von Richthofen's Flying Circus'.Their aircraft included the Albatros D.III and D.V and, later, the Fokker D.VII, although they are perhaps best known for their exploits in Fokker's Dr.I. Among the pilots were the most accomplished Air Service aces of the day, including Werner Voss and Ernst Udet.

In its 17-month lifespan the wing amassed 644 aerial victories, but 56 of its pilots were killed and 52 were wounded.

Often discounted as a copy of the Sopwith Triplane (at least one early example of which fell into German hands), the Dr.I obviously owed its conception to the British scout. However, when originally produced the design featured three cantilever wings without interplane struts.

Two fixed Spandau machine-guns were synchronised to fire through the propeller arc. They could be fired independently.

von Richthofen flew four triplanes in total, one of which (152/17) was displayed after the war in a Berlin museum. It was destroyed by Allied bombs in 1944.

The Fokker Dr.I (or F.I as it was originally known) was powered by either an Oberursel UR II or Thulin-built Le Rhône nine-cylinder rotary engine, rated at 82 kW (115 hp.), driving a two-bladed 2.6-m (8-ft. 6-in.) diameter wooden propeller.

On this aircraft the straight-sided national marking, known as the 'Balkenkreuz', had been recently applied, and traces of the original 'Iron Cross' were still visible.

Contrary to many reports, this aircraft was not all-red. It featured blue undersides, metal cowling and white wheels and vertical tail.

During late 1917 a number of pilots were killed after the main wing structure failed; this caused the Dr.I to be temporarily grounded.

DR.I

Arguably one of the best-known aircraft, this Dr.I (425/17) was the aircraft flown by von Richthofen when he was killed on 21 April 1918.

Dr.I

Type: single-seat fighting scout

Powerplant: one 82-kW (110-hp.) Oberursel UR II rotary piston engine

Maximum speed: 165 km/h (103 m.p.h.) at 4000 m (13,120 ft.)

Initial climb rate: 7.1 min to 3000 m (9840 ft.)

Endurance: 1 hr 30 min

Service ceiling: 6100 m (20,000 ft.)

Weights: empty 430 kg (948 lb.); maximum take-off 626 kg (1,380 lb.)

Armament: two fixed 7.92-mm LMG 08/15 on nose firing through propeller arc

Dimensions:
span	7.19 m	(23 ft. 7 in.)
length	5.77 m	(18 ft. 11 in.)
height	2.95 m	(9 ft. 8 in.)
wing area	18.66 m²	(201 sq. ft.)

ACTION DATA

MAXIMUM SPEED

The Albatros D.III was followed in JG 1 service by the Fokker Dr.I. This, in turn, was replaced by the Fokker D.VII towards the end of the war. The Dr.I introduced better manoeuvrability over the D.III.

Dr.I	165 km/h (103 m.p.h.)
D.III	165 km/h (103 m.p.h.)
D.VII	186 km/h (116 m.p.h.)

ENDURANCE

The rotary-engined Dr.I actually had less endurance than the D.III which it replaced. Greater power and handling improvements were viewed as more important to counter new British fighters like the Sopwith Triplane.

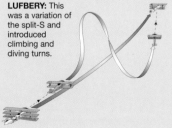

Dr.I	D.III	D.VII
1½ hours	2 hours	1½ hours

ENGINE POWER

While it is true that engine power increased steadily as the war progressed, resulting in improved performance, the later Fokker Dr.I actually had a smaller engine than the Albatros D.III as it was a much lighter aircraft.

 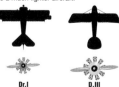

Dr.I	D.III	D.VII
82 kW (110 hp.)	119 kW (160 hp.)	138 kW (185 hp.)

Dogfight manoeuvres

TACTICAL EVOLUTION: As aircraft improved, so air combat manoeuvring developed.

SNAP TURN: Using engine torque to increase turn rate allowed the target to get behind his opponent.

IMMELMANN: Named after its inventor Max Immelmann, this climbing turn was used mainly as a means of escape.

SPLIT-S: The split-S was used by more experienced pilots as a variation of the snap turn and was intended to force the opponent to overshoot the target.

LUFBERY: This was a variation of the split-S and introduced climbing and diving turns.

GLOSTER

GAMECOCK

● Biplane fighter ● Wooden construction ● Aerobatic star

Gloster's Gamecock fighter burst onto the scene in the mid 1920s and, while far from beautiful, it astounded pilots with its performance. The Gamecock was the last wooden biplane fighter in Britain's Royal Air Force and typified the end of an era. Because of this, it embodied all that was known about air combat maneuverability. The Gamecock was meant for battle, but it also was extremely popular for its aerobatic qualities.

▲ The Gamecock's nine-cylinder Bristol Jupiter IV engine produced 317 kW (425 hp.) and turned a wooden propeller to give the aircraft a top speed of 248 km/h (154 m.p.h.). All RAF examples used this powerplant.

GLOSTER GAMECOCK

▼ Built under licence
Gloster supplied three aircraft to Finland and these were followed by another 15 built under licence. The last aircraft was retired in 1941.

▲ A pilot's dream
The aerobatic capabilities of the Gamecock were loved by its pilots. Wearing the spectacular markings of the era and being flown to the limit, these fighters were great air show performers.

◀ In RAF service
The Royal Air Force received almost 100 Gamecocks, which served with five squadrons. J7900 was one of the first production batch of 30 Gamecock Mk Is.

Aerodynamic problems ▼
Early test flights revealed wing problems at high speeds. To solve these and to make the aircraft safer, a V-shaped strut was fitted between the wings.

▲ Fighter development
The main difference between the Gamecock and World War I fighters was its increased power.

FACTS AND FIGURES

➤ The Gamecock was designed by H.P. Folland to meet British Air Ministry Specification 37/23.

➤ Developed from the Grebe, the Gamecock had a more powerful engine.

➤ The Gamecock first flew in 1925 and served in Finland as a trainer until 1941.

➤ The first squadron to be equipped with the Gamecock, No. 23, received its aircraft in May 1926.

➤ Many of the RAF's 100 Gamecock fighters were operational up to 1931.

➤ Before its first flight, progress in fighter design was overtaking the Gamecock.

PROFILE

The last wooden fighter

The most potent fighter in the RAF in the mid 1920s was the Gloster Gamecock, a pilot's airplane and responsible for many fine aerobatic displays. Although it had an ungainly, swollen shape and was sometimes prone to wing flutter problems (making it necessary to add strengthening struts on the outer wing), the Gamecock was universally admired by the pilots who flew it and was deemed to be almost the perfect fighter. Much like the biplane fighters of the Great War, but with far greater power, the Gamecock was able to fly circles around most comparable aircraft then in service.

The Gamecock was constantly improved throughout its service life (changes to the design of the tail had proven necessary in early testing) and naturally drew the attention of foreign observers who were watching the RAF.

Gloster supplied three Gamecocks to Finland which then built 15 more in 1929–30. Named Kukko in Finnish service, these were in frontline service from 1929 to 1935 and were then used as trainers until the last was retired in 1941.

An early Gamecock Mk I in service with No. 23 Squadron of the Royal Air Force. Aircraft such as this thrilled audiences at air shows during the late 1920s.

Gamecock Mk I

Type: Single-seat fighter.

Powerplant: One 317-kW (425-hp.) Bristol Jupiter VI nine-cylinder radial piston engine

Maximum speed: 248 km/h (154 m.p.h.)

Range: 1160 km (720 mi.)

Service ceiling: 6095 m (20,000 ft.)

Weapons: 2 fixed forward-firing 7.7-mm (.303 cal.) Vickers Mk I machine guns

Weights: Empty 873 kg (1,925 lb.); loaded 1103 kg (2,431 lb.)

Dimensions:
span	9.07 m (29 ft. 9 in.)
length	5.99 m (19 ft. 8 in.)
height	2.95 m (9 ft. 8 in.)
wing area	24.53 m² (264 sq. ft.)

GAMECOCK MK II

Known in Finnish service as the Kukko, the Gamecock Mk II had strengthened wings and other improvements.

The cylinder heads of the Bristol Jupiter VI engine protruded through the forward fuselage. A blast trough ahead of the machine gun protected the area from damage.

Unlike the Grebe, the open cockpit of the Gamecock was fitted with a windscreen, but Kukko pilots would have suffered in the cold of a Finnish winter.

The wooden construction of the Gamecock made it light and strong. During flight tests one aircraft reached 446 km/h (277 m.p.h.) in a dive and completed a 22-turn spin.

The prototype was fitted with a tail similar to that of the SE.5a. On production aircraft the tail was re-designed as shown.

The fixed main undercarriage featured suspension. The wheels were faired, but no other aerodynamic streamlining was attempted.

Ailerons were fitted to both sets of wings. These gave the Gamecock its outstanding agility and aerobatic performance. The Mk II no longer required the V-shaped strut.

This Mk II wears the national markings of Finland. Only three Mk IIs entered RAF service, but all of them were colorfully decorated with squadron markings.

A spring tailskid protected the rear fuselage on the ground. Tailwheels were quite uncommon on aircraft of this period.

ACTION DATA

POWER

The less powerful Jupiter IV of the Woodcock gave it inferior performance to the Gamecock. American fighter designs were more advanced at this time and used far more powerful engines. British engine designers rapidly improved their technology.

GAMECOCK Mk I	WOODCOCK Mk II	F4B-4
317 kW (425 hp.)	283 kW (380 hp.)	694 kW (930 hp.)

SPEED

The higher speed of the Boeing F4B-4 results from its more advanced design and extra power. The British fighters, though slower than the F4B-4, are evenly matched. The RAF was soon to receive aircraft of much higher performance such as the Fury.

GAMECOCK Mk I	248 km/h (154 m.p.h.)
WOODCOCK Mk II	225 km/h (140 m.p.h.)
F4B-4	303 km/h (188 m.p.h.)

CEILING

Altitude can be a significant advantage in a dogfight. Here the Gamecock falls behind, but any lack of altitude performance could be compensated for by its stunning maneuverability.

F4B-4
8200 m (26,900 ft.)

WOODCOCK Mk II
6858 m (22,500 ft.)

GAMECOCK Mk I
6095 m (20,000 ft.)

Gloster-built biplanes for the RAF

■ **GREBE:** This was the first radial-engine fighter to enter quantity production for the RAF and the predecessor of the Gamecock.

■ **GORCOCK:** Three Gorcocks were delivered in 1927. They were used for trials work and aided future fighter development.

■ **GAUNTLET:** The Gauntlet served successfully with the RAF in considerable numbers and was also widely exported.

■ **GLADIATOR:** Developed from the Gauntlet, this was the ultimate RAF biplane fighter with a 619-kW (830-hp.) engine and enclosed cockpit.

GLOSTER

GLADIATOR

● Single-seat fighter ● Last RAF and Royal Navy biplane fighter

Biplane fighters were already on the way out when the Gladiator development of the Gloster Gauntlet was proposed in 1933, but Britain's urgent need for combat aircraft led to orders for an eventual total of 581. These included 350 Gladiator Mk IIs, which had improved equipment and three-blade metal propellers in place of the Gladiator Mk I's two-bladed wooden airscrew. All had been delivered by April 1940 and a number went into combat.

▲ The Gladiator prototype flew for the first time in September 1934 as a private venture. The Air Ministry ordered the type the following year, with 480 being delivered. The Royal Navy took 60.

GLOSTER GLADIATOR

▲ Last flyer
The last surviving airworthy Gladiator is this Mk I, which belongs to the Shuttleworth Collection in Bedfordshire. Here it wears the colours of No. 247 Squadron, RAF, while they were flying defensive patrols over Plymouth.

▲ Twenty RAF squadrons
No fewer than 20 home-based RAF squadrons were equipped with the Gladiator from 1937 to 1940.

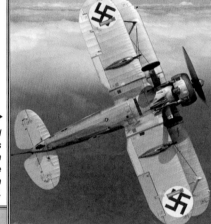

▼ Air display practice
Representing the RAF's fighter force of 1938, these tethered Gladiators practise for the 1938 Hendon air display.

Scandinavian Gladiators ▶
The Swedish and Finnish air forces bought Gladiators in the late 1930s. These saw action early in World War II.

◀ Battle of Britain
One of the last home-based Gladiator units was No. 247 Squadron, which flew the type until late 1940 over Plymouth.

FACTS AND FIGURES

➤ One Swedish squadron fighting with the Finns claimed 12 Soviet aircraft for only three losses.

➤ Gladiators entered RAF service in 1937, the year of the first Hurricane deliveries.

➤ The last RAF Gladiators, meteorological and liaison aircraft, were retired in 1944.

➤ The Sea Gladiators that defended Malta in early June 1940 were dubbed 'Faith', 'Hope' and 'Charity' by the Maltese.

➤ Sea Gladiators had catapult points, an arrester hook and a dinghy fairing fitted.

➤ Early Mk Is had two Vickers and two Lewis 7.7-mm (.303 cal.) machine-guns.

PROFILE

The last British biplane fighter

Despite being a biplane the Gladiator saw widespread action during the early stages of World War II. However, the results only underlined the type's obsolescence. The single squadron of Gladiators in Norway and the two squadrons based in France were all but wiped out during the German invasions in May and June 1940.

Other Gladiator squadrons fought in North Africa, Greece and Palestine in 1939 and 1940. Many were flown by Australian and South African units and a few were transferred to Egypt and Iraq. Another 36, which were supplied to China, joined the war against Japan in 1938.

The Sea Gladiator variant served aboard the aircraft-carriers *Courageous*, *Eagle* and *Glorious* and a handful were based in Malta when Italy joined the war in June 1940. For the next month, just four aircraft were the island's only defence against the Italians.

K5200 was the Gladiator prototype. The enclosed cockpit had yet to appear, although the gun armament was fitted at an early stage.

A major improvement on the Gladiator in terms of pilot comfort was the fully enclosed cockpit, which had a rear-sliding Perspex canopy.

The forward and rear spars of the mainplanes were made of high-tensile steel of 'dumb-bell' cross-section. The wing leading edge was made of duralumin.

The two-bladed wooden airscrew was a feature of the early Mk I Gladiators; Mk IIs were fitted with a three-bladed metal propeller.

Four fuselage- and wing-mounted 7.7-mm (.303 cal.) Browning machine-guns were fitted.

A silver dope finish was standard on RAF fighters between the wars. Often squadrons would add their individual markings to aircraft.

Behind the pilot's seat was the radio compartment, the aerials for the radio being strung between the wings and the tailfin.

Bristol's Mercury Mk IX radial engine also powered the earlier Gauntlet and other types like the twin-engined Blenheim bomber.

GLADIATOR MK I

K7985 was a Gladiator Mk I, one of a batch of 180 ordered in September 1935. Here it carries the well-known markings of No. 73 (Fighter) Squadron.

Like most fighters of the 1930s, the Gladiator was of basically metal construction with a fabric skin.

Gladiator Mk I

Type: single-seat interceptor

Powerplant: one 627-kW (840-hp.) Bristol Mercury Mk IX air-cooled radial engine

Maximum speed: 407 km/h (252 m.p.h.) at 4420 m (15,000 ft.)

Climb rate: 9.5 min to 6095 m (20,000 ft.)

Range: 547 km (339 mi.)

Service ceiling: 10,060 m (33,100 ft.)

Weights: empty 1565 kg (3,443 lb.); maximum take-off 2155 kg (4,741 lb.)

Armament: four 7.7-mm (.303 cal.) Browning machine-guns; two nose-mounted and two wing-mounted

Dimensions: span 9.83 m (32 ft. 3 in.)
length 8.36 m (27 ft. 5 in.)
height 3.15 m (10 ft. 4 in.)
wing area 30 m² (323 sq. ft.)

COMBAT DATA

MAXIMUM SPEED

Arriving on the scene at the end of the biplane era, the Gladiator was fast for an aircraft of this type. It had an advantage over the He 51, but a lower top speed than the CR.42 which saw considerable wartime service.

GLADIATOR Mk I	407 km/h (252 m.p.h.)
He 51	330 km/h (205 m.p.h.)
CR.42 FALCO	420 km/h (260 m.p.h.)

SERVICE CEILING

Again, the Gladiator and Falco had the edge over the earlier He 51. The monoplane was soon to make an impact, however. The first monoplane bombers were able to operate at higher altitudes.

GLADIATOR Mk I 10,060 m (33,100 ft.)

CR.42 FALCO 10,200 m (33,500 ft.)

He 51 7700 m (33,000 ft.)

ARMAMENT

Four machine-guns was about the limit for the last of the biplane fighters. These had to be fuselage-mounted or fitted under the wings. On monoplanes, guns were carried inside the wing assembly; monoplane wings were thicker and had more space.

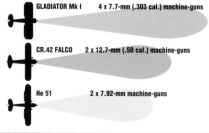

GLADIATOR Mk I — 4 x 7.7-mm (.303 cal.) machine-guns

CR.42 FALCO — 2 x 12.7-mm (.50 cal.) machine-guns

He 51 — 2 x 7.92-mm machine-guns

Gladiators around Europe

FINLAND: This Gladiator Mk II of the Suomen Ilmavoimat saw service in late 1939 and early 1940. Unlike the other Gladiator users, Finland flew its machines on the Axis side.

NORWAY: This Gladiator Mk II of the Norwegian Haerens Flyvevaben was based at Fornebeu, near Oslo, during April 1940. Ski landing gear was regularly fitted.

PORTUGAL: An important part of Portugal's airpower during World War II, this Gladiator II is shown in the markings of Esquadrilha de Caca de Base Aerea 2, flying from Ota in 1940.

GOTHA

G.IV AND G.V

● Long-range bomber ● Raids on Britain ● Pusher engines

So notorious did the Gotha bombers of World War I become that their name came to be applied generally to all large German bombers. It was the series of highly public daylight raids on Great Britain in 1917 that gained the Gotha name its notoriety. Developed from the earlier G.II and G.III, the G.IV and G.V variants were built in greater numbers and carried out the majority of the attacks, replacing the limited Zeppelin airship raids.

▲ Easily identifiable by their pusher engines and twin main wheels, the Gotha force became a common sight over southern England during 1917–18.

GOTHA G.IV AND G.V

▼ Safety at height
One of the primary reasons for the Gotha's success was the performance of its Mercedes engines, allowing it to operate at heights above 4600 m (15,000 ft.).

▲ Sting in the tail
The G.V's rear gunner could fire not only upwards and backwards, but downward through a specially designed 'tunnel' in the base of the fuselage.

▼ Reconnaissance Gotha
Although famed for their bomber designs, Gotha also built a wide range of land- and sea-planes during World War I. This example is a photo-reconnaissance G.VII.

▲ Bomber developments
As the war progressed Gotha sought to develop its bomber designs including the modified G.Vb, the G.VI and the G.VIII. This example is a G.IX, of which only two were built by LVG.

Massive wings ▶
The Gotha bomber types were characterised by their wide-span biplane wings. The ailerons on the top wing extend beyond the main wing structure, giving the wingtips a distinctive shape. The twin pusher engines are visible between the wings.

FACTS AND FIGURES

➤ The first G.IV raids on England were made by the 'Ostend Carrier-Pigeon' squadron in November 1916.

➤ Of 61 Gothas destroyed, 24 were lost to Allied defences and 37 in accidents.

➤ The G.IV and G.V were developed from the G.II and G.III designs of early 1916.

➤ With extra landing wheels fitted to the undercarriage chassis, the G.Vb was the last production 'Gotha twin'.

➤ Gotha also produced a wide variety of combat floatplanes during World War I.

➤ A number of G.Vs built by LVG were handed over to the Austrian government.

PROFILE

Gotha's giant bombers

Entering service in the autumn of 1916, the Gotha G.IV was not committed to major bombing raids on Britain until the spring of 1917. Yet in the period from May to November that year the Gotha force had remarkable success, and a low loss rate.

G.IV defensive armament consisted of two machine-guns whose fields of fire were co-ordinated with those of other bombers to defend against enemy fighters. A considerable toll was taken of British fighters

until effective evasive tactics had been evolved.

Although very little material damage was achieved by the Gotha raids, the effect on the British public was such that the government withdrew a number of front-line fighter squadrons from France to combat the threat. By September 1917 the British defences had improved enough to force the Gothas to revert to night raids, which continued until May 1918.

Gothas were also used to bomb positions on the Western

Front but it was the raids by Bombengeschwader 3 on southern England which made the Gothas famous. Altogether, 84,745 kg (186,440 lb.) of bombs were dropped in 22 raids.

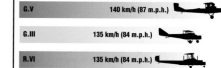

Left: As well as the effect the Gotha raids had on their targets on the ground and on the morale of the British people, they also kept many British fighter aircraft away from the Western Front on home defence duties.

Below: Among the Gotha's assets was an ability to withstand a large amount of punishment from enemy fighters. More Gothas were lost in accidents than to enemy action.

G.V

Type: twin-engined long-range day or night bomber

Powerplant: two 194-kW (260-hp.) Mercedes D !Va 6-cylinder in-line piston engines

Maximum speed: 140 km/h (87 m.p.h.) at 3660 m (12,000 ft.)

Initial climb rate: 28 min to 3000 m (9,800 ft.)

Range: 491 km (300 mi.)

Service ceiling: 6500 m (21,300 ft.)

Weights: empty 2740 kg (6,028 lb.); loaded 3975 kg (8,745 lb.)

Armament: single manually operated 7.92-mm Parabellum machine-guns in nose and rear cockpits plus up to 500 kg (1,100 lb.) of bombs.

Dimensions:
span	23.70 m	(77 ft. 9 in.)
length	11.86 m	(38 ft. 11 in.)
height	4.30 m	(14 ft. 1 in.)
wing area	89.5 m²	(963 sq. ft.)

G.IV

Operated by Kampfgeschwader 3 based at Ghent, this G.IV participated in daylight bombing raids on London during the spring and summer of 1917.

Sitting on the port side of the fuselage, the pilot looked over the front gunner's cockpit which was situated in the extreme nose. The main fuel tanks were situated immediately aft of the pilot's position.

The upper wings were composed of two panels joined at the centre. The two spruce main spars supported plywood ribs and the whole structure was covered with fabric.

Of fairly conventional construction, the fuselage was a one piece wooden structure of spruce longerons and spacers. The skin was plywood, and the whole structure was braced with stranded steel cables.

Constructed from light-gauge steel tubing, the tail unit was fabric-covered. The rudder was very large in comparison to the fin and was balanced to reduce the weight on the controls. Steel tube struts braced both the rudder and the tailplane. Beneath the rear fuselage was a steel-reinforced wooden tailskid.

Despite the aircraft's relatively large size, the bombs were mounted externally on removable racks. A maximum of 500 kg (1,100 lb.) could be carried.

Each undercarriage leg was fitted with two wheels which were sprung with long tension springs mounted inside the undercarriage leg.

COMBAT DATA

MAXIMUM SPEED

All large bombers of World War I were very slow, even by the standards of the day. Flying into a strong wind could double the time taken to reach a target.

G.V	140 km/h (87 m.p.h.)
G.III	135 km/h (84 m.p.h.)
R.VI	135 km/h (84 m.p.h.)

ARMAMENT

A well co-ordinated defensive strategy was a feature of the German bombing raids, forcing the British to re-evaluate their interception tactics.

G.V	2 x 7.92-mm machine-guns 500-kg (1,100-lb.) bombload
G.III	3 x 7.92 -mm machine-guns 1500-kg (3,300-lb.) bombload
R.VI	4 x 7.92-mm machine-guns 2000-kg (4,400-lb.) bombload

POWER

The R.VI was powered by four of the same engines which powered the twin-engined Gotha designs. This extra power allowed the Zeppelin design to carry a much bigger bombload, although it did not provide superior flight performance.

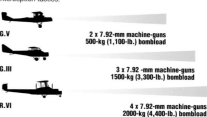

G.V	G.III	R.VI
388 kW (520 hp.)	388 kW (520 hp.)	776 kW (1,040 hp.)

Great War German bombers

■ **AEG G.IV:** Without the range or the lifting power of the Gotha designs, the AEG G.IV was used for tactical bombing on the Western Front.

■ **FRIEDRICHSHAFEN G.III:** Along with the Gotha designs, this aircraft formed the backbone of Germany's long-range bomber force.

■ **ZEPPELIN-STAAKEN V.G.O III:** One of the true German giants of World War I, this type was powered by six engines driving three airscrews.

■ **ZEPPELIN-STAAKEN TYPE 8301:** Although intended as a seaplane, the Type 8301 was fitted with wheels for trials as a bomber.

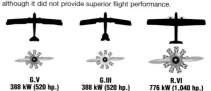

GRUMMAN

J2F DUCK

● Early Grumman amphibian ● Pacific rescue missions ● USCG service

▲ *Grumman's G-20 Duck design*
paved the way for a number of monoplane amphibian
designs, beginning with the twin-engined G-21 Goose
of 1937. Examples of each are still flying today.

This new family of single-engined biplane amphibians was among Grumman's first designs. The US Navy of the mid-1930s immediately found them ideally suited to utility duties aboard aircraft-carriers. Grumman Ducks were somewhat awkward-looking, but highly functional flying machines. Built by Grumman and Columbia, JF and J2F Ducks served with distinction in the Pacific island-fighting campaign during World War II, and around the world.

GRUMMAN J2F DUCK

▼ **Coast Guard JF-2**
Grumman's first amphibious design, the JF, made its maiden flight in 1933. From 1936, the type equipped US Navy utility squadrons aboard aircraft-carriers. The JF-2 rescue variant was built for the USCG.

▲ **Preserved J2F-6**
This preserved airworthy example of the J2F-6, built by Columbia Aircraft, wears the pre-war markings of Navy utility squadron VJ-4.

US Navy photo-ship ▲
Seen in 1942 colours, this J2F-5 also carries the markings of an Atlantic Fleet air photographic unit.

▲ **First US Navy deliveries**
BuNo. 0162 was the first J2F-1 delivered to the US Navy, arriving at Naval Air Station, Anacostia, in April 1936.

◄ **Duck!**
J2F tasks included target-towing, for which this Duck is equipped.

FACTS AND FIGURES

➤ The Duck was the first aircraft built after Leroy Grumman left Loening Aircraft to form his own company.

➤ Columbia Aircraft was still building these amphibians when World War II ended.

➤ Argentina, Colombia and Mexico received Ducks in the 1930s and 1940s.

➤ Between 1942 and 1945, US Navy and Marines Ducks rescued downed aircrew from the battle for Guadalcanal.

➤ A J2F-5 and five J2F-6s were operated by the USAF as OA-12s for air-sea rescue.

➤ As the Japanese invaded the Philippines, US Navy J2F-5s rescued VIPs.

PROFILE

First of the Grumman amphibians

After the attack on Pearl Harbor on 7 December 1941, a lone Grumman Duck set forth to search for the Japanese fleet, its radio operator armed with a bolt-action Springfield rifle. The single-engined Grumman Duck biplane was neither a fighter nor a bomber, but it found itself in action more than once in the Pacific. And, at the time of the US entry into World War II in 1941, the Duck was unique as the only biplane still in production for a US Navy operational role.

When originally ordered into production in 1932, these amphibians (JF-1 to JF-3 and

J2F-1 to J2F-6) were deemed quite advanced, with their all-metal construction and relatively clean lines. The US Navy, Marines and Coast Guard employed them for a variety of utility missions. Under pressure to deliver naval fighters and attack aircraft, Grumman transferred production to the nearby plant of the Columbia Aircraft Corporation.

Post-war, Ducks saw limited use and some were assigned to US Army Air Forces. A few have been preserved.

Below: At the US Navy's request, J2F-6 production was transferred to Columbia Aircraft on Long Island.

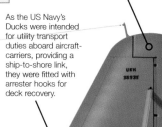

Above: USCG JFs and J2Fs served until the early 1950s, when they were phased out after some 17 years of service.

Ducks shared airframe design features, such as a semi-monocoque fuselage, with Grumman's first fighter design, the XFF-1.

Two or three crewmembers were carried aboard the US Navy's Ducks – apart from the pilot, there was an observer and, if required, a radio operator. The rear cockpit had provision for a 7.62-mm (.30 cal.) machine-gun, but this was seldom fitted. Two wing bomb racks were installed; in the J2F-5 and J2F-6, they were each able to carry a 147-kg (325-lb.) depth charge or bomb.

As the US Navy's Ducks were intended for utility transport duties aboard aircraft-carriers, providing a ship-to-shore link, they were fitted with arrester hooks for deck recovery.

The first JF-1 Ducks were powered by a Pratt & Whitney R-1830 Twin Wasp 14-cylinder radial engine driving a three-bladed propeller. However, JF-2s for the Coast Guard were fitted with Wright R-1820 Cyclone 9s. This engine became the standard Duck powerplant, the J2F-6 having a 783-kW (1,050-hp.) R-1820-54.

The large central amphibian float was faired into the J2F's fuselage. The fuselage had sufficient room for two passenger seats. The seats could be replaced with a stretcher in the casualty evacuation role.

J2F-6 DUCK

Columbia Aircraft built 330 J2F-6s, production ending in August 1945. In World War II, Pacific-based US Navy and Marine Corps J2Fs flew air-sea rescue missions.

J2F-6 Duck

Type: two/three-seat utility amphibian

Powerplant: one 783-kW (1,050-hp.) Wright R-1820-54 Cyclone 9 nine-cylinder radial piston engine

Maximum speed: 306 km/h (190 m.p.h.)

Cruising speed: 249 km/h (154 m.p.h.)

Initial climb rate: 405 m/min (1,328 f.p.m.)

Maximum range: 1370 km (850 mi.)

Normal range: 1085 km (673 mi.)

Service ceiling: 8140 m (26,700 ft.)

Weights: empty 2470 kg (5,430 lb.); maximum take-off 3307 kg (7,290 lb.)

Armament: usually unarmed, although provision was made for one 7.62-mm (.30 cal.) machine-gun in rear cockpit and up to 294 kg (647 lb.) of bombs or depth charges

Dimensions:
span	11.89 m	(40 ft.)
length	10.36 m	(34 ft.)
height	3.76 m	(12 ft. 4 in.)
wing area	38 m²	(409 sq. ft.)

ACTION DATA

CRUISING SPEED

Grumman's Duck had a good turn of speed, although this was marginally less than that of the Arado Ar 196. Aichi's 'Jake' was a significantly slower machine.

J2F-6 DUCK	249 km/h (165 m.p.h.)
Ar 196A-3	267 km/h (166 m.p.h.)
E13A1a 'JAKE'	222 km/h (138 m.p.h.)

POWER

Duck amphibians and 'Jake' floatplanes had a similar power rating. The Arado had a smaller engine, but was a smaller, lighter machine without the need for a powerful engine.

J2F-6 DUCK 783 kW (1,050 hp.)	Ar 196A-3 716 kW (960 hp.)	E13A1a 'JAKE' 790 kW (1,060 hp.)

RANGE

The Japanese Aichi E13A design had a 2000-km (1,300-mi.) range, useful for its naval reconnaissance role. Like the Duck and Ar 196, the E13A was employed from both ships and shore bases. Both the Arado and Aichi were floatplane designs; the J2F was a more versatile amphibian, able to operate from aircraft-carrier decks and land bases.

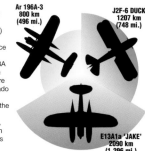

Ar 196A-3 800 km (496 mi.)

J2F-6 DUCK 1207 km (748 mi.)

E13A1a 'JAKE' 2090 km (1,296 mi.)

Grumman's amphibian family

■ **G-21 GOOSE:** Grumman's first twin-engined design, the G-21, flew in May 1937. In all, 345 were built for military and civil users. Wartime aircraft served with the USN, USCG and RAF.

■ **G-44 WIDGEON:** Grumman flew the Widgeon, which was cheaper than the Goose, in June 1940. Early examples saw military service; some civil G-44s remain airworthy today.

■ **G-73 MALLARD:** An enlarged variation of the G-21 design, the Mallard, first took to the air in 1946. All 59 built went to civil users, except for two received by the Egyptian air force in 1949.

■ **G-64/G-111 ALBATROSS:** Large numbers of this air-sea rescue amphibian, first flown in 1947, were delivered to the USN and USAF. Anti-submarine warfare versions were exported.

GRUMMAN

F2F/F3F

● Single-seater ● Carrier based ● Last USN biplane fighter

9575 F2F1
2-F-4

A natural development of the FF1 two-seat naval fighter of 1931, Grumman proposed a single-seat fighter, the F2F, in 1932. The larger F3F followed in 1934 and was destined to be the last biplane fighter ordered by the US Navy for delivery in 1937/38. These tubby biplanes, with their characteristic retractable landing gear (a Grumman patented design), were to keep the biplane era alive in the American fleet until late in 1940.

▲ The famous 'Fighting Two' squadron based on the USS Lexington flew F2F and F3Fs continuously from 1935 until 1940.

GRUMMAN **F2F/F3F**

▼ **Fleet fighter**
When the last F3F-2 was accepted in May 1938, all seven US Navy and Marine Corps fighter squadrons operated Grumman single-seaters. This situation lasted until December 1939.

▲ **New factory**
When 27 FF-1s were ordered, Grumman rented a new factory at Farmingdale to build them.

▼ **Red Rippers**
Production of 55 F2F-1s ended in October 1935, with nine aircraft going to VF-5B 'Red Rippers'.

▼ **Top guns**
The Mk III Mod 4 telescopic gunsight was mounted on top of the cowling, projecting forward from the small windscreen, for the two fixed, forward-firing (through the propeller) 7.62-mm (.30 cal.) Browning machine-guns that were fitted in the upper fuselage.

▼ **Last US Navy biplane fighter**
The bigger and more powerful F3F was the US Navy's basic carrier-borne fighter until the early-1940s. This F3F-2 served with VMF-2 Squadron.

2-MF-6

FACTS AND FIGURES

➤ The F2F and F3F were stressed to 9*g*, similar to that of the F-16 and F/A-18.

➤ Grumman's unique undercarriage design on the F2F/F3F became a distinctive feature of the F4F Wildcat carrier fighter.

➤ The first aircraft-carrier to have the F2F on board was the USS *Lexington* in 1935.

➤ Grumman delivered the last F2F in August 1935 and F3F in May 1939.

➤ The first two XF3Fs were destroyed in high-speed dives, the airframe being strengthened for production aircraft.

➤ A total of 140 F2Fs and F3Fs remained in service as station hacks in 1942.

PROFILE

The US Navy's 'Flying Barrels'

Taking the nickname 'Flying Barrel' on account of its deep forward fuselage and engine cowling, the Grumman biplane fighter was a legend in its time. The mainstay of the US carrier force immediately before World War II, it provided many young aviators, who would later hold command positions, with a sound training in shipboard fighter operations.

Starting life as the Grumman G-8 (later XF2F), the F2F-1 first entered service in 1935. One of the Navy's most illustrious fighter squadrons, VF-2B 'Fighting Two', helped prove the aircraft, which had a production run of 54.

Before the F2F entered service, Grumman anticipated future Navy requirements and secured orders for its G-11 (F3F). Similar to its predecessor, it had a longer fuselage and increased wingspan to enhance handling qualities. The first two XF3Fs crashed during flight tests, but an order for 35 F3F-1s was confirmed.

A larger diameter Cyclone engine powered the F3F-2 and this was the subject of an order for 81 aircraft for 1937/38 delivery. More engine power and other improvements produced the F3F-3, 27 of which were built. Few better tributes could be made to these biplanes than the longevity of service and late phase-out date of November 1943.

Left: This F3F carries the 'M' prefix to the squadron letter ('F') denoting a Marine Corps aircraft. In this case the aircraft belongs to Marine Fighter Squadron Two (VMF-2), indicated by the '2' prefix.

After front-line service the F3F-1s were used for pilot training at NAS Norfolk and Miami until February 1941.

F3F

Type: single-seat carrier fighter/bomber

Powerplant: one 708-kW (950-hp.) Wright R1820-2Z Cyclone air-cooled engine

Maximum speed: 425 km/h (264 m.p.h.)

Initial climb rate: 701 m/min (2,300 f.p.m.)

Range: 1328 km (824 mi.)

Service ceiling: 9205 m (30,200 ft.)

Weights: empty 1478 kg (3,252 lb.); loaded 2042 kg (4,492 lb.)

Armament: two 7.62-mm (.30 cal.) Browning machine-guns, plus two 52.6-kg (115-lb.) bombs

Dimensions:
span	9.75 m (32 ft.)
length	7.07 m (23 ft. 3 in.)
height	2.84 m (9 ft. 4 in.)
wing area	24.15 m² (260 sq. ft.)

F3F-2

With a more powerful Wright engine, the F3F-2 was the ultimate 'Flying Barrel'. This version had an improved speed, climb rate and performance range.

Two 7.62-mm (.30 cal.) Browning machine-guns were mounted forward of the cockpit and fired through the propeller arc.

The tube ahead of the pilot's windscreen is a Mk III Mod 4 telescopic gunsight.

Compared to the F2F, the F3F's fuselage was nearly 0.5 m (1 ft. 7 in.) longer, the wingspan was increased by 1.07 m (3 ft. 6 in.) and it had a slightly bigger tail unit; improved handling was the goal.

F3F-2 '1009' was one of a relatively small number of F3Fs to serve with the US Marine Corps units, in this case VMF-1.

F3F-2s used the 708-kW Wright R1820-22 Cyclone nine-cylinder single-row radial air-cooled engine.

Grumman's patent undercarriage had the mainwheels retracting into the fuselage behind the engine.

Watertight compartments in the lower fuselage provided flotation during an emergency water landing.

Grumman's naval fighters

■ **SF-1:** The US Navy ordered 33 SF-1 (G-6) scouts in 1932, the first being delivered to Squadron VS-3B 'Scouting Three' based on USS *Lexington* on 30 March 1934.

■ **F2F-1:** The first single-seat fighter from Grumman, the all-metal F2F-1 entered service with VF-2 aboard the USS *Lexington* in January 1935, serving until 1940.

■ **F4F WILDCAT:** One of the great naval fighters of World War II and the first monoplanes produced by Grumman, the XF4F was initially flown in February 1939 and was soon ordered.

COMBAT DATA

MAXIMUM SPEED

Grumman's reputation as a builder of fighters for the US Navy was just developing during the 1930s, the F3F going some way towards its enhancement. The F3F was a relatively quick aircraft, though the days of the biplane were numbered.

F3F	425 km/h (264 m.p.h.)
GLADIATOR	414 km/h (257 m.p.h.)
P-26 PEASHOOTER	377 km/h (234 m.p.h.)

RANGE

Naval aircraft must possess good range performance because of the nature of their operation, often some distance from an aircraft-carrier. Long range allows a good radius of operation and an increased time spent patrolling the skies on the lookout for enemy aircraft that may threaten the fleet. Both the P-26 and Gladiator were land-based machines.

GLADIATOR 710 km (440 mi.)

P-26 PEASHOOTER 579 km (358 mi.)

F3F 1328 km (530 mi.)

ARMAMENT

By American standards the F3F was typically armed with two machine-guns, while the British Gladiator demonstrates that fighter types of the period were generally better armed. This trend continued into the early years of World War II. Higher calibre machine-guns then became the norm.

F3F 2 x 7.62-mm (.30 cal.) MGs

GLADIATOR 4 x 7.7-mm (.303 cal.) MGs

P-26 PEASHOOTER 2 x 7.62-mm (.30 cal.) MGs

GRUMMAN

GOOSE/MALLARD

● Flying-boat ● Commercial flights ● Island hopping

T he Grumman Goose and Mallard were superb flying-boats built by a company better known for its carrier-based fighters. Development of the Goose began just before World War II, with that of the Mallard just after. Both were high-winged, twin-engined amphibians with two-step flying-boat hulls and retractable landing gear. These fine aircraft served as personal transport for many celebrities and as passenger liners for commuter airlines.

▲ Reflecting a bygone era, the Mallard is still operating as an airliner from the crystal blue waters off the Florida coastline. Here, a Turbo Mallard takes off at the start of another flight.

GRUMMAN GOOSE/MALLARD

▼ More power
In an effort to shorten the take-off run and also increase performance of the Grumman Goose, an extra pair of engines was installed on this example. The modification was not widely adopted.

▲ Land operations
With its engines at full power, a Grumman Goose prepares to lift off. The aircraft is fitted with a small undercarriage to allow amphibious operations.

◄ Executive model
After the end of World War II, Mallards were withdrawn from US Navy service and sold on the civil market. The interiors of the aircraft were completely refurbished to include a bar, sofas and sleeping quarters.

▼ Waterborne runway
Its passengers safely aboard, a Gruman Mallard eases its way into the water prior to a flight to Nassau.

▲ Former service
Having served with the US military forces during World War II the Goose aircraft were then sold to numerous small civilian operators.

FACTS AND FIGURES

➤ The Mallard was the only non-military product built by Grumman in the post-World War II period.

➤ During World War II, Grumman Goose aircraft were used for reconnaissance.

➤ A retractable undercarriage allows amphibious operations to be undertaken.

➤ Grumman Goose flying-boats were used by the US Coast Guard, Canadian and British forces.

➤ One Grumman Goose was operated by the Bolivian air force.

➤ Chalk's International Airline have now become Pan Am Air Bridge.

PROFILE

Grumman's fantastic flying-boats

The Grumman G-21A Goose was developed for commercial use before World War II, making its debut in 1937. A versatile utility craft and short-distance cargo and passenger type, the Goose saw military service with the US Army, Navy and Coast Guard. It later became a familiar sight around the world in post-war years.

The replacement for the Goose, the G-73 Mallard, followed in 1946. It was larger and more powerful, with provision for between 10 and 15 passengers. Both aircraft were ideally suited to a variety of commercial activities, including VIP transport.

The Mallard had the advantage of placing the pilot well forward of the engines, offering improved visibility and (with its greater power) better performance. Unfortunately, the post-war market for commercial amphibians proved to be smaller than Grumman anticipated, and only a few companies purchased these fine aircraft straight off the production line. They have shown enormous durability, however, and Gooses and Mallards are still operating in several places around the world today on commercial routes.

Above: Although it is dated, no modern equivalent has yet been found for the Grumman Goose. This example has been modified with adjustable wingtip floats.

Left: Restored with its former wartime markings, this Grumman Goose is active on the American warbird circuit. The aircraft presents an unusual sight in the air.

G-73 Mallard

Type: light amphibian flying-boat; commercial transport aircraft

Powerplant: two 447-kW (600-hp.) Pratt & Whitney R-1340-SH31 Wasp radial piston engines

Maximum speed: 346 km/h (215 m.p.h.)

Cruising speed: 290 km/h (180 m.p.h.)

Range: 2221 km (1,377 mi.) with maximum fuel load

Service ceiling: 7010 m (23,000 ft.)

Weights: empty 4241 kg (9,330 lb.); maximum take-off 5783 kg (12,723 lb.)

Accommodation: two flight crew; up to 15 passengers

Dimensions:
span	20.32 m	(66 ft. 8 in.)
length	14.73 m	(48 ft. 4 in.)
height	5.72 m	(18 ft. 9 in.)
wing area	41.25 m²	(444 sq. ft.)

A separate flight deck was provided for the aircrew, and the main accommodation for 15 seated passengers was located in the rear fuselage, in two compartments. Very often, the interiors of the aircraft were air-conditioned, heated and soundproofed to provide maximum comfort.

The two Wasp radial engines were positioned high on the wing, away from the corrosive salt spray generated by operations at sea.

Grumman's Mallard was exceptionally well-designed. With a fuselage consisting of an all-metal stressed-skin design, and the addition of a two-step hull, the aircraft proved to be immensely strong.

A large cargo door was positioned on the port-side rear fuselage, the high setting of which allowed cargo to be unloaded while the aircraft was on the water.

To improve handling on the water a large rudder was fitted to the Mallard. Chalk's International Airline aircraft carry a small American flag on their tail, signifying their country of origin.

Retractable landing gear gave the Mallard an amphibious capability; when retracted, the main wheels were recessed into the fuselage.

Rigid balancer floats were mounted on either side of the wings to provide stability for the Mallard when operating from the water. They also served as extra fuel tanks.

CHALK'S INTERNATIONAL

N2970

G-73 MALLARD

Chalk's International Airline was founded in 1919 and by the early 1990s was the oldest airline still operating under its original title. It now operates as Pan Am Air Bridge.

ACTION DATA

MAXIMUM SPEED

Small and lightweight, the Grumman G-21 Goose offers exceptional performance when compared to the larger G-73 Mallard. Later models were fitted with uprated engines to improve the speed of the small flying-boat.

G-73 MALLARD	346 km/h (215 m.p.h.)
DHC-3 OTTER	212 km/h (131 m.p.h.)
G-21 GOOSE	391 km/h (242 m.p.h.)

RANGE

Despite its small size, the Grumman G-21 Goose had exceptional range compared to the larger utility aircraft. Although fitted with additional fuel tanks in its stabilising floats, the G-73 Mallard was unable to match the Goose's performance.

G-73 MALLARD 2221 km (1,377 mi.)

DHC-3 OTTER 1048 km (650 mi.)

G-21 GOOSE 2575 km (1,597 mi.)

SERVICE CEILING

Equipped with two powerful Wasp radial engines, the G-73 Mallard had a surprisingly high service ceiling for a large flying-boat. It was often utilised for long-range overseas flights. With only a single engine, the DHC-3 Otter's performance was particularly poor.

G-73 MALLARD	DHC-3 OTTER	G-21 GOOSE
7010 m (23,000 ft.)	5485 m (18,000 ft.)	6100 m (20,000 ft.)

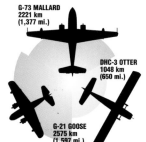

Riding the waves of success

■ **CANADAIR CL-215:** Developed for the specialised role of fire-bombing, the CL-215 has been purchased by a host of European countries. Later variants feature turboprop engines.

■ **MARTIN MARS:** Having had an extremely brief military career, the Mars flying-boats now serve as fire-bombers and operate from lakes in British Columbia, Canada.

■ **SHINMAYWA US-1:** Japan has operated flying-boats for a number of years for coastal patrols and anti-submarine duties. The type re-entered production in 1992.

HALBERSTADT

D.I-D.V

● Single-seat ● Fighting scout ● Exported to Turkey

From the end of 1915 until the conclusion of World War I, the Halberstadt series of fighting scouts were a common sight, participating in dogfights above the trenches on the Western Front. Although outclassed in 1916–17 by the Albatros D.I and Allied aircraft such as the Sopwith Pup and SPAD VII, the Halberstadts gave a good account of themselves and were certainly treated with respect by their Allied adversaries.

▲ *The major production versions of the Halberstadt series were the D.II and D.III. The D.III was basically an improved D.II with more agile handling and with the Mercedes engine replaced by an Argus.*

HALBERSTADT D.I-D.V

◀ **First in the line**
The D.I first flew in late 1915 and entered operations soon after. It was powered by a 74.5-kW (100-hp.) Mercedes engine.

▼ **Advanced design**
The D.Va featured a new tail design but did not enter large-scale production.

▼ **High-lift wings**
The wings on the D.III provided tremendous lift allowing a good rate-of-climb. To help prevent engine fumes entering the cockpit, the exhaust extended down the starboard side of the fuselage.

▼ **Family lines**
The Halberstadt series of fighters carried distinctive family traits including the triangular rudder which was attached by two steel struts and was believed to be prone to failure.

◀ **Turkish scout**
With modified centre-section struts and ailerons, the D.V was virtually identical to the D.III. This damaged example is one of a number which were supplied to Turkey.

FACTS AND FIGURES

➤ The unsuccessful D.I became a much better aircraft when fitted with the Mercedes engine and designated D.II.

➤ Only 100 D.IIs and D.IIIs were in front-line service by January 1915.

➤ The D.IV was the first in the series to be fitted with two machine-guns.

➤ Halberstadt also produced B series reconnaissance and CL series ground-attack aircraft during World War I.

➤ The D.V had the best handling of the series and was reputedly a delight to fly.

➤ D.IIs and D.IIIs were contract-built by the Aviatik and Hannover companies.

PROFILE

Halberstadt's fighting family

Although produced in only small numbers compared to Germany's illustrious Fokker and Albatros designs, the fighters of the Halberstadt series were well designed and performed admirably in combat during the mid-war years.

The single-gun D.I was the first Halberstadt fighting scout to appear but was quickly replaced in production by the improved D.II. To help solve the problem of fumes in the cockpit a number of different exhausts were fitted to this model including a long exhaust down the starboard side of the fuselage and later a chimney-type manifold exhausting over the top wing. The D.II was extremely strong and could take significant punishment for which pilots were extremely grateful, since they had no parachutes.

The D.III featured larger ailerons which improved the aircraft's manoeuvrability. It was these aircraft, along with Fokker D.IIIs and and D.IVs, which formed the basis of the first *Jastas* in the summer of 1916 and revolutionised air combat.

By the end of 1916 the D.II and D.III were obsolescent and production switched to the D.IV, which although capable did not receive large orders. The final version, the D.V, was basically a slightly modified D.III.

Left: This D.II was flown by the famous German ace Oswald Boelcke. He was killed in combat on 28 October 1916.

Below: The D.IV of 1917 owed many of its features, such as its neatly spinnered nose, to the firm's CL.II two-seater.

D.II

Type: single-seat fighting scout

Powerplant: one 89.5-kW (120-hp.) Mercedes D.II six-cylinder in-line engine

Maximum speed: 150 km/h (93 m.p.h.)

Initial climb rate: 4 min to 1000 m (3,300 ft.); 15 min to 3000 m (9,850 ft.)

Range: 250 km (155 mi.)

Service ceiling: 5975 m (19,600 ft.)

Weights: empty 520 kg (1,144 lb.); maximum take-off 730 kg (1,606 lb.)

Armament: one fixed forward-firing 7.92-mm LMG 08/15 machine-gun

Dimensions:
span	8.80 m (28 ft. 10 in.)
length	7.30 m (23 ft. 11 in.)
height	2.67 m (8 ft. 9 in.)
wing area	23.60 m² (254 sq. ft.)

D.V

Virtually a D.III airframe with a number of minor modifications, the D.V was used as a scout. A small number, such as this example, were supplied to the Turkish Government in late 1917 and early 1918.

The two-bay wing structure fitted to the D Series of scouts was extremely strong. Like the D.III, the D.V had larger ailerons for increased agility.

Delivered in late 1917 this example carries the Turkish insignia of the period and was used against Allied opposition during the last year of the war.

The aircraft's rudder was of approximately triangular profile and was braced by two steel struts. The elevators were of similar trapezoidal shape to those of its Fokker contemporaries.

The steel vee-type undercarriage chassis had two spreader bars welded from streamlined steel tube. The wheels were fitted with elastic-cord shock absorbers.

The fuselage was of a conventional wooden structure with hollow square-section longerons. Curved metal panels held the engine in place at the nose. The rear fuselage tapered in a wedge shape to a horizontal knife-edge and was fabric-covered; the front fuselage was plywood covered.

COMBAT DATA

MAXIMUM SPEED

The D.II had excellent climb performance and good manoeuvrability but this was at the expense of speed with the aircraft having a large amount of drag. Contemporary Allied fighters like the Nieuport 17 and Sopwith Pup were able to outrun the Halberstadt design if they got into difficulties during a dogfight.

HALBERSTADT D.II	150 km/h (93 m.p.h.)
SOPWITH PUP	180 km/h (112 m.p.h.)
NIEUPORT 17	170 km/h (105 m.p.h.)

CLIMB RATE

The Halberstadt D.II's wings had excellent lift qualities which allowed a good rate-of-climb although the corresponding increase in drag reduced the aircraft's speed performance. The Pup had the poorest rate of climb but the highest speed.

HALBERSTADT D.II	250 m/min (820 f.p.m.)
NIEUPORT 17	211 m/min (690 f.p.m.)
SOPWITH PUP	140 m/min (460f.p.m.)

SERVICE CEILING

The Halberstadt's excellent wing design gave the aircraft a superior service ceiling over its contemporaries. The good rate-of-climb was also a big asset in a dogfight allowing the aircraft to climb above and make diving attacks.

HALBERSTADT DII 5975 m (19,600 ft.)	SOPWITH PUP 5355 m (17,600 ft.)	NIEUPORT 17 5350 m (17,550 ft.)

Other Great War Halberstadts

CL.II: Designed to a light-escort and ground-attack specification, the CL.II first flew in 1917 and was built in considerable numbers.

CL.IV: In 1918 the German ground-attack aircraft fleet was undergoing rapid expansion and the capable CL.IV was built to fill this need.

CL.IV (ROLAND-BUILT): To satisfy the German demand for more of the excellent C.IV a sub-contract was undertaken by Roland.

CLS.I: Designed to succeed both the CL.II and CL.IV, the CLS.I was smaller, lighter and faster than its predecessors.

HANDLEY PAGE

O/100 AND O/400

● Long-range heavy bomber ● Built in large numbers ● Pioneer 'airliner'

A t the beginning of World War I, aircraft looked as if someone could tie a piece of string to them and fly them in a light breeze. In four short years the fighting plane had evolved into a potent military weapon, in such diverse forms as high-speed fighters and multi-engined long-range heavy bombers. Among the most powerful of them all were the Handley Page O/100 and the improved O/400.

▲ Warplanes began the war armed with a rifle and tiny bombs. By 1918 they were dropping monster 748-kg (1,650-lb.) weapons such as this. In Britain, the name Handley Page was virtually synonymous with large aircraft.

HANDLEY PAGE O/100 AND O/400

▲ Stuck in the mud
The O/400 series had a wide undercarriage, with fat tyres to take its weight. This aircraft was used by No. 207 Sqn at Ligescourt in 1918.

▲ Roaring Eagle
In place of Rolls-Royce Eagle engines, the O/400 could use the Sunbeam Maori or Liberty 12-N.

◀ Lift-off
The O/400 took off at about 80 km/h (50 m.p.h.). Its top speed was not much higher, due to high drag.

▼ Daring mission
Navy O/100 crews attacked the German battlecruiser Goeben in Stenia Bay, Turkey, in 1917.

Canal bomber ▶
This O/400 is seen on a practice flight over the Thames. Operational flights were made to attack the Zeebrugge canal, to stop it being used by U-boats.

◀ Civil service
The O/400 was used to carry passengers after World War I. G-EAKG was an ex-service aircraft bought by Handley Page Transport and used for flights to Paris.

FACTS AND FIGURES

➤ The first O/100 left the ground at 1.51 p.m. on 18 December 1915.

➤ In July 1916 an O/100 took 20 passengers to an altitude of 2000 m (6,500 ft.).

➤ In 1917 an O/100 was flown to the Middle East via Paris, Rome and the Balkans, and was used to bomb Constantinople.

➤ On the night of 14/15 September 1918, 40 Handley Page O/400s attacked military targets in the Saar.

➤ The O/400 could drop a 748-kg (1,650-lb.) bomb, then the heaviest British bomb.

➤ An O/400 was used in December 1918 to survey the route from Egypt to India.

Britain's first heavy bomber

Designed to an Admiralty specification, the big Handley Page bomber was Britain's largest aeroplane when it first entered service late in 1916. The first recorded mission took place on the night of 16/17 March 1917, when the 'Handley Page Squadron', as it was then known, made an attack on a German-held railway junction and marshalling yard.

The O/100 was powered by two 198-kW (265-hp.) Rolls-Royce Eagle engines. It originally had an enclosed cockpit and armour plate to protect engines and crew, but performance was sluggish and production aircraft had an open cockpit and no armour.

Production deliveries of the O/400 began in 1918. This was a much improved aircraft, having more powerful engines

and a revised fuel system, and could carry around a ton of bombs. Although only 46 O/100s had been built, more than 400 of its replacement were in service as the Armistice was signed. The US Army Air Service selected the O/400 as its standard heavy bomber and ordered 1,500, but only 107 were completed before the end of the war brought about the cancellation of the contract.

The O/400 was a massive aircraft by the standards of the time, and it was not until the Fairey Hendon of 1936 that the RAF again had a bomber of this size in service in numbers.

O/400

Type: long-range heavy bomber

Powerplant: two 268-kW (360-hp.) Rolls-Royce Eagle VIII V-12 piston engines

Maximum speed: 156 km/h (96 m.p.h.)

Ferry range: 1200 km (745 mi.)

Service ceiling: 2600 m (8,900 ft.)

Weights: empty 3719 kg (8,182 lb.); loaded 6350 kg (13,970 lb.)

Armament: up to five flexibly-mounted 7.7-mm (.303 cal.) Lewis guns, plus up to 907 kg (2,000 lb.) of bombs or one 748-kg (1,650-lb.) bomb

Dimensions:
span	30.48 m	(100 ft.)
length	19.16 m	(63 ft.)
height	6.71 m	(22 ft.)
wing area	153.1 m²	(164 sq. ft.)

O/400

The O/400 served with the Royal Naval Air Service and later the RAF with great success. It saw combat in Europe and Turkey and went on to support the British Army in Egypt and India.

Drag from the engine nacelles was a problem for the Handley Page designers. Moving the large radiators helped to alleviate this, but the O/400 was never a fast machine.

The wing was made of two large spruce spars, with hollow compression pieces between the front and rear spars.

Rolls-Royce Eagles were in short supply, so Sunbeam Cossack engines were sometimes installed.

A Lewis gun provided some protection for the observer in the rear cockpit. Crew members had armour protection, known as the 'bath'.

The fuselage was assembled from four main sections, with reinforced metal plates at the joints and internal wire bracing.

The nose gunner sat in an exposed forward cockpit, armed with a single Lewis gun. Trials of a Davis recoilless gun for attacking U-boats were not successful, as the gun often did more damage to the aircraft than to its target.

Unlike the upper wing, the lower wing had no ailerons.

The rear fuselage of the early O/100 prototypes experienced severe vibration problems when the aircraft reached 130 km/h (80 m.p.h.), but strengthening the structure provided a cure.

The elevators were fitted with large aerodynamic 'horn balances' to reduce the effort of controlling the aircraft.

Heavy bombers of World War I

■ CAPRONI Ca 3: Italy was a pioneering force in multi-engine aviation, and the highly successful Caproni series of biplane and triplane heavy bombers were used by France and Britain as well as by the Italian air force.

■ GOTHA G.IV: The G-type could carry up to 500 kg (1,100 lb.) of bombs, and bore the brunt of Germany's campaign against England in 1917 and 1918. Although several manufacturers produced such aircraft, they all became known to their enemies as 'Gothas'.

■ ZEPPELIN-STAAKEN R: The 32 R-type giant bombers built in Germany in the last two years of the war evolved into seven-man aircraft able to carry a significant bombload. They were used on the Eastern Front and in bombing raids on London.

COMBAT DATA

MAXIMUM SPEED

None of the early heavy bombers were fast. The O/400 was faster than the comparable but slightly smaller German Gotha, and both were much faster than the pioneering Russian Ilya Mouramets, designed by Igor Sikorsky before the war. The high drag produced by the biplane wings and bracing wires reduced speed.

O/400	156 km/h (96 m.p.h.)
GOTHA G.V	140 km/h (87 m.p.h.)
MOURAMETS	100 km/h (62 m.p.h.)

SERVICE CEILING

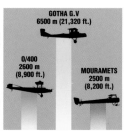

The O/400 was a little underpowered, and it was never able to climb very high when carrying a bombload. It did not have the advantage of the Gotha's exceptionally high ceiling, which meant that it was very difficult for British and French fighters to intercept. However, since the O/400 generally flew at night, its low ceiling was not a great handicap.

GOTHA G.V 6500 m (21,320 ft.)

O/400 2600 m (8,900 ft.)

MOURAMETS 2500 m (8,200 ft.)

WEAPONS LOAD

The O/400 was one of the first aircraft able to deliver around one ton of high explosive over appreciable distances. German 'R' class giants could carry more, but could not fly as far when carrying a heavy load. The big Russian bombers had good lifting ability, but rarely carried more than 10 small bombs.

O/400	GOTHA G.V	MOURAMETS
907 kg (2,000 lb.) of bombs	500 kg (1,100 lb.) of bombs	160 kg (350 lb.) of bombs

HANDLEY PAGE

H.P.42

● Early luxury airliner ● Long-haul routes ● British Empire services

▲ At a fuel stop in the desert, the crew of an H.P.42E supervise the replenishment of the aircraft's supplies. Such operations turned the journey into an adventure.

Looking at it today, the Handley Page H.P.42 seems strange, with its exposed engines and its odd-sized, biplane wings. But in the 1930s, when Imperial Airways was harnessing the new science of aviation to carry passengers over great distances, the H.P.42 was a trailblazer. Although far from the state of the art, it was the first true intercontinental airliner operating with elegance and style.

HANDLEY PAGE H.P.42

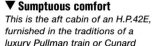

▼ **Sumptuous comfort**
This is the aft cabin of an H.P.42E, furnished in the traditions of a luxury Pullman train or Cunard liner of the time.

▲ **'Built-in headwind'**
With its two wings and the maze of struts connecting them, the H.P.42 was hardly aerodynamic. In spite of the power of its four engines, the big biplane could barely manage 200 km/h (126 m.p.h.).

An exclusive passage ▼
The H.P.42 made long-range air travel a realistic proposition. But it was fearfully expensive: you had to be well off to fly.

◄ **On-the-spot maintenance**
Imperial Airways crew were trained to handle any emergency. The simple yet sturdy construction of the H.P.42 allowed them to undertake virtually all essential maintenance en route.

▲ **Western class**
'Heracles' was one of the aircraft used only in the West, tailored for European routes with high-density seating.

FACTS AND FIGURES

➤ The H.P.42 'Heracles' logged its one-millionth mile (about 1.6 million km) on 23 July 1937.

➤ The craft known as the H.P.42W was actually designated the H.P.45.

➤ The H.P.42 was one of the first airliners equipped with a kitchen, toilets and heaters for passenger comfort.

➤ The H.P.42 was so slow that Anthony Fokker joked that they were equipped with built-in headwinds.

➤ H.P.42s were retired on 1 September 1939 after almost a decade of service without a single fatal accident.

➤ The H.P.42 made its first flight on 14 November 1930.

PROFILE

Flying the Imperial routes

A famous name in Britain, the Handley Page team gave the world the H.P.42E (Eastern) and H.P.42W (Western) airliners at a time when air travel was a new and exciting adventure. These big aircraft of gleaming metal, their broad wings braced by enormous girders, became ocean liners of the sky, the four Eastern ships opening up new routes to India and South Africa while the four Westerners pioneered long trips in Europe.

'Up front' were two pilots and a wireless operator. The men at the controls of the H.P.42 faced challenges: the aircraft made plenty of noise, shook like a washing machine, and was difficult to land. But the pilots also held a commanding view, and enjoyed excellent control over the aircraft when aloft. It was a thrilling aeroplane to fly.

All eight H.P.42s had evocative names – Hannibal, Heracles, Horsa, Hanno, Hadrian, Horatius, Hengist and Helena. All true pioneers and great aircraft.

'Hannibal' was the class leader of the four Eastern aircraft, fitted out to perform the arduous journey linking Cairo to the Empire. One route flew south to Lake Victoria, another headed east for India.

H.P.42W

Billed as the world's largest airliner at the time of its service entry, the H.P.42 was something of an anachronism, for already more streamlined airliners were being built. Nevertheless, it had an elegance which transcended its meagre performance, and it was instrumental in establishing air travel.

H.P.42W/H.P.45

Type: civil transport aircraft

Powerplant: four 414-kW (555-hp.) Bristol Jupiter XFBM nine-cylinder piston engines

Maximum speed: 204 km/h (126 m.p.h.)

Range: 805 km (500 mi.)

Service ceiling: 6400 m (21,000 ft.) with moderate load

Weights: empty 8047 kg (17,700 lb.); loaded 12,701 kg (28,000 lb.)

Accommodation: maximum 18 passengers forward and 20 aft (total 38) with minimal baggage

Dimensions:
span	39.62 m (129 ft. 8 in.)
length	28.09 m (91 ft. 2 in.)
height	5.04 m (16 ft. 6 in.)
wing area	277.6 m² (2,990 sq. ft.)

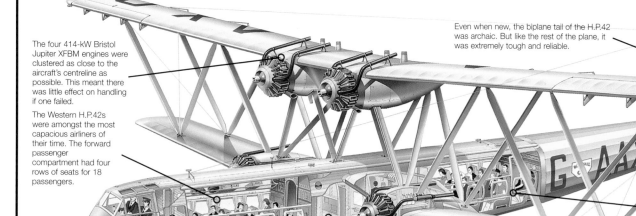

The four 414-kW Bristol Jupiter XFBM engines were clustered as close to the aircraft's centreline as possible. This meant there was little effect on handling if one failed.

The Western H.P.42s were amongst the most capacious airliners of their time. The forward passenger compartment had four rows of seats for 18 passengers.

Even when new, the biplane tail of the H.P.42 was archaic. But like the rest of the plane, it was extremely tough and reliable.

The huge wing allowed the H.P.42 to take off in a very short distance, usually less than 200 m (600 ft.). Often it was airborne while still on the taxiway after leaving the terminal, and long before it had reached the recognised runway.

In the rear fuselage was a further passenger saloon with five rows of four-abreast seats.

The flight deck at the front of the H.P.42W had room for two pilots. Behind them was a compartment for the wireless operator.

The H.P.42 was luxuriously equipped for its time. In the centre of the aircraft were two toilets and a bar.

The immensely strong undercarriage was not so important for the Western class, which mostly operated from well-prepared airfields. On the other hand, the Eastern class regularly negotiated boulders and ruts on rudimentary desert strips.

ACTION DATA

MAXIMUM SPEED

Airliners of the late 1920s and early 1930s were not the fastest of aircraft, and within a decade were to be completely outclassed by modern stressed-skin designs like the Douglas DC-3 and the Focke-Wulf Condor. But even though they were slow, they pioneered many of the world's long-range passenger routes.

F.VII
209 km/h (130 m.p.h.)

H.P.42
204 km/h (126 m.p.h.)

G.38
210 km/h (131 m.p.h.)

PAYLOAD

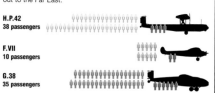

Although the massive Junkers G.38 was the biggest airliner in the world, it did not carry as many passengers as the long, slender fuselage of the H.P.42. The Fokker was much smaller, but competed directly with the Handley Page in opening the air routes out to the Far East.

H.P.42
38 passengers

F.VII
10 passengers

G.38
35 passengers

East to India

MEDITERRANEAN

CAIRO: This Egyptian airfield was the centre of Imperial's Empire land operations. From here H.P.42s flew south to the East African colonies, or east to the Indian sub-continent.

Cairo (Egypt)

DESERT REPLENISHMENT: The H.P.42 lacked range, and needed an interim stop in the Iraqi desert to pick up fuel.

ARABIA

Basra (Iraq)

Muharraq (Bahrain)

Sharjah (Trucial States)

Gwadar (Persia)

Karachi

INDIA: Taking the air route to India involved a considerable effort. Flying from Croydon in a D.H.86, passengers switched to a Short Rangoon flying-boat for the over-water trip from Brindisi in Italy to Egypt. From there, they transferred to the H.P.42 for the passage to India.

INDIA

HANDLEY PAGE

HEYFORD

● Biplane bomber ● Last of its kind ● Bomber trainer

▲ Heyfords were very much in the public eye in the 1930s, appearing at Hendon air pageants in impressive formations. This aircraft was reviewed by His Majesty King George VI and Air-Marshal Trenchard at the 1935 Jubilee Review at RAF Mildenhall.

Last of the RAF's biplane bombers, the Heyford had the unusual distinction of having the fuselage attached to the upper wing. Another oddity was the rear gunner's retractable 'dustbin' turret. After questions about whether bombing might be outlawed by the League of Nations, the Heyford entered service and flew as the RAF's premier night-bomber. But it had a short life, being introduced in 1933 and progressively withdrawn by 1939.

HANDLEY PAGE HEYFORD

▼ Improved Heyford
Handley Page were only too aware of the Heyford's failings, and the company improved the aircraft throughout its life. Problems with engine cooling were cured by fitting new nacelles.

▲ Flying monstrosity
With its top wing-mounted fuselage the Heyford was one of the RAF's most unconventional designs. However, this arrangement gave the aircraft excellent take-off performance.

Dustbin turret ▶
The retractable gun turret was produced in response to the opinions of RAF aircrew. The mock-up of the turret was built in just four hours.

▼ Nose high
The curious design resulted in a large 'ground angle' (high nose attitude), which in turn gave the Heyford a short landing roll and low touchdown speed.

◀ Fun to fly
For such a big aircraft, the Heyford was unusually agile and also had surprising structural strength, which is important for a bomber.

▼ Open cockpits
Heyford crews were exposed to the elements, making operating at its ceiling rather unpleasant.

FACTS AND FIGURES

➤ One Heyford pilot flew for an hour with his starboard propeller smashed by empty rounds from the nose gun.

➤ Early in 1940 at least seven Heyfords were still in use as bomber trainers.

➤ Heyfords took part in the first secret trials of the Hotspur assault glider.

➤ Heyfords were also used in trials of a 'frictionless take-off trolley and track' and new de-icing equipment.

➤ Six Heyfords crashed in one day in 1936 after encountering severe icing.

➤ Eleven RAF squadrons used Heyfords between 1933 and 1939.

PROFILE

Britain's last biplane bomber

Having made do with a variety of lamentable designs in the 1920s, the RAF required a big bomber to equip the bombing force that it considered so important. The Heyford's designers faced the challenge of having to use a biplane configuration and indifferent engines, knowing that monoplanes with much better powerplants would soon be produced. Variable-pitch airscrews were another feature

that was newly available but ruled out because they presented technical difficulties.

Despite looking very awkward, the Heyford was described by a test pilot as being 'devoid of vice' and 'possessing all the essential features required by a night-bomber'. It was an unusual aircraft, having the fuselage attached to the upper wing, and the bombs stored in a bulged compartment in the lower wing. The production

aircraft received Rolls-Royce Kestrel or Armstrong Siddeley Tiger engines, and various features to reduce drag, but the result was still a rather slow aircraft. Surprisingly, the Heyford had commendable agility and could even be looped. It was also easy to maintain and was quite strong. However, the monoplane spelled the end for the Heyford, and the last few were used as trainers in 1940.

One aviator managed to ground-loop a Heyford no less than two-and-a-half times on landing, and another survived a misadvertant high-speed dive caused by icing.

While crews generally liked the Heyford, the nose gunner was very exposed. Stieger and Hubbard nose turrets were tested but never adopted for service.

HP.50 HEYFORD

Wearing the 'Nivo' dark-green night-bomber scheme, this Heyford was operated by No. 10 Squadron, RAF.

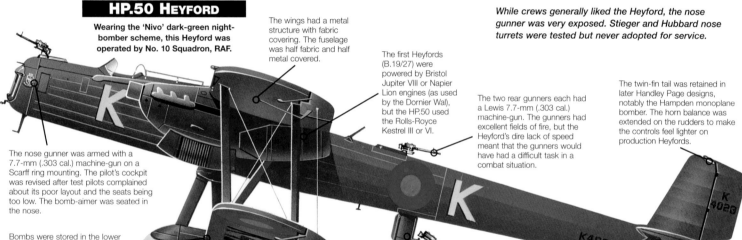

The wings had a metal structure with fabric covering. The fuselage was half fabric and half metal covered.

The first Heyfords (B.19/27) were powered by Bristol Jupiter VIII or Napier Lion engines (as used by the Dornier Wal), but the HP.50 used the Rolls-Royce Kestrel III or VI.

The two rear gunners each had a Lewis 7.7-mm (.303 cal.) machine-gun. The gunners had excellent fields of fire, but the Heyford's dire lack of speed meant that the gunners would have had a difficult task in a combat situation.

The twin-fin tail was retained in later Handley Page designs, notably the Hampden monoplane bomber. The horn balance was extended on the rudders to make the controls feel lighter on production Heyfords.

The nose gunner was armed with a 7.7-mm (.303 cal.) machine-gun on a Scarff ring mounting. The pilot's cockpit was revised after test pilots complained about its poor layout and the seats being too low. The bomb-aimer was seated in the nose.

Bombs were stored in the lower wing and thus could only be of rather small size. Normal bombload was four 227-kg (500-lb.) or ten 90-kg (200-lb.) weapons. There was very little ground clearance for the trailing edge of the wing.

The famous 'dustbin' turret was a very confined space, and the smaller gunners in a squadron were often 'volunteered' to fly in this position. Handley Page modified the turret to make more room for the gunner's knees.

RAF bombers of the 1930s

■ **ARMSTRONG WHITWORTH WHITLEY:** Whitleys formed the backbone of the night-bomber force at the outbreak of war.

■ **BRISTOL BOMBAY:** The Bombay flew in 1935 and remained in service long enough to see action in North Africa in the 1940s.

■ **FAIREY HENDON:** The first monoplane to enter service with the RAF, in 1936 the Hendon was soon replaced by the Wellington from 1938.

■ **HANDLEY PAGE HARROW:** A stop-gap between the Heyford and the Whitley, the Harrow entered service in 1937.

COMBAT DATA

RANGE

Designed as a strategic night-bomber, the Heyford had enough range to bomb targets in Europe from the UK. The Do 17 was designed for tactical support missions.

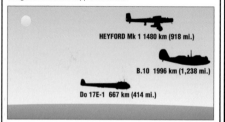

HEYFORD Mk 1 1480 km (918 mi.)

B.10 1996 km (1,238 mi.)

Do 17E-1 667 km (414 mi.)

MAXIMUM SPEED

No amount of power could make up for the enormous drag of the Heyford's biplane design. The sleek Do 17 was actually much faster than the fighters of its day, but by 1940 even this excellent aircraft could never outrun a pursuing fighter aircraft.

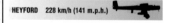

HEYFORD	228 km/h (141 m.p.h.)
B.10	343 km/h (213 m.p.h.)
Do 17E-1	347 km/h (215 m.p.h.)

BOMBLOAD

British bombers had high bombloads, gained at the expense of speed or equipment fit. The Heyford's bomb capacity was as large as any other aircraft in service in the mid-1930s outside the USSR.

HEYFORD Mk 1	B.10	Do 17E-1
1200 kg (2,640 lb.)	1025 kg (2,250 lb.)	750 kg (1,650 lb.)

HANRIOT

HD.1

● French biplane fighter ● Highly successful ● Maneuverable

This highly maneuverable biplane fighter was the first military aircraft designed and built by the company of René Hanriot, who started his French manufacturing enterprise on the eve of the Great War. The Hanriot HD.1 was a workman-like little aircraft built largely of wood with fabric covering. Although lightweight and lightly armed, it captured the enthusiasm of Belgian and Italian pilots and remained in Italian service until 1925.

▲ Having been eclipsed by the more powerful SPAD S.VII in France, the HD.1 achieved favor with the wartime forces of Belgium and Italy. The Belgians received 125 and the Italians more than 1000. Late in World War I, an HD.1 was modified with a float undercarriage to become the HD.2 floatplane fighter.

HANRIOT HD.1

▲ Streamlined design
The 89-kW (120-hp.) Le Rhône 9Jb rotary engine was neatly faired. Forward sections were covered in sheet metal.

▲ Staggered wings
Considerable stagger was adopted for the wings and a faired headrest for the pilot.

Battleship take off ▶
From a gun-turret platform on the USS Mississippi, the U.S. Navy flew HD.2 variants of the HD.1.

▲ Postwar developments
Hanriot continued to design and build aircraft into the 1930s. The HD.14 was a brilliant trainer.

Vickers armed ▶
A single machine gun armed the HD.1, and the cockpit boasted a luxuriously padded headrest.

FACTS AND FIGURES

➤ French records indicate that total production of the HD.1 was 1145 aircraft.

➤ The prototype HD.1 fighter completed its maiden flight in June 1916.

➤ The Hanriot HD.1 replaced the Nieuport Scout in several Belgian units.

➤ Belgian pilots began flying the Hanriot fighter in August 1917 and had considerable success with it.

➤ Macchi manufactured 901 of these fighters under license in Italy.

➤ An HD.1 was flown by the French navy from a battleship gun turret.

Original French fighter design

Designed by Emile Dupont, the HD.1 was its builder's first original product. Previously, the Hanriot firm, founded in 1916, had manufactured the Sopwith 1-1/2-Strutter reconnaissance biplane under license. The HD.1 had wings closely resembling those of the British aircraft and was characterized by its compact appearance and staggered wings of unequal span.

The HD.1 might have achieved greater success had it not been a competitor of the better-known SPAD S.VII, which performed extremely well. The HD.1 did not have enough power, despite its otherwise fine qualities, so Hanriot had to watch France order the SPAD instead. The Belgians and Italians, both desperately needed new fighters and settled on the HD.1. Macchi undertook production in Italy under licence.

The Belgian and Italian air arms flew the HD.1 with considerable success and it won the praise of Belgium's top ace Lieutenant Willy Coppens, who was among the first to fly it. After the First World War, a small number of these fighters turned up in other countries, such as Switzerland and Latin America, and the aircraft went on to form an important part of Italy's defences, six front-line squadrons facing Austria until at least the mid 1920s.

Above: Shown is a ghoulishly marked HD.1; probably after World War I. In addition to Swiss service, postwar HD.1s also found their way to South America and the U.S.

Above: Willy Coppens was largely responsible for the successful introduction of the HD.1 into Belgian service. His aircraft is preserved in a Belgian museum.

HD.1

Greatly impressed by tests carried out on a force-landed Italian HD.1, the Swiss purchased 16 war-surplus aircraft from Italy.

Pilots enjoyed the well-balanced controls and rugged construction.

Ailerons were fitted to the larger, forward staggered upper wing. They were large and powerful and gave outstanding agility.

An unusual feature among its contemporaries was the HD.1's lack of rigging wires or control cables around the tail surfaces.

Originally powered by an 82-kW (110-hp.) Le Rhône 9J, the HD.1 was delivered with the more powerful 9Jb. Engines up to 127 kW (170 hp.) were tried with little success.

Conventional construction techniques using wooden frames with fabric covering accounted for most of the fuselage and wings. Dural, a metal alloy, was used for covering the forward fuselage.

A framework of steel tubing, covered with fabric, was selected for the tailplane. The strength of the resulting structure may explain the lack of any support other than the single tail strut on either side of the fuselage.

HD.1

Type: Single-seat fighter scout

Powerplant: One 89-kW (120-hp.) Le Rhône 9Jb nine-cylinder rotary piston engine

Maximum speed: 183 km/h (114 m.p.h.)

Cruising speed: 156 km/h (97 m.p.h.)

Service ceiling: 6000 m (19,700 ft.)

Endurance: 2 hr 30 min

Weapons: 1 fixed forward-firing 7.7-mm (.303 cal.) Vickers machine gun with 110 rounds

Weights: Empty 399 kg (880 lb.); max take-off 649 kg (1,430 lb.)

Dimensions:
Span	8.69 m	(28 ft. 6 in.)
Length	5.84 m	(19 ft. 2 in.)
Height	2.85 m	(9 ft. 8 in.)
Wing area	18.21 m²	(196 sq. ft.)

ACTION DATA

ENDURANCE

World War I fighter tactics were either to act as escorts for reconnaissance and bomber types or to remain airborne in the hope of enemy contact. Long endurance was therefore desirable.

HD.1	ALBATROS D.I	SPAD S.VII
2¹/₂ hr	2¹/₂ hr	1¹/₂ hr

WEAPONS

A single Vickers machine gun was usually the preferred armament of Allied fighters; a second gun decreased performance. The Albatros was the slowest of these three.

HD.1 — 1 x 7.7-mm (.303 cal.) machine gun

ALBATROS D.I — 2 x 7.92-mm machine guns

SPAD S.VII — 1 x 7.7-mm (.303 cal.) machine gun

POWER

Extra power allowed the SPAD a stronger, heavier structure, which was more able to withstand the stresses of combat. Its strength and speed allowed it to become one of the War's most successful fighters, even though it could not match the agility of types like the HD.1. The Albatros D.1 led to a series of exceptional fighters.

HD.1 — 89 kW (120 hp.)

ALBATROS D.I — 119 kW (160 hp.)

SPAD S.VII — 134 kW (180 hp.)

Early 1920s contemporaries

SOPWITH PUP: Excellent maneuverability and altitude performance made the low-powered Pup a formidable fighter.

SPAD S.VII: Higher power allowed the SPAD to be fast and strong. It was less agile than other designs but nevertheless very successful.

NIEUPORT 17: Nieuport pilots used the excellent rate of climb and overwing gun of the 17 to attack enemy aircraft from below.

SOPWITH TRIPLANE: The Triplane had all the qualities of the Pup, combined with higher speed and greater climb rate.

HANSA-BRANDENBURG

W.12 AND W.29

● Seaplane ● Imperial German Navy ● Fighter scout

Hansa-Brandenburg gave Germany two highly effective seaplane fighters during the Great War. Designed by the brilliant Ernst Heinkel, the W.12 of 1917 was a two-seat fighter seaplane with an observer-gunner in the back seat. The W.29, which was introduced a year later, improved on this concept. Both Hansas were among the most successful seaplanes used by German naval flyers, destroying submarines and aircraft.

▲ *Inhibited by their floats, seaplanes were not usually the most capable fighters of the war, but the Hansa-Brandenburgs were among the most effective. They were dangerous to attack from any angle.*

▲ **British model**
This replica of a W.29 was based at Thorpe Park in Surrey. It was complete with replica LMG 7.92-mm machine-guns.

▲ **Replica fighter**
Finland built the W.29 under licence at a factory near Helsinki. Based at Viipuri in the late 1920s, a number were fitted with skis.

Final version ▶
The W.33 was basically a scaled-up version of the W.29, which used a more powerful 183-kW (245-hp.) engine. Twenty-six of these aircraft were built in the autumn of 1918.

▼ **Ready to roll**
For taxiing on land the W.12 was mounted on a trolley. The exhaust pipes fed into a collector box, routed over the upper wing.

▲ **Prototype**
The first W.12 was built in 1917, with flying trials limited by harsh weather. The early models were powered by Mercedes D.III engines.

FACTS AND FIGURES

➤ At an airfield north of the Arctic Circle, Finland was flying its version of the W.29 on skis as late as 1930.

➤ Seaplane fighters were being developed by Britain as recently as the 1960s.

➤ During the war years 146 W.12 and 78 W.29 seaplane fighters were built.

➤ A W.12 based at Zeebrugge destroyed the British non-rigid airship C.27 during December 1917.

➤ Improvements to the W.12 design increased endurance by adding fuel capacity.

➤ Hansa-Brandenburg designed more than 20 flying-boat types between 1914 and 1918.

PROFILE

Seaplane fighter goes to war

Seaplane fighters have fallen out of fashion, even though the idea has considerable merit. But in both world wars, these fighters carried out important duties.

The W.12 biplane and W.29 monoplane were both of wood and fabric construction, with the vertical tail behind and below the fuselage. When they went into combat, they provided their users with enormous firepower and speed, although range was limited. Almost any

landplane was better looking, but Ernst Heinkel's seaplanes were both trailblazers and successful warriors.

The W.12 was assigned to seaplane bases, where it enjoyed modest success combating Allied airships. Searching for improved performance, Heinkel decided on a single wing for the W.29, which began to enter service in 1918. The latter aircraft was even more successful, prompting the government of Finland to

manufacture its own version. The W.12 and W.29 contributed enormously to increasing the knowledge of the engineering community on how to build small, operational seaplanes for combat, and both had a fine fighting record.

Above: The unusual downward curved tail was designed to allow the gunner an unrestricted field of fire for his machine-gun.

Below: By late 1917 the W.12 was making an appearance at German seaplane bases in an attempt to fight off the increasing attentions of the Royal Navy. It soon proved successful in combat.

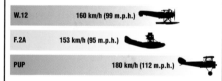

W.29

Type: two-seat fighter seaplane

Powerplant: one 112-kW (150-hp.) Benz Bz.III six-cylinder inline piston engine (W.12: one 119-kW (160-hp.) Mercedes D.III six-cylinder inline piston engine)

Maximum speed: 175 km/h (109 m.p.h.)

Endurance: 4 hours

Service ceiling: 5000 m (16,400 ft.)

Weights: empty 1000 kg (2,200 lb.); maximum take-off 1495 kg (3,289 lb.)

Armament: one or two fixed forward-firing 7.92-mm LMG 08/15 machine-guns and one 7.92-mm Parabellum machine-gun on pivoted mount in rear cockpit

Dimensions:
span	13.50 m (44 ft. 3 in.)
length	9.36 m (30 ft. 8 in.)
height	3.00 m (9 ft. 10 in.)
wing area	32.2 m² (346 sq. ft.)

Forward-firing armament consisted of one or two fixed LMG 08 machine-guns which were semi-recessed in the fuselage above the engine.

Defence was provided by a gunner in a rear cockpit equipped with a Parabellum machine-gun on a flexible mount.

The upswept rear fuselage and curved tailfin and rudder were distinct features of the W.12 and W.29. The red and white squares were a unit marking and not national identification.

Power was provided by a Mercedes D.III in the early versions of the W.12 and a Benz Bz.III in just over half of the production run.

The biplane wings were of equal length. The W.29 had a monoplane configuration that permitted higher speed and better manoeuvrability.

1414

W.12

Flown from Zeebrugge by Leutnant Becht of the Imperial German Navy Air Service, this W.12 flew defensive missions against British naval aircraft during 1918.

W.12s were fitted exclusively with floats, but some W.29s (especially those in Finland) had skis for ice operation; the bracing on the floats was very strong. Camouflage was painted on the upper surface.

COMBAT DATA

MAXIMUM SPEED

The single-seat Sopwith Pup is the fastest of the trio, however, it was lightly armed. The W.12 and the F.2A both had average performance for flying-boats of the period but the W.12 was more manoeuvrable.

W.12	160 km/h (99 m.p.h.)
F.2A	153 km/h (95 m.p.h.)
PUP	180 km/h (112 m.p.h.)

ENDURANCE

For naval aircraft of World War I endurance was vitally important as it allowed far ranging patrols over water. The F.2A had exceptional endurance and often destroyed airships or U-boats during patrols.

W.12	3½ hours
F.2A	6 hours
PUP	3 hours

ARMAMENT

Most land-based scouts of World War I were lightly armed with one or two machine-guns. The excellent W.12 had slightly heavier armament, but the larger F.2A could carry up to six guns.

W.12	F.2A	PUP
3 x 7.92-mm MGs	6 x 7.7-mm (.303 cal.) MGs	1 x 7.92-mm MGs

Attack on submarine C.25

■ **ON THE SURFACE:** A Royal Navy submarine, C.25, was caught off Harwich. A flight of Hansa-Brandenburg W.29s attacked and killed the captain, Lieutenant Bell, within minutes.

■ **NO ESCAPE:** Machine-gun fire riddled the hull, killing four more sailors. The hull was punctured, so the submarine could not dive. The crew replied with fire from a Lewis gun.

■ **UNDER TOW:** Submarine E.51 took the stricken C.25 under tow, but Oberleutnant Christiansen's W.29s kept up a fierce attack. Some of the aircraft dropped small bombs.

■ **WOUNDED:** The second coxswain was mortally wounded. He shouted 'never mind me sir, dive' as he fell, unaware that the captain was dead and the boat could not dive.

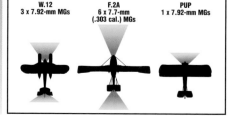

HAWKER

HART SERIES

● Basic pilot trainer ● Army co-operation ● Target tug

HAWKER HART SERIES

◀ Demon target tug
The Demon was replaced in front-line combat service by the Blenheim from 1938, but a few remained in service during World War II as target tugs. High-visibility markings were carried along with a target winch.

▼ Hart T trainer
Hart bombers remained in service in the Middle East during the war and soldiered on at home as trainers.

▲ Audax wartime trainer
This Audax of No. 11 Flying Training School flew from Little Rissington.

▼ Hart day bomber
The Hart saw action as day bomber and general-purpose biplane with the South Africans, and as an RAF communications aircraft until 1943.

▲ Audax decoys
These unserviceable Audax aircraft at Habbaniyah airfield in Iraq had their upper mainplanes removed in order to appear like serviceable Hurricanes to enemy aircraft above.

F aster than most fighters when it entered service in 1930, the Hart light bomber spawned a host of diverse derivatives. They included the Hart (Special) for the Middle East, the Hart (India) and the Hart (C) for communications work. The Hartbees was developed for South Africa, where 65 were built from 1935. Most Harts were replaced by modern types by September 1939, but some were still operational with front-line squadrons.

▲ The Audax
saw the most wartime action.
No. 237 Squadron flew against the Italians in East Africa in 1940. Others based at Habbaniyah saw use in the 1941 Iraqi revolt.

FACTS AND FIGURES

➤ So fast was the Hart bomber when it entered service, it was used as a development aircraft in fighter trials.

➤ A fighter variant of the Hart, the Demon carried three machine-guns.

➤ The Audax was widely exported, to Iraq, Persia and the Straits Settlements.

➤ The Hartbees was developed from the Hart specifically for the South African Air Force, where it was flown until 1946.

➤ In 1938 all Hind trainers had blind-flying hoods fitted for instrument training.

➤ The Osprey was essentially a navalised Hart for fleet reconnaissance/spotting.

PROFILE

War service in their twilight years

No. 5 Squadron, based at Lahore in India (now Pakistan), replaced its Wapitis with Harts in June 1940. In February 1941, after the Japanese had joined the war, the squadron was redeployed to Calcutta, where it operated another Hart derivative, the Audax, until September 1942.

A second India-based squadron, No. 27, became a training unit and swapped its Wapitis for Harts and Tiger Moths at Risalpur in October 1939. It operated the biplanes for a year before switching to operations with the Blenheim.

Four South African Air Force squadrons operated the Hartbees from Kenya and East Africa against the Italian forces in Ethiopia during 1940. Between June and September they were supported by the RAF's No. 237 Squadron, which deployed its Hart, Audax and Hardy ground-support aircraft from their bases at Nairobi as far as the Ethiopian border.

Above: Neutral Sweden's 42 licence-built, Perseus-engined Harts saw service throughout the war years.

At home in England, a few single Harts were used by communications squadrons based at Northolt and then at Hendon. The type was also used for training by the Glider Exercise Unit, which became No. 296 Squadron in January 1942. Based at Netheravon, No. 296 used its Harts and Hectors to tow Hotspur gliders on training flights.

Below: A development of the Hart, the Hind remained in wartime RAF service as a Volunteer Reserve Flying Training School light bomber trainer.

HIND

A number of Hind light bombers saw service during World War II, those based in the UK, like this one, being assigned such tasks as communications and glider towing. This aircraft was equipped as a blind-flying trainer.

A two-bladed, fixed-pitch propeller was the standard fitting to aircraft of the Hart family.

Rolls-Royce's tried and tested Kestrel 12-cylinder engine powered most members of the Hart family. Ratings between 400 kW (536 hp.) and 500 kW (670 hp.) were typical.

Hind bombers included a synchronised, forward-firing 7.7-mm (.303 cal.) Vickers machine-gun mounted on the left of the engine cowling and firing through the propeller arc.

Given its new role as a bomber trainer, the Hind retained its underwing bomb racks.

In the light day-bomber role for which it was designed the Hind had a crew of two, the rear cockpit usually being equipped with a Lewis 7.7-mm (.303 cal.) machine-gun for self defence.

During the early months of the war, RAF aircraft were fitted with gas detection patches, often on the upper surface of the wings, or in this case, the rear fuselage. In the event they were not needed.

Modifications made to the Hind bomber for the bomber trainer role included removal of all armament and the fitting of dual controls for an instructor.

Hart series aircraft colours

■ **AUDAX:** Production of the Audax ended in 1937 with 624 built. It served as an army co-operation aircraft and an advanced trainer.

■ **DEMON:** Operational in 1940, this example is one of 64 built for the Royal Australian Air Force. The Demon II was a trainer version of the fighter.

■ **HART:** First entering service in 1930, this Hart light bomber is seen with No. 57 Squadron, based at RAF Upper Heyford,1932–36.

■ **HART TRAINER:** Unarmed, this RAF Hart Trainer Series 2A is currently preserved at the RAF's Museum at Hendon, London.

Hart

Type: two-seat light bomber, close-support aircraft and trainer

Powerplant: one 391-kW (525-hp.) Rolls-Royce Kestrel IB, or 380-kW (510-hp.) Kestrel X (DR) liquid-cooled piston engine

Maximum speed: 296 km/h (184 m.p.h.) at 1525 m (5,000 ft.)

Range: 756 km (470 mi.)

Service ceiling: 6510 m (21,360 ft.)

Weights: empty 1148 kg (2,531 lb.); maximum take-off 2066 kg (4,555 lb.)

Armament: one or two forward-firing 7.7-mm (.303 cal.) machine-guns, one 7.7-mm machine-gun in rear cockpit; 236 kg (520 lb.) of bombs

Dimensions:
span	11.35 m	(37 ft. 3 in.)
length	8.94 m	(29 ft. 4 in.)
height	3.17 m	(10 ft. 5 in.)
wing area	32.33 m²	(348 sq. ft.)

ACTION DATA

MAXIMUM SPEED

The Hart was a very fast aircraft for its day, particularly bearing in mind its bomber status. When it first reached No. 33 Squadron, it was as much as 80 km/h faster than any contemporary bomber. The powerful Helldiver appeared at the beginning of the war.

HART	296 km/h (184 m.p.h.)
S.328	280 km/h (174 m.p.h.)
SBC-4 HELLDIVER	381 km/h (237 m.p.h.)

SERVICE CEILING

The Hart was not capable of such extreme altitudes as the Helldiver or S 328. However, during the war most of its army co-operation and training missions were flown at low level. The Curtiss SBC's ceiling was useful for its dive-bombing role.

HART 6510 m (21,360 ft.)
S.328 7200 m (23,620 ft.)
SBC-4 HELLDIVER 8320 m (27,300 ft.)

BOMBLOAD

For its day, the Hawker Hart carried a very useful bombload. By 1939, however, its offensive capabilities were less often called upon. Typical wartime roles were army observation, communications, liaison and aircrew training.

HART 236 kg (520 lb.)
S.328 500 kg (1,100 lb.)
SBC-4 HELLDIVER 454 kg (1,000 lb.)

HAWKER

HART/DEMON

● Inter-war two-seat light bomber ● Interceptor ● Foreign service

Policing British colonies in the Middle East and protecting the borders of India were two of the RAF's main tasks in the years between World Wars I and II. The Hart bomber proved ideal for this, being deployed rapidly to deal with emergencies and attack ground targets with guns and bombs. It was also fast enough to serve as the basis for the Demon fighter, and a whole generation of other combat and support aircraft.

▲ The Hart was used for a variety of tasks, from bombing and interception to training and army co-operation. In the latter role, the RAF used the Audax in the Middle East until 1941.

HAWKER **HART/DEMON**

◀ **Hinds in formation**
These Hind Mk Is equipped No. 40 Squadron based at Abingdon in Oxfordshire for just over two years, until they were replaced by Fairey Battles in 1938.

Bombers ▶
In February 1930, the RAF's No. 33 (B) Squadron was equipped with Hart bombers. In 1938, however, No. 33 became a fighter squadron.

▲ **Hart (India)**
The Hart (India) was built for action on the North West Frontier, the first examples arriving there in 1932.

▼ **Pegasus Hart with skis**
A Bristol Pegasus radial engine and enclosed cockpit were fitted to K3012 in 1934, to test a ski undercarriage in Canada.

▲ **Auxiliary Air Force on exercise**
No. 603 (City of Edinburgh) Squadron was one of eight Auxiliary Air Force units equipped with the Hart.

FACTS AND FIGURES

➤ Many RAF pilots who flew in World War II gained their 'wings' on Hart trainers between 1935 and 1939.

➤ Armstrong Whitworth, Gloster and Vickers also built Harts for the RAF.

➤ Audax army co-operation aircraft had an underfuselage message-collecting hook.

➤ One inter-war Hawker biplane remains airworthy today – a Hind belonging to the Shuttleworth Collection in Bedfordshire.

➤ No. 237 (Rhodesian) Squadron, RAF, flew the Audax during the 1941 Iraqi rebellion.

➤ Royal Navy Ospreys had folding wings for use aboard aircraft-carriers.

PROFILE

The versatile Hart family

First flown in 1928, the Hart entered service in 1930. Powerful and streamlined, it carried a two-man crew and could deliver up to 227 kg (500 lb.) of bombs. Gun armament consisted of a single forward-firing Vickers gun and a hand-aimed Lewis gun in the rear cockpit.

As well as the 452 standard bombers delivered by four companies in the early 1930s, specialised versions were developed for use in India and the Middle East. Another 500

aircraft were built as trainers.

The Hart's ability to outperform contemporary fighters also resulted in the development of the Demon two-seat interceptor, which was equipped for night flying. To enable the rear crewman to aim the gun against the force of the slipstream, later models of the Demon introduced a powered 'lobster-back' turret.

Other derivatives of the Hart included the Audax army co-operation aircraft and the

Above: In its heyday during the early months of the RAF's mid-1930s expansion, the Hind bomber was developed from the Hart but was powered by a more powerful Kestrel engine.

Osprey carrier-based fighter. Many remained in RAF service until the eve of World War II, and Harts also served with the air forces of several other countries, including India.

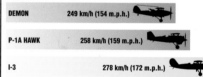

Above: Hawker's inter-war biplanes were widely exported. This Estonian Hart was one of eight delivered in 1932, and had interchangeable wheel and float undercarriages.

Hart

Type: two-seat light day-bomber

Powerplant: one 392-kW (525-hp.) Rolls-Royce Kestrel IB or 380-kW Kestrel X (DR) inline engine

Maximum speed: 277 km/h (172 m.p.h.) at 3048 m (10,000 ft.)

Climb rate: 8 minutes to 3048 m (10,000 ft.)

Range: 756 km (470 mi.)

Service ceiling: 6498 m (21,300 ft.)

Weights: empty 1148 kg (2,526 lb.); loaded 2066 kg (4,545 lb.)

Armament: one 7.7-mm (.303 cal.) machine-gun forward and one 7.7-mm machine-gun aft, plus up to 227 kg (500 lb.) of bombs

Dimensions:
span	11.35 m	(37 ft. 3 in.)
length	8.94 m	(29 ft. 4 in.)
height	3.17 m	(10 ft. 5 in.)
wing area	32.33 m²	(348 sq. ft.)

Twin Vickers 7.7-mm (.303 cal.) guns mounted ahead of the cockpit fired through the propeller arc.

'AUSTRALIAN DEMON'

Australia ordered 64 'Australian Demons', as they were known by Hawker. They were employed as army co-operation fighter-bombers and target tugs.

The Demon was a two-seater, with an observer/gunner occupying the rear seat. A 7.7-mm (.303 cal.) Lewis machine-gun could be fitted.

The Hart family were of all-metal construction with fabric covering.

The Rolls-Royce Kestrel VDR 12-cylinder vee engine powered the 'Australian Demon'. Producing 447 kW, it was more powerful than that fitted to RAF Demons.

The Demon's undercarriage was of the straight axle type with Vickers Oleo shock absorbers. Dunlop made the wheels and Palmer supplied the hydraulic brakes.

'Australian Demons' had provision for up to six electromagnetic bomb carriers under the wings.

A1-59 was one of the last 10 'Australian Demons' delivered and was equipped to perform target-towing duties. 'A1' was the serial prefix used by Demons.

COMBAT DATA

MAXIMUM SPEED

Although it was an interceptor, the Demon was a two-seater with a gunner behind the pilot. This extra weight and drag contributed to a slightly lower top speed than that of single-seaters.

DEMON	249 km/h (154 m.p.h.)
P-1A HAWK	258 km/h (159 m.p.h.)
I-3	278 km/h (172 m.p.h.)

ARMAMENT

With three machine-guns the Demon was well-armed. Two machine-guns of around 7.7-mm (.303) calibre were the norm on single-seat fighters during the early 1930s.

DEMON 3 x 7.7-mm (.303 cal.) machine-guns

P-1A HAWK 2 x 7.7-mm (.303 cal.) machine-guns

I-3 2 x 7.62-mm (.30 cal.) machine-guns

RANGE

The Demon's range was average for the interceptors of the day. Range was largely dependent on the space available for fuel aboard the aircraft.

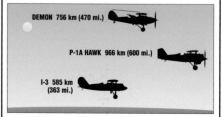

DEMON	756 km (470 mi.)
P-1A HAWK	966 km (600 mi.)
I-3	585 km (363 mi.)

Hart derivatives

■ **AUDAX:** Introduced in 1932, the Audax army co-operation aircraft served until 1941.

■ **HARDY:** The Hardy was a general-purpose model of the Audax. It served with the RAF in Iraq.

■ **OSPREY:** The Royal Navy's Osprey fighter-reconnaissance aircraft had folding wings.

■ **HIND:** A day-bomber derived from the Hart, the Hind was the last RAF biplane light bomber.

Hawker

Fury

- Single-seat fighter ● Cutting edge of RAF air defence

Serving the Royal Air Force in the defence of the homeland, the Hawker Fury symbolised the excitement of flying fighters in the 1930s. It was a clean, appealing biplane with speed, agility and an open cockpit. The pilot lived in a world of engine fumes and wind rushing through the wing braces. Incredibly, long after its streamlined shape had become dated, the Fury fought in World War II with South African pilots.

▲ *The Fury was renowned for its speed. This aircraft was dubbed the High-Speed Fury and was a company testbed for various engines and wing configurations, all of which were intended to increase the maximum performance of the type. Trials with this led to the Kestrel VI-powered Fury Mk II for the RAF.*

PHOTO FILE

Hawker Fury

Undercarriage developments ▶
In the interests of ever greater speed, the High-Speed Fury introduced these close-fitting wheel spats. Later aircraft had a single-strut landing gear offering less drag.

◀ Aerobatic mount
The Fury was a joy to fly, with beautifully harmonised controls. It was regularly displayed in aerobatic performances at the Hendon Air Pageant and other prestigious air shows.

◀ Massive propeller
Propeller technology lagged behind that of engines in the 1930s, so the Fury had to rely on a huge two-bladed airscrew.

▼ Civil testbed
Preceding the High-Speed Fury was this aircraft, known to Hawker as the Intermediate Fury. Unusually wearing a civilian registration, it was powered by a supercharged Goshawk engine.

▲ Export success
Large numbers of Furies were sold overseas, this being one of three built for Portugal.

FACTS AND FIGURES

- ➤ Three prototype Furies and 18 production aircraft all made initial flights in 1931.

- ➤ The improved Fury Mk II entered service with RAF No. 25 Squadron in 1936.

- ➤ Persia acquired Fury fighters and used some of these against the RAF during the Raschid Ali revolt of 1941.

- ➤ Three Furies were delivered to Spain with more powerful Hispano-Suiza engines.

- ➤ As late as 1940 a Fury pilot shot down a Messerschmitt Bf 109 in a dogfight.

- ➤ The closely-related Nimrod naval fighter appeared in Buenos Aires at the British Empire Trade Exhibition in 1931.

PROFILE

Hawker's famous fighting biplane

Graced with superbly clean and simple lines, the beautiful Fury biplane designed by the great Sydney Camm was the first RAF fighter able to fly over 200 m.p.h. (320 km/h). In the early 1930s, the daring men who flew the Fury were envied as the fortunate elite in 'the best flying club ever'.

The Fury went into RAF service in 1931 and was a superstar from the beginning. Its dramatic flying displays, including memorable tied-together aerobatics at Hendon, inspired several other countries to purchase this much-admired British fighter.

Dramatic advances were made to improve the Fury

design and improved engine, wing design and armament were introduced in new versions.

A close relative, the Nimrod, joined the Fleet Air Arm in the late 1930s. The few pilots who flew this remarkable craft in World War II fought courageously against great odds.

Owing to the steep angle of the fuselage, the Fury was notoriously difficult to taxi as the pilot could not see over the nose. In order to avoid obstacles he had to zigzag the aircraft on the ground.

Fury Mk II

Type: single-seat biplane fighter

Powerplant: one 477-kW (640-hp.) Rolls-Royce Kestrel VI 12-cylinder Vee piston engine

Maximum speed: 359 km/h (223 m.p.h.) at 5030 m (16,500 ft.)

Range: 435 km (270 mi.)

Service ceiling: 8990 m (29,500 ft.)

Weights: empty 1240 kg (2,728 lb.); maximum take-off 1637 kg (3,600 lb.)

Armament: two forward-firing synchronised 7.7-mm (.303 cal.) machine-guns

Dimensions: span 9.14 m (30 ft.)
length 8.15 m (26 ft. 8 in.)
height 3.10 m (10 ft. 2 in.)
wing area 23.41 m² (262 sq. ft.)

FURY MK I

Arguably the finest-looking biplane fighter, the Fury was also one of the fastest. It was very expensive to produce, so only three RAF squadrons flew the Mk I.

The front of the propeller spinner had a fitting for attachment to an external Hucks starter.

Between the undercarriage struts was the large bath for the radiator. The Kestrel engine was liquid-cooled, and such a radiator was necessary to dissipate the heat generated by the engine.

The key to the Fury's performance lay in its streamlined shape and the enormous power generated by the Rolls-Royce Kestrel II. Gun armament was no different to that of a World War I fighter: two Vickers 7.7-mm (.303 cal.) guns in the top decking of the fuselage, firing through the propeller arc.

In the late 1920s/early 1930s, RAF squadrons wore colourful unit markings, these being presented on the fuselage sides and on the wing panels. The black/white checkerboard signified No. 43 Squadron, the famous 'Fighting Cocks'.

K 3731

Fitting a radial engine (in this case a Panther on a Norwegian aircraft) greatly altered the look of the Fury.

ACTION DATA

MAXIMUM SPEED

For a short while the Fury was the world's fastest fighter, but the Fiat CR.32, arguably the best biplane fighter ever built, easily outperformed it. The P-26, first of the monoplane fighters, was just a shade quicker than the Fiat, and pointed the way forward for fighter development.

P-26 377 km/h (234 m.p.h.)
CR.32 375 km/h (232 m.p.h.)
FURY Mk II 359 km/h (223 m.p.h.)

SERVICE CEILING

The pre-war fighters were all still equipped with open cockpits, making flight at high altitude almost unbearable due to the cold. The thin atmosphere at these heights also led to the development of oxygen breathing apparatus, which began to appear in the mid-1930s.

P-26 8350 m (27,500 ft.)
CR.32 8800 m (28,850 ft.)
FURY Mk II 8990 m (29,500 ft.)

Inter-war biplane fighters of the RAF

■ **GLOSTER GREBE:** The Grebe entered service in 1923, replacing World War I–vintage Sopwith Snipes.

■ **HAWKER WOODCOCK:** The first aircraft to bear the Hawker name, the Woodcock served from 1925.

■ **ARMSTRONG WHITWORTH SISKIN IIIA:** Large numbers were delivered between 1926 and 1931.

■ **BRISTOL BULLDOG:** The main replacement for the Siskin, the Bulldog entered service in 1929.

■ **GLOSTER GAUNTLET:** Last of the open-cockpit biplanes, the Gauntlet reached the squadrons in 1935.

HEINKEL

HE 51

- Single-seat biplane ● Luftwaffe's first fighter ● Légion Condor

When the new Luftwaffe was rebuilt in the early 1930s, it required a fighter aircraft above all else. The Heinkel company had already designed biplane fighters for export, and it refined the HD 37 design to produce the He 51. This aircraft demonstrated the resurgence of air power in the Third Reich, especially when it was used during the civil war in Spain fighting against Republican forces.

▲ Like many biplane fighters of the 1930s, the He 51 was a fine machine when it was delivered in 1934, but was soon made obsolete by the appearance of much faster aircraft.

HEINKEL HE 51

▲ Légion Condor service
A total of 79 He 51s were delivered to Spain: 51 for the Nationalists and the remainder for the Légion Condor.

▼ Prototype Heinkel
Wearing the code D-IQEE, this He 51 was one of nine pre-production machines used for evaluation.

▲ Diving pair
Although far from ideal for the role, the He 51 equipped the first Stukagruppe dive-bombing units before the arrival of more suitable types like the Hs 123.

▲ Lively handling
The Heinkel had higher wing loading than earlier machines and was therefore less manoeuvrable. This caused a number of accidents.

▼ He 51B-2 floatplane
After a He 51A-1 was fitted with floats, 38 He 51B-2 floatplanes were built. This one was used by I/JG 136.

FACTS AND FIGURES

➤ To speed up production of the first 75 He 51A-1s, many were built under licence by AGO, Erla, Arado and Fieseler.

➤ The He 51's first victims in Spain were a Breguet XIX and two Hispano Nieuports.

➤ In April 1937 the Légion Condor replaced its He 51s with Bf 109Bs.

➤ Fighter chief Ernst Udet fought against an Ar 68 in a trial dogfight; the He 51 he flew was judged to have lost.

➤ The proposed high-altitude He 52E was never put into production.

➤ The He 49 and He 51 were the first Heinkel designs by the Günter brothers.

The Luftwaffe's first fighter

When the He 49a single-seat biplane first flew in November 1932, it was supposedly a civilian advanced trainer. However, its top speed of almost 320 km/h (200 m.p.h.) suggested leisurely intentions.

Its true role as the forerunner of the Luftwaffe's first fighter became clear when examples of the longer He 51 were delivered in mid-1934. The following year the new Luftwaffe was formed, with He 51As equipping its first fighter unit, Jagdgeschwader 'Richthofen'.

In 1936 the strengthened He 51B (some of which were equipped with floats) followed, plus 79 export He 51Cs which were delivered to Spain. The civil war there saw the He 51 in action for the first time, with the Légion Condor operating 28 of the Spanish machines fighting Soviet-built Polikarpovs. Later, the Luftwaffe took delivery of a number of He 51Cs with an improved radio and some flew close-support sorties in Poland in 1939. As a trainer the He 51 lasted until 1943.

This early He 51 has a civil registration and swastika marking, the former was to suggest a civil role for the aircraft.

The markings on this aircraft are typical of the late 1930s, the civil registration having been deleted once the establishment of the Luftwaffe had taken place. Note that the commandant's chevron marking is repeated on the wing.

HE 51B

This aircraft was flown by the Gruppe commandant of II/JG 132 'Richthofen' based at Döberitz.

Two 7.92-mm Rheinmetall MG 17 machine-guns were fitted above the engine to fire through the propeller arc.

Chevron markings on the fuselage and centre section indicated that it was flown by the unit's commandant.

One important improvement over the early He 49s was the extension of the rear fuselage and a broader tailfin in an effort to improve directional stability.

The wings were two-spar units with fabric covering, the upper surfaces carrying the ailerons and the lower surfaces carrying the trailing-edge flaps.

A powerful BMW VI inverted-Vee 12-cylinder piston engine rated at 559 kW propelled the He 51 to a top speed of 330 km/h (205 m.p.h.).

He 51B s and Cs were often fitted with an auxiliary fuel tank to increase their range, especially in the ground attack role.

The superstructure of the He 51 was metal, but the bulk of the skin was fabric as was common on fighters of the day.

He 51B-1

Type: single-seat biplane fighter

Powerplant: one 559-kW (750-hp.) BMW VI 7,3Z 12-cylinder liquid-cooled inverted-Vee piston engine

Maximum speed: 330 km/h (205 m.p.h.) at sea level

Cruising speed: 280 km/h (174 m.p.h.) at sea level

Range: 570 km (353 mi.)

Service ceiling: 7700 m (25,250 ft.)

Weights: empty 1460 kg (3,212 lb.); maximum take-off 1895 kg (4,169 lb.)

Armament: two 7.92-mm MG 17 machine-guns

Dimensions:
span 11.00 m (36 ft. 1 in.)
length 8.40 m (27 ft. 6 in.)
height 3.20 m (10 ft. 6 in.)
wing area 27.2 m² (293 sq. ft.)

COMBAT DATA

MAXIMUM SPEED

Speeds in the region of 350 km/h (220 m.p.h.) were fairly common for fighters of the day. It was not until the application of the monoplane to fighter aircraft in the late 1930s that speeds increased greatly. At a stroke the biplane became obsolete.

He 51B-1	330 km/h (205 m.p.h.)
CR.32	375 km/h (233 m.p.h.)
GAUNTLET	370 km/h (229 m.p.h.)

RANGE

Being a larger aircraft with a less powerful engine, the Fiat CR.32 had a greater fuel capacity and lower fuel consumption. This translated as greater range. One of the last British biplane designs, the Gauntlet was better still. A few were still in service in 1939.

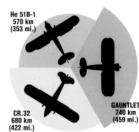

He 51B-1
570 km
(353 mi.)

CR.32
680 km
(422 mi.)

GAUNTLET
740 km
(459 mi.)

SERVICE CEILING

A combination of wing design, engine power and the relatively light weight of the airframe combined to give the Gloster Gauntlet the edge in ceiling capability. Service ceiling, the ability to maintain altitude and manoeuvrability at altitude, were important attributes, especially for a dogfighting aircraft.

He 51B-1
7700 m
(25,250 ft.)

GAUNTLET
10,210 m
(33,500 ft.)

CR.32
8800 m
(28,850 ft.)

European fighters of the 1930s

FIAT CR.32: Another type to see service with the Légion Condor, the CR.32 was designed by Celestion Rosatelli for the Italian air force and saw service in World War II.

GLOSTER GLADIATOR: Entering service in 1937, the Gladiator was to be the RAF's last biplane fighter. Despite its inferior performance a few remained in frontline use as late as 1942.

POLIKARPOV I-15: The last and best Polikarpov biplane fighter, a total of 550 were supplied to Republican Spain and flew against aircraft like the Fiat CR.32. Finland was also an operator.

HEINKEL

HE 59

● Air–sea rescue ● Torpedo bomber ● Maritime reconnaissance

In the early 1930s Germany possessed a small but industrious aircraft industry, and by far the most prolific of these companies was the Heinkel works at Warnemünde. When the expansion of the clandestine German air arm was launched in 1934, the He 59 was one of the first aircraft developed. After employment during the Spanish Civil War, flying night-bombing and reconnaissance sorties, the He 59 served in a wide variety of duties during World War II.

▲ When it first
appeared in the early 1930s, the
He 59 exceeded in size by a substantial margin
any aircraft previously produced by the Heinkel
company. It normally held a crew of four.

HEINKEL HE 59

▼ Legion Condor
Ten He 59B-2s were assigned to
naval reconnaissance squadron
AS/88 during the Spanish Civil War.

▲ Anti-ship sorties
The He 59 carried a single 700-kg (1.540-lb.) or 1000-kg (2,200-lb.) torpedo. Alternatively, 1000 kg (2,200 lb.) of bombs could be carried in the weapons bay.

▼ Open cockpit position
The He 59 was certainly not designed with crew comfort in mind. The bow and dorsal gunners as well as the pilot sat in an open position at the mercy of the elements.

▲ Rescue response
During the fierce fighting of the Battle of Britain, white-painted He 59C-2s were regularly called into action to rescue downed Luftwaffe pilots.

Land-based prototype ▶
Posing as a civilian freight aircraft, the first He 59 to fly was actually the second prototype. It was the only example to feature a wheeled undercarriage.

FACTS AND FIGURES

➤ The first flight was made by the He 59A in September 1931; the first float-equipped prototype did not fly until January 1932.

➤ Twelve He 59s were used to transport troops for a surprise attack on Rotterdam.

➤ The He 59E-1 was a photographic training variant with three camera positions.

➤ Some Spanish Civil War He 59s were fitted with 20-mm cannon for attacking road and rail communications.

➤ After the Spanish Civil War, three He 59s were handed over to the Spanish navy.

➤ Several He 59s were transferred to the Finnish air force for rescue duties.

PROFILE

Battle of Britain rescue craft

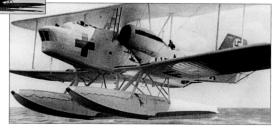

Left: In service with 3./Kü.Fl.Gr.106 of the coastal aviation group, this He 59B-2 operated in the North Sea area during 1939. It was used for controlling shipping in the North and Baltic Seas.

Conceived by Reinhold Mewes in 1930, the He 59 was developed as a general-purpose floatplane suitable for roles such as naval co-operation, maritime patrol and torpedo bombing. First flying in 1931, the He 59 masqueraded as a civilian freight transport to avoid the ban on the development of military aircraft in Germany.

Successful trials with the two prototypes (one wheeled, the other float-equipped) led to an order for the fully militarised He 59B-1 production version, featuring a bomb-aimer's position and defensive machine-guns.

Deliveries began in the summer of 1934, and during the next two years of intensive training the He 59B-1 was replaced in production by the improved B-2 and B-3 versions built under licence by Arado. In 1936 the He 59 became part of the Condor Legion force committed to the Spanish conflict, flying night-bombing attacks on important harbours.

In 1938 the He 59 was replaced in production by newer types but by the outbreak of World War II more than 100 were still in service. After brief front-line use many were modified to He 59C, D and E standard and flew air-sea rescue, training and transport tasks. By 1943 the type had all but disappeared from service.

Above: Sporting large red crosses and civil identities, He 59s were believed by Britain to be transporting agents onto the British mainland. After a number were shot down they returned to a military identity.

He 59B-2

Type: four-seat, twin-engined torpedo bomber, reconnaissance and air-sea rescue floatplane

Powerplant: two 492-kW (660-hp.) BMW VI 6,0 ZU 12-cylinder piston engines

Maximum speed: 220 km/h (137 m.p.h.) at sea level

Range: 1750 km (1,090 mi.)

Service ceiling: 3500 m (11,500 ft.)

Weights: empty 6215 kg (13,700 lb.); maximum take-off 9000 kg (19,840 lb.)

Armament: three 7.92-mm MG 15 machine-guns in nose, dorsal and ventral positions plus one torpedo or up to 1000 kg (2,200 lb.) of bombs

Dimensions:

span	23.70 m	(77 ft. 9 in.)
length	17.40 m	(57 ft. 1 in.)
height	7.10 m	(23 ft. 4 in.)
wing area	153.3 m²	(1,650 sq. ft.)

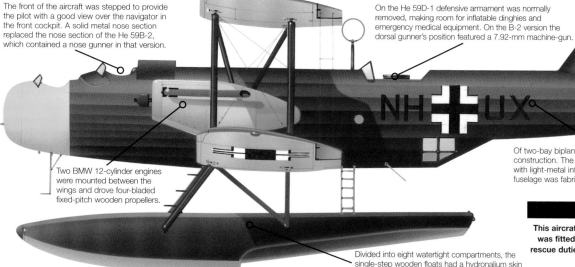

The front of the aircraft was stepped to provide the pilot with a good view over the navigator in the front cockpit. A solid metal nose section replaced the nose section of the He 59B-2, which contained a nose gunner in that version.

On the He 59D-1 defensive armament was normally removed, making room for inflatable dinghies and emergency medical equipment. On the B-2 version the dorsal gunner's position featured a 7.92-mm machine-gun.

Two BMW 12-cylinder engines were mounted between the wings and drove four-bladed fixed-pitch wooden propellers.

Of two-bay biplane design, the He 59 was of mixed construction. The two-spar wooden wings were braced with light-metal interplane struts. The welded steel-tube fuselage was fabric-covered, as were the control surfaces.

Divided into eight watertight compartments, the single-step wooden floats had a hydronalium skin and were braced to the fuselage at the wingroots.

HE 59D-1

This aircraft of the Seenotzentrale Agäisches Meer was fitted with emergency equipment for air-sea rescue duties in the Aegean Sea during 1941, saving downed Luftwaffe pilots.

COMBAT DATA

POWER

The Do 18 which replaced the He 59 was a more powerful and faster design. The Walrus was a single-engined, smaller, lighter design and was considerably slower.

He 59B-2 984 kW (1,320 hp.)	Do 18G-1 1312 kW (1,760 hp.)	WALRUS Mk II 578 kW (775 hp.)

RANGE

The Walrus was designed for operations close to its mother ship or in coastal waters and did not require a long range. The Do 18 had a much longer range and was able to patrol far out into the Atlantic Ocean. The He 59 operated close to the shore.

He 59B-2 1750 km (1,090 mi.)

Do 18G-1 3500 km (2,175 mi.)

WALRUS Mk II 966 km (600 mi.)

ARMAMENT

Designed originally for anti-shipping and reconnaissance duties, the He 59 had the best bombload of the three types. All three carried defensive machine-guns for protection against fighters.

He 59B-2	3 x 7.92-mm machine-guns 1000-kg (2,200-lb.) bombload
Do 18G-1	1 x 13-mm machine-gun 1 x 20-mm cannon 100-kg (220-lb.) bombload
WALRUS Mk II	3 x 7.7-mm (.303 cal.) machine-guns 345-kg (760-lb.) bombload

World War II rescue seaplanes

■ **CONSOLIDATED CATALINA:** Used for anti-shipping attacks and spotting as well as air-sea rescue, the PBY saved hundreds of airmen.

■ **DORNIER Do 18:** Replacing the He 59 in service, the Do 18N rescue version served in Denmark, France, Holland and Norway.

■ **DORNIER Do 24:** Being first delivered in the autumn of 1941, the Do 24 excelled in the air-sea rescue role thanks to its rugged design.

■ **SUPERMARINE WALRUS:** Obsolete before World War II, the 'Shagbat' became famous for daring rescues of downed Allied pilots.

HUGHES

H-4 'SPRUCE GOOSE'

- Largest aircraft ● Wooden construction ● Strategic transport

◄ The monster rises
At the end of the taxi trials, all of the guests left the aircraft. Hughes then took the 'Goose' out into the harbour for its one and only flight.

◄ Eight-engine power
Propelled by eight huge Pratt & Whitney 28-cylinder radial engines, Hughes' flying-boat had more than twice the power of a Boeing B-29 Superfortress heavy bomber.

▼ Launch day
'Spruce Goose' was launched from its 88.4-m (290-ft.) dry dock into Long Beach Harbor on 1 November 1947.

▼ Gathering dust
After its one flight, the mighty flying-boat was left in storage for 35 years, gathering dust and attracting fascinated tourists.

◄ Taxi trials
The HK-1 moved under its own power for the first time on 2 November. Hughes undertook a taxi trial with 18 crew, five officials and nine invited guests aboard before flying the H-4 himself.

For more than three decades the Hughes HFB-1 (H-4) Hercules was the biggest flying machine ever built. It was a towering achievement of entrepreneurial spirit and aviation pioneering, all the more remarkable because the behemoth was built without essential wartime materials. Popularly called the 'Spruce Goose' because of its wooden construction, Hughes' flying-boat was an incredible sight, which flew just once.

▲ Variously known as the HFB-1, H-4 or HK-1, the monster flying-boat designed by Howard Hughes was a giant in every way. Even the flight deck had more space than the passenger cabins of many airliners of the period.

FACTS AND FIGURES

➤ Hughes wrecked a Sikorsky S-43 while experimenting with centre-of-gravity and power settings for the HK-1.

➤ 'Spruce Goose' was flown just once, over Los Angeles harbour on 2 November 1947.

➤ The HK-1 was built in the world's largest wooden building at Culver Field.

➤ The huge flying-boat was taxi-tested with its eight engines controlled by four throttles harnessed in pairs.

➤ Hughes planned a larger flying-boat, the HFB-2, which was never built.

➤ 'Spruce Goose' was transported by barge to its present owners in Oregon.

The 'Spruce Goose' flies

In 1944, when Howard Hughes unveiled plans for the HFB-1 (Hughes Flying Boat First Design) or HK-1 (Hughes-Kaiser First Design) Hercules flying-boat, no one believed he was serious. He intended to build a seaborne giant that could carry up to 750 troops, without using steel or aluminium except in the engines. The airframe would be manufactured of non-strategic wood products. At that time, the Allies still thought that a large-scale invasion of Japan would be needed to bring the Pacific War to an end, and the H-4 would have been much in demand as a flying troopship.

Everything about the HK-1 flying-boat was big. When it was built, it was the largest aircraft in the world. Today, the Ukrainian Antonov An-225 is larger, but the Hughes flying-boat still has a greater wing span.

Hughes and his experts saw the flying-boat as a great, globe-girdling craft which would change the way people and cargo were moved across vast distances.

Left: The huge wingspan of the 'Spruce Goose' was as long as a soccer pitch. Street lighting had to be dismantled at great expense to allow the road transportation of such a huge aircraft for final assembly in Los Angeles.

In a sense, this is what was accomplished decades later by the Boeing 747 jetliner. Unfortunately, the very promising Hughes flying-boat was flown only once. Though it was a true pioneer, its potential was never fulfilled despite the genius of its design.

Above: The flight of the 'Spruce Goose' attracted great media interest, and Los Angeles harbour was packed with a flotilla of small boats. Little did they know that they would be the only people to see this great beast fly.

H-4 'SPRUCE GOOSE'

The massive aircraft gained its popular name from the derogatory comment of a senator investigating what he saw as a waste of public money. "It's a Spruce Goose," he said, "it'll never fly."

The 'Spruce Goose' was designed to be flown by two pilots. On its only flight the aircraft carried 18 working personnel, including flight engineers and flight test observers. There were also 15 airline-type seats on the upper deck for use by reporters and invited guests.

'Spruce Goose' was powered by eight Pratt & Whitney Wasp Major R-4360 radial engines, each delivering some 2240 kW (3,000 hp.). These were the most powerful conventional piston-driven engines ever built.

The leading edge of the massive wings housed a catwalk which allowed inflight access to the engine nacelles.

Tailplanes and fin were of wood construction, though the rudder and elevators were fabric covered. The massive tailplane was longer than the wing of a Lancaster bomber.

The reason that such a large aircraft could be built from wood was that the Hughes Corporation had recently developed the Duramold process, which laminated plywood and epoxy resin into a lightweight but very strong building material.

NX37602

Although the nose of the aircraft was solid, its structure was designed to be easily fitted with clamshell doors to allow the loading of outsize cargo.

Up to 53,000 litres (14,000 gal.) of fuel were carried in 14 underfloor tanks.

The only flight of the Hercules

1 TAXI TO TAKE OFF: Hughes was supposed to keep the flying-boat on the surface, but to engineer Dave Grant's surprise the multi-millionaire ordered 15° of flap – which was the take-off setting.

2 LIFT OFF: Accelerating through 150 km/h (93 m.p.h.), the huge boat began skimming across the surface. Then, to the delight of thousands of people watching from the shore, it lifted slowly and gracefully into the air.

3 TOUCHDOWN: Hughes eased his huge machine back onto the water. The flight had lasted less than a minute, never more than 25 m (80 ft.) above the water and covering less than 1.6 km (one mile).

KAWANISHI

H6K 'MAVIS'

● Maritime reconnaissance/bomber ● Long range ● Transport

I t was a Japanese navy need for an aircraft which could cover the vast expanses of the Pacific that inspired Kawanishi to design the 'Mavis'. Powered by four engines, the H6K, first flown in July 1936, was one of the most reliable and efficient of the flying-boats used by Japan during World War II. It also had a very long range and an endurance of more than 24 hours, making it ideally suited to long overwater missions.

▲ Although the 'Mavis' was undoubtedly one of the finest World War II flying-boats, it was notoriously difficult to service. Large platforms were erected by engineers for engine maintenance.

▼ Allied evaluation
Many Japanese aircraft were captured as the Allies overran Japanese bases in the Pacific. This H6K flew with the Allied Technical Air Intelligence Unit (ATAIU) which tested the capabilities of enemy types.

▲ Early introduction
In 1938 the first H6K1s entered service with the Imperial Japanese Navy after 18 months of flying and sea trials with four prototypes.

◀ Transport version
Code-named 'Tillie' by the Allies, the H6K4-L was a transport version with additional cabin windows. Armament was removed and sleeping berths were provided.

▼ Offensive armament
The H6K could carry two 800-kg (1,760-lb.) torpedoes or up to 1000 kg (2,200 lb.) of bombs attached to the struts.

▲ Series prototype
Originally named the Kawanishi Navy Experimental 9-Shi Large-size Flying-Boat, the 'Mavis' prototype was first flown on 14 July 1936, with test pilot Katsuji Kondo at the controls.

FACTS AND FIGURES

➤ Powered by four Nakajima Hikari engines, the prototype first flew in 1936 after three years of design work.

➤ The H6K was regarded as a success during the Sino-Japanese War of 1938–39.

➤ Total production of the H6K reached 215, of which 127 were H6K4s.

➤ As well as for maritime patrol, H6K4s were used against land targets in the Dutch East Indies during 1942.

➤ Transport versions were fitted with mail, cargo and passenger compartments.

➤ H6Ks were vulnerable to fighters as they lacked self-sealing fuel tanks and armour.

PROFILE

Reconnaissance for the Imperial Fleet

The initial production model of the 'Mavis', the H6K2, had a powered turret with a single machine-gun on top of the rear fuselage, plus manually operated guns in the nose and tail. The 10 built were delivered to the Japanese navy in 1939, but were subsequently converted for use as transports.

The main version was the H6K4, which had two blisters for machine-guns on the sides of the forward fuselage. There were 66 of this model in service at the time of the attack on Pearl Harbor, and during the Japanese conquests of early 1942 they were used widely both for bombing and maritime patrol.

In 1942 the H6K5 introduced 969.4-kW (1,300-hp.) engines, but by this time it was proving too vulnerable to Allied fighters, and its H8K replacement, the fastest flying-boat of the war, was already in production.

Altogether, 215 H6Ks were built before production ended in 1943. They included some 18 transports used by the Kaiyo (Ocean) division of Greater Japan Air Lines until 1945. A few survivors were used by the republican Indonesian air force during the post-war fight for independence and the civil war which followed.

Above: The final maritime reconnaissance version was the H6K5. Fitted with more powerful Mitsubishi Kinsei 53 radial engines, this version had a turret housing a 7.7-mm (.303 cal.) machine-gun aft of the flight deck.

Left: As Allied fighters improved during the course of the Pacific War, the lumbering H6Ks became easy targets. This example was downed in 1944 by Lieutenant John D. Keeling of VB-109, US Naval Reserve.

H6K5 'MAVIS'

As the final production version, the H6K5 was fitted with more powerful engines and improved armament. This example is seen in standard Imperial Japanese Navy colours.

H6K4 'Mavis'

Type: long-range reconnaissance, bomber or transport flying-boat

Powerplant: four 745.7-kW (1,000-hp.) Mitsubishi Kinsei 43 14-cylinder radial engines

Maximum speed: 340 km/h (211 m.p.h.) at 4000 m (13,100 ft.)

Climb rate: 5000 m (16,400 ft.) in 13 min 31 sec

Range: 6080 km (3,770 mi.)

Service ceiling: 9610 m (31,500 ft.)

Weights: 21,545 kg (47,400 lb.) max. take-off

Armament: four 7.7-mm (.303 cal.) machine guns (one each in nose, dorsal and fuselage-side mountings) plus one 20-mm cannon in tail; two 800-kg (1,760-lb.) torpedoes or 1000 kg (2,200 lb.) of bombs

Dimensions:
span	40.00 m (131 ft. 3 in.)
length	25.63 m (10 ft. 9 in.)
height	6.27 m (20 ft. 7 in.)
wing area	170 m² (1,829 sq. ft.)

Replacing the bow gun position, a turret containing a 7.7-mm (.303 cal.) machine-gun was added immediately aft of the flight deck. This position protected the aircraft from attack from above or head-on.

The final production versions were powered by Kinsei 51 or 53 radials which were 224 kW (300 hp.) more powerful than earlier versions.

Offensive armament was mounted on the parallel wing supporting struts and consisted of bombs or two torpedoes. The beam blisters on each side of the fuselage each contained a single, hand-held 7.7-mm (.303 cal.) Type 92 machine-gun.

After studying the American Sikorsky S-42, Kawanishi designed the H6K with a slender two-step hull. The parasol wing was mounted above the fuselage and a stabilising float was fitted to each wing.

The tail turret had a large glazed section giving the gunner good visibility. Armament comprised a hand-held 20-mm Type 99 Model 1 cannon.

In earlier versions of the 'Mavis' a 7.7-mm (.303 cal.) hand-held Type 92 machine-gun was mounted in an open bow position. This was removed in the H6K5 but observation windows remained.

After the first test flight the forward step of the hull was moved 50 cm (20 in.) rearwards. This modification was successful and the H6K had the best water-handling characteristics of any World War II flying-boat.

Kawanishi Seaplanes

■ **E7K 'ALF':** Flying anti-submarine, convoy escort and reconnaissance patrols in 1941-43, many E7K2s ended up in *kamikaze* attacks.

■ **E8K:** Designed in 1933 as a reconnaissance seaplane, the E8K lacked manoeuvrability and lost out to the Nakajima E8N1 biplane.

■ **E15K SHIUN 'NORM':** Repeated failures of the float assemblies were the main downfall of the Shiun (Violet Cloud). Only 15 were built.

■ **N1K KYOFU 'REX':** An ambitious design, the N1K suffered from a protracted development and only 97 of these floatplane fighters were built.

COMBAT DATA

RANGE

All three of these types were respected for their highly impressive range and endurance. The H6K was capable of remaining aloft for 24 hours and crew fatigue was often the limiting factor, rather than the endurance of the aircraft. Long range was especially important in order to cover the vast area of the Pacific theatre.

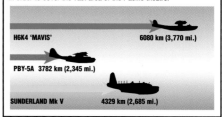

H6K4 'MAVIS'	6080 km (3,770 mi.)
PBY-5A	3782 km (2,345 mi.)
SUNDERLAND Mk V	4329 km (2,685 mi.)

KAWANISHI

H8K 'EMILY'

● Long-range flying-boat ● Maritime patrol bomber

Given the allied reporting name of 'Emily', the Kawanishi H8K was one of the most outstanding and advanced flying-boats to be built during World War II. Heavily armed and armoured, it had a very long range and flew superbly. Yet it was a complex machine, and the 167 examples built never fully replaced the Sikorsky-influenced H6K 'Mavis' with which the Imperial Japanese Navy had been equipped at the start of World War II.

▲ The H8K was similar to Britain's Short Sunderland in layout and role, but although the Sunderland was better known, the Japanese aircraft had superior performance. It was also far better than its Kawanishi predecessor, the H6K.

PHOTO FILE

KAWANISHI **H8K 'EMILY'**

▲ Float trials
The initial trials of the H8K showed some flaws in handling on water, but performance was otherwise very good and it was ordered into production.

Under attack ▶
This 'Emily' was shot up by an A-26 over Saipan in 1944. It made a hurried forced landing after the port inner engine caught fire.

▲ Transport
The H8K was turned into a transport capable of carrying up to 64 passengers. Mitsubishi MK4Q engines were installed and armament was reduced.

▲ High power
The main advantage of the H8K over the H6K was the amount of power. Top speed was markedly higher, and take-offs were shorter and much easier.

◀ Hitting the sea
Attacking even a stricken 'Emily' like this could be a hazardous business because of its heavy defensive armament of 20-mm cannon.

FACTS AND FIGURES

➤ The H8K prototype flew for the first time in January 1941.

➤ The first operational mission took place in 1942, when two aircraft set off from Wake Island to bomb Pearl Harbor.

➤ An H8K trials version was built with retractable floats and dorsal turret.

➤ Radar-equipped H8Ks sank at least three American submarines north of the Philippines in 1945.

➤ As a VIP transport the H8K could seat 29 passengers in great comfort.

➤ The 'Emily' could fly further than any other operational flying-boat of the war.

PROFILE

A floating flying fortress

The H8K prototype was first flown in 1941. It was designed to meet a 1938 requirement for a four-engined maritime reconnaissance flying-boat superior in all respects to the British Sunderland, then the best in the world. After modification improved the initially poor water handling qualities, the type was put into production as the Navy Type 2 Flying Boat Model 11. With armour protection, self-sealing fuel tanks, an armament that included 20-mm cannon and a maximum speed of over 430 km/h (270 m.p.h.), it represented a great advance over previous types.

The further improved H8K2 had more power, greater speed and its armament increased to five 20-mm cannon and four 7.7-mm (.303 cal.) machine-guns. This made it unquestionably one of the toughest opponents faced by the Allies in the Pacific. It was also one of the first Japanese aircraft to be fitted with anti-surface vessel radar, and achieved some success against American submarines late in the war.

Above: With an empire stretching across thousands of kilometres of the Pacific, the Japanese needed good flying-boats urgently. This need became acute when American naval supremacy began to deny Japanese shipping access to the sea lanes.

Left: Equipped with radar, the 'Emily' was one of the few serious threats to the US Navy submarines which were strangling Japan's seaborne lifelines.

H8K2 'Emily'

Type: long-range maritime reconnaissance flying-boat

Powerplant: four 1380-kW (1,850-hp.) Mitsubishi Kasei 22 14-cylinder radial piston engines

Maximum speed: 467 km/h (290 m.p.h.)

Range: 7180 km (4,450 mi.)

Service ceiling: 8760 m (28,700 ft.)

Weights: empty 18,380 kg (40,436 lb.); loaded 32,500 kg (71,500 lb.)

Armament: 20-mm (0.79-in.) cannon in bow, dorsal, tail turrets and on each beam; four 7.7-mm (.303 cal.) machine-guns from beam hatches; up to 2000 kg (4,400 lb.) of bombs or two 800-kg (1,760-lb.) torpedoes

Dimensions:
span	38.00 m	(124 ft. 7 in.)
length	28.13 m	(92 ft. 4 in.)
height	9.15 m	(30 ft.)
wing area	106 m²	(1,140 sq. ft.)

H8K2 'EMILY'

The H8K2 was the major production version of the 'Emily', with 112 boats being completed and entering service between 1942 and 1944.

Unlike many Japanese aircraft, the H8K had excellent armour protection for the crew.

Prototypes were powered by the Mitsubishi Mars MK4A engine, but later aircraft used the 1380-kW (1,850-hp.) MK4Q engine, driving Hamilton propellers.

The wing structure was all-metal, with a metal covering. The wing had slight dihedral for enhanced stability during long patrols.

The dorsal turret was powered and mounted a single 20-mm (0.79-in.) cannon.

Normally flown with a crew of 10, the H8K's capacious fuselage could hold up to 64 passengers.

The nose gunner operated a 20-mm (0.79-in.) cannon from his position, which was retained in the H8K transport.

The bulk fuel tanks in the hull were self-sealing and had a carbon dioxide fire suppression system.

The tail gunner operated a 20-mm cannon from the rear turret.

COMBAT DATA

CRUISING SPEED

Flying-boats are not the most streamlined of machines, and none of the really heavy examples were particularly fast. The specification for the H8K called for it to be able to outperform the British Sunderland, which it did. Both cruised faster than the massive German Bv 222.

H8K 'EMILY'	295 km/h (183 m.p.h.)
SUNDERLAND	285 km/h (177 m.p.h.)
Bv 222 WIKING	250 km/h (155 m.p.h.)

RANGE

Maritime reconnaissance requires the aircraft to stay in the air for long periods. The H8K was designed to operate over the vast expanses of the Pacific, and had a considerably longer range than its rivals. It could remain on patrol for an entire day and night, the only limiting factor being the endurance of the crew.

H8K 'EMILY' 7180 km (4,450 mi.)

Bv 222 WIKING 6000 km (3,700 mi.)

SUNDERLAND 4700 km (2,914 mi.)

DEFENSIVE ARMAMENT

The Short Sunderland was not an easy target in a fight and was nicknamed 'the Flying Porcupine' by the Luftwaffe. But the British aircraft's armament paled in comparison with that of the H8K. It took strong nerves on the part of an American fighter pilot to get in close to the 'Emily', with its powerful all-round armament of 20-mm (0.79-in.) cannon.

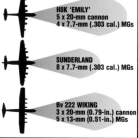

H8K 'EMILY' 5 x 20-mm cannon 4 x 7.7-mm (.303 cal.) MGs

SUNDERLAND 8 x 7.7-mm (.303 cal.) MGs

Bv 222 WIKING 3 x 20-mm (0.79-in.) cannon 5 x 13-mm (0.51-in.) MGs

Giants of the oceans

■ **SHORT SUNDERLAND:** Smaller and slower than the 'Emily', the British Sunderland performed a similar function and amassed a superb combat record.

■ **BLOHM & VOSS Bv 222 WIKING:** The huge six-engined Wiking served from the Arctic to the Mediterranean. It carried huge loads, but was vulnerable to Allied fighters.

■ **LATÉCOÈRE 631:** This elegant flying-boat was completed in occupied France and was immediately confiscated by the Germans. After the war it flew Atlantic passenger routes.

■ **CONSOLIDATED PB2Y CORONADO:** Reliable but sluggish, the Coronado was used by the US Navy as a long-range patroller, 44-seat transport and ambulance.

■ **MARTIN JRM MARS:** Ordered in 1938, only five examples of the US Navy's largest flying-boat were built. They were used from the end of the war as long-range cargo transports.

MACCHI

M.5-M.67

● Fighting floatplanes ● Schneider Trophy winners ● Transports

O ne of the most famous names in aviation, the Macchi company built a series of seaplanes which gained fame not only during World War I, but also through legendary Schneider Trophy victories of the 1920s and 1930s. It was in 1915 that the Macchi company was asked to design a flying-boat to match those of the Austrian opposition. This was built in just over one month and paved the way for the record-breaking aircraft of the following decades.

▲ First appearing in 1918, the M.7 was the ultimate Macchi flying-boat of World War I. Post-war, the aircraft was developed into the successful M.7bis racer and M.7ter fighter.

MACCHI M.5-M.67

Venice victory ▶
Piloted by Giovanni di Briganti, an M.7bis won the 1921 Schneider Trophy. No less than five M.7s of various versions took part in the race.

◀ **Trophy winner**
Piloted by Mario de Bernardi, this M.39 won the 1926 Schneider Trophy at Norfolk, Virginia.

▼ **Monoplane racer**
Designed by Mario Castoldi, the M.33 was third in the 1925 Schneider Trophy at Baltimore, Maryland.

▼ **Seaplane spotter**
Macchi's first twin-boom design was the M.12 armed reconnaissance and bomber flying-boat.

Famous fighter ▶
The highly agile, single-seat M.5 was the most successful Italian-designed fighter of World War I.

FACTS AND FIGURES

➤ Entering service in 1918, the M.7 served as the M.7ter in Italian training schools until as late as 1940.

➤ Three M.41s were delivered to Spain in 1936 and fought in the Civil War.

➤ The M.24 was used in torpedo-launching experiments during 1925.

➤ A number of M.3s were converted by Swiss company Ad Astra Aero for carrying passengers on pleasure flights.

➤ In 1929 one of the three Schneider Trophy M.67s crashed into Lake Garda.

➤ On 4 November 1927 the M.52 broke the 3-km (1.86-mile) world speed record at 479.29 km/h (297 m.p.h.).

Macchi's seaplane series

Macchi's first flying-boat design, the L.1 (L standing for Lohner), was basically a copy of an existing Austrian design. The company's first indigenous aircraft was the L.3 (later changed to M.3 in recognition of Macchi's design work). This aircraft, along with the M.5 and M.7 which were developments of this airframe, became highly successful fighters during World War I, matching any land-based opponent. They achieved export sales to the USA.

Post-war, the M.7 was developed into the M.7bis, which won the 1922 Schneider Trophy, and the M.7ter, of which more than 100 were built.

The success of the single hull, biplane wing, pusher-engine layout was to influence Macchi's designs over the next decade. Numerous designs were produced, each with more powerful engines and refined aerodynamics, culminating in the twin-engined M.24 commercial flying-boat capable of carrying eight passengers.

In 1925 Macchi began to specialise in floatplane racers. With financial backing from Mussolini, the company created the M.39 which won the 1926 Schneider Trophy and led, via the M.52 and M.67, to the world record-breaking M.C.72.

Below: Featuring a two-step hull, the M.24 was built as a reconnaissance bomber. The later M.24bis, as seen here, was designed for the civilian market.

Above: Developed for submarine-borne duties, the M.53 could be dismantled for storage aboard a submarine.

M.33

Designed for the 1925 Schneider Trophy air race, this example is one of two built. It later went on to serve with the Italian high-speed flight training school.

Power was provided by a single V12 in-line piston engine built by Curtiss in the United States. This powerful 19.7-litre (5.2-gal.) unit used fuel at a high rate which restricted range. However, since the aircraft was designed solely as a racing machine, range was not important.

The M.33 was of the high-wing configuration that was necessary to provide sufficient clearance for the outrigger floats. The wing was built in three major sections, with the outer units capable of mild flexing. Identifying features of the aircraft were the very long ailerons.

At a glance, the engine mounts appeared to be rather flimsy. Macchi realised that this area had potential for structural weakness and paid considerable attention to making the struts as strong as possible.

A very streamlined fuselage was a characteristic of the M.33. Most of the hull, including the centre-section, was built entirely from metal. The two main sections were extremely robust in order to absorb the considerable forces exerted by air flow over the wing and engine supports.

ACTION DATA

MAXIMUM SPEED

The progression in flying-boat design is reflected in the relative speeds of these three aircraft. The M.3 of 1916 was a fast aircraft for its time, and the M.18, which appeared more than a decade later, was not significantly faster. The higher speed of the M.C.77 of the 1930s was a result of rapid increases in engine power.

M.3 145 km/h (90 m.p.h.)
M.C.77 279 km/h (173 m.p.h.)
M.18 187 km/h (116 m.p.h.)

RANGE

As a maritime reconnaissance flying-boat, the M.C.77 required long range, which was achieved by placing large fuel tanks in the fuselage and wing. The M.3 was designed as a fighter and its endurance of more than three hours was impressive for the period.

M.3 450 km (279 mi.)
M.18 1000 km (620 mi.)
M.C.77 3000 km (1,860 mi.)

TAKE-OFF WEIGHT

The M.3 could carry four bombs, which meant its take-off weight was higher than that of most of its contemporaries. The much larger M.18 could not carry significantly more because of a lack of power. The M.C.77, with significantly more power, could carry a much bigger load, but a large proportion of the weight was fuel.

M.3 1350 kg (2,970 lb.)
M.C.77 4835 kg (10,637 lb.)
M.18 1785 kg (3,927 lb.)

Land-based Macchis

 ■ **M.14:** In 1918 Macchi designed and built this single-seat scout. Only two were completed before development work was abandoned.

 ■ **M.16:** This ultra-light sport aircraft first flew in 1919. In 1920 the M.16 established a world altitude record for aircraft in its class.

 ■ **M.20:** Similar in appearance to the M.16, the M.20 could be used as a sport or training aircraft. It twice won the prestigious Coppa d'Italia.

 ■ **M.70:** First flying in 1929, the M.70 competed for Italian orders for a new training aircraft. It had a remarkable minimum speed of 55 km/h (34 m.p.h.).

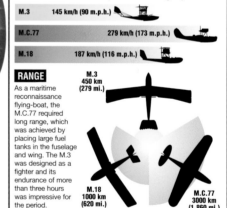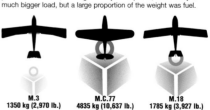

MARTIN
PBM MARINER

● Flying boat ● Amphibian ● Anti-submarine and SAR aircraft

One of the truly great flying boats of all time, the Martin PBM Mariner was produced in seaplane and amphibian versions. It was the most important naval aircraft in its class during World War II. Largely used as a replacement for the Consolidated PBY Catalina, which was perhaps the only better-known flying boat, the big, sturdy PBM Mariner served in every combat theatre. Many other countries used the Mariner well into the 1950s.

▲ *The amphibious capabilities of the later Mariner versions made them versatile aircraft. The high-mounted engines, search radar and gull wing were distinctive features.*

MARTIN PBM MARINER

▲ Search and rescue
Used in the search and rescue role after World War II, the Mariner served on into the 1950s with the U.S. Coast Guard and US Navy.

▼ Onto the ocean
Launched from a slipway at NAS Norfolk, Virginia, this Mariner is being prepared for a mission in late 1942. The aircraft is armed with eight machine guns.

▲ Rocket assistance
Rockets fixed to the fuselage sides helped heavily loaded aircraft get airborne. Drag from the water was a serious problem.

▼ Full power
The two huge Wright Cyclone engines haul the Mariner into the air on another long-range patrol mission.

Search radar ▶
Radar allowed the Mariner to hunt for submarines and ships. Later it was useful in the search and rescue role, operating far out to sea.

FACTS AND FIGURES

➤ The prototype for the Mariner series completed its maiden flight on 18 February 1939.

➤ British Mariners were returned to the US without seeing operational service.

➤ Seven PBMs sank the submarine U-615 near Aruba on 6 August 1943.

➤ The Navy first used RATO (rocket-assisted take-off) boosters to fly a stranded PBM off the Colorado river.

➤ A 3/8 scale model of the Mariner was flown before the prototype PBM flew.

➤ The Martin 162-A scale model was manned and had Chevrolet engines.

PROFILE

US Navy patrol flying boat

The Mariner was designed in 1937 when the US Navy wanted a new patrol flying boat. The big, gull-wing Mariner was sturdy and tough, and featured weapons bays in its engine nacelles.

The pilots and crew of the Mariner had tremendous confidence in a ship that had been optimized to give them the strongest chance of surviving combat and getting home safely. There were numerous combat actions in which the PBM Mariner excelled, beginning on

June 30, 1942, when a crew headed by Lieutenant Richard E. Schreder sank the German submarine U-158 near Bermuda. Exactly a dozen U-boats had been sent to the bottom of the sea by Mariners by the time the war ended. In the Pacific, Mariners fought just about everywhere, but were particularly active at Saipan and in the liberation of the Philippines. In the postwar era, Mariners took part in atomic weapons tests in the Pacific and fought in the 1950–53 Korean

War. Production of the Mariner ceased in 1949, but the aircraft remained a mainstay of the US Coast Guard for many years.

Below: The Royal Air Force received 27 Mariners. Fitted with British equipment, they were never used operationally and were returned to the United States.

Above: Although the Mariner could reach an altitude of 6095 m (20,000 ft.), patrols were normally flown at low level. Attacks on submarines were made at wave-top height using bombs and depth charges.

PBM-3D Mariner

Type: seven- or eight-seat patrol flying boat

Powerplant: two 1417 kW (1,900-hp.) Wright R-2600-22 Cyclone radial piston engines

Maximum speed: 338 km/h (210 m.p.h.) at 520 m (1,700 ft.)

Cruising speed: 303 km/h (188 m.p.h.) at 520 m (1,700 ft.)

Ceiling: 20,000 ft.

Combat radius: 722 mi.

Range: 2,235 mi.

Weights: Empty 33,106 lb.; max takeoff 57,878 lb.

Weapons: Eight .50 cal. (12.7-mm) machine guns in nose, dorsal turrets, waist and tail; plus up to 1,646 lb. of bombs, torpedoes or depth charges.

Dimensions:
span	35.97 m (118 ft.)
length	24.38 m (80 ft.)
height	8.23 m (27 ft.)
wing area	130.71 m² (1,407 sq. ft.)

PBM-5 Mariner

The PBM-5 variant was used postwar by the U.S. Navy and Coast Guard, mainly in the search and rescue role. This aircraft carries a Pacific theatre colour scheme.

The large search radar was enclosed by a streamlined fairing, mounted above and behind the cockpit.

The two Wright R-2600 engines were mounted high on the gull wings to keep the propellers clear of corrosive saltwater spray.

A fixed float under each wing kept the wingtips clear of the water and allowed a stable take-off and landing in rough seas.

The large engine nacelles were each able to carry up to 1,811 kg (3,993 lb.) of bombs, depth charges or air-dropped rescue equipment.

Nose, dorsal and tail turrets contained a total of six 12.7-mm (.50 cal.) machine guns. These were supplemented by two more guns in the waist positions.

The prototype mounted its twin fins and rudders on horizontal tailplanes. Those on production aircraft were angled upward, keeping them in line with the inboard section of the wings.

The boat-shaped underside was the key to easy operations from any large area of water. Early aircraft had retractable wing floats, while the PBM-5 was amphibious, with retractable wheeled landing gear.

ACTION DATA

WEAPONS

Carrying a heavier bomb load, the Mariner was designed to replace the smaller Catalina. Although it carried fewer bombs, the Sunderland had more defensive guns.

SUNDERLAND GR.Mk 5 463-kg (1,021-lb.) bomb load
10 x 7.62-mm (.30 cal.) machine guns

PBM-5A MARINER 1654-kg (3,646-lb.) bomb load
8 x 12.7-mm (.50 cal.) machine guns

PBY-5A CATALINA 374-kg (824-lb.) bomb load
1 x 12.7-mm (.50 cal.) machine gun
3 x 7.7-mm (.303 cal.) machine guns

RANGE

The Catalina was renowned for its excellent range. The Mariner comes a close second and both aircraft beat the Sunderland by almost 1000 km (620 mi.).

PBY-5A CATALINA 3774 km (2,345 mi.)

PBM-5A MARINER 3597 km (2,235 mi.)

SUNDERLAND GR.Mk 5 2842 km (1,766 mi.)

MAXIMUM TAKE-OFF WEIGHT

The Sunderland and Mariner are closely matched in weight. In the Mariner, however, far more of this weight consists of fuel and weapons. The lighter Catalina, although very successful, would have been more difficult to handle on open sea.

PBY-5A CATALINA 16,033 kg (35,347 lb.)

PBM-5A MARINER 26,218 kg (57,800 lb.)

SUNDERLAND GR.Mk 5 26,253 kg (57,878 lb.)

US Navy patrol aircraft

■ **LOCKHEED PV-2 HARPOON:** Developed from the Lodestar airliner, the PV-2 was a well-armed coastal patrol aircraft.

■ **CONSOLIDATED PBY CATALINA:** Hugely successful, the Catalina served throughout World War II in the long-range patrol mission.

■ **CONSOLIDATED PB4Y-2 PRIVATEER:** This was a long-range patrol version of the B-24 Liberator developed for the Navy.

■ **CONSOLIDATED PB2Y CORONADO:** Similar in size to the PBM, the PB2Y carried a heavier bomb load and had more power.

MARTIN

P5M MARLIN

● The last American flying-boat ● Anti-submarine/rescue

▲ *Military flying-boats are a rare breed today. The Martin Marlin was retired in 1966, after 14 years with the US Navy and Coast Guard. Of its contemporaries, only the Japanese ShinMaywa and the Russian Beriev Be-12 remain in service.*

T he USSR's 600-strong submarine force was considered a huge threat to the West in the 1950s. This estimate of Soviet undersea strength may have been a Cold War exaggeration, but it spurred the development of anti-submarine planes. The Martin P5M Marlin was the US Navy's last operational flying-boat, designed to stalk and kill submarines as they hid in the ocean's depths.

MARTIN P5M MARLIN

▼ **Sub-chaser**
The Marlin was designed to hunt enemy submarines, but could also be used to resupply friendly ones when needed.

◀ **Gull wing**
The gull-shaped profile of the Marlin's wing was retained from its predecessor, the Martin Mariner. It was designed to keep the propellers clear of the water's surface on landing.

Vietnam missions ▶
Designed for deep-water submarine hunting, the Marlin's only real combat use was in Vietnam. It monitored coastal shipping and performed search-and-rescue missions.

▼ **In the dock**
Amphibious dock landing ships were trialled with some success as Marlin bases. The US Navy tried to operate the seaplanes as strike aircraft, independent of land bases.

▲ **Stranded at sea**
Although Marlins usually operated from sheltered waters, sometimes they had to brave the open ocean. This one lost an engine, and had to taxi home to its base in Japan. The voyage took more than nine hours.

FACTS AND FIGURES

➤ The prototype Marlin flew on 30 May 1948. It entered service in April 1952.

➤ The only overseas operator of the Marlin was France, which acquired 10 P5M-2s under the Military Assistance Program.

➤ Although designed to carry two 20-mm cannon in the tail, most Marlins did not carry guns operationally.

➤ The P5M-2 (SP-5B) differed from the P5M-1 (P-5A) in having a T-shaped tail and more sophisticated equipment.

➤ One Marlin was evaluated with an auxiliary jet engine in its tail, as a possible retrofit to the entire fleet.

➤ US Coast Guard Marlins did not carry anti-submarine sensors or weapons.

PROFILE

Submarine hunter

The Glenn L. Martin Company was one of the great builders of flying-boats, those large aircraft with ship-like hulls which operate from water, free of dependency on fixed airfields. The P5M Marlin followed upon the great success of the company's PBM Mariner of World War II. The Marlin was a creature for the 1950s, intended to fly and fight on the world's great oceans. This aircraft was packed with detection gear to find submarines and with weapons to destroy them.

Marlins achieved a fine record with a dozen patrol squadrons while in service from 1952 to 1965. The familiar deep-blue paint on the Marlin became a combination of grey and white when the Navy shifted colours in 1955. In its final years (the P5M was re-named the P-5 in 1962) this reliable aircraft went to Vietnam, where it flew offshore patrols to choke off seaborne infiltration. In US

Coast Guard Service Marlins were used for rescuing downed pilots, using the aircraft's superb endurance to conduct long search missions, helping to save many lives. It was the US Navy's last operational flying-boat.

The original Marlin had a conventional tail. The P5M-2 of 1953 featured a T-tail and more powerful engines.

Marlins operated from a variety of land bases and ships. This P5M has run up onto an inflatable platform alongside the assault ship USS Ashland. This allowed the aircraft to be serviced without needing to be winched aboard.

P5M Marlin

Type: patrol flying-boat with 11-man crew

Powerplant: two 2573-kW (3,450-hp.) Wright R-3350-32WA Turbo-Compound radial engines

Maximum speed: 404 km/h (251 m.p.h.) at sea level

Combat radius: 3300 km (2,046 mi.)

Service ceiling: 7315 m (24,000 ft.)

Weights: empty 22,900 kg (50,380 lb.); loaded 38,555 kg (84,821 lb.)

Armament: four torpedoes, four 907-kg (2,000-lb.) bombs or mines, or smaller weapons up to 3629 kg (8,000 lb.) total carried internally, and up to eight 454-kg (1,000-lb.) bombs, mines or rocket projectiles carried externally

Dimensions:
span	36.02 m (118 ft. 2 in.)
length	30.66 m (100 ft. 7 in.)
height	9.97 m (32 ft. 8 in.)
wing area	130.66 m² (1,405 sq. ft.)

P5M-2 MARLIN

The French Aéronavale received 10 Marlin P5M-2s. Like many other nations, France replaced the seaplane with search-and-rescue helicopters and large land-based maritime patrol aircraft.

The cockpit of the Marlin housed the two pilots. The rest of the crew consisted of navigator, mission co-ordinator, electrician and six ASW specialists, who were housed in the capacious fuselage.

Weapons and sensors were carried in bays in the engine nacelles, and on eight underwing hardpoints. Weapon options included bombs, mines, depth charges or Mk 46 air-launched ASW torpedoes.

The tail 'stinger' housed a magnetic anomaly detecter (MAD). This tracked submarines by the distortions they caused in the Earth's magnetic field.

Early Marlins were armed with a pair of 20-mm cannon in the tail, but these were deleted in the improved P5M-2.

The APS-80 radar was the most powerful surface search unit of its day, capable of detecting a periscope at up to 90 km (56 mi.).

Power was provided by a pair of Wright R-3350 radial piston engines, each delivering 2573 kW (3,450 hp.).

Marlins carried both active and passive sonobuoys, deployed through hatches by the ASW technicians. Jezebel was a long-range low-frequency buoy which could detect a snorkelling diesel submarine at 150 km (93 mi.).

Taking off from water

The speed of flying-boats ploughing through the water is limited by water resistance. To take off they have to be skimming across the surface, which offers less resistance and allows much higher speeds to be attained. The hull is designed with a sharply-defined 'step'. At high enough speeds, the hull aquaplanes on the step and accelerates away to flying speed.

At rest, the Marlin floats low in the water.

Accelerating forward, hydrodynamic forces lift the hull higher, but speed is limited to about 65 km/h (40 knots).

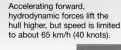

Once 'on the step' the Marlin hydroplanes across the surface of the water, and when flying speed is reached it takes off.

COMBAT DATA

MAXIMUM SPEED

The Marlin was designed before the advent of turboprops. The new engines were lighter and more powerful, which is reflected in the faster performance of the two more modern boats. The Beriev dates from the late 1950s and the ShinMaywa from the late 1960s and both will remain in service for many years to come.

P5M-2 MARLIN	404 km/h (251 m.p.h.)
Be-12 'MAIL'	600 km/h (372 m.p.h.)
PS-1	522 km/h (324 m.p.h.)

RANGE

Hunting submarines can be a time-consuming process. As a result, maritime patrol aircraft should have the ability to loiter economically on station for very long periods, which means they need equally long range enabling patrols to reach far out into the oceans.

Be-12 'MAIL' 7500 km (4,650 mi.)
P5M-2 MARLIN 3299 km (2,050 mi.)
PS-1 3800 km (2,356 mi.)

COMBAT LOAD

P5M-2 MARLIN 7250 kg (16,000 lb.)	Be-12 'MAIL' 5000 kg (11,000 lb.)	PS-1 600 kg (1,320 lb.) depth charges and four torpedoes

The size that enables maritime aircraft to carry large crews on long patrols means that the aircraft usually have the capacity to carry large amounts of anti-submarine weaponry. Both the Beriev and the Marlin could carry as much as contemporary bombers. The more modern Japanese boat had a much smaller warload.

MARTIN

PB2M MARS

● Maritime patrol ● Water-bomber ● Four-engine flying-boat

▲ Like so many large flying-boat projects in the late 1940s, the Mars was an excellent aircraft that became irrelevant when the war ended. The fact that two are still flying shows just how useful the Mars is.

F ew modern sights in aviation can equal that of a huge scarlet Martin Mars coming straight at you over a Canadian lake. These 50-year-old Navy veterans of World War II are among the biggest flying-boats ever built and hold the record as the largest aircraft used for fighting forest fires. Capable of dumping thousands of litres of water and foam to extinguish forest fires, the two remaining Mars 'boats' are survivors of six that were originally built.

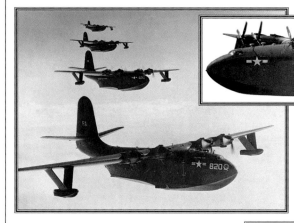

▲ **Mightier Mars**
The JRM-2 Mars, named 'Caroline Mars' by the Navy, was even heavier and more powerful than the first JRM-1s. It was fitted with Pratt & Whitney R-4360s, which were the most powerful engines in existence at the time.

▲ **Mars formation**
A rare sight even in the 1950s, this formation of four JRM-3s was headed by 'Philippine Mars' and 'Marianas Mars'. The JRM-1s were eventually upgraded to the same standard as the JRM-2, and were then known as JRM-3s.

▼ **'Hawaii Mars'**
Flying cargo between the mainland and Honolulu, the Mars could operate in worse conditions than land-based aircraft and carried its larger load more economically.

▲ **Pearl Harbor patrol**
The first Mars was berthed at the Naval Air Station at Alameda, California. It made the round trip to Pearl Harbor in Hawaii in just five days, including all servicing and cargo loading. The massive wing contained large fuel tanks.

FACTS AND FIGURES

➤ Designer Glenn Martin saw the Mars as a flying battleship, carrying enough bombs and troops to storm an enemy island.

➤ All six Mars flying-boats were named after islands, the first being 'Hawaii'.

➤ Until the B-36 bomber, the Mars was the largest aircraft used by the US military.

➤ The Mars might have had a future after World War II if airlines had not opted to use landplanes rather than flying-boats.

➤ The US Navy retired its last Mars in August 1956 despite its success.

➤ Mars flew three sorties a week between San Francisco and Honolulu.

PROFILE

Patrol aircraft turned water-bomber

Designed to meet a US Navy requirement for a patrol bomber, the Mars started life as the Martin Model 170 or XPB2M-1. The flying-boat was so large that inside it was fitted out like a ship with separate mess rooms for troops, officers' quarters, staterooms and berths.

Flying for the first time on 5 November 1941, the twin-tailed Mars prototype did not become the forerunner of a huge wartime fleet of combat aircraft as designer Glenn Martin had hoped. Instead, the Navy

asked for a transport and the XPB2M was stripped of its turrets and bombing equipment. In this role the Mars was impressive and the Navy began regular runs across the Pacific, packing thousands of kilograms of freight into the huge interior.

After the war the Navy ordered 20 examples of an XPB2M derivative designated JRM-1 and fitted with a single fin and rudder, but in the event only five were completed. The original 'Hawaii Mars' and 'Marshall Mars' were destroyed in crashes, and the other four,

joined by a single example of the heavier JRM-2, served until 1956.

When no post-war boom in civil flying-boat operations materialised, the five aircraft were sold to Forest Industries Flying Tankers of Canada for use as water-bombers.

Post-war flying-boats were killed off by the introduction of larger jet-powered and turboprop-powered landplanes. Those that survived, however, were found extremely useful for everything from rescue to fire bombing.

JRM-1 Mars

Type: long-range flying-boat

Powerplant: four 1715-kW (2,300-hp.) Wright Duplex Cyclone R-3350 radial piston engines

Maximum speed: 360 km/h (225 m.p.h.)

Range: 7039 km (4,360 mi.)

Service ceiling: 4450 m (14,600 ft.)

Weights: empty 34,279 kg (75,414 lb.); loaded 74,844 kg (164,657 lb.)

Dimensions:
span	60.96 m	(200 ft.)
length	35.76 m	(117 ft.)
height	11.73 m	(38 ft.)
wing area	342.15 m²	(3,681 sq. ft.)

The original twin-tail was replaced by a taller, single-fin unit with a large rudder. This was essential for good handling on the water in windy conditions.

Dihedral tailplanes help give the Mars stable and slow handling in pitch and roll. The rudder has a large trim tab to assist in control movement.

The Mars has a very spacious cockpit, entered via doors in the port and starboard side of the nose and stairs up to the flight deck.

JRM-1s were powered by Wright Cyclone engines, replaced by Pratt & Whitney R-4360s in JRM-2 'Caroline Mars'.

JRM-3 MARS

Still flying after more than 50 years of continuous operation, the last two Martin Mars flying-boats are 'Hawaii Mars' and 'Philippine Mars'.

High-wing designs were almost universal for flying-boats to ensure that the propellers and flying surfaces were as far above the water as possible. The long-span wing gives the Mars very long range.

A small access walkway was retained in the JRM-2 even though the rear fuselage had been extensively modified. Doorways to the rear fuselage are located ahead of the tailfin.

HAWII MARS

C-FLYL

The Mars' planing hull is an excellent design, giving the aircraft very good handling on the water and making take-off and landing surprisingly easy for such a massive aircraft.

For the water-bomber role, the Mars contains enormous water tanks fitted in the fuselage. These can be filled in as little as 15 seconds as the aircraft taxies across the surface of a lake.

The main cargo-bay door is located in the fuselage side. It was the size of this door rather than payload weight limitations that dictated what a Mars could carry.

The bulk of a flying-boat fuselage could accommodate very large loads. In 1949, 'Marshall Mars' carried no less than 315 passengers as well as its crew of seven.

ACTION DATA

MAXIMUM SPEED

Flying-boats require range, capacious fuselages and a boat hull, all factors which mitigate against a fast design. With streamlining and powerful engines, the flying-boats of the 1940s were reaching almost 400 km/h (250 m.p.h.), an impressive achievement.

JRM-1 MARS	**360 km/h (225 m.p.h.)**
SHETLAND	**424 km/h (263 m.p.h.)**
BV 222 VIKING	**382 km/h (237 m.p.h.)**

Flying firemen in North America

■ **GRUMMAN TURBO FIRECAT:** The Firecat is used extensively in North America as an effective fire-fighter even though it is a small land-based design. It has also been sold to France. The airframe is a turboprop variant of the naval S-2 Tracker anti-submarine warfare aircraft.

■ **DOUGLAS DC-6:** Fitted with a large canoe-shaped external fuel tank under the belly, this DC-6 named 'Spirit of '76' is another early post-war design which was pressed into service for fire bombing. Its tanks contain chemical fire-suppressant rather than water.

■ **CANADAIR CL-215:** Operated in Canada and across Europe, the CL-215 is one of the most common sights above a forest fire today. It was used by the French Sécurité Civile to fight the large fires near the Riviera region in 1985. It is also operated in Venezuela as a transport and in Thailand as a surveillance aircraft.

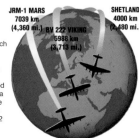

RANGE

American aircraft were often built with impressive range, which was essential as long trans-oceanic flights were needed to reach other countries. The Shetland was designed with British Empire sea routes in mind and the availability of frequent fuel stops. The BV 222 was almost as long-ranged as the Mars.

JRM-1 MARS 7039 km (4,360 mi.)

SHETLAND 4000 km (2,480 mi.)

BV 222 VIKING 5988 km (3,713 mi.)

MARTIN

P6M SeaMaster

● Jet maritime seaplane ● Martin's last warplane ● Minelayer

▲ The SeaMaster was an immensely strong aircraft designed to fly at high speed and low level to deliver its war load. It was to be Martin's last flying-boat. Only in Japan and Russia have military flying-boat designs been pursued since then.

Seaplane Striking Force was the name given to the US Navy's proposed units of minelaying maritime patrol aircraft equipped with the new generation of flying-boat, the Martin SeaMaster. However, the P6M was, in fact, a strategic, medium bomber. Inter-service rivalry had forced the Navy to disguise the real role of this seaplane from the Martin stable. Promising, but ultimately ill-conceived and accident-prone, the SeaMaster never entered squadron service.

MARTIN P6M SeaMaster

▲ Into the sunset
Pilots noted that the SeaMaster handled more like a fighter than a bomber, being very responsive and capable of supersonic speeds.

▲ Overtaken by events
The over-budget P6M ultimately fell victim to the funding requirements of nuclear submarines and their Polaris missiles. Its minelaying role was performed by other types.

▲ First prototype
Aircraft 138821 was the first P6M and was tragically lost with all crew on 7 December 1955.

◀ Seaplane bases
The US Navy began building a shore base and converting a seaplane tender for production P6Ms.

Strongly constructed ▶
To provide the strength required for high-speed flight at low level a thick aluminium wing skin was used. The skin at the root of the upper wing surface was up to 25-mm (1-in.) thick.

FACTS AND FIGURES

➤ The ejection of four crew from the second XP6M-1 was the first American multiple ejection.

➤ The P6M broke world altitude and speed records in its category on early flights.

➤ The P6M's hull design was tested on a modified XP5M Marlin prototype.

➤ The SeaMaster was more than 25 tons heavier than the giant wartime Martin PB2M Mars flying-boat.

➤ The SeaMaster was designed to operate in 1.8- to 2.75-metre (6 to 9-ft.) seas.

➤ World War II seaplane tender USS Albemarle was modified for use by P6Ms.

PROFILE

Last of the Martin seaplanes

Although deprived of the supercarrier *United States* by a Congress keen to cut peacetime defence budgets after 1945, the US Navy was eager to gain a nuclear capability to match that of the USAF. Martin was contracted to develop its new flying-boat, the P6M SeaMaster.

However, inter-service rivalry (the newly independent USAF tried to eliminate fixed-wing aircraft from the Army and Navy) was such that the nuclear role was played down. The Seaplane Strike Force (SSF) was thus devised to disguise the strategic bombing capability. SSF P6Ms would be deployed to lay mines

in the sea lanes around Soviet naval bases.

Refuelling en route if necessary, these graceful craft were required to carry a 14-ton payload over 2400 km (1,490 mi.) with a dash speed of 1100 km/h (683 m.p.h.) over a 185-km (115 mi.) leg running-in to the target.

Two prototypes were built, but after encouraging initial flights both were lost in accidents, knocking confidence and increasing costs. Further funding pressures meant that orders for this highly specialised machine were cancelled after just three P6M-2s had been delivered.

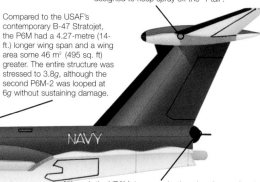

Below: On the hull below the 'Navy' legend is the starboard hydroflap, which was used as a rudder (one deployed) or brake (two deployed) on the water, or as a divebrake in the air.

Above: An important part of the SeaMaster system was its automatic beaching gear. The P6M simply taxied into the unit, electrical and hydraulic connections were made (for brakes and steering) and the aircraft went ashore.

P6M-2 SeaMaster

Initially 30 P6M-2s were ordered, but this figure was progressively cut back until only three were delivered to the Navy. The programme was cancelled in August 1959.

YP6M-1 SeaMaster

Type: mine-laying and maritime reconnaissance aircraft

Powerplant: four 57.8-kN (13,005-lb. thrust) Allison J71-A-6 afterburning turbojets

Maximum speed: 1107 km/h (687 m.p.h.) at 6706 m (22,000 ft.)

Combat radius: 2270 km (1409 mi.)

Service ceiling: 10668 m (35,000 ft.)

Weights: empty 38412 kg (84,700 lb.); maximum take-off in rough waters 72574 kg (160,025 lb.)

Armament: two 20-mm (0.79-in.) cannon in tail turret and up to 13607 kg (30,000 lb.) of mines and/or bombs

Dimensions:
span	31.30 m (102 ft. 6 in.)
length	40.93 m (134 ft. 4 in.)
height	10.33 m (33 ft. 10 in.)
wing area	176.51 m² (1900 sq. ft.)

The four crew (pilot, co-pilot, navigator/mine-layer and radio/armament defence operator) were seated in ejection seats, although these were not fitted to the first XP6M-1. Ahead of the cockpit was a nose radome for the main radar scanner.

The door of the watertight mine bay behind the cockpit rotated to open. The stores were attached to the inside of the door and were dropped when the door had rotated 180°. The SeaMaster sat low in the water – its wing floats were attached to the wingtips.

The SeaMaster did not perform to specification until the P6M-2 was fitted with 70.3-kN (15,817-lb. thrust) J75 engines. Two prototypes and four pre-production P6Ms used afterburning Allison J71s, mounted parallel to the fuselage on the first two aircraft. After the afterburners caused damage to the fuselage skin, the engines were canted 5° outwards.

Compared to the USAF's contemporary B-47 Stratojet, the P6M had a 4.27-metre (14-ft.) longer wing span and a wing area some 46 m² (495 sq. ft) greater. The entire structure was stressed to 3.8g, although the second P6M-2 was looped at 6g without sustaining damage.

After two accidents involving the prototypes (the first of which was fatal), the tailplane and its control surfaces were redesigned. The hull of the aircraft was designed to keep spray off the 'T-tail'.

Although the YP6M-1 pre-production aircraft were fitted with two 20-mm (0.78-in.) cannon in the tail turret (the fashion for bombers at the time) these were deleted on the P6M-2 production aircraft, leaving room for electronic countermeasures (ECM) equipment.

ACTION DATA

MAXIMUM LOW-LEVEL SPEED

The P6M was designed as a high-speed, low-level attack aircraft and thus possessed a good top speed. Search-and-rescue machines tend to patrol at more modest speeds.

XP6M-1 SEAMASTER	960 km/h (596 m.p.h.)
Be-10 'MALLOW'	912 km/h (566 m.p.h.)
Be-42	760 km/h (471 m.p.h.)

MAXIMUM THRUST

Even with afterburning turbojets the SeaMaster was underpowered. It was not until the production standard P6M-2 was available that the required performance was possible.

XP6M-1 SEAMASTER	231.2 kN (52,020 lb.)
Be-10 'MALLOW'	127.5 kN (28,6887 lb.)
Be-42 ALBATROS	284.4 kN (63,990 lb.)

RANGE

The Be-10 was an advanced aircraft in its day and set speed, distance and altitude records. However, its limited operational usefulness led to its early retirement. For its intended role the SeaMaster needed good range. The Albatros also has good range, which is essential for maritime patrol and search-and-rescue roles.

XP6M-1 SEAMASTER 4420 km (2,745 mi.)

Be-10 'MALLOW' 4800 km (2,980 mi.)

Be-42 ALBATROS 4100 km (2,546 mi.)

Jet-powered military flying-boats

■ **BERIEV Be-10 'MALLOW':** Little known in the West and the only aircraft of its class ever to go into operational service, the Be-10 was used in the Black Sea area from the early-1960s.

■ **BERIEV Be-42 ALBATROS:** Intended to replace the Be-12 turboprop in military maritime roles, the Be-42 flew in 1986. The status of Russian orders remains uncertain.

■ **CONVAIR XF2Y SEA DART:** The product of advanced research, the first of four Sea Dart jet seaplane fighter prototypes flew in 1953. Poor performance saw its cancellation in 1956.

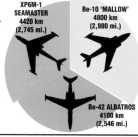

■ **SARO SR.A/1:** Despite an 824-km/h (512 m.p.h.) top speed, this twin-engined, pressurised fighter foundered for lack of official support. The first of three flew in 1947.

MITSUBISHI

F1M 'PETE'

● Observation ● Advanced trainer ● Floatplane

Designed to meet a 1934 Japanese naval requirement, Mitsubishi's F1M was to be the only observation seaplane in its class built in quantity for the navy. Highly manoeuvrable, the F1M2 production variant was used as an interceptor, dive-bomber, convoy escort and coastal patrol aircraft during World War II, such was its versatility. It was to earn a commendable reputation. The F1M2 was known as 'Pete' to the Allies.

▲ Production
of the F1M2 was initially undertaken by Mitsubishi Jukogyo K.K. Later on production was switched to the Dai-Nijuichi K.K. (21st Naval Air Arsenal) at Sasebo.

PHOTO FILE

MITSUBISHI **F1M 'PETE'**

◄ Ground-attack duties
Although mainly employed for coastal patrol and reconnaissance, the F1M2's three machine-guns and 120-kg (264-lb.) bomb load were also used for ground attack.

▼ Major production
The F1M2 was undoubtedly the most important Japanese observation floatplane of the war, with more than 1000 built.

▲ South Seas base
Two F1M2s are moored at an island base in the South Pacific ready for another sortie.

▼ On dry land
For servicing the 'Pete' was ferried from the water using a three-wheeled trolley.

◄ Singapore scrapyard
Like many Japanese aircraft, this F1M2 ended its days on the scrapheap at RAF Seletar.

FACTS AND FIGURES

➤ The F1M2 was officially known to the Japanese navy as the Navy Type 0 Observation Seaplane Model 11.

➤ A small number of F1M2s were delivered to Thailand for coastal patrol duties.

➤ A total of 1118 F1Ms were built, including the four F1M1 prototypes.

➤ Apart from Mitsubishi and Aichi, Kawanishi was also asked to build a seaplane prototype, but declined.

➤ The F1M was of all-metal construction with fabric-covered control surfaces.

➤ Experiments were carried out in which an F1M2 carried a 250-kg (550-lb.) bomb.

PROFILE

Imperial navy spotter

Mid-1936 saw the first flight of the F1M prototype, the first of four F1M1s. This flew alongside an Aichi design built to the same specification; both aircraft were powered by a Nakajima Hikari 1 nine-cylinder radial rated at 611 kW for take-off.

A remarkably 'clean' design, the F1M was a two-seat, single-bay biplane with a central float and stabilising floats beneath its wings. These features gave the aircraft excellent performance, but the F1M was far from perfect. Its biggest problems were a tendency to 'porpoise' on the water and a lack of directional stability in flight. Mitsubishi then set about redesigning the aircraft to cure these problems and re-powered the F1M with a 652-kW (875-hp.) Mitsubishi Zuisei 13, 14-cylinder radial in a longer cowling. The tail fin, rudder and wings were also altered.

This variant was ordered into production as the F1M2. Mitsubishi built 524 examples then Dai-Nijuichi Kaigun KoKusho (21st Naval Air Arsenal) added another 590.

Serving aboard seaplane tenders, cruisers and from shore bases, F1M2s were primarily reconnaissance, coastal patrol and convoy escort aircraft but performed various other combat and support roles, including training as the F1M2-K.

Above: Although it was a pre-war biplane design, the F1M2 served the Japanese throughout World War II.

Below: Seen after the war at RAF Seletar in Singapore, this F1M2 'Pete' (background) was captured in airworthy condition. It was, however, never flown again and was later scrapped.

A 652-kW (875-hp.) Mitsubishi Zuisei 13 engine drove the three-bladed propeller of the F1M2. Earlier F1M1 versions featured a two-bladed propeller and a 611-kW (820-hp.) Nakajima Hikari 1 nine-cylinder radial piston engine.

Two forward-firing 7.7-mm (.303 cal.) Type 97 machine-guns were sufficient for the observation role, but left the F1M under-armed when it was used as a fighter.

Little protection was afforded the pilot, who was sheltered only by a windscreen. A large cut-out in the upper wing centre section gave the pilot an acceptable view upwards, however.

A single 7.7-mm (.303 cal.) Type 92 machine-gun was provided for the observer. Flexibly mounted, the weapon allowed the rear crew member to protect the aircraft's rear hemisphere from attack.

In a style typical of Japanese floatplanes, the F1M featured a large central float, with a smaller float beneath each wing providing stability on the water.

F1M2 'PETE'

This F1M2 carries a typical Imperial Japanese Navy colour scheme of green over light grey. Japanese aircraft often carried a minimum of markings.

A rudder fitted at the extreme trailing edge of the central float allowed the pilot to steer the aircraft on water. Early F1M1 aircraft had shown a tendency to porpoise on the surface.

F1M2 'Pete'

Type: single-engined observation or training floatplane

Powerplant: one 652-kW (875-hp.) Mitsubishi Zuisei 13 14-cylinder radial engine

Maximum speed: 370 km/h (229 m.p.h.)

Range: 740 km (460 mi.)

Service ceiling: 9440 m (31,000 ft.)

Weights: empty 1928 kg (4,242 lb.); loaded 2550 kg (5,610 lb.)

Armament: two fixed forward-firing 7.7-mm (.303 cal.) Type 97 machine-guns and one flexible rear-firing 7.7-mm Type 92 machine-gun plus a normal bombload of two 60-kg (1320lb.) bombs

Dimensions:
span	11.00 m	(36 ft. 1 in.)
length	9.50 m	(31 ft. 2 in.)
height	4.00 m	(13 ft. 2 in.)
wing area	29.54 m²	(316 sq. ft.)

COMBAT DATA

SERVICE CEILING

The two Japanese floatplanes had a big advantage over their American counterpart as far as ceiling was concerned. High altitude flight allowed a larger field of view but also made the aircraft vulnerable to fighters.

F1M2 'PETE' 9440 m (31,000 ft.)
OS2U-3 KINGFISHER 3960 m (13,000 ft.)
N1K 'REX' 10,560 m (34,600 ft.)

MAXIMUM SPEED

A later and more powerful design, the Kawanishi N1K vastly out-performed the two older aircraft. Despite being of biplane design, the F1M2 had good performance for an aircraft in its class. The slow speed of the OS2U-3 left it at the mercy of enemy fighters.

F1M2 'PETE' 370 km/h (229 m.p.h.)
OS2U-3 KINGFISHER 264 km/h (164 m.p.h.)
N1K 'REX' 490 km/h (304 m.p.h.)

RANGE

For operations over the vastness of the Pacific Ocean range was the most important consideration. The 'Pete' with its less impressive range was mainly confined to patrolling coastal waters. The longer-ranged N1K was more versatile.

F1M2 'PETE' 740 km (460 mi.)
OS2U-3 KINGFISHER 1296 km (804 mi.)
N1K 'REX' 1665 km (1,032 mi.)

World War II Japanese floatplanes

■ **AICHI E16A ZUIUN 'PAUL':** This twin-float reconnaissance aircraft entered service in 1944 and suffered heavy losses to Allied fighters.

■ **AICHI E13A 'JAKE':** This all-metal reconnaissance floatplane was built in large numbers and had an impressive endurance.

■ **NAKAJIMA E8N 'DAVE':** Operating as a catapult-launched reconnaissance aircraft the E8N saw service from battleships and cruisers.

■ **MITSUBISHI A6M2-N:** A floatplane version of the famous 'Zero' fighter was developed although the float markedly reduced performance.

NIEUPORT

TYPE 17

- ● Scout fighter ● Favourite of aces ● Highly manoeuvrable

The Nieuport Type 17 was the first of the truly great fighters to carry its famous name into the skies of World War I. Derived from a series of light fighter scouts, the Nieuport was so successful that it was supplied to most of the Allied powers, including Russia and America. Many of the great aces of the war flew the type, which had particularly fine manoeuvrability and rate of climb. Nieuports were still flown after the war.

▲ *France produced some of the finest fighters of World War I. The experience gained in producing pre-war aircraft was reflected in the success of Nieuports, which were loved by pilots.*

NIEUPORT TYPE 17

▲ Swing start
The Le Rhône rotary could be hand-swung into action, with care and by a strong pilot.

▲ America's fighter
A lack of indigenous designs meant that the American forces purchased many French planes, including 298 Nieuport 28s. This model was flown by Eddie Rickenbacker, the top-scoring American ace.

◀ Lewis gun
Many Nieuports had a Lewis gun on top of the wing, fitted with the distinct flat magazine. This was reloaded by swinging the gun down on a rack, which was an awkward feature of the design.

▼ Large numbers
The demand for Nieuports was great, and huge numbers were produced. At many Allied air bases the Nieuports were the most numerous aircraft.

▲ Trusty design
Based on the proven Nieuport 11, the 17 had a more powerful Le Rhône or Clerget rotary and synchronised Vickers gun.

FACTS AND FIGURES

- ➤ At first the Type 17's gun fired above its propeller; a synchroniser enabled the gun to fire through the propeller.

- ➤ In 1910 Edouard de Nieuport began the company that made these fine planes.

- ➤ Canadian Major 'Billy' Bishop claimed many of his 72 kills in a Nieuport 17.

- ➤ The success of the Type 17 led to more Nieuport aircraft, including the famous Type 28 supplied to America in 1918.

- ➤ Earlier Nieuports included monoplanes, which could even perform loops.

- ➤ Nieuport 11s were built under licence in Italy and flown by 12 squadrons in 1917.

PROFILE

Nieuport's great fighter scouts

By the time war clouds loomed over Europe in 1914, Nieuport had been making innovative aircraft for half a decade. The first fighters were the Nieuport 11s, which gave the Allies a brief return to air superiority in 1915, as a result of their excellent manoeuvrability and climb rate. The Nieuport 17 was the next single-seater. It was stronger than the previous Model 11

and had more powerful Clerget or Le Rhône engines. The success of the type attracted much attention from abroad and the type was ordered by Belgium, Britain, Italy, Russia and the United States. With larger ailerons and a 60-kW (110-hp.) Le Rhône engine, the Type 21 was introduced in late 1917, and the Type 28 appeared in 1918.

Some of the famous aces of the war, among them

Nungesser, Ball and Bishop, flew the Nieuport Type 17. Like any aircraft made of wood and fabric, the plane could become a death trap if things went wrong. But in the right hands this aircraft was a real winner, as evidenced by its long list of successful aerial victories.

Left: The long slats on the struts of this Nieuport are the Le Prieur rocket rails used against airships. Eight of these weapons were carried, inclined to fire upwards, and were electrically triggered.

Right: American pilots liked the Nieuport 17, often decorating their aircraft with colourful artwork, like this Indian's head. The US pilots also flew other French fighters such as the SPAD.

Type 17

Type: single-seat fighter

Powerplant: one 89-kW (110-hp.) Le Rhône (Type 17) or one 97-kW (120-hp.) Clerget rotary piston engine (Type 17bis)

Maximum speed: 170 km/h (105 m.p.h.) at 1980 m (6,500 ft.)

Range: 250 km (155 mi.)

Service ceiling: 5350 m (17,550 ft.)

Weights: empty 374 kg (822 lb.); maximum take-off 560 kg (1,232 lb.)

Armament: one fixed forward-firing 7.7-mm (.303 cal.) Vickers or Lewis machine-gun

Dimensions:
span	8.20 m	(27 ft.)
length	5.96 m	(20 ft.)
height	2.44 m	(8 ft.)
wing area	14.75 m²	(159 sq. ft.)

TYPE 17C

The Imperial Russian Flying Corps used large numbers of Nieuport fighters. This Nieuport 17C was flown by No. XIX Gruppe, No. 1 Ostryad, and was subsequently captured by the Austrians.

Like all World War I fighters the Nieuport 17 had an open cockpit, which made flying at high altitude very uncomfortable.

The tails of the Nieuport 11, 17, 21 and 23 had a similar, distinct shape; the tail profile was more rounded in the Nieuport 24. The tail structure was wood, with fabric covering, and wire bracing helped to strengthen it. The large elevators and rudder helped give the Nieuport its legendary agility.

Distinct V-shaped struts were a recognition feature of the Nieuport 17. In the Nieuport 28, parallel struts were used. The 28 was not as popular as the 17 as it tended to shed its upper wing fabric in long dives and had engine problems.

One unusual feature of the Nieuport was the small width of its lower wing, only half as wide as the upper. The Nieuport 11 was even fitted with Le Prieur rockets to the wing struts, which were used for attacking balloons and airships.

Like their successors in World War II, Russian pilots in 1917 were fond of decorating their machines, and were glad to show their opponents who they were taking on.

Nieuport fighter scouts

■ NIEUPORT 27: Derived from the Type 17bis, the Nieuport 27 had a more powerful (89-kW (120-hp.)) Le Rhône engine and a circular-section fuselage. It was also purchased by Sweden.

■ NIEUPORT 28: The Type 28 had new wings, which were of almost equal size compared to the Type 17's unequal wings. The US Navy launched Type 28s from battleship gun turrets.

■ NIEUPORT-DELAGE Ni-D 29: This single-seat fighter made its first flight in 1918, and served with French forces throughout the 1920s. It was also built by SABCA of Belgium.

■ NIEUPORT-DELAGE Ni-D 52: Constructed largely of metal, the Ni-D 52 first appeared in 1927 and was used by Spain in the Civil War. The aircraft was developed into the Ni-D 62.

COMBAT DATA

MAXIMUM SPEED

Both the Nieuport and Sopwith Pup were powered by Le Rhône engines, giving them a good turn of speed. The later Albatros D.V had even greater speed.

NIEUPORT 17	170 km/h (105 m.p.h.)
SOPWITH PUP	180 km/h (112 m.p.h.)
ALBATROS D.III	165 km/h (102 m.p.h.)

ARMAMENT

Most German fighters had two machine-guns by 1916, giving them a decisive advantage in firepower. Pilots often chose the mix of ammunition that was used in their guns in World War I.

NIEUPORT 17
1 x 7.7-mm (.303 cal.) machine-gun

SOPWITH PUP
1 x 7.7-mm (.303 cal.) machine-gun

ALBATROS D.III
2 x 7.92-mm machine-guns

SERVICE CEILING

Pilots often mounted their offensive patrols at around 5000 m (16,500 ft.), despite the lack of heating or oxygen in their aircraft, which made flying in these open-cockpit fighters very uncomfortable. The Nieuport was particularly fast-climbing, which allowed it to gain a height advantage over its opponents.

NIEUPORT 17	ALBATROS D.III	SOPWITH PUP
5350 m (17,500 ft.)	5500 m (18,000 ft.)	5335 m (17,000 ft.)

NIEUPORT-DELAGE

NI-D 29

● Inter-war biplane fighter ● World speed record holder ● Air racer

▲ *In spite of a tendency to spin out of control the Ni-D 29 was regarded as an excellent fighter. The Nieuport-Delage aircraft served faithfully with the French Aviation Militaire and after a single example was sent to Japan as a pattern aircraft, Nakajima built 608 for the Imperial Japanese Army.*

After producing a series of outstanding fighters during World War I, the Nieuport company added the name of chief designer Gustave Delage to its model designations. The Ni-D 29, the first aircraft to carry the new designation, was too late to see combat during the war. In the years immediately after the war, however, racing versions set new world records for speed and altitude as well as winning several of the main air races.

NIEUPORT-DELAGE NI-D 29

▲ **Wartime ancestry**
Nieuport built a range of superb fighters during World War I. The Ni-D 29 clearly owed much to these earlier designs, but the adoption of an in-line engine considerably altered the contours of the forward fuselage.

▲ **Clean racing machine**
Several racing Ni-D 29s were cleaned up aerodynamically and flown without weapons. In addition, a few had shorter span wings, with only one set of interplane struts on each side.

▲ **Ungainly fighter**
With full military equipment and protruding exhausts, the Ni-D 29 was not a graceful aircraft.

▲ **Pilot protection**
A pronounced headrest protected the pilot in the event of the aircraft overturning on the ground.

Slim waist ▶
The fuselage tapered towards the rear, giving the aircraft a streamlined appearance.

FACTS AND FIGURES

➤ The first Ni-D 29s were delivered to French Aviation Militaire squadrons serving in Germany.

➤ Although the Ni-D 29 was popular with pilots, it did have a tendency to flat-spin.

➤ Nakajima Ko-4s flew during the Japanese occupation of Manchuria.

➤ Spain flew 30 Ni-D 29s, Belgium 108, Italy 181, Japan 609 and Sweden nine; Argentina also operated a few.

➤ French aircraft fought Rif insurgents in Morocco, alongside Spanish Ni-D 29s.

➤ An Ni-D 29G floatplane took part in the 1920 Monaco seaplane meeting.

Classic French fighter

With its in-line, rather than rotary, engine, the Ni-D 29 differed from the earlier Nieuports. Its achievements in 1920, when it pushed the world speed record beyond 300 km/h (185 m.p.h.), plus its high rate of climb and good handling won Nieuport-Delage an order to supply the French air force with the new fighter. Two-thirds of the 30

French fighter squadrons were equipped with the Ni-D 29C1 by 1923, and another five were using it by 1925. The type remained in service until 1928.

Nieuport's test pilot Sadi Lecointe, flying in the 1925 Moroccan campaign, formed an experimental flight of three machines which were modified with bomb racks for use as ground attack aircraft. In

November and December these aircraft dropped 5600 kg (12,320 lb.) of light bombs during 70 sorties.

The Ni-D 29 was also widely built under licence, especially in Japan, where Nakajima built the aircraft as the Ko-4.

Left: One of the more highly modified racing variants was the Ni-D 29V, which won the 1919 Coupe Deutsche and 1920 Gordon Bennet Trophy races. The aircraft had a span of only 6 m (20 ft.) and a boosted engine of 239 kW (320 hp.).

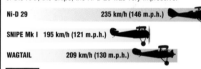

Above: This standard fighter variant shows the two-bay wings and extensive cable bracing. The two machine-guns were covered by streamlined fairings.

Ni-D 29

Type: biplane fighter

Powerplant: one 224-kW (300-hp.) Hispano-Suiza 8Fb liquid-cooled V-8 piston engine

Maximum speed: 235 km/h (146 m.p.h.)

Climb rate: 4000 m (13,120 ft.) in 9 min 44 sec

Range: 580 km (360 mi.)

Service ceiling: 8500 m (27,900 ft.)

Weights: empty equipped 760 kg (1,672 lb.); maximum take-off 1150 kg (2,530 lb.)

Armament: two fixed forward-firing 7.7-mm (.303 cal.) machine-guns

Dimensions: span   9.70 m (31 ft. 10 in.)
length   6.49 m (21 ft. 3 in.)
height   2.56 m (8 ft. 5 in.)
wing area 26.70 m² (287 sq. ft.)

Twin, fixed 7.7-mm (.303 cal.) machine-guns were mounted on the upper forward fuselage and fired through the propeller. This aircraft carries a tubular gunsight.

When first flown on 21 August 1921, the Ni-D 29 met all performance requirements except that of ceiling. In order to increase operational altitude, slightly longer wings were introduced.

Apart from his headrest, the only protection for the pilot came from a small windscreen and glazed side panels.

Wartime Nieuport designs used rotary engines, whereas the Ni-D 29 was powered by a V-8 in-line engine. This allowed a slimmer forward fuselage to be used.

To provide maximum agility, the prototype had ailerons fitted to the upper and lower wings. On production aircraft the upper set was eliminated and the lower set enlarged.

During World War I US volunteers formed the 'La Fayette' squadron as part of the French air force. The Sioux Indian's head badge has been used by the squadron ever since, most recently on the Mirage 2000N.

France's national colours were usually carried on the rudder of its air force fighters. Data, including the aircraft designation and weight details, were applied over these colours.

Ni-D 29

Eight companies, including Nieuport-Delage, delivered a total of 250 Ni-D 29s to the French air force. This aircraft served with 'La Fayette' squadron during the 1920s.

COMBAT DATA

MAXIMUM SPEED

Nieuport-Delage produced a fighter which was much faster than most of its rivals and which had sufficient performance to keep it in service into the late-1920s. Compared to the principal fighter of the RAF, the Snipe, the Ni-D 29 was very impressive.

Ni-D 29	235 km/h (146 m.p.h.)
SNIPE Mk I	195 km/h (121 m.p.h.)
WAGTAIL	209 km/h (130 m.p.h.)

POWER

With its powerful Hispano-Suiza engine, the Ni-D 29 was able to offer greater performance than contemporary fighters. As one of the most developed late-World War I fighters, the aircraft became one of the most important 1920s fighters.

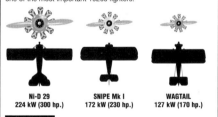

Ni-D 29	SNIPE Mk I	WAGTAIL
224 kW (300 hp.)	172 kW (230 hp.)	127 kW (170 hp.)

ARMAMENT

Fighter armament remained at a standard requirement of two fixed, forward-firing machine-guns for several years after World War I. The Snipe was a more versatile aircraft, being able to carry light bombs in the close support role.

Ni-D 29   2 x 7.7-mm (.303 cal.) machine-guns

SNIPE Mk I   2 x 7.7-mm (.303 cal.) machine-guns
2 x 11.3-kg (25-lb.) bombs

WAGTAIL   2 x 7.7-mm (.303 cal.) machine-guns

Nieuport-Delage designs

■ **Ni-D 52:** This fighter development of the Ni-D 42 appeared in 1927 in response to a Spanish requirement. In addition to the 34 aircraft that were bought, 92 were built under licence.

■ **Ni-D 62:** Representing a refined Ni-D 42, the 62 represented the most important French fighter in the 1930s. In May 1940, 143 of the outdated fighters were still on strength.

■ **Ni-D 82:** Revising the upper-wing planform of the Ni-D 42, Nieuport-Delage produced the single Ni-D 82. It was later modified, as seen here, to the parasol monoplane form.

■ **Ni-D 122:** First flown in the early 1930s, the Ni-D 122 fighter featured a graceful, elliptical wing and streamlined wheel spats. The aircraft was lost during a demonstration flight in 1933.

PFALZ

D.III – D.XII

● Biplane fighter family ● Western Front service ● Diverse designs

▲ Among a variety of biplane designs from Pfalz Flugzeug-Werke which did not enter service was the the D.VI. Those designs that did reach the squadrons were highly successful.

Starting out by building the French Morane L and H monoplanes under licence, Pfalz moved on to production of the D.I and D.II biplanes, which were licence-built versions of Roland designs. Their first original biplane design was the D.III of 1917. Within a year, however, Pfalz had progressed to the D.XII, a fighter built only in limited numbers, but one which was able to hold its own against the British Camel and SE5a.

PFALZ D.III – D.XII

▲ **Successful D.XII**
Pfalz entered the D.XII in fighter trials in June 1918. The aircraft equipped 10 units on the Western Front.

▲ **Improvements to the D.III**
The D.IIIa of 1918 differed from the D.III in having an increased tailplane area and a more efficient lower wing with rounded tips.

▲ **Captured D.III**
Seen in winter snow 'somewhere in France', this 1917-built D.III has fallen into Allied hands.

▲ **D.VIII with rotary engine**
The D.VIII fighter was built only in small numbers; a few had reached the Front for evaluation by August 1918.

Not for service ▶
With either a Oberursel U.III or Siemens-Halske Sh III of 119 kW, the D.VII suffered from a poor rate of climb, as did the smaller single-seat D.VI which preceded it.

FACTS AND FIGURES

➤ Some 600 D.III and D.IIIa fighters were delivered; by August 1918, 350 were in front-line service.

➤ Allied evaluation of a D.III noted that it handled better than the Albatros D.V.

➤ German aces Ernst Udet and Hans Weiss are thought to have favoured the D.XII.

➤ Such was the reputation of the Fokker D.VII, that the Pfalz D.XII was not welcomed by pilots.

➤ Pfalz biplane fighters were armed with twin Spandau forward-firing guns.

➤ The robust D.XII was unpopular with ground crews as it had complex rigging.

Unsung Western Front fighters

Less manoeuvrable than the Albatros and Fokker fighters of 1917, the Pfalz D.III was still a useful combat aircraft and around 600 were produced in the original and improved D.IIIa variants. It proved particularly suitable for diving attacks on Allied balloons and airships.

From a series of nearly a dozen subsequent designs, four prototypes were tested in the first round of fighter trials early in 1918. One of them, the rotary-engined D.VIII, was built in small

numbers, but Pfalz was already working on the D.XII.

In May and June, five versions of the D.XII were evaluated in a second series of trials. The BMW.IIIa-engined version had the best rate of climb, but this powerplant was reserved for the Fokker D.VII, so the version ordered used Mercedes engines.

The D.XII entered service alongside the Fokker D.VII, an aircraft with which it was always compared. The Pfalz proved

faster in a dive, although it was slower in a turn, and prone to stalling without warning. Nevertheless, it was an important aircraft which operated at a crucial stage of the war.

Above: The D.XII was a very different aircraft from the D.III, showing many design influences from the Fokker D.VII.

Left: Powered by a de Havilland Gipsy Major engine, this Pfalz D.III was one of two replicas built in the 1960s for the film Blue Max.

The well-respected and widely used Mercedes D.111 six-cylinder, water-cooled, in-line engine powered the Pfalz D.III, rated at 119 kW (160 hp.), and driving a two-bladed propeller. The later D.IIIa used a more powerful 134-kW (180-hp.) Mercedes D.IIIa engine.

D.III

Flown by Vizefeldwebel Barth of Jasta 10, this D.III was based at Heule in the summer of 1917. Jasta 10's staffel marking was a yellow nose.

Apart from metal panelling around the engine, the remainder of the fuselage was a wooden semi-monocoque structure. The framework was of spruce and plywood with a plywood skin. The latter was then fabric-covered and doped.

The tailplane structure was wooden with a fabric covering. It employed an inverted aerofoil section to aid dive recovery. The rudder was of welded steel tube.

Most D.IIIs were finished in *Silbergrau* aluminium dope. Each Jasta applied its own colourful staffel markings. Vizefeldwebel Barth added a personal dumb-bell marking to his aircraft.

A conventional vee-type undercarriage was fitted, the axle and spreaders between the wheels being encased in a streamlined fairing. The tailskid was sprung with elastic cord.

D.IIIa

Type: single-seat fighter

Powerplant: one 134-kW (180-hp.) Mercedes D.IIIa six-cylinder inline water-cooled engine

Maximum speed: 165 km/h (102 m.p.h.) at 3050 m (10,000 ft.)

Endurance: about 2 hours 30 min

Initial climb rate: 3.8 min to 915 m (3,000 ft.)

Service ceiling: 5180 m (17,000 ft.)

Weights: empty 695 kg (1,530 lb.); maximum take-off 935 kg (2,060 lb.)

Armament: two 7.92-mm LMG machine-guns

Dimensions: span 9.00 m (29 ft. 6 in.)
length 6.35 m (20 ft. 10 in.)
height 2.70 m (8 ft. 10 in.)
wing area 21.70 m² (233 sq. ft.)

COMBAT DATA

ENGINE POWER

Employing the tried-and-tested Mercedes D.III six-cylinder in-line engine, the Pfalz D.III had a reliable and reasonably powerful powerplant. While aircraft like the Sopwith Camel had comparatively small engines, they also had lighter airframes.

D.IIIa 134 kw (180 hp.)
S.XIII 164 kw (220 hp.)
F.1 CAMEL 97 kw (130 hp.)

SERVICE CEILING

The Pfalz had a lower service ceiling than other comparable fighters over the Western Front. The D.III was an unstable aircraft which contributed to its good manoeuvrability, but its lack of ceiling meant that it could not seize an altitude initiative as easily as Allied fighters during dogfights. The Spad S.XIII had a 1500-m (4,800-ft) service ceiling advantage.

S.XIII 6650 m (21,800 ft.)
F.1 CAMEL 5790 m (19,000 ft.)
D.IIIa 5180 m (17,000 ft.)

ENDURANCE

Endurance values of around two to two and a half hours were typical of fighters of the period. Such values varied greatly depending upon a number of factors, including the fuel load carried and the flying conditions encountered.

D.IIIa 2.5 hours
S.XIII 2 hours
F.1 CAMEL 2.5 hours

Pfalz fighter family

■ **Dr.I:** Starting life as a smaller, refined D.III called the D.VI, the Dr.I had an extra wing surface added to improve its climb rate.

■ **E.II:** Based on the Morane-Saulnier Type H, the E.I and E.II were armed single-seat scouts, powered by Oberursel rotary engines.

■ **E.III:** With Fokker gun synchronisation gear fitted, the E.II became the E.III. Built in small numbers, it was followed by the E.IV.

■ **E.V:** While the E.IV was a more powerful E.III, reliability problems saw it re-engined with a Mercedes rotary, but this was too late for the war.

POLIKARPOV

I-15/I-153

● Fighter biplane ● Fought in Spain and China ● Highly manoeuvrable

Designed by Polikarpov while he was in prison, the biplane I-15 'Chaika' (Seagull) was involved in many air battles in the 1930s from Mongolia to Spain. The aircraft was continually improved; the final I-153 was one of the most capable biplane fighters ever built. Displaying excellent manoeuvrability, the I-15 was still in service in large numbers in 1941, by which time it had been rendered obsolete.

▲ Polikarpov fighters fought with distinction in the late 1930s, taking on aircraft like the CR.32 and Ki-27. The I-15 was so manoeuvrable that it broke records, turning through 360° in only eight seconds. The design formed the basis of the later I-16 monoplane.

POLIKARPOV I-15/I-153

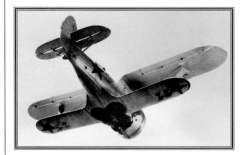

▲ Still fighting
The I-153 was still in action as late as 1943 dropping light bombs in the close support role. The type was flown by aces Grigory Rechkalov and Alexander Klubov before they flew MiG-3s.

▼ Starting up
These bomb-armed 'Chaikas' are being started up by trucks using a Hucks starter.

▼ Hidden in the woods
The Soviets were masters of camouflage, but that did not save these I-15s from destruction in 1941. Luftwaffe fighters decimated the Soviet biplanes.

◀ Fighting the invader
Finland's forces used 14 captured 'Chaikas' fitted with German radios and Browning machine-guns. With the advantage of having better pilots and the fact that they were often mistaken as friendly, the Finns wrought havoc against the Soviets.

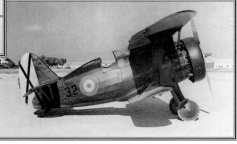

▲ Spanish tour
The 'Chaika' was the main Republican fighter in the Spanish Civil War, fighting Nationalist Fiat CR.32s. The two types were closely matched, although the I-15 had better firepower.

FACTS AND FIGURES

➤ More than 550 I-15s were supplied to the Spanish Republicans; they were known as 'Chato' (flat nose) to their opponents.

➤ I-153s were cleared to fire six RS-82 underwing rockets for ground attack.

➤ The 'Chaika' was flown by the Spanish ace Miguel Zamudio in the Civil War.

➤ A single I-15 variant was produced with rubber-sealed pressurised cockpits for high-altitude work.

➤ Two I-152s were rebuilt as 'Shturmovik' dedicated ground-attack prototypes.

➤ In October 1940 an I-153/DM-4 reached 440 km/h (273 m.p.h.) in a ramjet test flight.

PROFILE

Dogfighting in the 'Seagull'

When he designed a replacement for the earlier I-5, Polikarpov retained the biplane formula but created a gull-wing shape, leading to the nickname Seagull. Early versions were powered by an American Wright Cyclone engine driving a Russian propeller. First flown in 1933, the aircraft displayed astonishing agility.

Production began in 1934 and the armament was doubled to four guns with a high reserve of ammunition. The I-15 had an active combat life, fighting the Japanese at the battle of Khalkin Gol and in China. The aircraft also served the Republican cause in Spain, and fought on both sides in the Finnish campaign in 1940.

The Soviets tried to prolong the life of the I-15 with various improvements, such as revised cowlings and more powerful engines, for the I-15bis, I-152 and I-153 models. Even with turbocharged engines, however, the performance was not vastly improved, and Polikarpov turned to the monoplane I-16 which was very similar. Over 1,000 'Chaikas' were still in service with the USSR in 1941.

Above: The bizarre I-153/DM-4 was an experimental version used to test ramjet-assisted propulsion.

Left: Fitting a Cyclone engine in such a short airframe gave the I-15 its distinctive portly lines. The Soviet M-62 engine was used in the I-153 version.

I-15

Type: single-seat radial-engined biplane fighter and ground-attack aircraft

Powerplant: one 528-kW (708-hp.) Wright Cyclone F-3 radial piston engine

Maximum speed: 367 km/h (228 m.p.h.) at 3050 m (10,000 ft.)

Initial climb rate: over 900 m/min (2,950 f.p.m.)

Combat radius: 550 km (341 mi.)

Service ceiling: 9800 m (32,150 ft.)

Weights: empty 1130 kg (2,486 lb.); loaded 1390 kg (3,058 lb.)

Armament: four PV-1 7.62-mm (.30 cal.) machine-guns with 3,000 rounds; provision for four 20-kg (44-lb.) bombs or (I-153) six rockets

Dimensions: span 9.75 m (32 ft.)
length 6.10 m (20 ft.)
height 2.19 m (7 ft. 2 in.)
wing area 23.55 m² (253 sq. ft.)

I-15

One of the most successful biplane fighters ever, the I-15 was the main Spanish Republican fighter.

The 'Chaika' gained its nickname from the distinct shape of its upper wing. Many pilots disliked the gull-wing, saying the view was worse.

At an early stage in its production, the I-15 was equipped with seat armour. PV-1 guns were fitted in the fuselage sides in addition to the pair in original versions.

The multicoloured tail was the emblem of the Spanish Republican air force. The black cross of the Nationalists was later painted over this.

Such was the demand for the I-15 that the first examples had the original American engines, but most had Russian licence-built M-25 versions of the Wright Cyclone.

One outstanding feature was the undercarriage legs; the lower portion slid up and down inside the upper portion through an internal slot to provide wheel suspension.

The fuselage was constructed of KhMA gas-welded tube with light-alloy removable skin panels forwards of the windscreen and fabric covering behind.

COMBAT DATA

MAXIMUM SPEED

By the end of the 1930s fighters were approaching the feasible maximum speeds for biplane design. Even the first all-metal monoplane fighters which were entering service were at least as fast.

I-15	367 km/h (228 m.p.h.)
CR.32	375 km/h (233 m.p.h.)
GLADIATOR Mk I	410 km/h (254 m.p.h.)

ARMAMENT

Four-gun armament was a vital improvement in the last biplane fighters, as a lethal shot was less easy to attain due to the increasing speed and armour protection of enemy aircraft.

I-15	4 x 7.62-mm (.30 cal.) machine-guns
CR.32	2 x 7.7-mm (.303 cal.) machine-guns
GLADIATOR Mk I	4 x 7.7-mm (.303 cal.) machine-guns

SERVICE CEILING

The I-15 had a good climb rate and ceiling, and against a CR.32 pilots often had the edge in diving and climbing. With its pressurised cockpit the I-152GK could routinely operate at high altitudes.

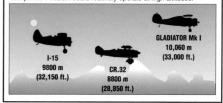

GLADIATOR Mk I 10,060 m (33,000 ft.)
I-15 9800 m (32,150 ft.)
CR.32 8800 m (28,850 ft.)

'Chaikas' at war

OUTSMARTING THE JAPANESE: During the Sino-Japanese War, which began in 1937, Chinese Nationalists flew their manoeuvrable I-15s against more advanced Japanese fighters.

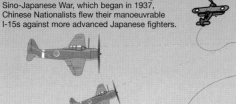

WITH REPUBLICAN FORCES: Spanish Republican forces equipped with I-15s came up against Nationalist and Condor Legion fighters from Germany during the Spanish Civil War.

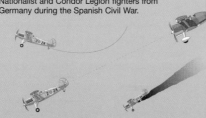

CAPTURED CHAIKAS: During World War II, Finland used 14 captured examples fitted with Browning guns and German radio to bomb Soviet positions.

POTEZ
25

● More than 4000 built ● General-purpose biplane ● Numerous variants

Built in large numbers and used by the air forces of more than 20 countries, the Potez 25 was developed from the earlier models 15S and 24, and flew for the first time early in 1925. During the following 10 years more than 4,000 were built, several hundred of them under licence for export customers, in over a dozen different versions. The Potez's career with the French air force ended in the mid-1930s, but some served elsewhere into the 1940s.

▲ In addition to its military applications, the Potez 25 found useful employment as a mail plane in South America during the 1930s. Aéropostale and its associated companies made regular mail flights, frequently taking the aircraft on hazardous routes over the Andes with considerable loads.

POTEZ 25

▲ Swiss 25 A.2
This Potez 25 A.2 observation aircraft was powered by a Lorraine-Dietrich 12Eb liquid-cooled engine.

▲ Potez 25 'Jupiter'
Switzerland operated a mixture of aircraft with liquid- and air-cooled engines. This aircraft has a 313-kW (420-hp.) Gnome-Rhône 9Ac Jupiter radial installed.

▲ Unequal-span wings
A common feature of all 25s was the design's unequal span mainplanes. Tail shapes varied; the Salmson radial-engined machines had an extended rudder.

▲ Salmson engine
A distinctively shaped engine cowling was a feature of the 388-kW (520-hp.) Salmson radial-powered Potez 25 versions.

Clean lines ▶
The clean lines of the Potez 25 are evident in this side-on view, though they are spoilt slightly by the radial engine.

FACTS AND FIGURES

➤ Licence production was undertaken in factories in Poland, Yugoslavia, Romania and Portugal.

➤ Apart from Potez, ANF Les Mureauz and Hanriot built 25s in France.

➤ China employed Potez 25s in action against the Japanese.

➤ A dozen countries, including the Soviet Union, took delivery of Potez 25s for test purposes.

➤ Ethiopian 25s saw action against the invading Italian troops in 1935.

➤ Civil-operated 25s were used by Hanriot and Caudron flying schools in France.

Widely used French design

Basic models of the Potez 25 built for the French Armée de l'Air were the A.2 reconnaissance aircraft, the B.2 bomber and the TOE for operations in overseas theatres. The B.2's bombload consisted of 12 12-kg (26-lb.) or four 50-kg (110-lb.) bombs under the fuselage, plus six 12-kg (26-lb.) bombs under the wings.

There were also civil derivatives of the aircraft. Some were used to carry mail in South America, and two were built with metal fuselages and extra fuel tanks as part of an unsuccessful attempt to make the first non-stop flight from Paris to New York. Designated 25-O (for Océan), they were designed to jettison their undercarriage after take-off and land on a strengthened skid on the underside of the fuselage. The 25H was a floatplane variant built in two forms, one with a large central float, the other with twin floats. Many engine types, both in-line and radial, were used with

power ratings in the 298- to 447-kW (400- to 600-hp.) range. Other operators included Afghanistan, Algeria, Argentina, Brazil, China, Ethiopia, Finland, Guatemala, Japan, Madagascar, Morocco, Poland, Portugal, Romania, Turkey, Uruguay, the USSR, and Yugoslavia.

Below: This Potez 25 TOE was among 2270 examples of this general-purpose variant built. They were designed for colonial use, but many saw home service with the French air force.

Above: Like its other aircraft, Switzerland's large fleet of French-built Potez 25s was long-serving, the last flying until 1940.

25 A.2

During the Gran Chaco War of 1932-35, this aircraft operated from Isla Poi with 2º Escuadrón de Reconocimiento y Bombardeo, Paraguayan air force. In this conflict Paraguay disputed the sovereignty of Chaco Boreal with neighbouring Bolivia.

A variety of engine types was fitted to Potez 25s, to drive a wooden fixed-pitch propeller.

Pilot and observer were accommodated close together in tandem cockpits beneath a cut-out in the trailing edge of the upper wing centre-section.

Twin Lewis 7.7-mm (.303 cal.) machine-guns were mounted on a TO 7 ring in the observer's cockpit. Another was fixed to fire forward.

Designed by Louis Coroller, the Potez 25 was derived from the Potez 24 A.2-category fighter aircraft.

Potez 25s were fitted with a new cross-axle landing gear with specially designed shock absorbers. The undercarriage wheels were formed with metal spokes and fitted with rubber tyres.

Bombloads of around 200 kg (440 lb.) could be carried by the Potez 25 on underfuselage racks, further enhancing the type's versatility. The 25 B.2 variant was specifically designed for the role.

A refined 25 prototype was flown for the first time from the new Méaulte factory in early 1925.

25 TOE

Type: two-seat general-purpose biplane

Powerplant: one 335-kW (450-hp.) Lorraine-Dietrich 12Eb liquid-cooled piston engine

Maximum speed: 208 km/h (129 m.p.h.) at sea level

Range: 1260 km (780 mi.)

Service ceiling: 5800 m (19,000 ft.)

Weights: empty equipped 1510 kg (3,322 lb.); maximum take-off 2500 kg (5,500 lb.)

Armament: one fixed forward-firing 7.7-mm (.303 cal.) Vickers machine-gun and two 7.7-mm Vickers machine-guns on trainable single mounting in observer's cockpit, plus 200 kg (440 lb.) of bombs

Dimensions:
span 14.14 m (46 ft. 4 in.)
length 9.10 m (29 ft. 10 in.)
height 3.67 m (12 ft. 1 in.)
wing area 47.00 m² (506 sq. ft.)

COMBAT DATA

MAXIMUM SPEED

Compared to other general-purpose types of the inter-war period, the Potez 25 had a good top speed. With a bombload this would be considerably reduced.

25 TOE 208 km/h (129 m.p.h.)
WAPITI Mk IIA 217 km/h (135 m.p.h.)
IIIF Mk IV 193 km/h (120 m.p.h.)

POWER

Engines of varying power were fitted to Potez 25s, the 25 TOE having a Lorraine rated at 335 kW (450 hp.). Westland's Wapiti had a larger engine, while that of the Fairey IIIF was of a similar rating.

25 TOE 335 kW (450 hp.)
WAPITI Mk IIA 373 kW (500 hp.)
IIIF Mk IV 339 kW (455 hp.)

RANGE

The Potez 25's range figure fell between those of the Fairey IIIF and Westland Wapiti. The Wapiti was a modest performer at 579 km (360 mi.), while the IIIF was designed for maritime patrols of almost 2500 km (1,550 mi.) (though this would be considerably less with a full weapons load).

25 TOE 1260 km (780 mi.)
WAPITI Mk IIA 579 km (360 mi.)
IIIF Mk IV 2446 km (1,515 mi.)

Aircraft of the Chaco War

■ **BREDA Ba.44:** This transport design, bearing a remarkable resemblance to the de Havilland DH.84, served the Paraguayan forces.

■ **FIAT CR.30:** A small number of these Italian biplane fighters served with the Paraguayan air force, opposing Bolivian Curtiss Hawk IAs.

■ **CURTISS TYPE 18T:** Designed for the US Navy, one example of this two-seat triplane was imported by Bolivia in 1919.

■ **JUNKERS W.34:** Transport aircraft like this one were converted to bombers by the Bolivian air force. Many pilots were mercenaries.

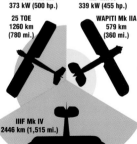

ROYAL AIRCRAFT FACTORY

B.E.2

● Two-seat reconnaissance ● Western Front light bomber

Developed at the Farnborough home of the Royal Aircraft Factory, the original B.E.2 was flown for the first time in February 1912 and remained in service until the end of World War I. By the start of the war at least three Royal Flying Corps squadrons were using the unarmed B.E.2a, and later versions, armed but still lacking in manoeuvrability, were operational on the Western Front in 1917.

▲ The inherent stability of the B.E.2, an important feature in the reconnaissance role, proved to be the type's downfall, especially during the 'Fokker Scourge' of 1915/16.

ROYAL AIRCRAFT FACTORY **B.E.2**

▼ Wartime service
In service throughout World War I, the B.E.2 served initially as a spotter aircraft, Zeppelin interceptor and light bomber until its vulnerability forced remaining aircraft to be redeployed to a training role.

▲ B.E.12 fighter
The B.E.12a was an attempt to build a single-seat fighter based on the B.E.2's airframe. A bigger engine was fitted but its agility was still poor.

▼ In the bomber role
This RFC B.E.2c 'Tasmania' carries a small load of bombs.

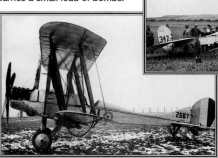

◄ Post-war service
After 1918 many B.E.2s, like other wartime RFC types, found their way into Britain's fledgling civil aviation market.

◄ Artillery spotter
B.E.2s made their mark as reconnaissance aircraft during the first months of 1915.

▲ A gift from Imperial lands
This B.E.2c carries the wording 'Presented by the Indian Nobles'. Presentation aircraft such as this were paid for by wealthy benefactors.

FACTS AND FIGURES

➤ Geoffrey de Havilland, later a famous manufacturer himself, flew the first B.E.2 in trials.

➤ The first B.E.2, a development of the earlier B.E.1, was built and flown in 1912.

➤ Two B.E.2s are in British museums; one is at the Imperial War Museum.

➤ B.E. stood for 'Blériot Experimental', as the B.E.1 was rebuilt from a damaged Blériot monoplane.

➤ Most B.E.2s were built under subcontract in factories other than Farnborough's.

➤ B.E.2s made the first reconnaissance flight by an RFC aircraft in World War I.

PROFILE

RFC's vulnerable two-seat spotter

After the outbreak of war in August 1914, B.E.2as were the first British aircraft to land in France. Like the B.E.2bs that followed, they had no defensive armament but were used for bombing with a single 45-kg (100-lb.) bomb or up to three smaller bombs.

The B.E.2c was a more stable aircraft, making it suitable for reconnaissance and bombing but limiting its manoeuvrability. It proved a good interceptor of Zeppelin airships, and it claimed to have downed at least four. But against the Fokker Eindecker, with its forward-firing armament, the B.E.2 suffered heavy losses over the Western Front in 1915.

The B.E.2c was also handicapped by having only a trainable gun in the front cockpit. The B.E.2d of 1916 reversed the crew positions to seat the observer in the rear and added a forward-firing gun. The later B.E.2e reverted to the original arrangement, however.

More than 3,000 B.E.2s were built by more than 20 manufacturers. They served in the Aegean, North Africa and the Middle East, as well as in France.

Below: Blackburn was among several firms that built more than 3000 B.E.2s during World War I.

Above: Built by Denny and Brothers in Dumbarton, Scotland, this B.E.2e was flown by Australian airline QANTAS.

B.E.2c

Type: two-seat reconnaissance and light-bombing aircraft

Powerplant: one 67-kW (90-hp.) RAF 1a eight-cylinder air-cooled inline engine

Maximum speed: 138 km/h (86 m.p.h.) at sea level

Climb rate: 1066 m (3,500 ft.) in 10 mins

Service ceiling: 3050 m (10,000 ft.)

Weights: empty 621 kg (1,366 lb.); loaded 1077 kg (2,370 lb.)

Armament: one trainable 7.7-mm (.303 cal.) machine-gun, up to 100 kg (220 lb.) of bombs or rockets

Dimensions:
span	11.30 m (37 ft.)
length	8.30 m (27 ft. 3 in.)
height	3.40 m (11 ft. 2 in.)
wing area	34.47 m² (371 sq. ft.)

B.E.2c

One of a batch of 100 B.E.2c aircraft built by Ruston, Proctor and Company Limited, 2713 was fitted with a 67-kW (90-hp.) Royal Aircraft Factory 1a engine.

A number of World War I designs featured tall, upturned exhaust pipes. These kept potentially harmful, hot, exhaust gases away from the fragile fuselage sides and cockpit area.

In most of the two-seat B.E.2s the pilot sat in the rear cockpit with the observer/gunner in the front armed with one or two Lewis 7.7-mm (.303 cal.) machine-guns.

National markings were usually prominently displayed on military aircraft of the Great War period. Note the large roundels under the wings and the brightly painted rudder markings. The aircraft's serial number is displayed on the forward section of the tailfin.

Most B.E.2s were fitted with eight-cylinder Royal Aircraft Factory 1a engines, although the first examples had a Renault powerplant of the same configuration.

Although 'B.E.' originally stood for Blériot Experimental, these letters were applied to a number of early RAF designs, the letters later standing for 'Bomber Experimental'.

The relatively flimsy construction of the B.E.2 was a reflection of its early design and the fact that it was intended as a slow and stable observation platform.

COMBAT DATA

MAXIMUM SPEED

Speed was not a strongpoint of the B.E.2 or any of the other early reconnaissance types of the Great War. Stability and endurance were seen as more important attributes. This, however, counted against these machines when fast, agile and well-armed fighters began to appear in the skies over France.

B.E.2e	145 km/h (90 m.p.h.)
ALBATROS C.I	140 km/h (87 m.p.h.)
AVIATIK C.I	142 km/h (88 m.p.h.)

ENDURANCE

The B.E.2 had excellent endurance, which made it a very useful type in its intended reconnaissance and artillery spotting roles. This was also useful in the training role, allowing long flights. Both the German types also had useful endurance, with the Aviatik being the better of the two.

B.E.2e	ALBATROS C.I	AVIATIK C.I
4 hours	2½ hours	3 hours

ARMAMENT

In common with other observation aircraft of the period, the B.E.2 had a single machine-gun for self-defence which was operated by the observer. B.E.2 crews also used them in an offensive role against Zeppelins. When up against fighters with forward-firing guns this armament fit was to prove extremely inadequate.

B.E.2e	1 x 7.7-mm (.303 cal.) machine-gun
ALBATROS C.I	1 x 7.92-mm machine-gun
AVIATIK C.I	1 x 7.92-mm machine-gun

World War I Royal Aircraft Factory designs

■ **F.E.2b:** Entering service in France in 1915, the F.E.2b was an interim solution to the problem of providing forward-firing armament.

■ **R.E.7:** Introduced in 1916 and judged to be unsuitable for reconnaissance, R.E.7s became light bombers and could carry a 152-kg bombload.

■ **R.E.8:** Popularly known as the 'Harry Tate', this aircraft was in many ways a scaled-up B.E.2. Unfortunately it was just as ungainly.

■ **S.E.5:** The S.E.5 and S.E.5a both entered service in France in 1917 and became formidable fighters after early teething problems.

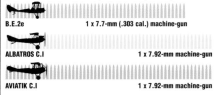

ROYAL AIRCRAFT FACTORY

F.E.2

● Pusher engine design ● Two-seat fighter ● Night bomber

As a companion to the Airco DH.2, the Farman Experimental 2b (F.E.2b) pusher-fighter was a vital component of the Royal Flying Corps' scout force over the Western Front in 1916. The German Fokker Eindekker had been taking a terrible toll of Allied aircraft and the introduction of the F.E.2b helped redress the balance. With an excellent field of fire and an ability to carry a useful bombload, the F.E.2 also served as a day and night bomber.

▲ *This F.E.2b built by Weir was used for experiments in the use of airborne searchlights for home defence at night. A generator-powered light was attached to two 7.7-mm (.303 cal.) Lewis guns.*

ROYAL AIRCRAFT FACTORY F.E.2

Under repair▶
The simple construction of World War I fighters meant that many could be repaired after serious crashes. This F.E.2 from No. 18 Squadron, RFC, is seen after a landing accident in France.

◀ Tandem seating
The pilot sitting in the rear cockpit had a good view over the gunner.

Coastal patrol ▶
Based at the Isle of Grain at the mouth of the Thames for anti-submarine patrols, this F.E.2b is seen with flotation bags.

◀ F.E.2d prototype
The F.E.2d was fitted with a bigger Rolls-Royce Eagle engine.

F.E.2b at war ▶
Without the obstruction of an engine and propeller in front of them, the pilot and observer had an excellent all-round view. Although the aircraft did not have remarkable performance, it proved to be effective against the Fokker Eindekker.

FACTS AND FIGURES

➤ The revised F.E.2 of 1913 was destroyed in a fatal crash in February 1914 when the pilot, R. Kemp, lost control in a dive.

➤ On 18 June 1916 a No. 25 Squadron F.E.2b claimed the German ace Max Immelmann.

➤ Most of No. 20 Squadron's record 600 kills from 1914 to 1918 were made by the F.E.2b.

➤ After withdrawal from daylight operations, the F.E.2b became the RFC's standard night bomber until August 1918.

➤ On 31 May 1918 a coastal patrol F.E.2b sank U-boat *UC 49* with two 45-kg bombs.

➤ In 1916-17 816 F.E.2s were allocated to fighter duties and 395 to bomber duties.

PROFILE

The RFC's finest pusher fighter

Uniquely among Royal Aircraft Factory machines, the F.E.2 existed in two entirely dissimilar forms. The first F.E.2 was actually a rebuilt F.E.1 and first flew in 1911. In 1913 this aircraft was entirely redesigned and rebuilt, and was the first in the successful series of wartime F.E.2 fighters.

The first major production version was the F.E.2b which featured twin-Lewis gun

armament and entered operational service with No. 6 Squadron, RFC, in September 1915. The arrival of these aircraft in France throughout the autumn of 1915 marked the beginning of the Eindekker's decline.

Although slower than other types, the F.E.2b proved to be an excellent gun platform and the introduction of the larger 119.3-kW (160-hp.) Beardmore engine kept the aircraft competitive until the spring of 1917.

Other versions included the specialist F.E.2c night-fighter, in which the positions of the pilot and observer were reversed to give the pilot the best possible view forward for night landings, and the F.E.2d powered by a Rolls-Royce Eagle engine.

Left: During 1917-18 the F.E.2b became an important ground-attack type. This No. 149 Squadron example is being loaded with a 50.8-kg (112-lb.) high-explosive bomb beneath the fuselage

Below: Night bombing raids were carried out by the F.E.2b. This one is fully 'bombed-up' for another sortie.

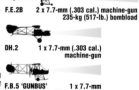

F.E.2b

Type: two-seat fighter and fighter-bomber

Powerplant: one 119.3-kW (160-hp.) Beardmore liquid-cooled in-line engine

Maximum speed: 147 km/h (91 m.p.h.)

Initial climb rate: 39 min 44 sec to 3048 m (10,000 ft.)

Endurance: 3 hours

Service ceiling: 3353 m (11,000 ft.)

Weights: empty 935 kg (2,057 lb.); maximum take-off 1378 kg (3,032 lb.)

Armament: one or two 7.7-mm (.303 cal.) Lewis machine-guns plus up to 235 kg (517 lb.) of bombs carried externally

Dimensions:
span	14.55 m (47 ft. 9 in.)
length	9.83 m (32 ft. 3 in.)
height	3.85 m (12 ft. 8 in.)
wing area	45.89 m² (494 sq. ft.)

On the F.E.2b the pilot sat in the rear cockpit with the observer/gunner in the front. The observer fired either a trainable Lewis gun mounted on the front of the cockpit or one mounted on a pillar between the cockpits, which he fired by standing up and facing backwards.

The wooden structure of the biplane wings was covered with doped fabric. The first F.E.2bs had wings of R.A.F.6 section, which were later replaced by R.A.F.14 section wings with a larger angle of incidence.

F.E.2B

F.E.2bs were used by 16 Royal Flying Corps squadrons on the Western Front in France, along with six home defence squadrons. Other RFC F.E.2bs were used for coastal patrol and night training.

A number of different powerplants were fitted to the F.E.2 series. The F.E.2b was initially powered by an 89.5-kW (120-hp.) Beardmore engine; later F.E.2bs used a 119.3-kW (160-hp.) unit. The F.E.2d was powered by the much larger 186.4-kW (250-hp.) Rolls-Royce Eagle.

The tail empennage was fabric-covered and was mounted at the end of two pairs of converging wooden booms. A wooden tailskid prevented damage to the rear of the aircraft.

A5448

COMBAT DATA

MAXIMUM SPEED

Pusher designs were generally slower than their tractor-engined counterparts, but this drawback was overcome in the F.E.2 by its excellent field of fire and manoeuvrability. The later F.E.2 and DH.2 were far faster than the earlier F.B.5.

F.E.2b	147 km/h (90 m.p.h.)
DH.2	150 km/h (93 m.p.h.)
F.B.5 'GUNBUS'	113 km/h (70 m.p.h.)

ARMAMENT

The F.E.2b is the only one of the types which was extensively used for bombing. It would usually carry Cooper bombs beneath the wings and could also carry a high explosive bomb beneath the fuselage. The F.E.2 had double the firepower of the other types.

F.E.2B — 2 x 7.7-mm (.303 cal.) machine-gun 235-kg (517-lb.) bombload

DH.2 — 1 x 7.7-mm (.303 cal.) machine-gun

F.B.5 'GUNBUS' — 1 x 7.7-mm (.303 cal.) machine-gun

SERVICE CEILING

Flying at high altitudes was extremely uncomfortable in open-cockpit aircraft because of the cold. However, it was important to gain tactical advantage over enemy aircraft and height could be converted to speed. The DH.2 was a lighter single-seat design and had the best ceiling. The F.B.5 was at a disadvantage.

F.E.2b — 3353 m (11,000 ft.)
DH.2 — 4265 m (14,000 ft.)
F.B.5 — 2743 m (9,000 ft.)

Piston pusher fighters

■ **AIRCO DH.1:** Geoffrey de Havilland's first design after joining Airco was this two-seat reconnaissance fighter which served until 1917.

■ **RAF F.E.8:** More than 180 F.E.8s served with the Royal Flying Corps from 1916, but were quickly declared obsolete.

■ **VICKERS F.B.5 'GUNBUS':** The Fighting Biplane No. 5 (F.B.5) was designed specifically as a fighter and entered service in 1915.

■ **VICKERS TYPE 161:** In 1929 the Air Ministry was looking for designs to carry the 37-mm C.O.W. gun. The Type 161 first flew in 1931.

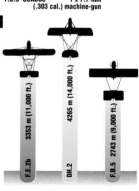

ROYAL AIRCRAFT FACTORY

R.E.8

● Reconnaissance bomber ● World War I ● Europe and Middle East

More than 4000 R.E.8s were produced during World War I. Like other aircraft produced by the Royal Aircraft Factory (which became the Royal Aircraft Establishment in 1918 to avoid confusion with the newly formed RAF), they were designed to be stable in flight, but were thus short on manoeuvrability. However, with a useful gun armament and light bombs, they were to be the RFC's most widely used reconnaissance type.

▲ *As they replaced the B.E. series two-seaters, it was hoped that the new R.E.8s would improve the fortunes of the RFC's reconnaissance units and their crews. However, losses were still high.*

ROYAL AIRCRAFT FACTORY R.E.8

▼ Presentation aircraft
Lamberhurst was a late production R.E.8 built by the Siddeley-Deasy Motor Co. Ltd, at Coventry. Apart from the Royal Aircraft Factory, five companies built R.E.8s.

▲ Defensive machine-guns
The R.E.8 had much better armament than the B.E.2. It was fitted with forward-firing Vickers and rear-mounted Lewis machine-guns.

'Somewhere in France' ▶
Surrounded by friendly troops, this No. 9 Squadron, RFC, aircraft has come to grief, possibly after a tangle with the enemy or an engine failure.

▼ Mesopotamia, 1918
As well as the Western Front, R.E.8s served in the Middle East and Italy during World War I. These No. 63 Squadron, RAF aircraft are seen in Mesopotamia, where the unit remained until 1920.

▲ Widely employed
The most widely used of the RFC's reconnaissance types, the R.E.8 was employed by only one Allied country. Belgium took delivery of 22 in July 1917. Replacement began after 10 months.

FACTS AND FIGURES

➤ In a pun on the aircraft's designation, the R.E.8 was nicknamed the 'Harry Tate' after a music-hall comedian of the day.

➤ Two R.E.8s have survived; one is at the Imperial War Museum, Duxford.

➤ Night bombing was undertaken by R.E.8s at the Battle of Ypres.

➤ After the two prototypes, 4430 R.E.8s were ordered; by late 1918, 4077 had been delivered and the others were cancelled.

➤ During August 1917, a number of RFC R.E.8s shot down German single-seaters.

➤ Plans to fit Rolls-Royce Eagles to R.E.8s were cancelled due to engine shortages.

PROFILE

'Harry Tate' on the Western Front

After the R.E.8 prototype had been tested in France in mid-1916, large-scale production was ordered. R.E. stood for Reconnaissance Experimental, but the aircraft was actually used in a host of roles, including artillery spotting, ground strafing, light bombing and supply-dropping to troops.

The first squadron equipped with the type arrived on the Western Front in November 1916. By the end of 1917 there were 18 R.E.8 squadrons. Early models tended to spin easily, but a bigger tailfin cured the problem.

More than 2000 were used in France, while another 300 served in the Middle East. They bombed the Turkish forces in Palestine, and carried supplies in Mesopotamia. Others were used in Italy and Russia and by the Belgian air force.

Although it equipped 19 RAF squadrons in 1918, the R.E.8 was retired quickly once the fighting was over. Although an easy target for German fighters, it had become a standard type because of the sheer numbers built.

Below: Evidently under repair, this R.E.8 carries the markings of No. 34 Squadron, RFC, based at Villers-Brettoneux during the spring of 1917.

Above: Named Spitfire, *this unarmed R.E.8 was with No. 35 Reserve Squadron, based in Britain.*

A prominent feature of the R.E.8 was its exhaust system, which directed smoke and fumes above the top wing and away from the aircraft's crew.

Having apparently forgotten the lessons learned during the service life of the B.E.2, the R.E.8 was an inherently stable aircraft, ideal for artillery spotting, but vulnerable to attack by agile enemy fighters.

R.E.8

C5048 was one of a batch of 100 'Harry Tates' built by Coventry Ordnance Works Limited. This aircraft was operated by No. 16 Squadron, RFC, in France during 1917/18.

Defensive armament consisted of two machine-guns: a fixed, synchronised, forward-firing 7.7-mm (.303 cal.) Vickers controlled by the pilot, and a pivoting 7.7-mm Lewis mounted on a Scarff ring in the observer's cockpit. On some aircraft the latter carried twin Lewis guns.

After the type was introduced in small quantities in France in 1916, a number were lost in accidents. Investigations revealed a tendency to spin, which was rectified by increasing the area of the tail fin. This aircraft has the revised fin.

Standard R.E.8s were fitted with an air-cooled 12-cylinder Royal Aircraft Factory 4a engine rated at 112 kW (140 hp.) and driving a four-bladed propeller. A small number of aircraft were fitted with a 149-kW RAF 4d engine; a few others had Hispano-Suiza powerplants.

RFC R.E.8s had a bombload capacity of 102 kg (224 lb.), made up of two 51-kg (112 lb.) bombs or more lighter bombs.

The airframe was a conventional wire-braced, fabric-covered wooden structure. The mainplanes were of unequal span. Military equipment included a camera and a wireless transmitter.

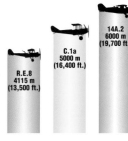

ACTION DATA

SERVICE CEILING

Compared to other designs like the Rumpler C.1a and Breguet 14A.2, the R.E.8 had a limited service ceiling of just over 4115 m (13,000 ft.). This made the aircraft more vulnerable to attack from high-flying enemy fighters approaching from 'out of the sun' to surprise their quarry.

R.E.8
4115 m
(13,500 ft.)

C.1a
5000 m
(16,400 ft.)

14A.2
6000 m
(19,700 ft.)

ENDURANCE

R.E.8s had a good endurance, useful for the reconnaissance and artillery spotting roles. This allowed sorties over greater distances with longer 'loiter' times over the target.

R.E.8
4 hours 15 min

C.1a
4 hours

14A.2
3 hours

ARMAMENT

'Harry Tates' compared well with other reconnaissance and light bomber types, having a defensive armament of two (or three in some cases) machine-guns and a 102-kg bombload.

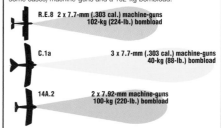

R.E.8   2 x 7.7-mm (.303 cal.) machine-guns
102-kg (224-lb.) bombload

C.1a   3 x 7.7-mm (.303 cal.) machine-guns
40-kg (88-lb.) bombload

14A.2   2 x 7.92-mm machine-guns
100-kg (220-lb.) bombload

Warplanes over Palestine

■ **ALBATROS C.III:** Once the C.III was outclassed over the Western Front in 1917, this reconnaissance type was sent to Palestine.

■ **AIRCO DH.2:** The RFC's first true single-seat fighter, the pusher-prop DH.2 was among more types sent to Palestine from 1916.

■ **RAF B.E.2:** Predecessors of the R.E.8, B.E.2s were among the first British aircraft committed to the Middle East in 1915.

■ **RUMPLER C.IV:** A few C.IV reconnaissance aircraft were sent to Palestine in 1917 to 'spot' for Turkish artillery forces.

ROYAL AIRCRAFT FACTORY

S.E.5A

- Single-seat scout biplane fighter ● Flown by Britain's top aces

Designed by H.P. Folland at the Royal Aircraft Factory in Farnborough, the S.E.5a was one of the finest scout aircraft to fly in World War I. Despite early teething troubles, it went on to achieve great success in the hands of aces like William 'Billy' Bishop, Ray Collishaw and Edward 'Mick' Mannock. Beautifully proportioned in spite of its angular lines, the S.E.5a was very fast and provided a very stable gun platform, qualities which more than compensated for its slight lack of agility.

▲ The S.E.5a was easy to fly, without the handling vices of more agile scouts. This was vital in an era when as many pilots were killed in accidents as in air combat.

ROYAL AIRCRAFT FACTORY S.E.5A

▲ Replica pair
Precise in every detail, these two S.E.5as are in fact replicas. They were flown in Canada and the United States in the 1970s.

▲ The Aces' favourite
Although not the best dogfighter of the time, the S.E.5a was fast. This made it the preferred aircraft of the aces, most of whom achieved success by stalking their targets from behind.

Kill record ▶
A pilot proudly records his squadron's grim tally of victims. The S.E.5 gave the Allies an aircraft capable of taking on and beating Germany's best.

▲ Still flying after 80 years
This immaculate S.E.5a is part of the Shuttleworth Trust collection at Old Warden in England, and is one of the few original aircraft still flying.

▼ Squadron on show
Posing for a photograph, a squadron shows off its new machines. The S.E.5 was an aircraft to be proud of, and together with the Sopwith Camel did much to regain Allied air superiority during late 1917.

▲ Bad landing
American pilots flew the S.E.5 as well as various French aircraft. They suffered an equally appalling loss rate as their Allies.

FACTS AND FIGURES

- ➤ The S.E.5 entered service on the Western Front in March 1917, followed by the more reliable S.E.5a in June.

- ➤ Major 'Mick' Mannock racked up 50 of his 73 aerial victories flying the S.E.5a.

- ➤ Elliott Springs became an early American ace flying S.E.5 scouts.

- ➤ The tough little S.E.5 was so rugged that one pilot flew it through the side of a house and emerged unhurt.

- ➤ By 1918 the S.E.5a was flown by 21 British and two American squadrons.

- ➤ Production of the S.E.5 and S.E.5a totalled 5205 aircraft.

PROFILE

The saviour of the Royal Flying Corps

The S.E.5 was one of the classic fighters of World War I. Though less manoeuvrable than Britain's other World War I 'great', the Sopwith Camel, the S.E.5 was much faster. It reached the Front in France during 'bloody April' 1917, the blackest month of the war in terms of casualties for the Royal Flying Corps. The S.E.5 was more than a match for the German Albatross, which until then had ruled the skies.

The improved S.E.5a was plagued by problems of an inadequately developed engine and other difficulties, but once these shortcomings were wiped away it excelled in battle, being both fast and an extremely stable gun platform. Flown by most of the top British and Commonwealth aces of World War I, the S.E.5a also equipped units of the American Expeditionary Force.

S.E.5A

The S.E.5, together with the Sopwith Camel, turned the tide of the air war at a time when Allied losses had risen to truly catastrophic levels. This aircraft was flown by Major Edward Mannock, Britain's most successful ace.

The S.E.5a was unusual in having only a single fixed forward-firing weapon. The Vickers machine-gun was mounted above the engine on the starboard side, synchronised to fire through the propeller.

The 149-kW (200-hp.) Hispano-Suiza engine gave the S.E.5a its superior speed. It had teething problems however, and most aircraft had the less temperamental Wolseley Viper engine fitted instead.

As with all aircraft in the early years of flying, the S.E.5a was equipped with a sturdy fixed undercarriage.

The Lewis gun mounted on the wing was magazine-fed, and could be swung down on a rail to change its magazine. It could also fire upwards.

Visibility from the S.E.5's cockpit was excellent, although the long in-line engine obscured the view ahead more than in its snub-nosed contemporary, the Sopwith Camel.

All RFC aircraft carried large and vivid national markings, but like their counterparts in World War II they still found that 'friendly' ground troops would shoot at them.

Aircraft in World War I were built as light as possible to save weight, the skeleton usually being of wood with a fabric skin.

The in-line engine and beautifully-proportioned wing made the S.E.5a an inherently more stable airframe than the Camel, which gained a reputation as a killer of inexperienced young pilots.

Wood and fabric construction meant that the S.E.5 was as much of a death trap as its contemporaries if it caught fire, but it did have exceptional structural strength.

The wedge-shaped tail, which was much more modern-looking than those of its contemporaries, was a key recognition feature of the S.E.5.

S.E.5a

Type: single-seat fighter

Powerplant: one 149-kW (200-hp.) Hispano-Suiza V-8 piston engine

Maximum speed: 218 km/h (135 m.p.h.)

Endurance: 2 hours and 30 minutes

Service ceiling: 6705 m (22,000 ft.)

Weights: empty 635 kg (1,397 lb.); loaded 887 kg (1,951 lb.)

Armament: one forward-firing synchronised 7.7-mm (.303 cal.) Vickers machine-gun and one 7.7-mm Lewis gun mounted over the centre section of the upper wing, plus up to four 18.6-kg (40-lb.) bombs

Dimensions:
span	8.12 m (26 ft. 7 in.)
length	6.38 m (20 ft. 11 in.)
height	2.90 m (9 ft. 6 in.)
wing area	22.67 m² (244 sq. ft.)

COMBAT DATA

MAXIMUM SPEED

The development of aircraft during World War I was rapid, with fighters like the S.E.5a of 1917 being twice as fast as those which had gone to war less than three years before. The S.E.5 was one of the fastest fighters of its time.

S.E.5a	218 km/h (135 m.p.h.)
SPAD XIII	218 km/h (135 m.p.h.)
FOKKER DVII	195 km/h (121 m.p.h.)

ENDURANCE

British warplanes almost invariably conducted long, aggressive patrols deep behind enemy lines. They needed much greater endurance than their German opponents, which were more defensive, rarely crossing into hostile territory.

S.E.5a 2.5 hours

SPAD XIII 2 hours

FOKKER DVII 1.5 hours

ARMAMENT

The machine-gun was as much of an influence in the air as it was in the muddy battles on the ground. Most top-class scouts had a pair of guns synchronised to fire through the propeller. The S.E.5 was unusual in that one of its guns was mounted above the wing, and could be aimed upwards into the belly of an enemy aircraft.

S.E.5a 1 x Vickers 7.7-mm (.303 cal.) 1 x Lewis 7.7-mm (.303 cal.) machine-gun

Fokker DVII 2 x 7.92-mm machine-guns

SPAD XIII 2 x 7.7-mm (.303 cal.) Vickers machine-guns

Aces high in the S.E.5

■ **ALBERT BALL:** The first British pilot to become nationally known as an ace, Ball switched from Nieuports to the S.E.5 early in 1917, scoring 34 of his 44 victories on the type. An intensely religious loner, Ball disappeared on 7 May 1917. His death remains a mystery, although some experts think that he was shot down by Lothar von Richthofen.

■ **JAMES McCUDDEN:** Originally a non-commissioned aircraft mechanic, McCudden became a pilot in 1916. Commissioned in January 1917, he joined the famous No. 56 Squadron flying S.E.5s, and was an immediate success. Like Ball, he was a loner, preferring to stalk his prey unaccompanied. He was killed in an accident when his score stood at 57.

■ **EDWARD MANNOCK:** Mannock transferred to the Royal Flying Corps in 1916 despite being all but blind in one eye. A ruthless fighter, he was an inspiring leader who made sure his pilots received the best possible combat training. He was shot down by ground fire in July 1918 when his score stood at 73, the highest by a British pilot. His body was never found.

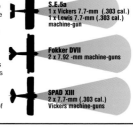

211

RUMPLER

C.I

● First of the C-types ● Service on all fronts ● Photo reconnaissance

In the early stages of World War I, the Rumpler B.I biplane was widely used as an unarmed scout and reconnaissance aircraft. By 1915, it was becoming obvious that armament was essential for survival over the Western Front. Accordingly, Rumpler developed the C.I – the C-type designation being applied to armed two-seat biplanes with an engine of 112 kW (150 hp.) or more – with a single ring-mounted Parabellum machine-gun in the rear cockpit.

▲ Thanks to its unusual construction, the C.I offered both crew members an excellent field of view. It performed some of the first photographic reconnaissance missions.

RUMPLER C.I

Two-spar wing ▶
Sunlight streaming through the canvas covering of this Rumpler's wings throws the internal structure into silhouette. Each wing had two spars and a series of plywood ribs.

▼ Exhaust installation
A feature of the C.I and C.Ia was the tall exhaust installation. This fed the exhaust gases upwards and over the upper wing, keeping the cockpit free of noxious fumes.

▲ Captured Rumpler
Several aircraft from both sides fell into enemy hands. This C.I carries British roundels.

▼ Field improvements
This C.I has been fitted with crude skis. Simply attached to the wheels, the skis would have been easily removable, but tricky to use.

Wing cut-outs ▶
Experience had shown that the observer often had a less than ideal view from the rear cockpit. Hence, Rumpler put large cut-outs in the wing centre-sections, improving the view considerably.

FACTS AND FIGURES

➤ During the 1917 battle for Gaza, a white cloth was laid on the ground whenever a C.I was required to land for instructions.

➤ British prisoners reported the devastation caused by C.I bombing.

➤ Bayerische Rumpler-Werke took responsibility for the trainer version.

➤ Photo reconnaissance was difficult in Gaza, since the heat damaged photographic plates.

➤ After World War I, some C.Is were converted into passenger aircraft.

➤ The German navy received 98 6B 1 and 6B 2 aircraft, based on the C.I.

PROFILE

Multi-role Rumpler

A fter the C.I's service entry in 1915, it soon became clear that the single ring-mounted Parabellum machine-gun in the observer's cockpit offered insufficient firepower. Thus, in common with most C-types, a forward-firing Spandau machine-gun was mounted on the left side of the forward fuselage.

Increasingly accurate Allied anti-aircraft defences meant that greater altitude was required of

the C-types. In response, Rumpler introduced the C.Ia, with a 134-kW (180-hp.) Argus As.III engine, which was otherwise almost identical to the C.I. Both types were built by several German manufacturers, and were widely used, serving in Macedonia, Salonika and Palestine as well as over the Western Front.

By the autumn of 1916, there were approximately 250 C.Is and

C.Ias in squadron service. They earned a reputation for being very difficult to shoot down, and were the first German aircraft to be used for photographic reconnaissance. Some were still in service 18 months later, although mostly in the training role. In 1918 Rumpler also produced a specialised dual-control trainer, powered by a 112-kW (150-hp) Bz.III engine, with all armament deleted.

Right: Twin floats distinguished the 6B 1 floatplanes, which were otherwise similar to the C.I. The 6B 2 introduced the tail surfaces of the Rumpler C.III.

Below: Although it was no great performer in the air, the C.I had a good reputation and was considered a difficult adversary.

C.Ia

Type: two-seat reconnaissance/general-purpose aircraft

Powerplant: one 134-kW (180-hp.) Argus As.III 6-cylinder water-cooled in-line piston engine

Maximum speed: 150 km/h (93 m.p.h.) at sea level

Endurance: 4 hours

Service ceiling: 5000 m (16,200 ft.)

Weights: empty 793 kg (1,745 lb.); maximum take-off 1300 kg (2,860 lb.)

Armament: one fixed forward-firing 7.92-mm LMG 08/15 machine-gun and one 7.92-mm Parabellum machine-gun in the rear cockpit, plus 100 kg (220 lb.) of light bombs

Dimensions:
span	12.15 m	(39 ft. 10 in.)
length	7.85 m	(25 ft. 9 in.)
height	3.05 m	(10 ft.)
wing area	35.70 m²	(356 sq. ft.)

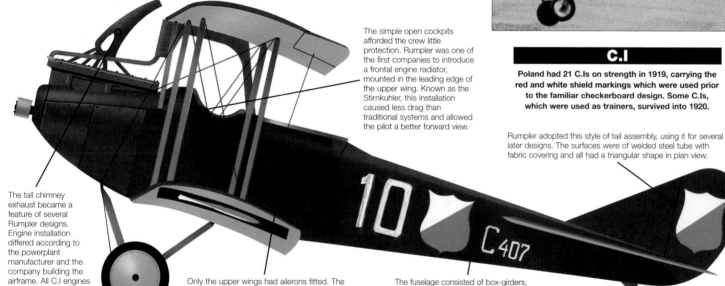

The simple open cockpits afforded the crew little protection. Rumpler was one of the first companies to introduce a frontal engine radiator, mounted in the leading edge of the upper wing. Known as the Stirnkuhler, this installation caused less drag than traditional systems and allowed the pilot a better forward view.

The tall chimney exhaust became a feature of several Rumpler designs. Engine installation differed according to the powerplant manufacturer and the company building the airframe. All C.I engines were six-cylinder units, fitted with the cylinder heads exposed.

Only the upper wings had ailerons fitted. The surfaces were controlled by a wire which ran through the lower wing and vertically upwards to connect with the aileron.

The fuselage consisted of box-girders, covered by ply sheeting forwards and fabric to the rear. Steel was employed for the framework forward of the cockpit.

C.I

Poland had 21 C.Is on strength in 1919, carrying the red and white shield markings which were used prior to the familiar checkerboard design. Some C.Is, which were used as trainers, survived into 1920.

Rumpler adopted this style of tail assembly, using it for several later designs. The surfaces were of welded steel tube with fabric covering and all had a triangular shape in plan view.

ACTION DATA

MAXIMUM SPEED

Rumpler was one of the first companies to introduce a successful C-type into service. Hannover introduced the CL.IIIA late in the war, which offered greater performance than the earlier types.

RUMPLER C.Ia	150 km/h (93 m.p.h.)
AVIATIK C.I	142 km/h (88 m.p.h.)
CL.IIIA	165 km/h (102 m.p.h.)

ENDURANCE

On reconnaissance missions, endurance was important if a number of targets were to be covered or if the progress of a campaign was to be monitored.

RUMPLER C.Ia 4 hours   **AVIATIK C.I** 3 hours   **CL.IIIA** 3 hours

SERVICE CEILING

Flying at a high altitude was the only method of reducing the danger posed by anti-aircraft artillery. Most C-types received more powerful engines during their careers. The C.Ia was moved from the Western Front in the later stages of the war because of its vulnerability and the availability of more advanced types.

CL.IIIA 7498 m (24,600 ft.)

RUMPLER C.Ia 5000 m (16,200 ft.)

AVIATIK C.I 3500 m (11,500 ft.)

Wartime Rumplers

■ **C.V:** Developed from the C.III, the C.V acted as an intermediate type before the C.VII was introduced. This machine fell into Allied hands.

■ **6A 2:** Powered by a 119-kW (160-hp.) Mercedes engine, the 6A 2 of 1916 was a two-seat experimental fighter.

■ **7D 7:** Developed from the 7D 4, the 7D 7 was one of several prototypes developed to test systems for the D.I.

■ **D.I:** Marking the culmination of a series of Rumpler single-seat fighter designs, the D.I was not adopted for service.

SAUNDERS-ROE

PRINCESS

- Last of the great passenger flying-boats ● Magnificent failure

▲ *The Princess, like the Brabazon, was another example of a technological wonder that had almost no relevance at all to the requirements of airlines in the 1950s and should never have been built.*

A vision of a futuristic age of air travel that might have been, the Saunders-Roe SR.45 Princess was a magnificent flying-boat of the post-war era, and was to be the world's largest pressurised aircraft and turboprop. It was an enormous technical achievement, but the Princess suffered from nagging problems with its powerplant and it arrived on the scene after flying-boats no longer offered advantages over landplanes.

PHOTO FILE

SAUNDERS-ROE PRINCESS

◀ **Clean design**
The Princess was powered by engines located in pairs in the wing, driving the propellers via long shafts. This was an elegant aerodynamic solution, but it made the wing very complex and heavy.

▲ **Air show star**
The Princess flew at Farnborough to delight the crowds. At higher speeds the floats would have been retracted into the wingtips.

◀ **Saunders-Roe slipway**
The Princess shared its slipway at Cowes with the SRA-1 fighter. The Princess handled well on water, but the need for large flying-boats, like floatplane fighters, did not really exist.

▼ **Under construction**
The huge size of the Princess meant that it was built more like a ship than an aircraft. The twin pressurised hulls were constructed first, mounted one on top of the other, and the rest of the airframe was then assembled around them.

▲ **Waiting for engines**
The technical snag with the Princess was the disastrous Bristol Proteus turboprop. Even when the airframe was complete, the engines were delayed and were much weaker than expected.

FACTS AND FIGURES

➤ The first Princess made a delayed maiden flight on 22 August 1952.

➤ Its 65,920-litre (17,140-gal.) fuel capacity was housed entirely in wing tanks.

➤ By 1952 British Overseas Airways Corporation, the only potential customer, decided to operate landplanes only.

➤ A proposition to use six Tyne turboprops would have solved any power problems.

➤ The US Navy seriously considered using the three Princess prototypes to test an atomic powerplant.

➤ The only Princess to fly was towed to a salvage yard in 1967 and scrapped.

Britain's magnificent maritime failure

As the Princess thundered over Southampton Water on an early test flight, it looked down on the ocean liners it was designed to replace. This huge, majestic aircraft with its double-deck fuselage and 10 engines in six nacelles was intended as an ocean liner of the sky, to offer luxurious travel to the privileged and the discerning.

The dream died because no turboprop engine available in 1950 could offer the power the Princess needed – and because land-based aircraft then coming along, including the Boeing Stratocruiser, offered a similar standard of service at far lower cost to the operator.

The ambitious thinking behind the Princess led, in fact, to plans for a landplane version, as well as a 'Twin Princess' with two full-sized fuselages and 14 engines which would have been used as a cargo-hauler.

In the end, these grandiose plans came to nothing. At one stage the three Princess prototypes were to be converted into RAF troop transports. But this dream also died, and only the first prototype was ever flown.

The Princess belonged to the maritime world of Southampton. In many ways it had more in common with the ocean liners which it flew over than with the airliners with whom it would have shared the airways.

Princess prototype

Type: long-range passenger flying-boat

Powerplant: 10 2386-kW (3,200-hp.) Bristol Proteus 600 turboprops (eight in coupled units, plus two single units)

Maximum speed: 579 km/h (360 m.p.h.)

Range: estimated 3000 km (1,860 mi.)

Service ceiling: estimated 10,000 m (33,000 ft.)

Weights: take-off 156,492 kg (344,282 lb.)

Accommodation: flight crew of two pilots, two flight engineers, one navigator and one radio operator. As conceived for trans-ocean airline travel, the Princess would have handled 105 passengers in first class; as an RAF troop transport it would have carried 200 fully-equipped combat soldiers and all their equipment

Dimensions:
span	66.90 m (219 ft.)
length	45.11 m (148 ft.)
height	17.00 m (56 ft.)
wing area	487 m² (5,240 sq. ft.)

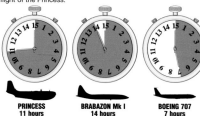

The Princess was an incredible sight. But no matter how majestic its appearance, it was doomed to fail, beaten by the harsh demands of economics and market forces.

SR.45 PRINCESS

The Princess prototype, G-ALUN, was the only one that flew out of the three built. The other two were put into storage on completion.

The flight deck housed two pilots, a navigator, two flight engineers and a radio operator.

Passenger accommodation was divided between two decks, with spiral staircases between them fore and aft. The rear cabin even had pull-down beds in the area where modern airliners have overhead baggage lockers.

The wing leading edges were de-iced thermally, using air piped from the exhaust manifolds.

The tailplane was de-iced by kerosene-burning heaters with their own fuel supply, fed by an air intake in the base of the fin.

Powered control units in the rear of the hull operated the three-section electro-hydraulically operated rudder and twin-section elevators.

Princess

G-ALUN

The Princess used a capacious hold in the lower hull to carry cargo and baggage.

The hull bottom was an efficient hydrodynamic design. Take-offs and landings were notably smooth.

Giant cargo carrier

■ One of the more outlandish schemes to salvage the Princess programme was to develop a giant cargo carrier. Joining a pair of hulls with a common central wing would have created a transport able to carry 400 troops or 50 tons of cargo.

Princess landplane

■ A more practical proposition involved redesigning the hull with wheels and a rear loading ramp. Power would have been provided by six Tyne turboprops. Although the resulting airlifter would have been highly capable, the plans perished with the rest of the Princess programme.

ACTION DATA

TRANSATLANTIC TIME

To be fair to the aviation committees of the 1940s which first planned the Princess and the equally large but futile Brabazon, few people could have foreseen the revolution that the jet would bring to airliner performance. But by the early 1950s the Comet had sounded the death knell for such monsters, and the superb Boeing Model 707 was in the air less than two years after the first flight of the Princess.

PRINCESS 11 hours	BRABAZON Mk I 14 hours	BOEING 707 7 hours

SHORT

MAYO COMPOSITE

● Long-range record holder ● Floatplane and mothership ● Mailplane

Short's Mayo Composite was an attempt to provide long-range air mail services by using two aircraft teamed together to carry out a single mission. This was a daring concept which looked bizarre. It was also a challenge to pilots, but it worked. During its brief moment of glory in the late 1930s, the Short Mayo combination established a long-distance duration record for seaplanes that will probably never be broken.

▲ *An ingenious attempt at solving the problem of establishing a high-speed transatlantic mail route, the remarkable Short Mayo Composite performed brilliantly.*

SHORT MAYO COMPOSITE

▼ Pylon support
A complicated pylon structure held the 'Mercury' securely on the S.21's back until separation.

▲ Short S.20 'Mercury'
'Mercury' was a completely new design and emerged as a sleek, four-engined floatplane with a long range.

Combining the aircraft ▶
'Mercury' is secured on top of its 'Maia' mothership. In its fully laden state, with fuel and 454 kg (1,000 lb.) of mail, the S.20 could not take off under its own power.

▼ Separation
'Mercury' was released at cruising altitude by the S.21. Although potentially dangerous, this operation never caused problems.

▲ Eight-engined take-off
A vital component of the Mayo Composite, the S.21 was based on the design of the successful 'Empire' flying-boat.

FACTS AND FIGURES

➤ With all eight engines running for take-off, the Short Mayo Composite had a total power output of 3760 kW (5,040 hp.).

➤ The normal cruising range of the loaded 'Mercury' was 6116 km (3,800 mi.).

➤ 'Mercury' was launched over Dundee, Scotland, for the record-breaking flight.

➤ On 6 February 1938 'Mercury' completed its first commercial, non-stop journey to Montreal in 20 hours 20 minutes.

➤ Changes in aerospace technology mean that the S.20's record may stand for ever.

➤ The second separation of the Mayo Composite was performed for the press.

PROFILE

Unique transatlantic mailplane

For its time it was one of the most incredible records in the history of aviation: 9652 km (5,984 mi.), from Dundee to the Orange River in South Africa.

In the 1930s, tests proved that an Imperial Airways 'Empire' flying-boat could achieve a transatlantic crossing if its entire payload only consisted of fuel, leaving no room for cargo or passengers. Since an aircraft can fly at a greater weight than at which it can take off, Robert Mayo proposed that a small, heavily loaded mailplane could be carried to operational altitude above a larger 'mother-plane' and then released to complete its long-range task.

Short designed and built a composite unit by modifying an 'Empire' flying-boat to carry the S.20 long-range twin floatplane. The system was a success, but World War II ended any further development.

'Maia' receives attention at its moorings. The S.21 flying-boat was destroyed by enemy action in May 1941, while the S.20 'Mercury' survived the war, but was later broken up.

MAYO COMPOSITE

Short Brothers built only one each of the S.20 'Mercury' (G-ADHJ) and the S.21 'Maia' (G-ADHK). Both aircraft were finished in their natural metal colour with Imperial Airways titles.

Napier Rapier H engines, each of 254 kW (340 hp.), drove two-bladed propellers to power the S.20. On the flight to South Africa a cowling broke away adding extra drag to the problems posed by headwinds.

An ingenious design, the pylon had to hold 'Mercury' securely but hinder the launch sequence as little as possible. This composite may have inspired the German Mistel projects.

'Mercury' was flown by a pilot and co-pilot, the latter also acting as the radio operator. For the record-breaking flight to South Africa the small S.20 weighed 12,474 kg (27,443 lb.).

Three-bladed propellers fitted to Bristol Pegasus radial engines drove the S.21. The lower aircraft was only required to fly the short distance for launch before it returned to base.

For the long-distance record attempt the floats were modified to hold extra fuel. Headwinds caused greater than expected fuel consumption, however.

To give the optimum water performance and to make lift-off as easy as possible, 'Maia' had a smooth two-step flying-boat hull.

S.20 'Mercury'

Type: long-range floatplane mail carrier

Powerplant: four 254-kW (340-hp.) Napier Rapier H piston engines

Maximum speed: 339 km/h (210 m.p.h.); 314 km/h (194 m.p.h.) at maximum weight

Normal range: 6116 km (3,800 mi.)

Extended range: record flight 9652 km (5,984 mi.)

Weights: empty 4614 kg (10,150 lb.); maximum 7030 kg (15,466 lb.); normal Mayo Composite launch 9443 kg (20,775 lb.); record launch 12,474 kg (26,752 lb.)

Payload: 454 kg (1,000 lb.)

Dimensions:
span 22.20 m (73 ft.)
length 15.50 m (51 ft.)
wing area 56.80m² (611 sq. ft.)

S.21 'Maia'

Type: flying-boat mother-plane for long-range upper component

Powerplant: four 686-kW (919-hp.) Bristol Pegasus XC radial piston engines

Maximum speed: 322 km/h (200 m.p.h.)

Range: 1360 km (843 mi.)

Service ceiling: 6100 m (20,000 ft.)

Weights: empty 11,234 kg (24,715 lb.); maximum take-off 17,252 kg (37,954 lb.); maximum for Mayo Composite launching 12,580 kg (27,676 lb.)

Dimensions:
span 34.70 m (114 ft.)
length 25.90 m (85 ft.)
wing area 162.50 m² (1,748 sq. ft.)

The Mayo Composite concept

1 TAKE-OFF: Too heavily loaded to lift-off under its own power, the S.20 'Mercury' was hauled aloft by the S.21 'Maia'. Immediately after launch the 'mother-plane' returned to base.

2 SEPARATION: 'Mercury', still with a large fuel reserve, was released by 'Maia' at cruising altitude.

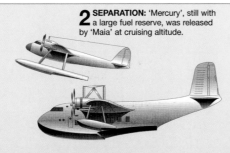

3 'MERCURY' LANDS ALONE: At the end of its long flight the S.20 landed on any suitable stretch of water. Return flights had to be made in stages since the 'mother-plane' was not available to carry 'Mercury' to altitude. This would have been a problem if the composite had entered regular service.

Record-breaking flight

DUNDEE

FLIGHT TO SOUTH AFRICA: Flying from Dundee, Scotland, to South Africa was a hazardous journey. Problems en route prevented 'Mercury' reaching its intended destination of Cape Town, and the crew were perhaps lucky to reach the Orange River unscathed.

ORANGE RIVER

SHORT

SINGAPORE

● Maritime patrol ● Long range ● Excellent safety record

Typical of flying-boats of the 1930s, the Short Singapore was a large, sturdy and functional machine with enormous potential for both civil and military use. It never lived up to its promise, however. The Singapore biplane is best known for demonstrating the ability of aircraft in its class to make marathon long-distance flights. Less well remembered is that it also achieved modest success as an armed military reconnaissance craft.

▲ The Singapore's unusual engine arrangement consisted of four Rolls-Royce Kestrels in tandem tractor-pusher pairs. This design principle was stated by Horace Short in 1911.

SHORT SINGAPORE

▲ Patrolling the Empire
With its excellent range, the Singapore Mk III was regarded as the most suitable aircraft to patrol the main trade and shipping routes of the British Empire. This example later served in Singapore.

▲ Biplane boat
The Singapore was the last biplane flying-boat to see operational service with the RAF.

▲ Scandinavian cruise
The only Singapore I first flew in 1926. It performed well on the RAF's Scandinavian cruise of 1927 and was later used by Alan Cobham on his flight around Africa.

▲ Operational trials
The first true production aircraft, K4577, underwent armament and equipment trials with the Marine Aircraft Experimental Establishment at Felixstowe.

Rochester works ▶
The Singapore II, seen on No. 3 slipway at Rochester, first flew in March 1930.

FACTS AND FIGURES

➤ Despite the Air Ministry specification calling for a three-engined design, Short's four-engined Singapore eventually won.

➤ The first production Singapore Mk III made its initial flight in March 1935.

➤ Singapore production included three prototypes and 33 service aircraft.

➤ Singapore flying-boats served with Nos 203, 205, 209, 210 and 230 Squadrons of the RAF.

➤ Nineteen Singapore aircraft remained in service at the start of World War II.

➤ The Japanese used design features from the Singapore in their own flying-boats.

Patrolling the British Empire

Even some experts have difficulty in recognising the Short Singapore flying-boat of the 1930s. But the aircraft made a mark in history in a modest way and contributed to aviation knowledge.

Short Brothers had great hopes for the Singapore prototype, but its main claim to fame was that it was used by adventurer Alan Cobham for his 37,015-km (22,950-mi.) survey flight around the African continent.

The Singapore II, which came on the scene in 1930, was also the subject of ambitious hopes that were essentially unfulfilled. The Mk III, which appeared

soon afterward, was more successful and resulted in an Air Ministry order for four developmental aircraft.

Testing led to a production order, and nearly three dozen Singapore flying-boats joined British military service in the mid-1930s. The aircraft, although representing outdated technology, combined reliability with the ability to undertake impressive long-distance patrol missions. Despite its obsolescence, Japan thought the

Singapore was a practical design which was worth copying. New Zealand purchased four ex-RAF Mk IIIs, which served faithfully on patrol missions from Fiji until April 1943.

Below: The Singapore Mk II was originally fitted with a single tailfin. This arrangement was found to be inadequate after the loss of one engine, and a triple-fin arrangement was used.

Above: The first Singapore Mk III was K3592, which flew development and acceptance trials. It later served with No. 205 Squadron at Seletar, Singapore.

SINGAPORE MK III

K4578 was coded '4' when it served with No. 203 Squadron. The squadron was based first at Aden and then Basrah before returning to Aden in 1939.

Singapore Mk III

Type: six-seat reconnaissance flying-boat

Powerplant: four 418-kW (560-hp.) Rolls-Royce Kestrel Mk VIII/IX V-12 piston engines (two tractor/two pusher)

Maximum speed: 233 km/h (145 m.p.h.)

Range: 1610 km (1,000 mi.)

Service ceiling: 4570 m (15,000 ft.)

Weights: empty 8355 kg (18,381 lb.); maximum take-off 12,474 kg (27,443 lb.)

Accommodation: crew of six, consisting of two pilots, navigator, radio operator/gunner and two gunners

Armament: three 7.7-mm (.303 cal.) Lewis machine-guns, including nose and tail guns, plus up to 908 kg (2,00 lb.) of bombs or survey equipment

Dimensions:
span	27.43 m (90 ft.)
length	23.16 m (76 ft.)
height	7.19 m (23 ft. 6 in.)
wing area	170.38 m² (1,833 sq. ft.)

The Singapore II flew with Rolls-Royce F.XII engines. The definitive Mk III was powered by four Kestrel Mk IX in-line engines.

The crew entered the aircraft via a large door on the starboard side. The original open cockpit was later enclosed by a glass 'greenhouse'.

The biplane wings created a great deal of lift. Drag was reduced by strengthening the wingroots which negated the need for extensive bracing.

The Singapore Mk III was of all-metal construction. The planing hull was so strong that it could withstand impacts of up to 9*g*.

The dorsal gun position housed a 7.7-mm (.303 cal.) Lewis gun, with 485 rounds of ammunition, mounted on a Scarff ring.

The Singapore Mk III was modified from the Singapore II by the introduction of a deeper hull which featured a pointed step.

When brought onto land via a slipway, the Singapore sat on either detachable wheels or a trolley.

The triple-fin arrangement allowed the installation of a gunner's cockpit with a 7.7-mm (.303 cal.) machine-gun in the extreme rear of the hull.

COMBAT DATA

POWER

Not surprisingly, the amount of power each aircraft produced was proportional to the number of engines. The four-engined Singapore had more than twice the power of the smaller twin-engined Scapa.

SINGAPORE Mk III 1672 kW (2,240 hp.)

SCAPA 783 kW (1,049 hp.)

RANGOON 1208 kW (1,619 hp.)

ARMAMENT

Typical defensive armament for British flying-boats of the period was three 7.7-mm (.303 cal.) Lewis guns usually mounted on Scarff rings. The larger Singapore could carry the greatest bombload.

SINGAPORE Mk III — 3 x 7.7-mm (.303 cal.) machine-guns 908-kg (2,000-lb.) bombload

SCAPA — 3 x 7.7-mm (.303 cal.) machine-guns 454-kg (1,000-lb.) bombload

RANGOON — 3 x 7.7-mm (.303 cal.) machine-guns 454-kg (1,000-lb.) bombload

RANGE

Long range is vital for a maritime patrol craft. The Singapore and Scapa both had impressive range and endurance, enabling them to cover large expanses of ocean. The Rangoon had shorter reach and tended to patrol smaller stretches of water such as the North Sea.

SINGAPORE Mk III 1610 km (1,000 mi.)

SCAPA 1770 km (1,100 mi.)

RANGOON 1046 km (650 mi.)

Short biplane flying-boats

■ N.3 CROMARTY: The Cromarty was the first flying-boat of Short Brothers' design and took to the air in April 1921. Only one example was built and it was scrapped in 1922.

■ CALCUTTA: Designed primarily for long-distance Empire sea routes flown by Imperial Airways, this three-engined flying-boat had accommodation for 15 passengers.

■ RANGOON: This was a naval reconnaissance version of the Calcutta. Six were built for the RAF and entered service in 1931. Defensive armament consisted of three machine-guns.

■ SARAFAND: With a similar engine layout to the Singapore, but having three instead of two tractor/pusher combinations, the single Sarafand was said to have been trouble-free and viceless.

SHORT
S.23 C-CLASS

● Flying-boat ● Trans-oceanic travel ● Mail service

The Short S.23 C-Class was a major technical advance in flying-boat design. It offered the latest features of the time – all metal structure, electrical flaps, variable-pitch propellers, a sleeping cabin, a promenade lounge and a steward's pantry. The S.23 entered service in 1937 and graced the skies for Imperial Airways and Qantas Empire Airways, among others. A trip in this aircraft was a memorable experience for any air traveller.

▲ 'Coriolanus' was beached for the last time in 1948, having flown over 4 million kilometres (2.5 million miles). Short's C-Classes were the last commercially successful flying-boats to fly in the British Empire.

SHORT S.23 C-CLASS

▲ **Setting out**
The C-Class flew as far afield as Cape Town, Egypt and Karachi, in addition to the European routes. Most of the cargo was mail, but passengers were also carried.

▲ **Lifted ashore**
Before the slipway was built at Queen's Island, 'Clio' had to be hoisted clear of the water by crane. When the slipway was completed, 'Clio' (renamed AX639 in RAF colours) was the first flying-boat to use it.

▲ **Rest and refit**
'Canopus' deserved its overhauls, having made many flights to Rome with British Imperial Airways.

▲ **Wartime colours**
Several C-Class aircraft were used as long-range transports in the war; some were lost in action.

Long service ▶
Travelling across the Empire built up huge numbers of flying hours, and 'Cameronian' flew 15,652 before it was scrapped.

FACTS AND FIGURES

➤ A Qantas S.23 flew the first commercial service between Australia and Southampton on 5 July 1938.

➤ First flight of an S.23 C-Class boat (Canopus) took place in July 1936.

➤ The Short S.23 was 26 km/h faster than the standard RAF fighter of its era.

➤ Among several S.23s impressed into RAF service, two became anti-submarine patrol aircraft.

➤ Together, the S.23, S.30 and S.33 were called Empire flying-boats.

➤ Thirteen of the Empire flying-boats were still airworthy at the end of World War II.

PROFILE

Flying ocean liners

When this magnificent flying-boat first appeared, it looked so promising that 28 were ordered before the first had even flown. The first boats in service operated from the new Imperial Airways flying-boat base at Hythe, Kent, where they provided air services to Australia, Bermuda, Egypt, Malaya, the United States and East and South Africa. The S.23 did not quite have the range for the transatlantic route, but its

inadequacies led to early tests with flight refuelling. Short also developed the later S.30 and S.33 for longer flights. Thirty-one of Short's 42 Empire flying-boats were the S.23 C-Class (along with nine S.30s and two S.33s), which soon spread its wings far and wide. Australia at first resisted introducing flying-boats on its air routes, but by the late-1930s the S.23, then considered the most advanced aircraft of this type in the world, was performing well 'down under'. British Overseas

Airways Corporation (BOAC) used the S.23 for heavy-duty wartime service, hauling people over long distances, and some were modified for patrol work.

Above: G-AFCZ, known as 'Clare', was lost in unknown circumstances after leaving Lagos, Nigeria, in 1942 while serving with BOAC.

Above: The first of the Empire boats, G-ADHL was later known as 'Canopus'. It was used for surveying the North Atlantic route and had extra long-range fuel tanks fitted.

S.23 C-Class

Type: mail/passenger flying-boat airliner

Powerplant: four 686-kW (920-hp.) Bristol Pegasus XC radial piston engines

Maximum speed: 322 km/h (200 m.p.h.)

Range: 1223 km (760 mi.)

Service ceiling: 6095 m (20,000 ft.)

Weights: empty 10,659 kg (23,500 lb.); normal loaded 17,655 kg (38,923 lb.); maximum take-off 19,732 kg (43,500 lb.)

Accommodation: two pilots, flight engineer, staff, and provision for up to 24 passengers or 3556 kg (7,840 lb.) of freight; later, the aircraft carried 17 passengers and 2000 kg (4,400 lb.) of mail

Dimensions: span   34.75 m (114 ft.)
length   26.82 m (88 ft.)
height   9.70 m (31 ft. 10 in.)
wing area 139.35 m² (1,506 sq. ft.)

S.23 C-CLASS

G-AETY, known as 'Clio', flew mail from Southampton to Alexandria before being pressed into service as AX659 in 1940, after being modified for coastal reconnaissance with ASV radar by Short at Belfast.

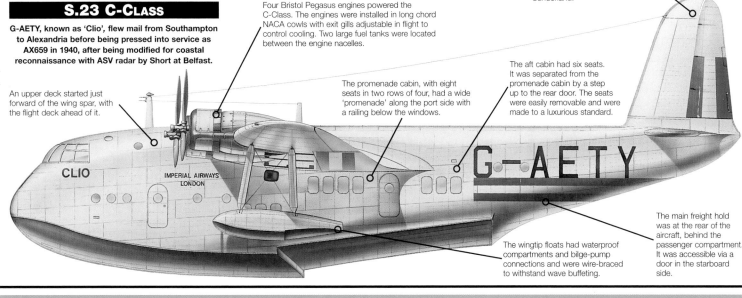

An upper deck started just forward of the wing spar, with the flight deck ahead of it.

Four Bristol Pegasus engines powered the C-Class. The engines were installed in long chord NACA cowls with exit gills adjustable in flight to control cooling. Two large fuel tanks were located between the engine nacelles.

The promenade cabin, with eight seats in two rows of four, had a wide 'promenade' along the port side with a railing below the windows.

The aft cabin had six seats. It was separated from the promenade cabin by a step up to the rear door. The seats were easily removable and were made to a luxurious standard.

The distinctive tall tail of the C-Class was a feature that remained on later Shorts designs such as the wartime Sunderland.

The main freight hold was at the rear of the aircraft, behind the passenger compartment. It was accessible via a door in the starboard side.

The wingtip floats had waterproof compartments and bilge-pump connections and were wire-braced to withstand wave buffeting.

CLIO

IMPERIAL AIRWAYS LONDON

G-AETY

ACTION DATA

MAXIMUM SPEED

The requirement to land on water governed aerodynamics far more than the need for speed, which passengers did not expect in the 1930s. The powerful engines and streamlined fuselage gave the C-Class a respectable speed advantage over its rivals, and allowed it to compete with many land-based designs. On long routes to the Far East, travelling time was measured in days rather than hours, but the mail service was still far faster than in the days of shipping.

S.23 C-CLASS	322 km/h (200 m.p.h.)
Do R4 'WAL'	210 km/h (130 m.p.h.)
S-42	233 km/h (145 m.p.h.)

RANGE

C-Class flying-boats were relatively short ranged compared to their rivals, one reason being that the routes they flew to their destinations had a large number of refuelling stations in the British Empire. The Dornier flew to South America with fewer stops.

S.23 C-CLASS	1223 km (760 mi.)
Do R4 'WAL'	2000 km (1,243 mi.)
S-42	4000 km (2,485 mi.)

PASSENGER LOAD

Large flying-boats like the C-Class had impressive passenger facilities for their day. During the war years, the luxury passenger facilities of the inter-war period were dispensed with, giving the aircraft the ability to carry as many as 10 more passengers than the contemporary Dornier R4 'Wal'. The Sikorsky was a smaller aircraft carrying fewer passengers but had longer range.

S.23 C-CLASS 24 passengers

Do R4 'WAL' 19 passengers

S-42 12 passengers

Short's floating flyers

■ **1914 S.80:** Flown up the Nile as far as Khartoum in 1914, the S.80's first flight had taken place the previous year. It was able to carry up to four passengers thanks to its Gnome engine.

■ **1929 VALETTA:** Carrying 17 passengers in comfort, the twin-float Valetta was an advanced design, the largest floatplane of its day. It was later converted to a landplane.

■ **1931 KENT:** An enlarged version of the Short Calcutta, three Kents were built for Imperial Airways. Seating 15 passengers in comfort, the Kents also carried mail cargo.

■ **1934 SINGAPORE III:** These improved Singapores were used on civil routes to the Far East and also served with the RAF, replacing Short Southamptons.

SHORT

SUNDERLAND

● Maritime patrol ● Anti-submarine ● Long-range flying-boat

Derived from the pre-war Empire flying-boat, the Sunderland became a legend in World War II as the main patrol flying-boat of British Commonwealth forces. It was tough and reliable, performing just about any maritime task including U-boat hunting, air-sea rescue and transport. Adversaries found the Sunderland a prickly customer and nicknamed it 'The Flying Porcupine'. The Sunderland was the only RAF aircraft to serve in the Korean War.

▲ The rugged Sunderland was one of the finest flying-boats of the war. Its vital role in fighting the U-boat blockade around Britain made it one of the most important weapons in the RAF's arsenal.

SHORT SUNDERLAND

▲ Maritime heritage
Short Brothers' expertise in flying-boat design was perfected with 'Empire'-type boats before the war. The Sunderland first flew in October 1937, and the type was operational by 1938.

▼ Run ashore
The Sunderland, as a flying-boat, had no undercarriage. Repair work on land meant that it had to be beached on a landing trolley and fitted on chocks.

▲ Coastal patrol
Sunderlands operated from some of the most remote areas in Europe and Asia. The crew had the comfort of knowing that they could always land on the sea if the engines failed.

▲ In the hull
The huge interior allowed space for weapon and flare stowage, crew rest areas, a galley, radio and radar, and plenty of fuel.

◄ On the slipway
The addition of radar to the Sunderland Mk II was a key turning point in the war against the U-boats, giving Royal Air Force Coastal Command the ability to hunt by day or by night. This new Mk II was the first built by Shorts in Belfast. The four radar aerials are visible along the aircraft's spine.

▲ Depth-charged
This attack in the Bay of Biscay in 1943 sent a U-boat to the bottom. Radar-equipped Sunderlands forced U-boats to cross the bay submerged.

FACTS AND FIGURES

➤ The prototype Sunderland made its maiden flight from the River Medway on 16 October 1937.

➤ One Sunderland won a battle with eight Ju 88 fighters, shooting down two.

➤ The Sunderland was the first flying-boat to have power-operated gun turrets.

➤ Shorts produced 721 Sunderlands between 1937 and 1945, and 17 Royal Air Force squadrons flew them.

➤ Sunderlands delivered 4,955 tonnes (4,877 tons) of supplies during the Berlin Airlift.

➤ France was the last country to fly military Sunderlands, retiring them in 1960.

PROFILE

The flying porcupine

When the Short Sunderland entered service in 1938, this big seaplane gave the RAF the endurance for gruelling 20-hour patrols. During the war Sunderlands undertook many dangerous missions, including evacuating Crete by making trips with up to 82 armed passengers plus a 10-man crew. As the war progressed, improved Sunderlands introduced search radar with huge antennas atop

the rear fuselage; no other aircraft was more capable at stalking and attacking U-boats.

The Sunderland carried bombs and depth charges internally, then cranked them out on underwing pylons when preparing to attack. Its gunners could rake the deck of an enemy submarine, preventing its crew from manning their own weapons.

Some Sunderlands became stripped, high-speed transports for British Overseas Airways

Corporation. During the 1948 Berlin Airlift Sunderlands lifted almost five million kilograms of freight flying hazardous mercy missions.

The final Sunderland introduced Pratt & Whitney R-1890-90B Twin Wasp engines to replace the reliable but somewhat underpowered Pegasus. This impressive aircraft remained the standard RAF ocean flying-boat until its retirement in 1959.

Sunderland Mk III

Type: long-range reconnaissance and anti-submarine flying-boat

Powerplant: four 794-kW (1,064-hp.) Bristol Pegasus XVIII nine-cylinder radial piston engines

Maximum speed: 341 km/h (211 m.p.h.)

Range: 4828 km (2,993 mi.)

Service ceiling: 5300 m (17,930 ft.)

Weights: empty 15,663 kg (34,459 lb.); loaded 26,308 kg (57,878 lb.)

Armament: eight 7.7-mm (.303 cal.) Browning machine-guns in nose, dorsal and quad tail turrets; some fitted with four fixed forward-firing 7.7-mm and twin 12.7-mm (.50 cal.) Brownings in waist; 2250 kg (4,950 lb.) of bombs, depth charges, mines or pyrotechnics

Dimensions:
span	34.38 m (113 ft.)
length	26.01 m (85 ft.)
height	9.79 m (32 ft.)
wing area	138.14 m² (1,486 sq. ft.)

On land, the Sunderland looked clumsy and heavy. But its performance in the air surprised many enemy pilots, who learned to treat this aircraft with respect.

SUNDERLAND MK III

This Sunderland Mk III is seen in the markings of No. 228 Squadron RAF during its deployment to the Mediterranean in 1940 and 1941.

The powered Frazer-Nash nose turret mounted two 7.7-mm (.303 cal.) machine-guns. It could be retracted into the nose.

Most Sunderlands were powered by Bristol Pegasus nine-cylinder radial engines, replaced in the final variant by more powerful Pratt & Whitney R-1890 14-cylinder radials.

The mid-upper turret replaced the single hand-held guns fired from beam windows of the Mk I.

The aft section of the fuselage contained the crew's quarters, bomb stowage and galley area.

The aerials of the ASV Mk II surface-search radar were mounted on the upper fuselage.

The fin and tailplane were metal-framed and skinned, with fabric-covered control surfaces.

The rear gunner's turret mounted four 7.7-mm (.303 cal.) machine-guns. Unlike tail gunners in other aircraft, he had easy access to the main hull.

NJ188

Royal Air Force flying-boats of the 1930s

■ **SHORT SINGAPORE Mk III:** Developed from the Singapore Mk I of 1926, the Singapore Mk III patrol boat served from 1935 to 1941. With a speed of 230 km/h (143 m.p.h.), it could carry a ton of bombs over a range of 1600 km (1,992 mi.).

■ **SUPERMARINE STRANRAER:** The last of Supermarine's classic series of biplane flying-boats, the twin-engined Stranraer was operational from December 1936 to 1940. Smaller than the Singapore, it had a 454-kg (1,000-lb.) bombload.

■ **SARO LONDON:** Ordered to a 1931 maritime reconnaissance requirement, the London was Britain's last front-line biplane, serving in home waters and the Mediterranean until late 1941. It had a range of 2800 km (1,736 mi.).

COMBAT DATA

ENDURANCE

Although it served all over the world, the Sunderland's main area of operations was the Atlantic, where it partnered the American-built Catalina and where its great German rival was the Focke-Wulf Fw 200 Condor. All three aircraft were well suited to maritime patrol, where the prime performance requirement was to be able to monitor large areas of ocean for extremely long periods of time.

SUNDERLAND 20 hours
CONDOR 14 hours
CATALINA 21.5 hours

SIKORSKY

ILYA MUROMETS

● Heavy bomber ● Record-breaker ● Numerous variants

Igor Ivanovitch Sikorsky was born in Kiev in 1889 and became one of Russia's most famous aircraft designers of the pre-revolution era. In 1909, he experimented with unsuccessful rotary-wing aircraft. By 1910, he had developed his first fixed-wing aircraft and the success of these early types led to his appointment as chief engineer of the Russo-Baltic Wagon Works (RBVZ). By 1913, he had developed the Ilya Muromets series of bombers which saw service in World War I.

▲ One of the most innovative designers of all time, Sikorsky developed combat aircraft for Russia before emigrating to the USA and designing flying-boats and helicopters.

PHOTO FILE

SIKORSKY ILYA MUROMETS

▼ Great War bomber
The size of the Ilya Muromets allowed it to carry a large bombload. Igor Sikorsky is seen standing next to the man with the clipboard.

▲ Ahead of their time
In their day, the Ilya Muromets were very advanced aircraft and demonstrated some features that would become a hallmark of later heavy bombers.

◀ Piggy-back ride
The first Ilya Muromets is seen here on its maiden flight carrying two brave passengers on its fuselage. A similar escapade five days earlier ended in near disaster because of poor lift from the wings.

▼ Extra endurance
To increase the aircraft's range, two fuel tanks were fitted above the top wing on this variant.

▲ Multiple versions
The Ilya Muromets was produced in more than 25 versions. This one features a fully-glazed nose, improving visibility.

FACTS AND FIGURES

➤ On 12 February 1914, the aircraft broke the world height-with-payload record, carrying 16 people to 2000 m (6,560 ft.).

➤ The Russkii Vityaz recorded 53 flights before being damaged on the ground.

➤ The Ilya Muromets was the first aircraft with an enclosed cabin, nose to tail.

➤ After the 1917 revolution, Sikorsky fled to the USA where he suffered great hardship until he formed a new company in 1924.

➤ The type's first combat mission was flown on 15 February 1915.

➤ In September 1916, an Ilya Muromets shot down three German fighters on one sortie.

PROFILE

First of the giant Soviet bombers

Above: The Ilya Muromets was flown with wheels and skis in 1913. In the spring of 1914, the aircraft was evaluated as a floatplane.

When RBVZ took on young designer Igor Sikorsky, he had already designed a number of experimental types (S-1 to S-6A), achieving his first flight in the S-3 biplane in November 1910.

Once the RBVZ had formed an aircraft division, Sikorsky became instrumental in shaping its new designs. After designing a number of moderately successful types, many of which he flew himself, Sikorsky began work on a large strategic reconnaissance biplane named the *Russkii Vityaz* (Russian

Knight). Also known as 'Le Grand', this twin-engined machine was the largest aircraft in the world when it first flew on 15 March 1913. In May of that year the aircraft was fitted with two additional engines to become the first four-engined aircraft to fly.

This remarkable aircraft formed the basis of the Ilya Muromets series of heavy bombers which were used by the Imperial Russian army during World War I. Bristling with guns, 80 of these aircraft were produced in dozens of

different variants including floatplane and ski-equipped versions.

Named after a legendary hero from Kiev, only two Ilya Muromets were shot down during the war and a number of the surviving craft went on to serve into the 1920s as Bolshevik trainers and transports.

Above: First flown by Sikorsky in March 1913, the Russkii Vityaz was originally named Bolshoi Baltiiskii. The aircraft was fitted with a sofa, table and toilet.

Ilya Muromets E2

Type: four-engined biplane heavy bomber

Powerplant: four 164-kW (220-hp.) Renault piston engines

Maximum speed: 137 km/h (85 m.p.h.)

Take-off run: 450 m (1,475 ft.)

Range: 560 km (348 mi.)

Service ceiling: 3200 m (10,500 ft.)

Weights: empty 5000 kg (11,000 lb.); loaded 7460 kg (16,450 lb.)

Armament: up to six machine-guns of various makes including Maxim, Lewis, Madsen and Browning

Dimensions: span 34.50 m (113 ft. 2 in.)
length 18.80 m (61 ft. 8 in.)
wing area 220 m² (2,368 sq. ft.)

An identifying feature of the Ilya Muromets was an extremely snub nose and extensive cockpit glazing which wrapped around the sides.

Most of the rear fuselage consisted of four main spars, two on the top and two along the bottom. Connecting them were a series of diagonally-mounted spars which increased the strength of the airframe and reduced flexing. Fabric covered most of the skeletal frame.

In an effort to generate as much lift as possible, the IM-V featured a huge tailplane, which was greater in chord than the main wing. It was a complex design and featured extensive bracing. Mounted just forward of the tail unit was an enormous tail skid.

To cope with the rough state of Soviet airfields at the time, the IM-V was fitted with wheels and skis. Dual tyres were necessary for effective weight distribution.

Powerplants differed, depending on the variant. The Type V, featured four in-line liquid-cooled Sunbeam engines, each producing up to 167 kW (224 hp.). Others could be fitted with Salmson radials or the powerful Renault V-12 in-line engines.

Production of these giant aircraft eventually totalled 80. They were originally built as reconnaissance aircraft, but were later converted for other roles. A large bombload could be carried, but because of the size and shape of the fuselage, only small bombs could be accommodated.

This particular aircraft, actually an IM-V variant, is typical of the Ilya Muromets in use as long-range bombers. By 1918, they were becoming obsolete and were soon withdrawn from front-line service.

ACTION DATA

MAXIMUM SPEED

Compared to other heavy bombers of the period, the Ilya Muromets were blessed with surprising performance, although this depended on the type of engines fitted. The IM-V, with its four Sunbeam engines, could fly at speeds of up to 137 km/h (85 m.p.h.).

ILYA MUROMETS-V	137 km/h (85 m.p.h.)
0/100	122 km/h (76 m.p.h.)
R.IV	125 km/h (78 m.p.h.)

WINGSPAN

Although it had a wing which spanned a gigantic (for the time) 34.5 m (113 ft. 2 in.), the Ilya Muromets were not the longest-spanned aircraft of the World War I era, the R.IV featuring a much larger wing.

ILYA MUROMETS-V	34.50 m (113 ft. 2 in.)
0/100	30.50 m (100 ft.)
R.IV	42.20 m (138 ft. 5 in.)

ARMAMENT

Both the Ilya Muromets and the R.IV could be heavily armed, with machine-guns, making them difficult to shoot down. One of the Soviet machines actually managed to shoot down three German fighters. The Handley Page 0/100 had only light armament.

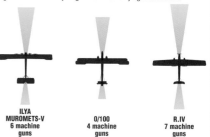

ILYA MUROMETS-V 6 machine guns	0/100 4 machine guns	R.IV 7 machine guns

Sikorsky's early designs

■ **S-1:** Sikorsky's first attempts at building flying machines were the S-1 and S-2 co-axial helicopters. On its first attempt to fly, the S-1 lifted but toppled over. The S-2 never managed to leave the ground. After these two unsuccessful attempts Sikorsky turned to fixed-wing aircraft. In the 1940s he returned to work on helicopters and produced some of the world's greatest designs.

■ **S-3:** Sikorsky's first fixed-wing design was the S-3. In November 1910 he completed a number of short flights.

■ **S-29A:** After his emigration to the US, Sikorsky's first design was the S-29A. This twin-engined transport first flew in May 1924.

SOPWITH

PUP

● RFC fighter ● Home defence ● Synchronised machine-gun

▲ Pilots appreciated the handling and synchronised armament of the Pup, which allowed them to gain an advantage over contemporary German fighters and two-seat C-type scouts.

J ust as the Hurricane has been overshadowed by the Spitfire, so the Pup has been pushed into second place by its illustrious successor, the Camel. Sopwith's Pup was a fine fighting scout, however, and it revolutionised Royal Flying Corps (RFC) tactics by introducing machine-gun armament synchronised to fire through the propeller disc. Principally a naval aircraft, the Pup equipped three squadrons of the RFC in France.

SOPWITH PUP

◄ Pup preservation
Many veteran and vintage aircraft are flown by The Shuttleworth Collection in the UK, including this original Pup.

Post-war prototype ▶
Photographed in 1925, the Pup prototype survived World War I. The Dove, a two-seat civil version of the Pup, sold badly.

▼ Lightweight elegance
Despite its low power, the Pup offered good performance and manoeuvrability. This was largely because of its lightweight but strong internal structure.

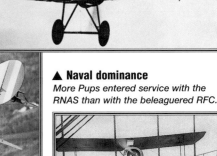

▲ Naval dominance
More Pups entered service with the RNAS than with the beleaguered RFC.

Shipboard modifications ▶
Several Pups suffered failures of their narrow wheels, leading to replacement with skids on some ship-based aircraft.

FACTS AND FIGURES

➤ Most Pups were built by one of three companies: Whitehead Aircraft, William Beardmore or Standard Motors.

➤ On its 9 February 1916 first flight, the Pup was piloted by Harry Hawker.

➤ No. 54 Squadron, the first RFC Pup unit, arrived in France on 24 December 1916.

➤ In the home defence role, the Pup was used to intercept Gotha G IV bombers attacking southeast England.

➤ Some home defence Pups received 74.6-kW (100-hp.) Gnome Monosoupape engines.

➤ Pup production reached a total of 1770 airframes from all sources.

PROFILE

Turning the German tide

Appearing here during the late 1990s as N6181, the Shuttleworth Collection's Pup is a regular air show performer.

At the close of 1915, Germany's fighting scouts were more than a match for any Allied aircraft. In recognition of the enemy's superiority, design of the Pup was initiated.

T.O.M. Sopwith's new fighter was officially known as the Scout, but its similarity to a scaled-down version of the same company's 1½ Strutter led to the aircraft being nicknamed 'Pup'. The type's major innovation was its employment of Sopwith-Kauper synchronising equipment. This enabled the pilot to aim the whole aircraft at an enemy machine, greatly simplifying combat and allowing the Pup to gain ascendancy over its German rivals. While other Allied types were easy prey, Pups were strenuously avoided.

Since Sopwith was committed to production of the 1½ Strutter, Pup production was handled by three sub-contractors, with first deliveries to the Royal Naval Air Service (RNAS) occurring in September 1916. Pups were slow to reach the RFC, in spite of mounting losses, since Sopwith was traditionally an RNAS supplier and the government was unwilling to divert its designs to the RFC. Hence, only three squadrons of RFC Pups fought in France, with others serving at home. Perhaps if more had been delivered, the return to ascendancy of the German scouts early in 1917 would have been avoided.

While its synchronised machine-gun initially represented a major advance, the Pup was soon to find itself too lightly armed. The Camel rectified this with its twin-gun armament.

Metal sheeting covered the forward part of the fuselage aft of the engine. The neat fairing was also of metal and closely faired the Le Rhône engine. All aircraft employed a twin-bladed wooden propeller.

Using conventional wood and fabric construction, Sopwith gave the Pup an unusually strong structure. This helped it perform tight manoeuvres, while its light weight allowed reasonable performance with little power. The split axle main undercarriage was of a type used widely by Sopwith.

During missions of up to three hours duration, the pilot was given minimum protection by the Pup's cockpit. Pilots found the aircraft easy to fly and highly effective in combat, however.

In common with the majority of World War I combat aircraft, the Pup employed a simple tail skid. This was easier to maintain than a tail wheel and kept weight to a minimum.

A635

PUP

This brightly marked aircraft was on the strength of No. 46 Squadron, RFC during 1917. The machine was based at Izel-le-Hameau, France, and typifies the finish of the few that reached the RFC.

Pup

Type: single-seat fighter

Powerplant: one 60-kW (80-hp.) Le Rhône rotary piston engine

Maximum speed: 180 km/h (112 m.p.h.) at sea level

Climb rate: climb to 4907 m (16,100 ft.) in 35 min

Service ceiling: 5335 m (17,500 ft.)

Weights: empty 357 kg (785 lb.); maximum take-off 556 kg (1,223 lb.)

Armament: one fixed forward-firing, synchronised 7.7-mm (.303 cal.) Vickers machine-gun and up to four 11.3-kg (25-lb.) Cooper bombs

Dimensions:
span	8.08 m	(26 ft. 6 in.)
length	6.04 m	(19 ft. 10 in.)
height	2.87 m	(9 ft. 5 in.)
wing area	23.60 m²	(254 sq. ft.)

COMBAT DATA

MAXIMUM SPEED

At sea level the Pup could not match the excellent speed of the SPAD S.VII. It was far more agile, however, and had a great advantage in speed over the Halberstadt D.II which was a close German contemporary of the Sopwith type.

SPAD S.VII	192 km/h (119 m.p.h.)
PUP	180 km/h (112 m.p.h.)
D.II	145 km/h (90 m.p.h.)

SERVICE CEILING

Although it suffered from an inferior service ceiling, the Pup more than compensated with its impressive agility. Attacking from altitude usually gives an advantage in combat, but German aircraft were very wary of the Pup at all heights.

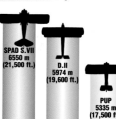

SPAD S.VII 6550 m (21,500 ft.)
D.II 5974 m (19,600 ft.)
PUP 5335 m (17,500 ft.)

ARMAMENT

Utilising its limited bomb capacity, the Pup was able to take on a secondary ground-attack role. This made it a more versatile aircraft than either the SPAD or D.II. With its synchronised machine-gun, the Pup was a formidable fighter.

SPAD S.VII — 1 x 7.7-mm (.303 cal.) machine-gun

PUP — 1 x 7.7-mm (.303 cal.) machine-gun / 4 x 11-kg (25-lb.) bombs

D.II — 1 x 7.92-mm machine-gun

Fighting Scouts of late 1916

■ **ALBATROS D.I:** Having done much to assert the superiority of German aircraft, the D.I was a serious adversary for the Pup.

■ **HALBERSTADT D.II:** By late 1916, the D.II was becoming obsolete and was no match for the Sopwith Pup.

■ **NIEUPORT 17:** Originally fitted with a single machine-gun firing above the propeller, the Type 17 was the mount of many Allied aces.

■ **SPAD S.VII:** A powerful engine and streamlined airframe guaranteed the success of the S.VII from its appearance in late 1916.

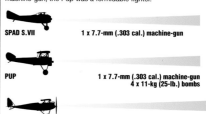

SOPWITH

PUP NAVAL FIGHTER

● Carrier fighter ● Scout ● Navy pioneer

Naval aviation began when a handful of adventurers went to sea in the wood and fabric Sopwith Pup, perfecting the technique of operating from ships' decks. Techniques for launch included take-off from platforms mounted on top of battleship gun turrets, and the first experiments were also made with deck landings. Although these were a success, leading to the first real aircraft-carrier, early naval pilots often paid the ultimate price for their daring challenges.

▲ The pioneers of naval flight were brave and enthusiastic men, who took considerable risks to prove the concept of launching from ships. The value of carrier-launched aircraft was not realised at the time, but the future of naval warfare was to be totally changed by it.

SOPWITH PUP

▲ Splash down
Before aircraft began landing on the decks of ships pilots had no choice but to ditch, which was extremely dangerous.

Platform launch ▶
Trials were carried out with launching platforms on cruisers, but turbulence from the ship's funnel was a major problem.

▲ Over the edge
The pilot was killed when this Pup ran off the edge of the deck during a trials flight. The crew dashed after the aircraft in an attempt to catch it.

▼ Pup in America
The US Navy took a keen interest in ship-launced aircraft. This aircraft was flown in Guantanamo Bay in Cuba from the USS Ohio. The launch was made from the ship's 355-mm (14-in.) gun turret.

▲ 1¹/₂ Strutter
This Sopwith 1¹/₂ Strutter was launched from a cruiser using launch rails on the bow. The skid undercarriage was a new feature.

FACTS AND FIGURES

➤ By the end of World War I ten Pups were flying from aircraft-carriers and 13 from battleships and cruisers.

➤ About 1770 Pups were manufactured, many for home defence of Great Britain.

➤ A two-seat civil version of the Pup, the Sopwith Dove, was unsuccessful.

➤ On 28 June 1917 Flt Cdr Rutland flew a Pup from a 5.95-m (19-ft. 6-in.) platform protruding from the light cruiser Yarmouth.

➤ Flying a Pup from the Yarmouth, Flt Sub. Lt B. A. Smart shot down the Zeppelin L-23.

➤ The Pup was known officially as the Sopwith Scout.

PROFILE

First of the carrier fighters

Although it looked strange, launching from gun turrets was actually quite useful because the aircraft could take off into wind regardless of the ship's course.

One of the most exciting areas of aviation involved the Sopwith Pup – the first aircraft ever to land on a ship at sea. It happened on 2 August 1917 when Squadron Commander E. H. Dunning matched the speed and path of his aircraft with that of the steaming aircraft-carrier *Furious*, and touched down on the ship.

Thus the Royal Naval Air Service (RNAS) began pioneering the operation of aircraft from vessels on the ocean.

The Sopwith Pup was ideal for this challenging effort. An elegant little biplane with wings of equal span, the Pup entered service with Britain's flying corps and navy in 1916. The Pup is remembered today as a true gem of a fighter aircraft,

almost totally devoid of faults and effective with its forward-firing, synchronised machine-gun. At the time of its introduction, the Pup was able to remain manoeuvrable and responsive at a greater height than any other fighter.

Flying at sea was hazardous, and the trials killed many men. Naval aviators were as much an elite then as today.

Pups used a 60-kW (80-hp.) Le Rhône rotary engine, a relatively low-powered engine even by the standards of 1916.

In common with aircraft of the period, the Pup was largely of wooden construction and fabric covered.

As the first naval Pups were required to ditch in the sea after a sortie, flotation bags were fitted under the wings to aid recovery of the aircraft.

PUP

This Royal Flying Corps (RFC) Pup is one of a batch of 350 delivered during 1917/18. About 290 Pups served with the RNAS, including a number diverted from RFC contracts.

Squadron Commander Dunning's third attempt to land an aircraft on the forward flight deck of a ship resulted in his death.

One of the advantages of the fabric-covered fuselage was that damage from hostile machine-gun fire was easily and quickly repaired.

Its low wing loading meant the Pup could hold its height better than any Allied or enemy aircraft of the period and was still manoeuvrable at altitudes of around 4500 m (14,760 ft).

Certain standard British markings of the period were common to RFC and RNAS aircraft, namely the fuselage roundel and striped rudder. Naval aircraft tended to carry their serial number on the fuselage, however, under the leading edge of the tailplane.

Skid undercarriages were fitted to early naval Pups. A system of fore-and-aft wires on the ship's deck engaged 'dog-lead' clips on the Pup's undercarriage to stop the aircraft.

While RFC Pups used a synchronised Vickers machine-gun firing through the propeller, those flying from ships had a single Lewis machine-gun firing upwards and eight strut-mounted Le Prieur rockets.

Pup

Type: single-seat fighter

Powerplant: one 60-kW (80-hp.) Le Rhône rotary engine or one 75-kW (100-hp.) Gnome Monosoupape rotary engine

Maximum speed: 180 km/h (112 m.p.h.)

Service ceiling: 5335 m (17,500 ft.)

Endurance: 3 hours

Weights: empty 357 kg (785 lb.); maximum take-off 556 kg (1,223 lb.)

Armament: one forward-firing synchronised 7.7-mm (.303 cal.) Vickers machine-gun, plus up to four 11.3-kg (25-lb.) bombs

Dimensions:
span	8.08 m	(26 ft. 6 in.)
length	6.04 m	(19 ft. 10 in.)
height	2.87 m	(9 ft. 5 in.)
wing area	23.60 m²	(254 sq. ft.)

COMBAT DATA

MAXIMUM SPEED

Compared to other scout aircraft of the period the Pup had a slight edge in top speed and therefore climb rate. This and the ability to maintain height were important in dogfight situations.

PUP	180 km/h (112 m.p.h.)
ALBATROS D.III	165 km/h (103 m.p.h.)
NIEUPORT 17	170 km/h (105 m.p.h.)

ARMAMENT

The German Albatros family was well-armed. Later Allied aircraft had better armament – usually two machine-guns. Naval Pups could also carry rockets for attacking Zeppelins.

PUP	1 x 7.7-mm (.303 cal.) machine-gun
ALBATROS D.III	2 x 7.92-mm machine-guns
NIEUPORT 17	1 x 7.7-mm (.303 cal.) machine-gun

SERVICE CEILING

All three types had comparable service ceilings, although the important factor was not how high the aircraft could fly but how the aircraft performed at altitude. The Pup was acknowledged as having good handling above 4500 m (14,760 ft.) due to low wing loading.

PUP 5335 m (17,500 ft.)	**ALBATROS D.III** 5486 m (18,000 ft.)	**NIEUPORT 17** 5350 m (17,550 ft.)

Sopwith naval aircraft of World War I

■ **TABLOID:** One of the outstanding aircraft produced before 1914, the land-based Tabloid entered naval service that year and was used by the RNAS to bomb Zeppelin sheds in 1914.

■ **TYPE 860 SEAPLANE:** One of a family of large single-engined seaplanes built for the RNAS, the torpedo-armed Type 860 patrolled home waters during 1915 and 1916.

■ **BABY:** Delivered between 1915 and 1916, Babies operated from seaplane-carriers in the North Sea and Mediterranean. Bombing raids were carried out using two 30-kg bombs.

■ **CUCKOO:** The first landplane torpedo-carrier able to operate from a flight deck, the Cuckoo entered service aboard the *Argus* just before the Armistice and was too late to see action.

SOPWITH

CAMEL

● Fighter scout ● Close support fighter ● Flown by aces

I t was a wicked, snub-nosed killer. The Sopwith Camel gave Britain a fighter capable of defeating any adversary in the 'Kaiser's War'. But the Camel was not for the faint-hearted, and was mastered only with the most superb flying skills. The Camel's bad habits were also its strength: because propeller, engine and armament were concentrated up front, the Camel was difficult to fly but was also incredibly manoeuvrable in a dogfight.

▲ The Camel at last
gave Allied fighter pilots an aircraft that could take on the German Albatros and Fokker scouts, and did much to restore morale.

SOPWITH CAMEL

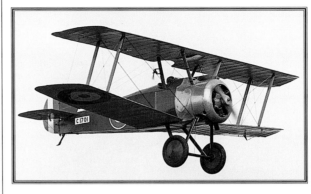

▲ Deck launch
The Camel was used in carrier trials by HMS Pegasus in November 1919. The sailors watching from the lower deck obviously doubted whether the experiment would work.

▲ Supreme dogfighter
Combining a good climb rate with twin-gun firepower and immense agility, the Camel helped restore Allied fortunes in the sky after the disastrous defeats of April 1917.

Airborne take-off ▶
This Camel was dropped from the airship R.23 as part of a bizarre experiment to give airships defence against enemy fighters.

▲ Camel replica
Although 5490 Camels were completed in the last two years of World War I, none have survived in flying condition. The only Camels to be seen in the air today are replicas.

◀ Down in no-man's land
This Camel crashed between the Canadian and German lines at Villers le Roye in August 1918. The belts of machine-gun ammunition have been dragged clear of the aircraft for use by the soldiers. Although the Camel was a tough opponent, it was also a tough aircraft to fly, and many novice pilots died in spinning incidents.

FACTS AND FIGURES

➤ The Camel prototype was first flown by Harry Hawker in January 1917.

➤ Camel production totalled 5,490, with 1325 produced in 1917 and 4165 in 1918.

➤ Sopwith Camels destroyed 1294 enemy aircraft during World War I, more than any other aircraft of the conflict.

➤ The Camel pilot sat in a wicker chair without a restraining seat belt.

➤ The US Navy tested the Sopwith Camel as a ship-borne fighter aboard the battleships Texas and Arkansas.

➤ The Camel was flown by Canadian ace pilots 'Billy' Barker and Roy Brown.

PROFILE

Sopwith's finest fighting scout

The Camel was introduced in 1917, initially as a fighter for the Royal Naval Air Service and soon afterward for the Royal Flying Corps. From its first appearance at the Battle of Ypres, the Camel proved itself to be an agile and potent pursuit craft.

Many rotary engines were flown in the Camel and numerous versions were built, including a night-fighter with a pair of Lewis guns mounted above the top wing centre section.

Most Camels lifted off noisily from grass strips to fly to the Front and beyond, to engage Fokker, Pfalz and other German warplanes. Some of these high-performing Sopwiths had special tasks, however: several went to sea aboard the aircraft-carriers HMS *Furious* and *Pegasus* or were catapulted from atop turrets on other warships. Two Camels were modified for trials as parasite fighters, carried aboard the airship R.23.

Camels served in several foreign air forces, including those of Belgium and Greece as well as with the American Expeditionary Force.

Britain led the world in taking aircraft to sea. This Camel was launched during trials in the Forth estuary from the carrier HMS Furious.

CAMEL

This Camel served on the Western Front in 1918 with 'B' flight, 210 Squadron RAF, previously 10 (Naval) Squadron RNAS.

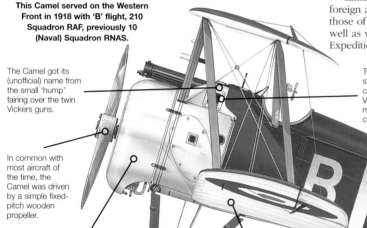

The Camel got its (unofficial) name from the small 'hump' fairing over the twin Vickers guns.

In common with most aircraft of the time, the Camel was driven by a simple fixed-pitch wooden propeller.

Camels used a number of different engines including the Clerget, Le Rhone 9J and Gnome Monosoupape.

Twin ammunition feed chutes led from stowage bins to the guns, which were cocked by large levers. Although the Vickers guns were generally reliable, many pilots kept a hammer in the cockpit to enable them to clear jams.

Part of the upper wing was cut out to give the pilot better visibility upwards.

The elevator had a large 'notch' cut in it to allow free movement of the rudder.

Mastering rudder control was all-important to Camel pilots, for it allowed them to make violent turns without producing spectacular and often fatal spins.

The forward fuselage contained the engine, fuel, pilot and guns. This concentration of weight and the high torque led to the tricky handling that made Camels infamous.

The outer fuselage skin was aluminium around the engine, plywood around the centre section and fabric around the rear section.

A simple tailskid was fitted, with an elastic cord shock-absorber.

Camel F.I

Type: single-seat fighting scout

Powerplant: one 97-kW (130-hp.) Clerget nine-cylinder air-cooled rotary piston engine

Maximum speed: 188 km/h (117 m.p.h.) at sea level

Climb rate: 10 min to 3000 m (9,850 ft.)

Endurance: 2 hr 30 min

Service ceiling: 5790 m (19,000 ft.)

Weights: empty 421 kg (926 lb.); maximum take-off 659 kg (1,450 lb.)

Armament: two 7.7-mm (.303 cal.) Vickers machine-guns on nose synchronised to fire through the propeller, plus four 11.35-kg (25-lb.) bombs carried on external racks beneath the fuselage

Dimensions:
span	8.53 m	(28 ft.)
length	5.72 m	(19 ft.)
height	2.60 m	(9 ft.)
wing area	21.46 m²	(231 sq. ft.)

COMBAT DATA

MAXIMUM SPEED

The Camel was reasonably fast and had a speed advantage over the Albatros D.V which appeared at the same time. Other Allied fighters like the SPAD and the S.E.5 were considerably quicker, but lacked the Camel's incredible agility.

CAMEL	188 km/h (117 m.p.h.)
ALBATROS D.V	165 km/h (102 m.p.h.)
SPAD XIII	215 km/h (133 m.p.h.)

ENDURANCE

British fighters were generally more aggressive than their opponents, and scouts usually operated over enemy territory. They needed to be able to stay in the air longer than German machines which, with a few notable exceptions, patrolled close to their home airfields.

CAMEL	ALBATROS D.V	SPAD XIII
2 hours 30 minutes	2 hours	2 hours

ARMAMENT

Most fighters of 1916 had a single machine-gun synchronised to fire through the propeller blades. The Camel's generation of scouts invariably carried two guns, which was to remain the standard fighter armament for the next 15 years.

CAMEL	2 x 7.7-mm (.303 cal.) machine-guns
ALBATROS D.V	2 x 7.92-mm machine-guns
SPAD XIII	2 x 7.7-mm (.303 cal.) machine-guns

Sopwith single-seat scouts

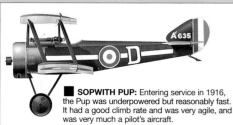

SOPWITH PUP: Entering service in 1916, the Pup was underpowered but reasonably fast. It had a good climb rate and was very agile, and was very much a pilot's aircraft.

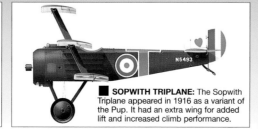

SOPWITH TRIPLANE: The Sopwith Triplane appeared in 1916 as a variant of the Pup. It had an extra wing for added lift and increased climb performance.

SOPWITH SNIPE: A development of the Camel with more power, more speed and more forgiving handling, the Snipe entered service in the last months of the war.

SOPWITH

TRIPLANE

● Agile dogfighter ● First combat triplane ● Naval service

S opwith's Triplane flew for the first time in May 1916, just as the Sopwith Pup was joining the action on the Western Front. Six months later the first Sopwith Camel flew. As a result of appearing between these two famous fighters, the Triplane was built in only limited numbers. Even so, it made quite an impact on the fighting in France in spring 1917, claiming a large number of victories and inspiring several German fighter triplane designs.

▲ Making its combat debut in France during February 1917, the Triplane was feared by the enemy. Manfred von Richthofen stated that the Triplane was 'the best Allied fighter at that time'.

SOPWITH TRIPLANE

▲ Hispano-Suiza power
N509 was built with a 112-kW (150-hp.) Hispano-Suiza engine.

▲ High climber
With three wings providing vast amounts of lift, the Triplane could climb faster than its contemporaries.

Small-scale production ▶
Despite its superb flying qualities only 150 Triplanes were built. The majority flew with the RNAS.

▲ Airworthy again
The only Triplanes that are still flying are replicas. This example is owned by the Fighter Collection at Duxford.

▲ Lone survivor
The only authentic Triplane still in existence is preserved at the RAF Museum, Hendon.

Respected fighter ▶
The Triplane was highly regarded by the Germans and led Fokker to build a triplane known as the Dr.1.

FACTS AND FIGURES

➤ The structure of the Triplane was very similar to its highly successful predecessor, the Sopwith Pup.

➤ Harry Hawker looped the Triplane just three minutes into its first flight.

➤ The 150 Triplanes produced were built by three different companies.

➤ One of the 16 victories Raymond Collishaw claimed in June 1917 was the famous German ace Allmenroder.

➤ Despite being successful the Triplane saw only seven months of front-line service.

➤ Five Triplanes were delivered to France and one to Russia.

PROFILE

World's first fighting triplane

The purpose of the Triplane's triple wings was to give pilots a better view than they had from the Pup's cockpit while retaining the earlier fighter's manoeuvrability. The wings were shorter and much narrower than those of the Pup, with the central wing level with the top of the fuselage and the top wing high above it.

No more than 150 Triplanes were built and in British service all were flown by the Royal Naval Air Service (RNAS). The RNAS had formed its own land-based fighter units to help meet the urgent need for more fighter squadrons on the Western Front, and exchanged its Spad VIIs for Triplanes ordered by the Royal Flying Corps.

By the spring of 1917, five squadrons were equipped with the Triplane on the Western Front. No. 10 Squadron was particularly successful, with 'B' Flight managing to down 87 enemy aircraft in just 55 days. All five squadrons re-equipped with Camels later in the year.

Away from the Western Front, one Triplane operated with RNAS forces in the Aegean and another was fitted with skis for service in Russia. One version was fitted with bigger wings and a Hispano-Suiza V-8 engine, but only two were built.

The triplane design was regarded with much suspicion when first introduced. However, pilots soon found the 'extra wing' gave the aircraft a superb rate of climb and good agility. The wood and fabric wings were supported by continuous broad-chord wooden interplane struts. Ailerons were fitted to all three wings.

Above: Triplanes were well-liked by Royal Navy pilots. Their front-line career was shortened by the disproportionate amount of repair work required for minor damage.

Below: Raymond Collishaw, one of the most famous Triplane pilots, shot down 16 enemy fighters in June 1917 in his Triplane Black Maria.

Most production Triplanes were powered by the 96.9-kW (130-hp.) Clerget 9B engine which gave the aircraft excellent performance. Several airframes were tested with a Le Rhône 9J engine, but this was not successful.

A single Vickers machine-gun was mounted centrally in front of the cockpit. It was intended that Triplanes constructed by Oakley & Co. would have twin Vickers guns, greatly increasing firepower, but none of these machines saw operational service.

On the first prototypes the entire tail assembly was identical to that of the Sopwith Pup, but the Triplane had the refinement of an adjustable tailplane. However, in February 1917 a smaller tailplane and elevators were fitted which improved the Triplane's control response and enabled the aircraft to be dived vertically.

'BLACK MARIA'

N533

Like most World War I combat aircraft, the Triplane was constructed from wood and doped fabric, which gave a light, but strong, airframe. The pilot sat in an open cockpit with the middle wing level with the pilot's eyes.

TRIPLANE

N533 was one of batch of six Sopwith Triplanes built by Clayton & Shuttleworth. 'N'-prefixed serial numbers were allocated to RNAS aircraft between 1916 and 1930.

Triplane

Type: single-seat fighting scout

Powerplant: one 96.9-kW (130-hp.) Clerget 9B nine-cylinder air-cooled rotary engine

Maximum speed: 188 km/h (116 m.p.h.) at 1830 m (6,000 ft.)

Endurance: 2 hr 45 min

Initial climb rate: 10 min 35 sec to 3050 m (10,000 ft.)

Service ceiling: 6250 m (20,500 ft.)

Weights: empty 450 kg (20,500 ft.); maximum take-off 642 kg (1,412 lb.)

Armament: one 7.7-mm (.303 cal.) nose-mounted Vickers machine-gun

Dimensions:
span	8.08 m	(26 ft. 6 in.)
length	5.94 m	(18 ft. 6 in.)
height	3.20 m	(10 ft. 6 in.)
wing area	21.46 m²	(231 sq. ft.)

COMBAT DATA

MAXIMUM SPEED

The Sopwith Triplane possessed excellent speed characteristics and was faster than the later Fokker Triplane. The slower Nieuport Type 11 was in service when the Triplane was introduced and lacked the power, and therefore the speed, of the later Triplanes.

TRIPLANE	188 km/h (117 m.p.h.)	
Dr.1 TRIPLANE	165 km/h (102 m.p.h.)	
TYPE 11	155 km/h (96 m.p.h.)	

ENDURANCE

The Triplane's Clerget engine was economical and gave the aircraft excellent endurance, which was vital for long patrols over enemy lines. The Type 11 was also a good performer in this respect. Dr.1s, like many German designs, lacked endurance.

TRIPLANE	Dr.1 TRIPLANE	TYPE 11
2 hours 45 min	1 hour 30 min	2 hours 30 min

SERVICE CEILING

Both Triplane designs had an impressive service ceiling thanks to powerful engines and the high lift generated by three wings. The earlier Nieuport could not reach these altitudes. However, by 1917 ceiling was dictated by the cold temperatures and lack of oxygen and their effects on the pilots at altitude, rather than the aircraft's performance.

TRIPLANE 6250 m (20,500 ft.)	TYPE 11 4500 m (14,800 ft.)	Dr.1 TRIPLANE 6095 m (20,000 ft.)

Great War naval fighters

■ **MORANE PARASOL:** The most famous feat by a naval Parasol fighter was by F./Sub-Lt Warneford of No. 1 Squadron, RNAS, who downed Zeppelin L.Z. 37 in this machine.

■ **NIEUPORT TYPE 11:** Entering service in 1915, the Type 11 saw much combat. RNAS pilot Sqn Cdr Bell Davies won the V.C. for rescuing a downed pilot under fire.

■ **SOPWITH 2F.1 CAMEL** The Camel 2F.1 was designed specifically as a shipboard fighter and saw action against Zeppelins from aircraft-carriers such as HMS *Furious*.

SOPWITH

SNIPE

● World War I ● RAF fighter of the early 1920s ● Camel successor

A lthough it was involved in combat for only the last few weeks of World War I, the Snipe was, however, clearly the best Allied fighter of the conflict. Designed in 1917 to use a new 171.5-kW (230-hp.) rotary engine, it resembled the Sopwith Camel but was not as difficult to handle. It became the RAF's standard fighter in the early-1920s, serving in Egypt, Iraq and India as well as with home-based air-defence squadrons.

▲ Joining combat only briefly at the end of World War I, the Snipe still managed to impress with its exceptional handling qualities. Many experts consider it to have been the greatest single-seat fighter of the conflict. Snipes went on to form the backbone of the post-war RAF.

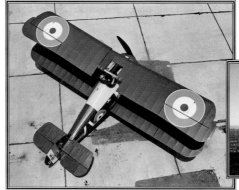

◀ Restored Snipe
Pilots had a degree of upwards visibility through the large cut-out in the upper wing. This was important to see attacks from above.

▲ Camel origins
Although the Snipe shared the Camel's manoeuvrability, it did not have the earlier fighter's tricky handling qualities. The Snipe had more power and two sets of wing struts on each side.

◀ Starting the Snipe
The Huck's starter consisted of a long spindle chain-driven from the car's engine and attached to the Snipe's propeller boss.

Service into the 1920s ▶
Snipes served as front-line RAF fighters until 1926. During this period many of the squadrons adopted flamboyant unit markings.

◀ Vickers armament
The Snipe was armed with twin forward-firing 7.7-mm (.303 cal.) machine-guns, aimed by the sight between the guns of this restored aircraft.

FACTS AND FIGURES

➤ Major W. G. Barker received the Victoria Cross for destroying four enemy aircraft in one action, even though he was wounded.

➤ After the war, No. 25 Squadron took its Snipes to Constantinople for a year.

➤ Snipes continued to serve as trainers for some time after 1926.

➤ Due to the B.R.2 engine not being ready, the prototype Snipe flew with the B.R.1 as fitted to the Camel.

➤ An attack aircraft, the Salamander, was developed from the Snipe.

➤ An A.B.C. Dragonfly I-powered Snipe, called the Dragon, was not successful.

Top World War I fighter design

Although it retained the humped forward fuselage that had earned the Camel its name, the 7F.1 Snipe's larger engine meant that the fuselage was deeper

and on the third prototype longer wings were added.

Its combat career may have been brief, but Major W. G. Barker earned the Victoria Cross while flying a Snipe.

On 27 October 1918, in a series of dogfights with a total of 15 Fokker D.VIIIs, he shot down four of the enemy aircraft.

As well as the standard single-seater, there was a long-range bomber escort version, the 7F.1A, which had an endurance of 4½ hours.

A small number of Snipes were fitted with arrestor hooks and flotation bags for deck landing trials. There were also about 40 two-seat trainer conversions, five of which formed the RAF's first formation aerobatic team flown by instructor pilots.

Like most fighters of the time, the Snipe had a two-bladed wooden propeller. The propeller of Major Barker's aircraft was shattered when the aircraft 'nosed-over' on landing.

Internally the Snipe had an all-wooden structure. This was covered by a combination of plywood, fabric and sheet metal.

Flying initially with a Bentley B.R.1 engine, the first prototype looked almost identical to a Camel. All later Snipes used the B.R.2 as their powerplant and were the RAF's last rotary-engined fighters.

It was not until the third prototype that two-bay wings were fitted. The lower wing was staggered backwards to give the pilot a better view downwards, which was especially important during trench bombing missions.

This unusual fin and rudder arrangement was used on the second prototype and early production machines; all other Snipes had a Camel-like tail.

The tail of Major Barker's aircraft was seriously damaged, probably when it overturned.

E8102

Above: Decorated with the colourful markings of the time and demonstrating exceptional performance, the Snipe was a popular performer at 1920s RAF pageants.

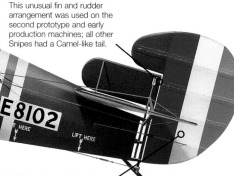

Left: Showing obvious similarities to the Camel, the Snipe was an all-round better performer. It retained the two-gun Vickers armament, as shown on this American museum replica.

SNIPE MK I

Major W. G. Barker, a Canadian temporarily on attachment to No. 201 Squadron, won the Victoria Cross flying this aircraft. Barker managed to cross back into friendly territory at very low level before he crash-landed his Snipe.

Snipe Mk I

Type: single-seat biplane fighter

Powerplant: one 171.5-kW (230-hp.) Bentley B.R.2 nine-cylinder air-cooled rotary engine

Maximum speed: 195 km/h (121 m.p.h.)

Climb rate: climb to 3048 m (10,000 ft.) in 27.3 min

Endurance: 3 hours

Service ceiling: 6248 m (20,500 ft.)

Weight: 914 kg (2,010 lb.) maximum take-off

Armament: two 7.7-mm (.303 cal.) machine-guns in forward fuselage, one 51-kg (112-lb.) or four 9-kg (20-lb.) bombs

Dimensions: span 9.47 m (31 ft.)
length 6.05 m (19 ft. 10 in.)
height 2.90 m (9 ft. 6 in.)
wing area 25.08 m² (270 sq. ft.)

COMBAT DATA

MAXIMUM SPEED

The SPAD was respected for its exceptional speed, but the Snipe was not far behind and was far more manoeuvrable. The Albatros represented one of the final developments of a long line.

SNIPE Mk I	195 km/h (121 m.p.h.)
SPAD S.XIII	224 km/h (139 m.p.h.)
ALBATROS D.V	186 km/h (115 m.p.h.)

ENGINE POWER

A powerful Bentley engine gave the Snipe a good rate of climb and enough power to carry light bombs in a secondary attack role. The SPAD and Albatros did not serve long after the war.

| SNIPE Mk I | S.XIII | D.V |
| 171.5 kW (230 hp.) | 164 kW (220 hp.) | 149 kW (200 hp.) |

SERVICE CEILING

A high-flying aircraft is able to dive on the enemy, attacking at great speed and maintaining momentum throughout the engagement. High initial altitude was crucial to Barker's successful attack.

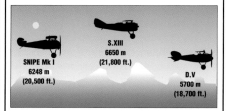

SNIPE Mk I 6248 m (20,500 ft.) — S.XIII 6650 m (21,800 ft.) — D.V 5700 m (18,700 ft.)

Victoria Cross winners' aircraft

ROYAL AIRCRAFT FACTORY B.E.2: Rhodes-Moorhouse of No. 2 Squadron, Royal Flying Corps, was honoured for a 1915 raid.

BRISTOL SCOUT: Major Lanoe G. Hawker was awarded the VC for a successful combat in which he was armed only with a cavalry rifle.

NIEUPORT 17 SCOUT: Captain Albert Ball was one of the Allies' most successful single-seater pilots, receiving the VC posthumously.

ROYAL AIRCRAFT FACTORY S.E.5A: Major Edward Mannock achieved 61 victories and was posthumously honoured in 1919.

SPAD

S.VII & S.XII

● World War I fighter ● Sturdy construction ● Flown by aces

Many consider the SPAD S.VII and S.XII to have been the best Allied fighters of the late stages of World War I. Previous fighter scouts had often been flimsy and prone to breaking up during aerial manoeuvres, but the sturdy SPAD was different. Flown by aces such as the Frenchman Georges Guynemer and Italian Francesco Barraca, the S.VII played a crucial part in helping to wrest supremacy in the air from the Germans.

▲ *SPAD first made its mark building two-seat pusher biplanes, though in 1915 the company turned its attention to fighters. What emerged was the S.VII, one of the best fighters of World War I.*

SPAD S.VII & S.XII

▲ Braving the weather
Operating conditions on the Western Front were harsh, especially in winter.

◄ Built tough
Appearances were not at all deceptive; the S.VII was as sturdy as it looked.

Key to success ▶
What made the S.VII special was its powerful Hispano-Suiza in-line V8 engine and its streamlined airframe.

▼ International popularity
The S.VII was such an improvement over earlier fighters that it found favour with other nations. The Royal Flying Corps used the little machine once initial problems had been solved.

▲ American fliers
In France, the American Expeditionary Force acquired a handful of SPAD S.VIIs, though they were primarily used to train new pilots for the later S.XIII which was supplied in larger numbers. Some went across the Atlantic after the Armistice.

FACTS AND FIGURES

➤ SPAD was originally the name of an aircraft manufacturing company. When Blériot took it over, the initials remained.

➤ Some 300 of all S.XII variants were built, a small number of them as float-planes.

➤ Armand Pinsard was the first pilot to score a 'kill' in a S.VII on 23 August 1916.

➤ After a series of fatal crashes caused by weak airframes, the Royal Flying Corps initially refused to accept S.VIIs.

➤ S.VIIs were built under licence at Brooklands, near Weybridge in the UK.

➤ Several examples of this famous fighter are preserved in Europe and the USA.

PROFILE

A new fighter for a new war

Taking to the air in April 1916, the arrival of the SPAD S.VII could not have been better timed. The 'war of attrition' was living up to its name as thousands were killed on the battlefield. In the air pilots battled constantly, but the Germans enjoyed an advantage with their Albatros and Fokker scouts. The arrival of the SPAD S.VII on the Western Front gave the Allied flyers an aircraft with which they could meet the enemy on equal terms.

The first unit to receive the S.VII was Escadrille (Squadron) N. 26 in August 1916, with one of its pilots making the first recorded victory in the little machine later the same month.

In combat, the S.VII soon established itself and was blessed with an excellent rate of climb, but most of all it gained celebrity as a steady gun platform enabling pilots to score many 'kills'. An improved variant, the S.XII, was built under the encouragement of the French ace

Georges Guynemer and entered service in 1917. Guynemer scored four victories in the new machine, but it did not prove popular, and only 300 were delivered. Later development culminated in the S.XIII.

Above: Aircraft flown by the aces, especially the Americans and the French, often wore bright markings.

Below: Seen wearing the markings of Captain Eddie Rickenbacker's famous mount, this is actually a replica of an S.XIII, a much improved S.VII. This variant became the most famous.

S.VII

This colourful S.VII is a post-war aircraft, assigned to the commanding officer of XIII Grupo, Regia Aeronautica (Italian air force) in 1924.

For the time, the wing had a remarkably thin aerofoil section and, unlike many other designs, featured ailerons on the upper wing only. Two sets of struts were mounted between the wings on each side, with a third set acting as tie struts for the bracing and flying wires. Construction was entirely of wood.

Underneath the smooth exterior was a very strong airframe with four major box sections. The S.VII was heavier than some of its contemporaries but it was soon discovered that S.VIIs could be sent up to meet the opposition time and again, and be able to engage in dogfights without the risk of breaking up in the air.

In common with most Allied fighter scouts of World War I, SPAD S.VIIs often wore bright colours on their rudders, usually representing the national flag of the service that used them. Even after the war, Italian examples, such as this one, continued to wear the Tricolore.

Powering the SPAD S.VII was a 134-kW (180-hp.) Hispano-Suiza 8Ab V8 engine. A powerful and initially reliable engine, it made a perfect marriage with the sleek airframe. On the front line, however, SPADs were often plagued by overheating engines, something which was never rectified during their service careers.

Apart from the forward fuselage panelling, the airframe was covered in doped fabric. This particular machine is actually unpainted, the beige finish being the natural colour of the fabric material.

COMBAT DATA

POWER

At the time of its appearance in 1916, the power of the SPAD S.VII was heartily welcomed. It at last put Allied pilots on an equal footing with their German adversaries.

S.VII
134 kW (180 hp.)

F.1 CAMEL
97 kW (130 hp.)

D.VII
138 kW (185 hp.)

ENDURANCE

With many of the aerial battles taking place over enemy-held territory, Allied aircraft such as the S.VII and the Sopwith F.1 Camel needed greater endurance in order to engage in combat.

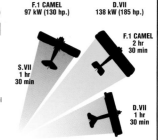

F.1 CAMEL
2 hr 30 min

S.VII
1 hr 30 min

D.VII
1 hr 30 min

ARMAMENT

If there was a drawback to the SPAD S.VII it lay in its lack of powerful armament. The Camel was harder hitting, but also more difficult to fly. The Fokker D.VII also sported two guns.

S.VII   1 x 7.7-mm (.303 cal.) machine-gun

F.1 CAMEL   2 x 7.7-mm (.303 cal.) machine-guns

D.VII   2 x 7.92-mm machine-guns

European SPAD S.VIIs

■ **FINLAND:** After the end of World War I, S.VIIs continued in service for a few years, particularly with nations such as Finland.

■ **GREAT BRITAIN:** This particular S.VII was a French machine acquired by the RFC in 1917.

■ **ITALY:** Some SPADs in post-war Italian service were painted in this dark green colour scheme with a white band on the tail.

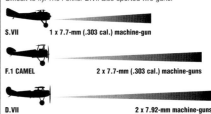

SPAD

S.XIII

● Best of the SPADs ● Flown by aces ● Biplane fighter

O ne of the finest fighters of
World War I, the SPAD S.XIII was
the culmination of a long line
of SPAD fighters. Heavy, fast and very
rugged, the S.XIII was immediately
successful, taking on the best German
designs over the Western Front. It saw
action with the new American squadrons
in 1918, and became the favoured mount
of many aces. The S.XIII was so good that
it remained in service after the war.

▲ One of the most flamboyant units of World War
I, the Escadrille Lafayette gained considerable
success with its SPAD S.XIIIs. The aircraft was not
as agile as many contemporaries, but gained a
reputation for its high speed and strength.

SPAD S.XIII

▲ Crashed SPAD
The SPAD had a reputation as
a rugged aircraft, but no fighter
could survive a crash like this.

▲ Adornments
American pilots adorned their
aircraft with bold emblems,
including the Indian's head of
the Escadrille Lafayette.

▼ SPAD seven
The similar S.VII was actually
a much less powerful aircraft
with a single gun.

▲ Museum piece
A few SPADs remain as museum exhibits as a
testimony to the design. A flying full-size replica
is also on display in the United States.

Bull nose ▶
Pilots loved the SPAD for its
performance and also for its
solid, threatening appearance.
The success of the aircraft owed
a great deal to the very powerful
Hispano-Suiza engine.

FACTS AND FIGURES

➤ The top-scoring American ace of
World War I was Eddie Rickenbacker, who
gained many of his 26 kills in a S.XIII.

➤ SPAD was an abbreviation of Societé Pour
L'Aviation et ses Dérives.

➤ SPADs were also used by the British Royal
Flying Corps and Royal Air Force.

➤ Orders for S.XIIIs at the end of the war
amounted to 10,000 aircraft; these were
cancelled after the Armistice.

➤ After the war SPAD S.XIIIs were exported
to Czechoslovakia, Japan and Poland.

➤ The SPAD was also flown by French aces
like Fonck, Guynemer and Nungesser.

PROFILE

Biggest and fastest SPAD

Louis Bleriot took over the SPAD company when it went bankrupt and went on to produce a highly acclaimed family of fighter aircraft. After experimenting with radical and unsuccessful designs with a gunner in front the propeller, the company produced the SPAD S.VII, a conventional design with an eight-cylinder Vee engine. First flown in 1916, this aircraft was widely used by the Allies, including the American forces.

The success of the S.VII led to the much more powerful S.XIII with a longer-span wing and improved ailerons. The prototype first flew in April 1917, a time when the Allies were suffering badly from the latest German aircraft. It was rushed into service quickly and met with instant success; the aircraft was required in great numbers and sub-contractors began producing them in the thousands.

A single-seat photo-reconnaissance version, the SPAD S.XVII, was produced just as the war ended. It had two cameras and only a single machine-gun. The projected S.XXI was cancelled as the war came to an end.

Below: The S.XX was a two-seat spotter-scout aircraft. It failed to live up to the reputation of the single-seat SPAD designs.

Above: After the war SPADs were highly popular for sport flying because of their good performance. This aircraft was flown in the Detroit races in 1922.

S.XIII

Type: single-seat Vee-engined fighter biplane and scout aircraft

Powerplant: one 164-kW (220-hp.) Hispano-Suiza 8Be eight-cylinder Vee engine

Maximum speed: 224 km/h (130 m.p.h.)

Endurance: 2 hr

Range: 400 km (250 mi.) (estimated)

Service ceiling: 6650 m (21,800 ft.)

Weights: maximum take-off 845 kg (1,859 lb.)

Armament: two Vickers 7.7-mm (.303 cal.) water-cooled machine-guns

Dimensions:
span	8.10 m (26 ft. 7 in.)
length	6.30 m (20 ft. 8 in.)
height	2.35 m (7 ft. 8 in.)
wing area	20.00 m² (199 sq. ft.)

S.XIII

Probably the finest French fighter of the war, the S.XIII was the favoured aircraft of the Escadrille Lafayette.

The S.XIII was better armed than most Allied fighters, having two Vickers machine-guns instead of the single gun of earlier types. The cockpit was very close to the upper wing surface.

The Lafayette Escadrille was an American-staffed squadron consisting of volunteer pilots fighting for the French air force. The unit included aces such as Raoul Lufbery, who shot down 17 enemy aircraft.

Like the S.VII, the S.XIII had a long, sloping fin with a ribbed trailing edge. The aircraft had large, powerful rudder and elevator surfaces.

The S.XIII's success was mainly due to the power of the Hispano-Suiza engine. The previous two-seat SPAD had an unreliable engine.

Many aircraft had tailwheels by 1917, but the S.XIII retained a simple skid. The fuselage structure was very strong; this was one of the reasons that the American Skyraider pilots in Vietnam nicknamed their similarly rugged aircraft the 'SPAD'.

COMBAT DATA

MAXIMUM SPEED

With its closely cowled fuselage and very powerful engine, the S.XIII could outrun almost any other fighter. The Camel and D.VII had lower all-out speed, but both were more agile. This was an important factor as most combat degenerated into turning dogfights.

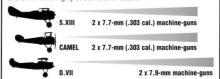

S.XIII	224 km/h (140 m.p.h.)
CAMEL	185 km/h (115 m.p.h.)
D.VII	200 km/h (124 m.p.h.)

ARMAMENT

By 1917 fighter designers on the Allied side had caught up with their German counterparts who had been arming their fighters with twin guns for a long time. The Vickers guns fitted to the Camel and S.XIII were highly effective and reliable.

S.XIII	2 x 7.7-mm (.303 cal.) machine-guns
CAMEL	2 x 7.7-mm (.303 cal.) machine-guns
D.VII	2 x 7.9-mm machine-guns

ENDURANCE

Endurance was less important to these dedicated air combat machines than to patrol and observation aircraft. It was still a vital commodity, however; a pilot who had to break off combat for lack of fuel was vulnerable as he turned towards base. Long endurance also meant that a fighter could fly further over enemy territory, denying more of the front-line to their observation balloons. Two hours' combat flying was sufficient for most pilots.

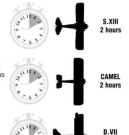

S.XIII	2 hours
CAMEL	2 hours
D.VII	1 ½ hours

Best fighters of World War I

■ **SPAD VII:** The VII was probably the second-best SPAD fighter after the model S.XIII. It was fitted with only one gun, but had similar handling and ruggedness and a high top speed.

■ **FOKKER D.VII:** A good claimant for the title of best fighter of World War I, the D.VII was such a good performer that the Allies specifically ordered their confiscation after the war.

■ **SOPWITH CAMEL:** Fast and extremely agile, the twin-gun Camel was a tricky aircraft for novice pilots, gaining a reputation for spinning easily. It was highly successful in combat, however.

SUPERMARINE

WALRUS

● Naval spotter ● Air-sea rescue ● Catapult launched

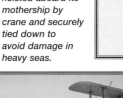

▲ Air-sea rescue was vital during the Battle of Britain as Fighter Command's pilot resources were becoming desperately low. Many grateful pilots were rescued by the trusty Walrus.

Like a dinosaur stepping through a time warp, the Supermarine Walrus was a piece of history caught up in World War II. Resembling an aircraft of the 1920s (except for its enclosed cockpit), the biplane had fabric surfaces, a wooden hull (on the Mk II version) and a single pusher engine. It was an anachronism, but to a pilot downed at sea, suffering from cold and hunger, it was a welcome sight.

PHOTO FILE

SUPERMARINE WALRUS

▲ Catapult launch
Ship-based Walruses were launched from a catapult. Australia operated the aircraft under the name Seagull Mk V.

▲ Back onboard
After a sortie the Walrus would be hoisted aboard its mothership by crane and securely tied down to avoid damage in heavy seas.

▲ Watertight hull
After taking off from land the wheels retract into wells in the wing allowing the aircraft to operate on water.

▲ 'Shagbat' rescue
More than 2000 survivors were rescued by Walruses. Landings were often made in mine-infested enemy waters.

◀ Ugly duckling
Although not an elegant aircraft, the sedate Walrus established a reputation for reliability and an ability to withstand damage.

FACTS AND FIGURES

➤ One Walrus based aboard a Royal Navy cruiser completed 16 separate rescues in one day.

➤ The name Walrus was allocated when the RAF ordered it in May 1935.

➤ The Walrus first flew in June 1933 and was called the Seagull Mk V.

➤ The Walrus was used by seven home and four Middle East rescue squadrons and a single mine-spotting squadron.

➤ Walrus production totalled 746, of which 461 were built by Saunders-Roe.

➤ The Anson and Lysander often worked with the Walrus in air-sea rescues.

PROFILE

Picked up by a 'Shagbat'

Supermarine was an expert manufacturer of seaplanes, and the Walrus was a great aircraft, although it was out-of-date by the time World War II began.

The earlier Seagull amphibian was developed into a version powered by the Bristol Pegasus engine, 24 of which were ordered by Australia. Evaluation of this aircraft led to it being adopted for service with Britain's Fleet Air Arm as the Walrus.

Supermarine-built Walruses had metal hulls, but more than half of the total number built were produced by Saunders-Roe which manufactured them with wooden surfaces.

Entering service with the Fleet Air Arm in 1936, the Walrus, which was stressed for catapult launching, equipped battleships and cruisers of the Australian, British and New Zealand navies, and was operational in practically every theatre of the war.

The Walrus, known to wartime servicemen as the 'Shagbat', also played an important air-sea rescue role in Royal Air Force service, rescuing many downed aircrew.

Left: Powered by a pusher engine and fitted with biplane wings, the Walrus was no faster than a World War I fighter. However, its ability to land on water and pick up survivors made it ideal for air-sea rescue.

Above: Walruses served wherever the Royal Navy was active. Here the crew paddle their aircraft towards a crane aboard HMS Belfast in the freezing conditions of an Icelandic fjord.

Walrus Mk II

Type: four-seat spotter reconnaissance amphibian

Powerplant: one 578-kW (620-hp.) Bristol Pegasus VI radial piston engine

Maximum speed: 217 km/h (135 m.p.h.) at 1524 m (5,000 ft.)

Range: 966 km (600 mi.)

Service ceiling: 5210 m (17,100 ft.)

Weights: empty 2223 kg (4,890 lb.); maximum take-off 3266 kg (7,185 lb.)

Armament: one 7.7-mm (.303 cal.) Vickers 'K' gun in bow and one or two similar weapons amidships, plus up 272 kg (600 lb.) of bombs carried beneath the wings, or two Mk VIII depth charges

Dimensions:
span	13.97 m	(45 ft. 10 in.)
length	11.35 m	(37 ft. 3 in.)
height	4.65 m	(15 ft. 3 in.)
wing area	56.67 m²	(610 sq. ft.)

WALRUS MK I

As well as RAF land-based squadrons the Walrus was also operated by the Royal Navy from cruisers and battleships. This example of No. 700 Squadron served aboard HMS Belfast in the early 1940s.

The open bow cockpit contained a 7.7-mm (.303 cal.) Vickers 'K' or Lewis machine-gun mounted on a Scarff ring. Marine rescue gear was also stored in the cockpit together with the bow mooring line.

The enclosed cockpit housed the pilot in the left seat with the co-pilot/observer on the right. Between and behind the pilots seats was the navigator's compartment.

The equal-span, single-bay biplane wings folded around the rear spar hinges on the centre section and hull. Ailerons were fitted to all four wings and bomb racks for carrying up to 345 kg (760 lb.) of bombs or depth charges were incorporated beneath the lower wing.

The Mk I was fitted with a 462-kW (620-hp.) Bristol Pegasus IIM2 engine. The later Mk II was fitted with the more powerful Pegasus VI.

Supermarine built the Mk I versions which all had an anodically-treated aluminium alloy hull. The Mk IIs were built by Saunders-Roe and had wooden hulls.

ROYAL NAVY X9556

The aft-gunner's cockpit, with a machine-gun fitted on a flexible mount, was positioned behind the wings.

A large rudder was necessary to provide good manoeuvrability on the water when retrieving survivors.

COMBAT DATA

MAXIMUM SPEED

Speed was not a factor in the design of these aircraft and all three were easy prey for patrolling fighters. Despite its slow speed the Walrus could operate from a short runway.

WALRUS Mk II	217 km/h (135 m.p.h.)
He 59B-2	220 km/h (135 m.p.h.)
E7K2 'ALF'	275 km/h (170 m.p.h.)

RANGE

Designed for coastal patrol the Walrus only had the range for rescuing crew close to the UK coastline. The Kawanishi and He 51 had the range to patrol greater areas of ocean.

WALRUS Mk II 966 km (600 mi.)

He 59B-2 1750 km (1,085 mi.)

E7K2 'ALF' 1480 km (918 mi.)

BOMBLOAD

The more powerful He 59 could carry over twice the weight in bombs compared to the Walrus. It was also used for mine-laying. The E7K2 could only carry four small bombs beneath its wings.

WALRUS Mk II	He 59B-2	E7K2 'ALF'
345 kg (760 lb.)	1000 kg (2,200 lb.)	120 kg (264 lb.)

Walrus rescue in the Channel

During the Battle of Britain RAF rescue procedures were shambolic. However, after a review in 1941 co-ordinated rescue operations saved the lives of many aircrew.

1 SHOOTDOWN: If an English pilot was downed in the Channel he would either ditch his aircraft or parachute into the water. He would already be wearing a life jacket and would inflate his life raft once in the water.

2 SPOTTING SURVIVORS: When the pilot was spotted in the sea a Walrus was summoned to pick him up. The survivor used sea dye and launched flares to attract the attention of the crew.

3 PICK UP: The Walrus pilot landed his aircraft as close to the downed pilot as possible, often having to avoid mines and enemy fire. A line was then thrown to the dinghy which was towed to the aircraft. The survivor was pulled aboard the Walrus, which then left the area as quickly as possible.

THOMAS-MORSE

SCOUT

● Purpose-built ● Pursuit trainer ● Movie star

Thomas-Morse produced the highly praised Scout throughout the Great War, culminating in the S4C. This was a sprightly, nimble aircraft which was once intended to spy on the enemy, but which was actually used to train pilots. The S4C Scout was one of the most successful US-developed aircraft of the 1914–1918 era and remained a familiar sight at civilian air shows throughout the 1930s.

▲ The Thomas-Morse Scout, a single-seat scout aircraft for training pursuit pilots bound for the Western Front, appeared on the eve of the USA's entry into World War I.

THOMAS-MORSE SCOUT

▲ Tricky handling
Despite its primary role as a trainer, the S4 was tail-heavy and was difficult to control. It could prove quite a handful for a novice.

▼ World War I Kaydet
The Thomas-Morse Scout was the 1917 equivalent of the later Boeing PT-13 and was also built in huge numbers.

▲ Purpose-built trainer
A characteristic of the 'Tommy' was that it was designed especially for training pursuit pilots. Previous trainers were often tired, or surplus, front-line aircraft. The S4C variant (shown above) was produced in the greatest numbers.

◄ Totally new
When the first S4 took to the air in June 1917, nothing like it had ever been built before in the United States. A 74.57-kW (100-hp.) Gnome rotary engine powered the first prototype.

Sopwith style cues ►
The chief designer of the Scout, Douglas Thomas, had previously worked for Sopwith. It was, therefore, not surprising that the American aircraft bore a strong resemblance to Sopwith designs, notably the Tabloid.

FACTS AND FIGURES

➤ The Scout was an 'equal' biplane, with upper and lower wings of exactly the same span.

➤ Float-equipped S5s had to have their floats repaired after each flight.

➤ Scouts starred in several films, including *Hell's Angels* and *Dawn Patrol*.

➤ A popular modification to privately-owned 'Tommies' was to turn them into two- or three-seat sport aircraft.

➤ The S9, with side-by-side seating, was the last Scout; only one was built.

➤ Only one Scout in 10 was test-flown before being delivered to a unit.

Super abundant Scout

The Thomas-Morse Scout was initially designed as a combat aircraft, but was used instead as an advanced solo trainer. The US Army's training programme was not well organised during World War I and not all pilots received proper instruction. A large number were fortunate enough to progress to the Scout, however, and sharpened their flying skills on a fine aircraft that performed well and was similar to warplanes that were being used in action over the Front.

Although designed by Douglas Thomas for combat, the Scout was quickly converted for use in the rapidly expanding effort to train young cadets. In general, the Scout was a pleasant aircraft to fly, although it had a tendency to bounce on landing and was difficult to loop. Nevertheless, it provided pilots with good preparation for the Front.

Although the Armistice signalled an end of production, the Scout was durable and remained on the aviation scene for decades after the war.

Left: Floats were tested on the S4 prototype and the US Navy acquired six S5s. Performance of the S5 was inferior to that of its land-based counterparts.

Right: The rudder control on the ground was so ineffective that the ailerons were used for directional control during take-off and landing.

S4C

Type: single-seat pursuit trainer and scout aircraft

Powerplant: one 60-kW (80-hp.) Le Rhone C-9 (built under licence by Union Switch & Signal)

Maximum speed: 152 km/h (94 m.p.h.)

Initial climb rate: 138 m/min (450 f.p.m.)

Service ceiling: 4876 m (16,000 ft.)

Fuel weight: 73.02 kg (161 lb.)

Weights: empty 437 kg (961 lb.); loaded 623 kg (1,371 lb.)

Armament: one 7.7-mm (.303 cal.) forward-firing Marlin machine-gun or a gun camera, smokescreen or radio equipment

Dimensions:
span	8.07 m	(26 ft. 5 in.)
length	6.05 m	(19 ft. 10 in.)
height	2.69 m	(8 ft. 10 in.)
wing area	21.73 m² (234 sq. ft.)	

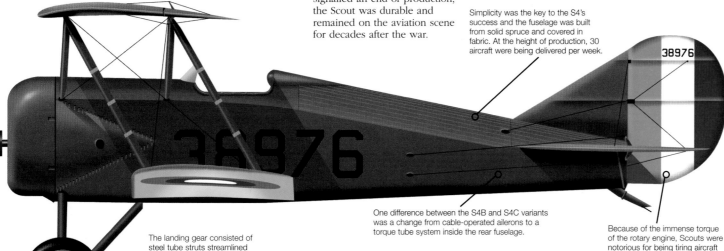

Simplicity was the key to the S4's success and the fuselage was built from solid spruce and covered in fabric. At the height of production, 30 aircraft were being delivered per week.

One difference between the S4B and S4C variants was a change from cable-operated ailerons to a torque tube system inside the rear fuselage.

Because of the immense torque of the rotary engine, Scouts were notorious for being tiring aircraft to fly over long distances. Considerable rudder input was required during take-off to counteract the torque. Sometimes the pilot would have to brace his arm between his stomach and the cockpit wall.

The landing gear consisted of steel tube struts streamlined with spruce wood. The axle-bearer was constructed of ash and was slotted to hold the axle assembly. In common with contemporary practice, high-pressure tyres were fitted.

S4C SCOUT

This anonymous-looking aircraft was typical of the S4Cs that equipped the Signal Corps in 1917–18. The standard finish was overall olive drab green. Military serial numbers were carried in black on both sides.

OTHER THOMAS-MORSE DESIGNS

MB-7: After the Scout, Thomas-Morse turned its attention to building successors. Three different prototypes, designated MB-1, MB-2 and MB-3, were built for evaluation purposes. The MB-3 was the most successful during flight tests due, in part, to its powerful 224-kW Wright-Hispano in-line engine. About 200 MB-3s were built and other variants, such as the MB-3M advanced trainer, the MB-6 and MB-7 (above) racing aircraft, were developed from it.

XP-13: During the 1920s, Thomas-Morse continued as a small aircraft manufacturer, whose efforts also centred on adopting new materials for aircraft construction. This culminated in a series of biplanes which made extensive use of aluminium alloy. One such aircraft was the XP-13 Viper single-seat fighter. Powered by a 447-kW Wright-Hispano engine, it offered superb performance, but was destroyed in a crash.

Other scout aircraft of World War I

■ **A.E.G D-I:** This little fighter was A.E.G's first single-seat scout aircraft and was distinguished by its 'ear'-type radiators.

■ **ROYAL AIRCRAFT FACTORY B.E. 2C:** These were in service by the time World War I began and were easy targets for the Germans.

■ **BRANDENBURG KDW:** Only a small number of these single-seat seaplane scouts were built, between late 1917 and early 1918.

■ **BRISTOL SCOUT:** Similar in concept to the S4C, the early Scouts were simple aircraft that were also powered by Gnome radial engines.

VICKERS

VIMY

● Strategic bomber ● Middle East service ● Pioneer flights

Named after a famous World War I battle, the Vimy achieved a dramatic 'first' when Britain's Alcock and Brown flew one eastward on the first crossing of the Atlantic. The Vickers Vimy bomber arrived too late for World War I, but served with the RAF, mainly in the Middle East, from 1918 to 1931. A flight to Australia and a semi-successful expedition to Cape Town in February 1920 capped off a number of achievements by this great aircraft.

▲ In the later years of World War I, controversy raged over the merits and morality of strategic bombing. However, once German bombers appeared over Britain in 1917, the RAF was prompted to order more than 1000 Vimys.

VICKERS VIMY

▼ **Vimy ambulance**
Built in 1921 for the RAF in the Middle East, the Vimy Ambulance was a Vimy Commercial equipped to carry four stretchers or eight sitting casualties.

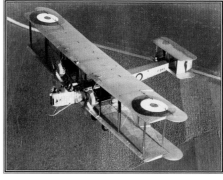

▲ **Home-based Vimy**
Most Vimy bomber units were based in the Middle East. No. 9 Squadron, however, flew Vimys for 14 months from RAF Manston during 1924/25.

Replica recreates flight ▶
In 1994 this replica re-enacted the trail-blazing flight made in 1919 from England to Australia.

▼ **Vimy Mk II prototype**
The Mk II's Eagle engines gave the new bomber reliability.

To South Africa…just ▶
In early 1920 two South African air force pilots attempted to fly civil Vimy G-UABA Silver Queen from England to Cape Town. After crashing in North Africa, they borrowed an RAF Vimy, but engine failure forced them to complete the flight in a DH.9.

FACTS AND FIGURES

➤ To help to establish civil aviation in China, 40 Vimy Commercials were imported; most appear not to have flown.

➤ Total Vimy production is believed to have reached 232 between 1917 and 1924.

➤ Vimy production was sub-contracted to firms like Westland and Morgan.

➤ Vickers designed the Vimy with the help of the world's first commercially owned wind tunnel, in St Albans, Hertfordshire.

➤ An RAF Vimy reached France in 1918 but arrived too late to make raids on Berlin.

➤ Vimys built during 1918 were fitted with torpedoes for anti-submarine duties.

PROFILE

Strategic reach for the RAF

Although made famous by the transatlantic flight of 1919, the Vimy was designed during World War I as a strategic bomber for the Royal Flying Corps (RAF from 1918).

Bombing of this nature was the subject of much debate during the later years of the war. However, British hesitation to commit itself to this new type of warfare was soon overcome when German air force bombers appeared over London in 1917. Bombers like the Handley Page O/400 were ordered into production, as were new prototypes like the Vickers FB.27.

Able to lift heavier loads than the much bigger and more powerful O/400, large numbers of Vimy aircraft were planned. But, by the time the Armistice had been signed in 1918, only one had reached France. The end of the war brought many cancellations; just over 200 were built, most powered by the ever-reliable Rolls-Royce Eagle engine.

Above: The Smith brothers and their mechanics pose in front of a Vimy at Brooklands before their 1919 flight to Australia.

Most Vimy bombers served in the Middle East, but by the end of the 1920s training was their main role.

Below: The RAF continued to employ the Vimy for training long after its retirement as a bomber. It was used to train searchlight crews until 1938.

VIMY MK IV

One of 25 of a batch of 75 ordered from Westland Aircraft Works, Vimy H5066 and the rest of the fleet were intended to be fitted with Liberty engines, but were built with Rolls-Royce Eagles.

Vimy Mk IV

Type: heavy bomber

Powerplant: two 269-kW (360-hp.) Rolls-Royce Eagle VIII V-12 water-cooled engines

Maximum speed: 166 km/h (103 m.p.h.) at sea level

Range: 1464 km (900 mi.) at 130 km/h (80 m.p.h.); more on record flights

Service ceiling: 2135 m (7,000 ft.)

Weights: empty 3221 kg (7,086 lb.); loaded 5670 kg (12,474 lb.)

Armament: two to four 7.7-mm (.303 cal.) Lewis Mk III machine-guns with twelve 97-round ammunition drums in nose, dorsal and ventral positions, plus bombload of 1123 kg (2,476 lb.)

Dimensions: span 20.75 m (68 ft. 1in.)
length 13.27 m (43 ft. 6 in.)
height 4.76 m (15 ft. 7 in.)
wing area 123.56 m² (1,330 sq. ft.)

Four prototype Vimys were built, each with a different type of engine. Those fitted to the first three aircraft were underpowered and, in some cases, unreliable. Rolls-Royce's liquid-cooled, 12-cylinder Eagle of 269 kW (360 hp.), fitted to the fourth example, was the most promising and was fitted to most production aircraft.

The Vimy had four crew: a pilot and observer/bomb aimer/nose gunner, a rear gunner and a ventral gunner. As the ventral gun was not always fitted, the latter was sometimes not carried.

In production form the Vimy followed conventional design practice of the time, with a wire-braced biplane structure and rear stabiliser arrangement. The front fuselage structure was of steel tube, the rear of wood.

Three 7.7-mm (.303 cal.) Lewis machine-guns were generally fitted to RAF Vimy bombers: one in the nose and dorsal positions, each mounted on Scarff rings, and a third in a ventral mounting.

The Vimy was able to lift a heavier load than the much larger Handley Page O/400. Maximum bombload was 1123 kg (2,476 lb.), typically made up of 18 x 51-kg (112-lb.) bombs under the wings and 2 x 104-kg (230-lb.) bombs under the fuselage.

A small window was fitted on either side of the lower fuselage for the ventral gunner, so that he could see to change the gun's ammunition drums. The Lewis machine-gun was fired through an opening in the bottom of the fuselage.

Late production Vimys with Eagle engines were originally referred to as Mk IVs (as was the fourth Vimy prototype, also fitted with the Rolls-Royce powerplants). In 1923 most surviving Eagle-engined Vimys were redesignated Mk IIs.

COMBAT DATA

MAXIMUM SPEED

The Handley Page V/1500 and de Havilland DH.10 Amiens were contemporaries of the Vimy, the former being a larger, heavier aircraft and the latter considerably smaller. The DH.10 had more powerful engines than the larger Vimy and was therefore faster.

VIMY Mk IV	166 km/h (103 m.p.h.)
V/1500	159 km/h (99 m.p.h.)
DH.10 AMIENS Mk II	185 km/h (115 m.p.h.)

ARMAMENT

Each of these bombers carried a bombload in keeping with its size, with the V/1500 being able to carry over three tonnes (three tons) of bombs. The larger aircraft required more protection against fighters and were therefore fitted with extra machine-guns.

VIMY Mk IV	2 x 7.7-mm (.303 cal.) machine-guns 1123-kg (2,476-In.) bombload
V/1500	4 x 7.7-mm (.303 cal.) machine-guns 3402-kg (7,485-lb.) bombload
DH.10 AMIENS Mk II	2 x 7.7-mm (.303 cal.) machine-guns 408-kg (900-lb.) bombload

POWER

The V/1500 had four Rolls-Royce Eagle engines in paired, push-pull configuration. The Amiens used two Liberty engines with slightly more power than the Eagles fitted to the Vimy. Both types were among the most widely used liquid-cooled engines of the period.

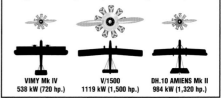

VIMY Mk IV	V/1500	DH.10 AMIENS Mk II
538 kW (720 hp.)	1119 kW (1,500 hp.)	984 kW (1,320 hp.)

Vickers Vimy variants

■ **VIMY Mk I:** After their withdrawal from front-line units in the 1920s, many Vimys were relegated to flying and parachute training. A number were re-engined with air-cooled radials.

■ **VIMY (CIVIL):** There were at least six civil-registered Vimy 'bombers', including those used on the pioneering flights of 1919 and 1920. G-EAOU was originally an RAF aircraft.

■ **VIMY COMMERCIAL:** A spacious new fuselage allowed the Commercial to carry up to 10 passengers or 2,200 kg (4,900 lb.) of freight. This example spent five years on European routes.

VOUGHT

OS2U KINGFISHER

● Two-seat observation/scout aircraft ● Search-and-rescue

Hundreds of Allied airmen owe their lives to Vought OS2U Kingfisher crews who made many rescues in World War II. Before the advent of the helicopter, a downed flier regarded the sight of an OS2U Kingfisher with a sigh of relief. The Kingfisher, operated on wheeled landing gear or floats, was valuable to the Allies in anti-submarine and reconnaissance roles, but it is as a search-and-rescue aircraft that it is most widely remembered.

▲ *Some 1500 Kingfishers were built, 300 of these by the Naval Aircraft Factory in Philadelphia as the OS2N. The last examples left the production line in 1942.*

PHOTO FILE

VOUGHT OS2U KINGFISHER

▲ OS2Us at Pearl Harbor
Of the six Kingfishers that reached the Pearl Harbor Battle Force by the end of 1940, a number were destroyed on December 7, 1941.

▲ Stable platform
Kingfishers were renowned for their stability at sea, a valuable attribute for an aircraft of its type. Engine reliability and range were also important.

◄ Preserved Kingfisher
Here an OS2U is preserved onboard the battleship USS Alabama, which would have carried up to three in service.

▼ Fleet Air Arm bird
Supplied under Lend-Lease arrangements, 100 OS2Us were delivered to the British Fleet for use onboard cruisers and as trainers.

▲ Over 1000 OS2Us
The main production model was the OS2U-3, which featured extra fuel tanks in the wings and better armor protection for the pilot and observer.

FACTS AND FIGURES

➤ On entering service in 1940, OS2Us were the U.S. Navy's first catapult-launched monoplane observation aircraft.

➤ One hundred Kingfishers served with the Royal Navy between 1941 and 1947.

➤ The Kingfisher first flew as a landplane in March 1938 and on floats in May.

➤ Several battleships preserved as museums in the United States have restored OS2Us onboard.

➤ OS2Us were used in the Aleutians as dive-bombers against Japanese targets.

➤ Some Fleet Air Arm Kingfishers were based in the West Indies for training use.

PROFILE

Sharp eyes of the Navy

Designed to replace a biplane, the Vought OS2U Kingfisher was modern for the late 1930s, employing spot-welding and other advanced construction techniques.

The US Navy needed a reliable aircraft that could be launched from a ship's catapults on rescue and reconnaissance missions, and in designing the Kingfisher Vought drew on their wealth of experience in observation aircraft. OS2Us were also useful as anti-submarine craft flown by inshore patrol squadrons.

The pilot and observer/gunner had a high perch with excellent visibility. Though slow and somewhat underpowered, the Kingfisher was stable and thoroughly reliable. On at least one occasion, a Kingfisher outmaneuvered and shot down a Japanese Zero fighter. During fighting at the island of Yap, an OS2U rescued a three-man bomber crew within eyesight of Japanese shore gunners, then taxied five miles to take the men to a ship.

Other users included the Royal Navy, the forces of Australia and several South American countries.

The bulk of OS2Us built were mounted on floats for service from catapult-equipped cruisers.

The Australian markings on A48-4 are based on Fleet Air Arm camouflage and feature early-style British national markings. Later in the Pacific war, RAAF aircraft adopted a blue and white roundel and fin flash.

OS2U-3 Kingfisher

Type: two-seat observation aircraft

Powerplant: one 336-kW (450-hp.) Pratt & Whitney R-985-AN-2 radial piston engine

Maximum speed: 264 km/h (164 m.p.h.) at 1767 m (5,500 ft.)

Range: 1287 km (800 mi.)

Service ceiling: 396 m (1,300 ft.)

Weights: empty 1867 kg (4,115 lb.); max take-off 2716 kg (5,988 lb.)

Weapons: two .303 cal. (7.62-mm) machine guns, with one forward-firing and one on trainable mount in rear cockpit; plus two 100-lb. or 325-lb. bombs on underwing racks.

Dimensions: span 10.97 m (36 ft.)
length 10.36 m (34 ft.)
height 4.57 m (15 ft.)
wing area 24.34 m² (262 sq. ft.)

KINGFISHER MK I

En route to the Netherlands East Indies when these islands were over-run by the Japanese, 18 of 24 Vought VS-310s were absorbed by the Royal Australian Air Force as Kingfisher Mk Is.

The two crew in the OS2U were the pilot and observer/radio operator/gunner. A large area of plexiglass in the cockpit canopies provided a good all-round view.

Two defensive 7.62-mm (.303 cal.) machine guns were usually fitted to Kingfishers; one flexibly-mounted in the rear cockpit, the other fixed to fire forward. Underwing racks were fitted for up to 295 kg (650 lb.) of bombs.

Pratt & Whitney's reliable R-985 Wasp Junior rated at 336 kW (450 hp.) powered most Kingfishers. This well-known engine also powered the Beech Model 18 (C-45) twin-engine trainer/transport.

A48-4

Intended to replace the land-based O3U Corsair biplane, the OS2U introduced a number of new construction techniques, including spot welding of metal components.

The large centerline float was stabilized by the outboard floats; one under each wing. When returning to a USN cruiser after a catapult launch, OS2Us taxied on to a recovery sled towed by the ship and were then hoisted aboard by crane.

ACTION DATA

RANGE

One of the outstanding floatplanes of the war, Aichi's E13A1 'Jake' had good range and speed performance. Its range (and therefore endurance) was almost twice that of the Ar 196 and considerably more than the Kingfisher. Most were operated at sea.

OS2U-3 KINGFISHER 1287 km (800 mi.)
Ar 196A-3 1067 km (663 mi.)
E13A1a 'JAKE' 2086 km (1,296 mi.)

SPEED

The Kingfisher was perhaps the slowest of the comparable World War II floatplanes. The 'Jake' had a margin of 110 km/h (70 m.p.h.) over the OS2U, largely due to its much larger engine, which was rated almost three times that of the latter.

OS2U-3 264 km/h (164 m.p.h.)
Ar 196A-3 309 km/h (192 m.p.h.)
E13A1a 'JAKE' 375 km/h (233 m.p.h.)

WEAPONS

By far the best armed of these types was the Arado Ar 196, with its two cannon and machine guns. The Kingfisher, however, was able to carry a much larger bomb load – almost three times as much as the Ar 196 – but about the same load as the 'Jake'.

OS2U-3 KINGFISHER 2 x 7.62-mm (.30 cal.) MGs 295-kg (650-lb.) bomb load
Ar 196A-3 2 x 20-mm cannon 2 x 7.92-mm MGs 100-kg (220-lb.) bomb load
E13A1a 'Jake' 1 x 7.7-mm (.303 cal.) MG 250-kg (550-lb.) bomb load

Kingfisher deployment

LAND BASED: The option of wheeled undercarriage allowed the Kingfisher to be shore based. The Royal Navy used these aircraft for training purposes.

ON FLOATS: Kingfishers were in their element on the water. Their floats allowed them to be deployed from catapult-equipped cruisers. After a sortie, the OS2U simply alighted on the water next to the ship and was lifted aboard again by crane. Floats also allowed the Kingfisher to land during a sortie, to pick up a downed pilot for example.

CATAPULT LAUNCH: Special catapults were fitted to U.S. Navy and Royal Navy ships intending to use the Kingfisher. These were swung out from the side of the vessel and the aircraft launched over the water.

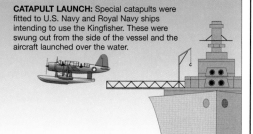

WESTLAND
WAPITI

● RAF general-purpose type ● Indian and Iraqi service ● Radial engine

With World War I at an end, the newly formed RAF found the idea of a general-purpose aircraft very attractive – defence spending had been cut, so a new aircraft needed to be 'multi-role'. In 1918 the RAF was saddled with wartime designs and by 1926 the DH.9A needed replacing. To complicate matters, however, Air Ministry Specification 26/27 required that the new aircraft use as many DH.9A parts as possible – another economy measure.

▲ Although defence budgets were cut after 1918, the RAF needed a replacement for a number of wartime models. Wapitis became the mainstay of the RAF's overseas deployments.

WESTLAND WAPITI

▲ Australian Wapiti Mk IA
In early 1929 the RAAF took delivery of the first of 28 Wapitis, some for use as trainers. RAAF Director of Training, Sqn Ldr Smart, said: 'The Wapiti is ideal for desert flying in Australia'.

▲ 'Bombed up'
Although a general-purpose type for overseas use, the Wapiti also gave valuable service as a day-bomber for the Auxiliary Air Force.

External fuel ▶
To extend the Wapiti's endurance and range, trials were undertaken with external fuel tanks. Each tank had a propeller-driven pump.

◀ On floats
A number of Wapiti Mk IIAs were fitted with Short's-built floats for trials. Wapitis could also be adapted for a ski undercarriage.

Civil-registered Wapiti Mk V ▶
In 1930 the Wapiti Mk V prototype was registered G-AAWA, fitted with floats and shipped to Buenos Aires for the 1931 British Exhibition and a sales tour of a number of South American states.

FACTS AND FIGURES

➤ An RAF Wapiti Mk IIA was used as a receiver aircraft during the in-flight refuelling trials of 1934.

➤ From 1929 the Prince of Wales used a specially equipped VIP Wapiti Mk IA.

➤ Wapiti Mk Vs were still employed in the army co-operation role as late as 1940.

➤ Wapiti prototype J8495 was mistakenly built with a fuselage that was 0.61 m (2 ft.) shorter than was originally intended.

➤ Wapitis served the air forces of Australia and South Africa.

➤ Heavily modified Wapiti Mk V/VII G-AAWA was later redesignated as a Wallace Mk I.

PROFILE

Biplane with a general purpose

Seven companies put forward eight different designs to meet the 1926 specification for a new general-purpose aircraft. All were to employ an all-metal airframe and use the Napier Lion engine.

Westland's Wapiti design actually used neither (at least initially), although it did incorporate de Havilland DH.9A components. Powered by a more modern 313-kW Bristol Jupiter radial, the prototype flew on 7 March 1927 and took part in trials with five other designs. In late 1927, 25 Wapiti Mk Is were ordered for service trials at home and with No. 84 Squadron in India. This marked the beginning of an almost 10-year association with the RAF's 'policing' squadrons in Iraq and on the Northwest Frontier.

An all-metal structure was finally introduced in the Mk II. Ten of these were built for No. 84 Squadron, before 430 Mk IIAs, with a 358-kW (480-hp.) Jupiter engine, were ordered. The first was delivered in 1930 and served in the bombing, supply-dropping and army co-operation roles.

Above: Pictured in the 1930s, a Wapiti Mk IIA of No. 30 Squadron flies over the city of Mosul, Iraq.

Below: The main Wapiti variant in RAF service was the Mk IIA. Of the 558 Wapitis built, 430 were Mk IIAs. These three aircraft from No. 55 Squadron, RAF, were among the Wapitis serving over the Northwest Frontier of India.

WAPITI MK IIA

From 1929 Wapiti Mk IIAs replaced the de Havilland DH.9As of No. 30 Squadron, RAF, on 'policing' duties in Iraq. Based at Mosul, the unit flew Wapitis until 1935, when they were replaced by the Hawker Hardy.

No. 30 Squadron's badge featured a date palm tree, which also adorned the tail of its aircraft. The unit was formed in 1914 for service in Egypt and remained in the Middle East until 1942.

Two 7.7-mm (.303 cal.) machine-guns were fitted for defence. A Lewis gun was mounted on a Scarff ring in the rear cockpit, while a fixed Vickers gun was controlled by the pilot and fired forward through the propeller arc.

Wapiti prototype J8495 used a set of virtually unaltered DH.9A wings and a modified DH.9A tailfin.

K1398

Despite the requirement that the RAF's new aircraft should employ the Napier Lion engine, the majority of Wapiti production machines were fitted with the Bristol Jupiter, a newer design with more development potential. The Wapiti Mk III built for the South African air force employed an Armstrong Whitworth Jaguar 14-cylinder, two-row radial, while two civil-registered Mk Vs and four Chinese Mk VIIIs used AW Panther engines.

Universal carriers under the wings and fuselage could hold various combinations of 51-kg (112-lb.), 104-/113-kg (229-250-lb.) or 9-kg (20-lb.) bombs up to a total of 263 kg (580 lb.).

Wapiti Mk IIs differed from Mk Is in having a detachable control column in the rear cockpit (but no rudder bar) for use in emergencies.

COMBAT DATA

POWER

A contemporary of the Wapiti, the Heinkel He 46 army co-operation aircraft had a much more powerful engine, but it was of similar weight and carried a smaller bomb load. It was, however, a slightly faster machine.

WAPITI Mk IIA	He 46C-1	Ro.37bis
358 kW (480 hp.)	485 kW (650 hp.)	418 kW (560 hp.)

MAXIMUM SPEED

Compared to other biplane types of the inter-war years, the Wapiti was relatively slow; more than 113 km/h (70 m.p.h.) slower than the Meridionali Ro.37 reconnaissance fighter.

WAPITI 217 km/h (135 m.p.h.)

He 46C-1 250 km/h (155 m.p.h.)

Ro.37bis 330 km/h (205 m.p.h.)

Specification 26/27 competitors

BEAVER: With a Napier Lion engine, Bristol's design was derived from the Type 93 Boarhound and did not use DH.9A parts. Another design was submitted, but was never built.

GORAL: Powered by a Bristol Jupiter engine, Gloster's design also used DH.9A wings. Although the Goral was rejected, Gloster went on to build the all-metal wings for the Wapiti Mk II/IIA.

HOUND: de Havilland's DH.65 suffered from a lack of internal stowage space and unacceptable handling on the ground. It was, however, the fastest of the trialists and used the Napier Lion.

VALIANT: Test pilots at RAF Martlesham Heath preferred the Vickers Valiant, but as it used no DH.9A parts, it was (like the Fairey Ferret III) more expensive than the other designs.

WRIGHT

FLYER

- History's first powered heavier-than-air flight ● Home-built aircraft

H istory was made when the Wright brothers flew their 'Flyer' a few metres over the sands of Kitty Hawk, North Carolina, in 1903. This short hop, in an aircraft that was less powerful and slower than a modern motor scooter, began the age of powered flight in heavier-than-air aircraft. The flight was less than the wing span of a modern airliner, but it opened up a whole new era of aviation.

▲ *Flying the first aircraft was nothing like flying modern aeroplanes. The builders and pilots devised their own control systems, built their own engines and airframes, and all too frequently caused their own deaths.*

250

WRIGHT FLYER

▲ Rail-launched
The Wright brothers' first experiments had been on dry sand which allowed take-offs on skids, but they had to find a way to reduce drag. One answer was a wooden railway, later replaced by wheels.

▲ Gliding record
In 1911, Orville returned to Kitty Hawk for the last time to set a world gliding record. He stayed aloft for 9 minutes and 45 seconds before landing safely.

▼ On camera
Keen to record their achievements, the brothers often filmed their flights. Here, Wilbur is seen photographing Orville during a test flight at Fort Myers in 1909.

▲ Wheeled undercarriage
The model 'R' was a sophisticated machine for its day, with twin propellers and wheels in place of the skids. The racing 'Baby Wright' was derived from this model.

◀ Passenger carrier ▶
The later Wright machines ('B' to 'R') could carry a passenger and had dual flying controls. The French aviation pioneer Paul Zens was Wilbur Wright's companion on this flight from Le Mans in 1908.

FACTS AND FIGURES

- ➤ The Smithsonian Institute refused to recognise the Wrights' achievement until the early 1950s.

- ➤ The Wright brothers opened their own flying school to train pilots.

- ➤ Wilbur Wright often kept his bowler hat on while flying his slow aircraft.

- ➤ Flyer III of 1905 had new propellers and a more powerful engine, and could be controlled easier than earlier 'Flyers'.

- ➤ Wilbur Wright had such a strong faith that he refused to fly on Sundays.

- ➤ The 'Flyer' Model D was a single-seater, two of which were sold to the US Army.

PROFILE

The first true powered aeroplane

Building experimental flying machines was a pursuit of cranks in the eyes of most people in 1903, but the Wright brothers were determined to achieve their goal of producing a practical, powered and controllable aircraft. Using the knowledge of previous aviation pioneers, they started building models and then small gliders, before rejecting many of the ideas as useless. With new plans of their own, such as controlling the aircraft with 'wing warping'

and designing their own tiny engines, they produced the 'Flyer', a derivative of their 'Glider No. 1' of 1899.

Orville Wright took the controls of the 'Flyer' on 17 December 1903, a blustery day on the remote Kill Devil Hill. Mounted on a wooden railway track and watched only by a handful of local spectators, the 'Flyer' slowly climbed into the air and flew nearly 40 m (120 ft.) before safely landing. The brothers made four more flights that

day, one lasting almost a minute.

Going on to demonstrate their flying machines to sceptical audiences all over Europe, they built bigger and better aircraft, cautiously correcting previous failures before going on to another flight. Thus, Wilbur Wright avoided being killed in an aeroplane crash like so many of his contemporary pioneers, instead succumbing to typhoid fever in his mid-40s.

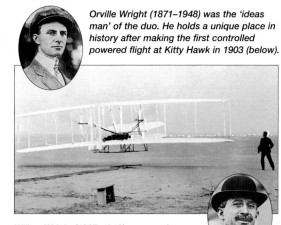

Orville Wright (1871–1948) was the 'ideas man' of the duo. He holds a unique place in history after making the first controlled powered flight at Kitty Hawk in 1903 (below).

Wilbur Wright (1867–1912) was a quiet man, who once said that a parrot, the bird that talked the most, did not fly very high.

Wright Flyer 1903

Type: experimental heavier-than-air powered biplane glider

Powerplant: home-built four-cylinder in-line piston engine delivering 9 kW (12 hp.)

Maximum speed: c. 50 km/h (31 m.p.h.)

Height on initial flight: c. 3 m (10 ft.)

Distance on initial flight: 36.5 m (120 ft.)

Duration of initial flight: 12 sec

Take-off weight: c. 340 kg (750 lb.)

Dimensions:
span	12.29 m (40 ft.)
length	6.43 m (21 ft.)
height	2.81 m (9 ft.)
wing area	c. 35 m² (510 sq. ft.)

WRIGHT FLYER

The Wright Flyer was based on earlier Wright glider designs. The 'Flyer' made history when Orville Wright flew it at Kill Devil Hill, Kitty Hawk, North Carolina, on 17 December 1903.

The 'elevators first' layout was soon dispensed with. This layout has recently found favour with aircraft designers, and can be seen on many fighters.

Early Wright gliders were fitted with skids rather than wheels, with the 'Flyer' being built to the same pattern.

Wright-designed aircraft had no flaps or ailerons. Control was provided by warping the thin wood and fabric wings.

The Wrights built their own engines. The first 'Flyers' were powered by 9-kW (12-hp.) engines, with later ones having 16-kW (20-hp.) engines.

The structure was braced with wire for rigidity.

The wooden rudder was covered in fabric. In early Wright machines it was connected to the wing warping apparatus by cables, but was later controlled separately.

The Wrights had to carve their own chain-driven propeller, a fixed-pitch wooden unit.

FIRST FLIGHTS

Man has probably dreamed of flight for as long as he has dreamed of anything. From the first caveman watching bats flitting out into the night, through the ancient Greeks and their myths of Daedalus and Icarus, to writers like Cyrano de Bergerac in the 17th century who fantasised about going to the moon in a carriage pulled by swans. But it was not until the 18th century, when the Montgolfier brothers harnessed the power of hot air in a balloon, that these dreams became an as-yet imperfectly achieved reality.

Dare-devils all over Europe followed the Montgolfier example, often with fatal results. Soon, people were experimenting with hydrogen to lift their balloons – much more controllable than hot air, but far more dangerous.

From there, the logical step was to fit some form of propulsion and steering mechanism. Experiments along these lines culminated in the last decade of the 19th century with steerable balloons, or dirigibles. Had anybody been taking bets in those days, most people would have put money on this being the future of flight. Few would have taken notice of the work being carried out by two mechanics in America, who were to achieve so much at Kitty Hawk in 1903.

The most important flight in history

LAUNCH RAMP: The Wright Flyer had no wheels. It took off by skidding along a polished wooden railway track.

HEAD WIND: The Wrights had chosen Kitty Hawk, on the North Carolina coast, for their flying experiments because it had a consistent steady wind blowing in off the Atlantic.

INTO THE AIR: There was a headwind of 43 km/h (21 m.p.h.) when, with Wilbur Wright at the controls, the 'Flyer' lifted into the air from the end of the launch rail.

ONE SMALL STEP: Although Wright was in the air for only 12 seconds, during which time the aeroplane covered 36.5 m (120 ft.), the short hop was one of the greatest events in history. For the first time, man had flown under power in a heavier-than-air machine, and the way was paved for the 20th century's aviation revolution.

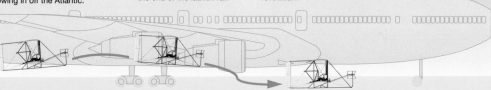

Zeppelin

Staaken R

- Four-engined pioneer ● Heavy bomber ● Raids over Britain

In aviation no ordeal can compare with the demands of a seven-hour flight aboard the collosal Zeppelin Staaken R-series bomber; the boldest design of the Great War. The name of Count von Zeppelin is usually associated with dirigible airships, but this heavier-than-air warplane was just as striking as anything else made by the company. In long-range flights over Britain, the Staaken made history conducting the first strategic bombing missions.

▲ Staaken R.VI 30/16 is prepared for flight, with Oberleutnant Meyer in the foreground. The Staaken crews developed tactics for long-range night bombing that were a completely new mode of warfare.

Zeppelin Staaken R

▲ **Modified version**
The Staaken R.IV was a modified VGO.III. The name changed to Staaken after the factory moved.

Inside the giant ▶
The enclosed cockpit contained radio and advanced equipment for navigation.

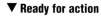

▲ **Long range**
Missions over Britain from bases in Belgium took several hours and were highly demanding, but these were also the safest. The short-range attacks over France were more dangerous due to better defence there.

▼ **Ready for action**
In 1916 the smaller VGO.III was already heavily committed to action over the Eastern Front, carrying out raids on railway installations near Riga.

▲ **Gunner's seat**
Staakens had excellent gun positions, and fighters attacking them usually received a curtain of accurate return fire. By the end of hostilities the addition of a Becker 20-mm cannon was considered.

FACTS AND FIGURES

➤ The final R-series, built after the war, was banned by the Allied Control Commission and scrapped in 1922.

➤ Zeppelin's first heavy bomber made its maiden flight on 11 April 1915.

➤ A final R-plane raid against Britain planned for August 1918 was cancelled.

➤ The R.IV was so much bigger than other aircraft that British pilots often opened fire on them from too far away.

➤ R-planes dropped 27,190 kg (59,818 lb.) of bombs on Britain.

➤ Only three Staakens were shot down over Britain, all by anti-aircraft guns.

Zeppelin's giant night-bomber

When the Great War began, Count von Zeppelin developed heavy bombers which he expected to strongly influence the conflict. Zeppelin worked on three aircraft, all with distinctive slab sides and biplane tail, before turning to the R-series (R for Riesenflugzeug). The first production R series aircraft was delivered in June 1917.

The distinctive lines of Zeppelin's bombers were unforgettable. Several companies turned their industrial prowess toward constructing these giant bombers, and even a two-float seaplane version was built.

The Zeppelin carried out missions over France and Russia in support of the German army, but its most famous missions were the 11 raids over Britain, often accompanied by Gotha bombers. The Staaken crews developed new navigation techniques, including the use of radio, and dropped huge 1000-kg (2,200-lb.) bombs, never seen before. The British had to divert large numbers of guns and fighters to face the new threat. This caused more disruption than the actual bombing, which

did little damage. The Allies were highly impressed by the Staakens, and hurriedly developed similar aircraft like the Handley Page series of bombers.

Below: Construction of the VGO.III began in October 1915, using Mercedes D.III engines in place of the less reliable Maybach units. Two engines in the nose drove one propeller through a central combining gearbox.

Above: The ultimate R-plane was the R.VI, of which 18 were built. The R.VI squadrons carried out bombing missions on the Western Front, suffering high losses.

Staaken R.IV

Type: seven-crew heavy bomber

Powerplant: two 119-kW (160-hp.) Mercedes D.III and four 164-kW (220-hp.) Benz Bz.IV inline piston engines

Maximum speed: 125 km/h (78 m.p.h.)

Endurance: 6 or 7 hours

Service ceiling: 3700 m (12, 150 ft.)

Weights: empty 8772 kg (19,298 lb.); maximum take-off 13,035 kg (28,677 lb.)

Armament: up to seven 7.92-mm Parabellum machine-guns, plus a maximum short-range bombload of 2123 kg (4,670 lb.)

Dimensions:
span	42.20 m (138 ft. 5 in.)
length	23.20 m (76 ft. 1 in.)
height	6.80 m (22 ft. 4 in.)
wing area	332 m² (3,572 sq. ft.)

STAAKEN R.IV

The wing engines were fitted in a pusher-type configuration, with radiators mounted above the engines. The R.IV was the only R-plane with coupled engines to see service on both fronts up to the end of the war.

A great deal of thought went into the defence of the R.IV. Guns were fitted in the upper wing, accessible by a ladder, and in the rear fuselage where two gunners sat side by side.

One improvement over the R.III was to move the tail surfaces above the line of the fuselage. Tail damage almost inevitably occurred in any accident of the R.III.

Assigned to Rfa 501 stationed near Ghent, the R.IV took part in raids on targets including London, the Thames Estuary, Calais, Morville and Bolougne. Rfa 500 also operated the R.IV, which saw service over the Eastern Front just before Russia surrendered in 1917.

The nose contained a forward engineer's compartment to allow inflight maintenance.

Almost the same wing structure was used in the R.IV as in the R.III, with the exception that the lower wing dihedral was decreased.

The ventral gun was useful for firing at enemy searchlight positions during night raids.

The lower tail spars extended under the top fuselage longeron, a feature retained on later R-series aircraft. The whole airframe (except around the engines) was covered in fabric, with the distinct polygon pattern common to German aircraft at the time. Occasionally this pattern was overpainted. Although the aircraft had a nosewheel, a tail skid was retained to prevent damage during take-off.

COMBAT DATA

MAXIMUM SPEED

Large and ungainly biplane designs like the Staaken were very slow. The primary requirements for the design were to obtain sufficient power and wing area to lift a useful load. This required large span wings and big engine radiators, which created large amounts of drag.

STAAKEN R.IV	125 km/h (78 m.p.h.)	
MOUROMETS	137 km/h (85 m.p.h.)	
0/100	122 km/h (76 m.p.h.)	

WING AREA

The size of the R.IV is vividly illustrated by comparing its wing area to that of its contemporaries. The need for lift meant that designers had to produce aircraft with large wing areas to compensate for lack of power. High speed was not a realistic requirement.

STAAKEN R.IV	**MOUROMETS**	**0/100**
332 m²	220 m²	153 m²
(3,572 sq. ft.)	(2,367 sq. ft.)	(1,646 sq. ft.)

ARMAMENT

Fighter pilots who took on a Staaken were taking their lives in their hands, and many were driven back or killed by the accurate and powerful fire of the aircraft's gunners. The Ilya Mouromets gave similar problems to German and Austrian pilots.

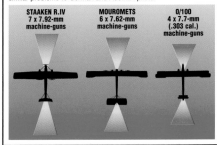

STAAKEN R.IV	**MOUROMETS**	**0/100**
7 x 7.92-mm machine-guns	6 x 7.62-mm machine-guns	4 x 7.7-mm (.303 cal.) machine-guns

Long-range bombers of the Great War

■ **ILYA MOUROMETS:** Designed by Igor Sikorsky, the Ilya Mouromets was used for bombing by the Imperial Russian Air Service. One shot down three German fighters.

■ **CAPRONI Ca.36:** This twin-engined design was a derivative of the wartime Ca.3, which first flew in 1914. Over 150 large Capronis were built, and the Ca.36 was still in production after the war.

■ **GOTHA G.V:** A twin-engined design much smaller than the R-planes, the Gothas formed the backbone of the bomber fleet against Britain, and took part in raids alongside the R.IVs.

■ **VICKERS VIMY:** The British equivalent to the Gotha, the Vimy would have taken part in raids against Germany if the war had continued, but only three were ready by October 1918.

INDEX